WITHDRAWN

THE ALBERT SHAW LECTURES ON DIPLOMATIC HISTORY

Under the Auspices of the

WALTER HINES PAGE SCHOOL OF INTERNATIONAL RELATIONS

By the liberality of Albert Shaw, Ph. D., of New York City, the Johns Hopkins University has been enabled to provide an annual course of lectures on Diplomatic History. The lectures, while continuing to be included in the regular work of the Department of History, have since the establishment of the Page School of International Relations, in 1930, been placed under its auspices.

THE
MONROE DOCTRINE
1826–1867

LONDON: HUMPHREY MILFORD
OXFORD UNIVERSITY PRESS

THE ALBERT SHAW LECTURES ON DIPLOMATIC HISTORY, 1932
THE WALTER HINES PAGE SCHOOL OF INTERNATIONAL RELATIONS

THE
MONROE DOCTRINE
1826–1867

BY

DEXTER PERKINS

*Watson Professor of History
in The University of Rochester*

BALTIMORE
THE JOHNS HOPKINS PRESS
1933

COMPOSED AND PRINTED IN THE UNITED STATES OF AMERICA
BY THE LORD BALTIMORE PRESS, BALTIMORE, MARYLAND

PREFACE

The study of the origins and immediate effects of
the Monroe declaration of December 2, 1823, which I
undertook some years ago, revealed to me so much that
was of the highest interest that it has inevitably
tempted me to proceed further. In the field of diplomatic history, as in other phases of the story of American life, no task can be more attractive than that of
tracing the evolution and consolidation of fundamental
principles. And in the case of the Monroe Doctrine, in
answer to the contention that to do this is to retrace
familiar ground, it may be stated that in studying the
development of this great shibboleth, as in studying its
first enunciation, insufficient attention has been paid to
a great variety of the materials available. The archives
of foreign powers have never been adequately explored.
The debates in Congress and the reactions of American public opinion have been no less neglected. Increasing familiarity with these materials only deepens
the conviction that there is room for a more thorough
study of the evolution, from 1826 down to the present
day, of a dogma which has played a vital part in the
history of the United States. This work I hope may
prove a contribution to that end, and I shall seek to
follow it with two more volumes which deal with the
period after 1867.

In dealing with such a subject as the Monroe Doctrine
questions of interpretation inevitably arise. It is possi-

ble, for example, to relate the policy of the United States towards Hawaii, and still more the policy of the United States towards Cuba, to the principles of 1823. But in relation to both these problems, my researches tend to show that the connection was not definite and explicit in the period covered by this study. In the pronouncements of American statesmen and politicians on Hawaii and on Cuba, there are almost no direct appeals to Monroe's famous declaration. I have, therefore, thought it permissible to postpone the story of the gradual association of the Doctrine with American policy in these two areas, and shall examine the matter in my third volume.

In the carrying out of my task, I have received aid from so many quarters as to make it impossible to render full acknowledgment. To Dr. John H. Latané, who extended to me the invitation to give the substance of this book as the Albert Shaw lectures, I owe the first word of appreciation. The work would no doubt have profited much from his wide knowledge and friendly criticism, had it not been for his untimely death just as it was going to the press. I must record, too, my appreciation of the cordial interest of Dr. John V. A. MacMurray, Director of the Walter Hines Page School of International Relations, and of Dr. W. Stull Holt, Associate in History at The Johns Hopkins University. To Professor A. M. Schlesinger and to Professor J. P. Baxter, 3rd, of Harvard University, both of whom read the manuscript, I feel a special obligation. Their critical judgment and wide knowledge have been invaluable, and their appreciative comment and friendly interest a source of much encouragement. In the State Department at Washington I have met always with a cordial reception, and have found especially helpful Mrs. Maddin Summers, whose efficient and sympathetic administration of the archives of the Department is putting more and more American scholars in her debt. At the Ministère des Affaires Etrangères and the London Public Record Office, I have met with unfailing courtesy and helpfulness from the officials in charge. I must acknowledge with gratitude the services of Professor R. R. Hill, who secured access for me to the archives of the Ministerio del Estado at Madrid, and of Señor José Antonio Artiz, who performed with efficiency and promptitude the work of copying many important despatches from this source. The remarkable service of the Library of Congress in securing photostats of manuscripts in foreign archives, a work directed by the dean of American historical scholars, Dr. J. F. Jameson, and inaugurated with the greatest energy and efficiency by Professor S. F. Bemis, has put much material at my disposal from the Haus-Archiv of the Emperor Maximilian. Finally, my secretary, Miss Alice M. Morrissey, has done yeoman service in the verification of references, and in the careful and scholarly preparation of the manuscript for the press.

DEXTER PERKINS.

Rochester, N. Y.
June, 1932.

CONTENTS

CHAPTER I

The Period of Quiescence

Though the foreign policy of the United States has undergone the necessary modifications of time and circumstance, it is not too much to say that it has been dominated by, if not always directed by, a single principle. This principle is the principle of the two spheres, the principle that the Old World and the New represent separate areas of international action, and that the less political contact there is between them the better. It is easy to trace the development of this principle from the earliest days of the republic. One finds evidences of it in the manifest reluctance with which, even under the stress of the Revolution, the thirteen colonies turned to an outside power for aid. One finds evidences of it in the provisions of the Constitution with regard to foreign affairs, and in particular with regard to the making of treaties. And when the new régime was ushered in in 1789, the early experience of its governors confirmed and deepened a point of view that had already found expression. The nation was called upon to steer its foreign policy through the mazes of a European war. Domestic faction and foreign intrigue threatened the very foundations of the new state. Taught by the experience of his own administrations, George Washington in his famous Farewell Address laid down the principle (which derived additional authority, of

course, from his great name) that it was best to have
as little political intercourse with foreign nations as
possible.

During the next thirty years this principle was becoming more and more firmly fixed in the consciousness of American statesmen. It was not yet unswerv-
ingly applied; Washington, himself, for example, had
adverted to the possibility of temporary alliances with
European nations; Jefferson, on first hearing of the
cession of Louisiana by Spain to France, was ready to
contemplate an alliance with Great Britain; and proposals to guarantee the Spanish dominions in North
America, in exchange for the cession of the Floridas,
are a clear deviation from the doctrine of the two
spheres. But the warning against " entangling alliances "
was reiterated by Jefferson in his first inaugural; and
when in 1812 the United States took up arms against
Great Britain, it made no connection whatsoever with
Britain's secular enemy. In the meantime circumstances
were making it more and more reasonable, not only to
keep aloof from European affairs, but to act upon the
principle that Europe should keep aloof from America.
The cession of Louisiana immensely diminished the
European holdings upon the American continent. In
1808 blazed forth those revolts in the Spanish colonies
which were to bring into being throughout Central and
South America a galaxy of independent states. At the
end of the Napoleonic wars, Europe turned more and
more toward reaction. In such a situation, it was natural enough that the United States should hold aloof
from the newly constituted Holy Alliance, despite the

views of some peace enthusiasts, that it should recognize the Spanish colonies when their independence seemed secure, and that it should, when there seemed to be some danger of their reconquest, warn European nations from any such interference in the affairs of the New World. The famous presidential message of December 2, 1823, that has since come to be known as the Monroe Doctrine, was but the logical counterpart to the maxim of no entangling alliances, and to abstinence from participation in the politics of Europe.

Noninterference in European affairs, the warning to Europe not to meddle unduly in the affairs of America, these are the two grand divisions of the principle of the two spheres. Either one of them deserves to be the subject of more study than it has yet received. The evolution of each ought to be carefully traced from the early period of American diplomacy down to the present time. My present purpose, however, is a more restricted one. Having examined, in a previous volume, the inception of the Monroe Doctrine, I shall now undertake to follow its development for a period of some forty years, from the debates on the Congress of Panama in 1826 down to the evacuation of Mexico by the French in 1867.

At the beginning of this period, the Monroe Doctrine had not yet become " doctrine " at all. The message of 1823 had been hailed with enthusiasm by the people of the United States; but executive and legislative alike had refused to turn it into any kind of binding pledge, being obviously anxious to retain entire liberty of action as to its practical application. In Europe the message had influenced not at all, one may say, the policies of the continental powers, and had aroused the jealousy, but not commanded the respect, of Great Britain; and in the newborn states of the American continent its value, while admitted, was rated as unimportant as compared with the powerful protection of England. In 1867 on the other hand, the principles of Monroe's pronouncement had taken deep root in the consciousness of the American people; they were known and to a very considerable degree respected abroad, and they had been more than once invoked by the governments of Latin America. The evolution of these forty years is thus a matter of high historic interest.

In the years from 1826 to 1843, however, which form the earliest period for our examination, the Doctrine plays a very subordinate rôle. The debates in Congress in 1825 and 1826 must have familiarized American political leaders and American public opinion with the principles enunciated in 1823; but in general those principles were not applied, at any rate on the scale which was to prevail later; and Europe and Latin America conducted their diplomatic intercourse with one another with a rather complete disregard of the doctrine of the two spheres. The period is interesting, then, from the negative rather than from the positive point of view, because it illustrates how little the principles of Monroe had been extended, rather than because it marks their steady extension. From this point of view I shall proceed to examine it.

The original message of 1823 had laid down the doctrine of two spheres in two separate paragraphs and with regard to two unrelated questions. On the one hand, Monroe had served a warning against the reconquest of the Spanish colonies ; on the other, John Quincy Adams had seen to it that there was incorporated into the presidential pronouncement a warning against further European colonization in the New World.

This second paragraph was destined to be the more important in the development of the Monroe Doctrine. It was given wider publicity by the efforts of Adams to secure for it continental acceptance at the time of the Panama Congress ; and it has been cited again and again in the evolution of the principles of 1823. The examination of the period from 1826 to 1841 may properly begin, then, with an examination of those cases in which the Adams principle was more or less directly violated, or in which, at any rate, a public opinion more sensitive and more highly indoctrinated would have undoubtedly believed it to be violated.

The most conspicuous of these cases has to do with the encroachments of Great Britain. When the non-colonization principle was originally enunciated, the British Foreign Secretary, George Canning, had promptly refused to accept it as binding ; and in April of 1824 in the negotiations on the Oregon question, it was emphatically and formally repudiated by the British plenipotentiaries. The policy of the British government was indeed very far from accepting the doctrine of the two spheres, or American hegemony in the New World. In the course of the fifteen years which followed on the Doctrine, the British took possession, or repossession, as might be claimed, of the Falkland Islands, and extended their already existent interests in Central America.

With regard to the case of the Falkland Islands, the essential facts are as follows. The sovereignty of these islands was in the course of the latter half of the eighteenth century the subject of a bitter dispute between Great Britain and Spain.[1] Though the British maintained at a later date that they had never waived their claims, they did in fact abandon the islands in 1774, leaving Spain to exercise the rights of jurisdiction there until the end of her colonial rule in the New World. Then, naturally enough, the Argentine government succeeded to the rights of the former mother-country, and in 1820 an officer of the Argentine navy took possession of the territory. An attempt at settlement was made in 1823 and failed. Three years later, with the encouragement of the Argentine government, Don Luis Vernet, of French origin, but long a resident of Hamburg, succeeded in establishing a colony upon East Falkland; in 1828 the same individual was granted a monopoly of the fisheries in the archipelago, and in the next year he was appointed governor. The exercise of his authority led to a quarrel with the United States. When he attempted to exclude American whaling vessels from the

[1] For a very scholarly and detailed account of this controversy, see Julius L. Goebel. *The Struggle for the Falkland Islands. A Study in Legal and Diplomatic History* (New Haven, 1927). Another excellent account is by Paul Groussac, *Les Iles Malouines. Nouvel Exposé d'un Vieux Litige* (Buenos Ayres, 1910). For a brief summary, see Adolfo Saldías. *Historia de la Confederación Argentina—Rosas y su Epoca* (5 vols., Paris, 1881-87), II, 67-91.

Falklands, his establishment was broken up by Commander Duncan of the U. S. S. "Lexington," and a rupture between the Argentine and American governments soon followed.[2] At this propitious moment the British reasserted their ancient claims of sovereignty. On January 2, 1833, the British corvette "Clio" appeared at Puerto Luis, and its commander announced to the commander of the Argentine goelette in the harbor that he had come to take possession of the islands as belonging to His Britannic Majesty. Resistance was useless, and on the following morning the flag of La Plata was hauled down, and the Union Jack hoisted in its stead.[3]

The action of the British on this occasion must be regarded as a clear violation of the Monroe Doctrine if the title to the islands is assumed to rest in the Argentine government. The exhaustive and scholarly researches of Dr. Julius Goebel have established beyond a peradventure of a doubt that such an assumption would be entirely correct. But neither in 1833 nor at any later

[2] For many of the documents in connection with this case, see *British and Foreign State Papers*, XX, 311-441. And for a convenient summary of the correspondence see J. B. Moore, *A Digest of International Law* (Washington, 1906, 8 vols.) I, 876-890. Livingston's instructions in connection with this matter are given in *ibid.*, pp. 876-882. See State Department Instructions. American States, XIV, 235 *et seq.* See also Adelaide Hasse, *Index to U. S. Documents relating to Foreign Affairs*, I. 572.

[3] The correspondence which followed between the British and Argentine governments is best found in *British and Foreign State Papers*, XXII, 1366-94. See also V. G. Quesada, *Recuerdos de mi Vida Diplomática* (Buenos Ayres, 1904), pp. 221-292, and the works already cited, Goebel and Groussac.

date has the United States ever taken the view that the principles of the President's famous declaration were involved.

On reflection, however, it will not appear surprising that such was the case. There were numerous reasons, any one of them almost convincing in itself, why the Jackson administration should not have taken any vigorous action, or made any protest at the conduct of the British. In hardly any instance would the application of Monroe's tenets have been less consistent with a definite national interest of the United States. The islands were extremely remote; their possession by the British could threaten no American interest; indeed the business of American whalers might and probably would thrive better under a British occupation than under an Argentine monopoly. Furthermore, the title to the islands might at the time have fairly been assumed to be doubtful, and the administration, as its later action showed, hardly possessed the materials for a decisive judgment on the matter. Again, it must be remembered, in 1833 the diplomatic relations of the United States with the Argentine government were entirely suspended, as a result of the raid of the " Lexington." In such circumstances it was hardly to be expected either that the authorities at Buenos Ayres would invoke the aid of the American government, or, on the other hand, that such aid would be spontaneously offered.[4] Finally, the admis-

[4] The raid of the "Lexington" led the Jackson administration to send to Buenos Ayres a Massachusetts lawyer, Francis Baylies, for the liquidation of the ensuing dispute. Baylies engaged in an extremely spirited, but not particularly diplomatic,

sion of the Argentine claims to the islands would have opened the door to a claim against the American government itself for the action of the American commander in breaking up Vernet's settlement.

It is not strange, therefore, that the British action was not the cause of any diplomatic representations to the Foreign Office by the Jackson administration. The only step that was taken was to set on foot an inquiry through the American minister to Spain as to the legal title involved; [5] but this inquiry was not pressed to any conclusion, and the whole matter lapsed. It had, so far as I have been able to ascertain, caused not a ripple upon the surface of American public opinion; it was not widely discussed in the press; and it was never mentioned in Congress. There was no reason why Edward Livingston, Jackson's Secretary of State, should have sought to take vigorous action. Not even the most dogmatic adherent of the doctrine of the two spheres is likely to regret this inertia. The question of the Falkland Islands has never interested, and does not now interest, the people of the United States.

It has not been the same, however, with the question of Central America. Here is a part of the world in which the rival interests of Great Britain and the United States have more than once clashed, and clashed in no

exchange of notes with Foreign Minister Anchorena. In the course of this exchange, he used the Brisish title as an argument. See *British and Foreign State Papers,* XX, 345-46. The correspondence, as I have already indicated, is given in the same volume *in extenso.*

[5] Quesada, *op. cit.,* p. 200.

uncertain fashion. Yet in the period which we have under review, encroachments on the part of the British appear to have passed largely unnoticed, and entirely unresented, at Washington. To these encroachments it is now necessary to turn.

The first of the areas involved is that now known as the province of British Honduras, or Belize. British interests in this region go back to the latter half of the seventeenth century, when settlements, formed largely with the purpose of cutting logwood, were formed along the coasts. The exact status of these settlements remained indeterminate until the treaty of 1783, between Great Britain and Spain. By this treaty the region between the Rio Hondo on the north, and the Belize River on the south, was recognized as one in which the British might exercise special privileges, though the title was definitely recognized as belonging to Spain. Subsequent treaties, in 1786 and 1814, confirmed these arrangements, and extended the southern boundary of the British settlements to the River Sibun. Within this region, then, the subjects of the British Crown exercised certain limited legal rights at the time when President Monroe delivered the famous message of December 2, 1823.[6]

If those rights had not been in any way stretched or distorted, it is obvious that the settlement of British Honduras would not have come at all within the pro-

[6] For an excellent discussion, see M. W. Williams, *Anglo-American Isthmian Diplomacy* (Washington, 1916), especially chs. 1 and 2.

scriptions of the Monroe Doctrine. President Monroe had explicitly stated in making his declaration of principles that there was no intention to interfere with existing rights. Succeeding administrations must naturally have followed the same course.

But the position of the British in Belize tended to change with time. In the first place, the settlers soon extended their settlements still further to the southward, until, by 1821, they had reached the River Sarstoon. For some years the home government at London remained indifferent to this expansion. But when, in 1833, the government of Central America, which had, of course, succeeded to the rights of Spain, protested against the encroachments of the settlers, Lord Palmerston, then Foreign Secretary, flatly refused to discuss the boundary question. The next year, when the Central Americans sent one Colonel Galindo to London to negotiate upon the matter, he was denied reception, and his mission ended in a thorough rebuff. By the year 1836 the Colonial Office, at any rate, was definitely claiming the Sarstoon to be the southern boundary of Belize, and the jurisdiction of the Central American government was never exercised within this limit.[7] These encroach-

[7] In E. G. Squier. *Notes on Central America. Their Geography, Topography, Climate, Population, Resources, Productions, Commerce, Political Organization, Aborigines, Etc., Etc., comprising Chapters on Honduras, San Salvador, Nicaragua, Costa Rica, Guatemala, Belize, the Bay Islands, the Mosquito Shore, and the Honduras Inter-Oceanic Railway* (New York, 1855), p. 62. See also Frederick Crowe. *The Gospel in Central America; containing a Sketch of the Country, Physical and Geographical—Historical and Political—Moral and Relig-*

ments south of the Sibun were from the first illegal, and might have been made the occasion at any time for the assertion of the Monroe Doctrine.

But even within the limits prescribed by the treaties of 1783, 1786, and 1814, British authority naturally tended to outgrow the treaty stipulations. On the basis of the limited privileges originally conceded, a self-governing colony began to define itself. The government in London moved with great prudence, it is true, and was, throughout the period we are discussing, reluctant to alter the legal status of Belize; but the authorities of the settlement itself were not so cautious. It is clear that they exercised full governmental authority within the region, and in 1840, the superintendent, Alexander Macdonald, declared the law of England to be the law of the " settlement or colony of British Honduras," with the approval, if not at the instance, of his superiors in London.

The relations of the United States with the distracted republics of Central America were so spasmodic and so far from close in the decade of the thirties that it would not have been surprising if the gradual extension of British authority had passed entirely unnoticed at Washington. But the question of Belize was, as a matter of fact, brought to the attention of the State Department by the Central Americans themselves. The Colonel Galindo, already mentioned as charged with a mission from the Central American government to London,

_ious: A History of the Baptist Mission in British Honduras and of the Introduction of the Bible into the Spanish American Republic of Guatemala (London, 1850), pp. 201-2.

stopped on his way to Europe in Washington in July of 1835. On this occasion he delivered to Mr. Forsyth, then Secretary of State, a communication from the foreign minister of Central America, dated December 30, 1834. This note did not mention the declaration of 1823 in specific terms, but it contained this significant sentence. " Suffer me to remind you that it has always been an object of the policy of the United States that there should be no European settlements upon the American continents." Passing on to express the " danger and alarm " which the " violation of that principle " might cause, the note frankly solicited the mediation of the American government.[8] To this plea, however, the administration of Andrew Jackson made no positive answer. Galindo was informed that it was not deemed expedient to interfere in the matter.

The truth of the matter is that Galindo had been anticipated by the British minister at Washington, Vaughan. Vaughan had received advance notice of the projected mission from Chatfield, the British consul-general in Central America. He had therefore solicited an interview with Forsyth, and had frankly raised the question of Belize. He had, he reported to his government, " no difficulty " in convincing the Secretary of State that no American interest was involved in the question, and in securing the assurance that the Central American emissary would not be given a hearing at all.[9]

[8] Washington, Dept. of State, Special Agents, Galindo.
[9] Williams, *op. cit.*, p. 34. London, P. R. O., C. O., Honduras, vol. 47, July 4, 1835.

One step, however, Forsyth did take in opposition to the views of the British government. Contemporaneously with the events which have been described, the British government was seeking to get a clear title to the region in controversy by direct negotiation with Spain. In March of 1835, Villiers, the British representative at Madrid, was instructed to negotiate to this end.[10] These negotiations the American minister, Barry, about to depart for the Spanish capital, was instructed vigorously to oppose, as " injurious to the rights of Central America." [11] Barry died on the way to his post, and his successor, Eaton, who reached Madrid never saw fit to take up the matter, but the incident is an interesting one as an evidence of at least a faint and flickering interest in the British policy in Central America.

Before taking leave of this episode, it is worth while to add a word or two with regard to the Secretary of State who played a part in it. John Forsyth had been a member of the Congress which debated at such length the sending of the mission to Panama; and he had at that time denounced the non-colonization principle in vigorous terms. It was, he declared, " based upon assertions of fact, which I trust we shall never be called upon to establish, and of principles that are fallacious." [12]

[10] *Ibid.*, p. 35. London, P. R. O., F. O., Spain, vol. 439, no. 19, March 12, 1835.

[11] Washington, Dept. of State, Instructions, Spain, vol. 14, p. 70, June 30, 1835. Quoted in Moore, *A Digest of International Law,* VI, 442.

[12] *Register of Debates,* 19th Cong., 1st Sess., part 2, col. 2317. See also my earlier work, *The Monroe Doctrine, 1823-26* (Cambridge, 1927), p. 217.

It may be that he still held to the same view, and that he perceived no vital national interest of the United States which was impaired by the British encroachments in Belize, or that, if he did perceive it, he could see in 1835 as in 1826 no particular use in appealing to a general principle established by doubtful reasoning and hardly likely to be accepted as binding by the nation to whom it was addressed. It is even possible, indeed, that Forsyth may have known of the distaste which the non-colonization principle inspired in Canning at the time at which it was enunciated. A cool, cautious, and conservative man, his own memories, his own past attitude, and his whole temper help to explain the coolness with which he regarded Galindo's appeal, and the very modest steps which he took to defend the rights of the government of Central America.

The attitude thus assumed by Forsyth in 1835 was maintained throughout his long incumbency in the State Department. When, in 1839, John L. Stephens was sent out as a special agent in Central America, he received no instructions whatever touching on the question of Belize, and the tone of his intercourse with the Superintendent of the colony, Macdonald, whom he visited, shows clearly enough that there was not the slightest disposition at Washington to quarrel with Great Britain over the matter. [13] A similar caution was maintained by Forsyth's successors. In June, 1841, Daniel Webster,

[13] Washington, Dept. of State, Special Agents. Stephens's instructions are dated August 13, 1839. See also J. L. Stephens, *Incidents of Travel in Central America, Chiapas, and Yucatan* (New York, 1848), (2 vols.). I, 14, and 21-23.

then Secretary of State in the administration of John
Tyler, instructed Murphy, a new special agent to Central
America, to inform himself with regard to the merits
of the controversy over the territory,[14] but although the
information was transmitted to Washington, the American government remained entirely quiescent. Indeed,
to anticipate the subject of later chapters, the Polk
administration, certainly not one of the least aggressive
in our history, sent an American consul to Belize, and
permitted him to secure his exequatur from the British
authorities, thus impliedly recognizing the British title
to the region. It was not until the time of Franklin
Pierce that the United States challenged the British
pretensions. In the period with which we are now dealing there was as yet none of that generalized sensitiveness to even the smallest hint of European aggrandizement in America which later was to make it so easy, one
might almost say so inevitable, for any administration
to invoke the Monroe Doctrine. There was no important
material interest involved. Indeed, it may even be
doubted whether the American public was interested
in the slightest degree in what was going on in Central
America.

The British encroachments in Belize do not stand
alone. Indeed, a clearer case of actual aggression, one
with regard to which the Monroe Doctrine was later to
be invoked, was that of the Bay Islands. These islands,
of which the most important is Ruatan, lie off the coast

[14] Washington, Dept. of State, Instructions, American States,
vol. 15.

of Honduras. Fertile territory, with excellent harbors, they had long been coveted by the British settlers on the mainland, and by the British agents in Central America. In 1830 the superintendent at Belize had actually seized Ruatan, on the excuse that the Central America authorities had refused to return fugitive slaves, but the British government had not sustained its representative. But in 1838 the question was reopened. A group of liberated slaves from the Cayman Islands settled upon the island, and appealed to Macdonald, the aggressive superintendent of Belize, to protect them. Macdonald willingly responded, and although for a time the government of Honduras resisted, and attempted to maintain its sovereignty, the effort was fruitless. For this time London sustained the local authorities, and Chatfield, the British minister, was instructed that the British government did not deem it necessary to discuss the question of title.[15] From this time on the British remained in control.

The seizure of Ruatan was never the occasion for any appeal to the United States by the Central American authorities. The Central American federation, indeed, was at this time rapidly dissolving. Both the remnant of a government that was left, and the authorities of Honduras, were no doubt too busy with their own affairs to pay much attention to the United States. Nor did the British action receive any attention from American consular representatives in Central America, or from

[15] London, P. R. O., F. O., Central America, vol. 22, no. 7, Sept. 21, 1839. For this episode see Williams, *op. cit.*, pp. 37-9

the special agent, John L. Stephens. No act of aggression against a Latin American state has ever so completely escaped the attention of Washington, perhaps, as did the one which we have just described.

It was much the same, moreover, with what was going on further to the southward in the region known as the Mosquito Coast. For a long time the British had had some kind of shadowy rights there. In 1740 they had actually established themselves in control, secured the assent of the leading Mosquitoes to the transfer of the sovereignty of the shore to Great Britain, and set up a local ruler under their control. But by the treaties of 1783 and 1786 with Spain they were induced to give up all relations with the Mosquitoes, and for some time thereafter, though a contraband trade existed, and though leading Mosquitoes were entertained by the authorities at Belize, the government at London showed no especial interest in the region. With the expulsion of the Spaniards from Central America, however, the interest of the British began to revive. In 1816 the Mosquito " king " was crowned at Belize, and the precedent was followed in the case of his successors. The custom of giving presents was revived in 1830. In 1837 the Colonial Office ordered that the Indians be protected from Central American encroachments. And in 1840 the always enterprising Macdonald, in all probability stimulated by the American mission of Stephens,[16]

[16] See London, P. R. O., C. O., Honduras, vol. 57. Macdonald to Lord John Russell, August 25, 1840.

" The Americans are anxious above all things to possess that part of the shore where the St. Juan flows into the sea, which

began to interest himself in the region. In August, 1841, the port of San Juan, at the mouth of the river of that name, was seized in the name of the painted savage who at that precise moment rejoiced in the title of King of Mosquitia. The Nicaraguans were not permanently dispossessed, but in the correspondence which followed Lord Aberdeen made it clear beyond peradventure that the British government regarded the mouth of the San Juan River as within the territory of its protégés.[17]

In the attitude of the British Foreign Office in dealing with this question, there is not any indication of concern as to the attitude of the United States. True, the governor of Jamaica, who exercised a measure of supervision over the superintendent of Belize, seems to have feared that movements of aggression on the Mosquito Shore might excite the jealousy of the American authorities.[18] But his views cannot be said to have carried any weight, and in the instructions of the Colonial Office and the Foreign Office there is no reference to the possibility of American resentment, and *a fortiori,* no reference to the principles of 1823. The

---

if they acquired and created a communication by the Lake Nicaragua to the Pacific we might bid farewell to the high commercial footing we at present enjoy, and allow a power not indisposed to cripple our energies a fair stage for the execution of their hostile designs.

" Our alliance with the Mosquito Nation is of long standing, and a stronger recognition of it would promote our commercial prosperity and strengthen our national and political power."

17 London, P. R. O., F. O., Central America, vol. 29, April 13, 1842.

18 London, P. R. O., F. O., Central America, vol. 15, No. 27, July 5 and November 19, 1841.

3

British government behaved in this part of the world precisely as if the Monroe Doctrine had never been invented. And so did the American government itself. The dogma of non-colonization remained unused, as it had in the case of Belize and in the case of Ruatan.[19]

There is one more case involving the non-colonization principle which must be considered before we pass to other aspects of the subject. The attempt of France to encroach upon the territory of Brazil, extending the limits of French Guiana to the eastward, and the diplomatic controversy which followed, has passed virtually unnoticed by students of the Monroe Doctrine.[20] The background of this controversy, as of so many similar ones, lies in a series of more or less contradictory treaties, involving the region between the Oyapoc and the Araguary rivers, the final construction of which, by the arbitration of 1897, awarded the territory to Brazil. Taking advantage of the troubled condition of

[19] The special agent, Murphy, sent out in 1841, reported the facts of British aggression to his government. But he seems to have generated very little emotion on the subject. See on this matter his despatch of December 6, 1841, in Washington, Dept. of State, Central America, Despatches, vol. 2.

[20] For a discussion of this question see J. C. da Silva, *L'Oyapoc et l'Amazone. Questionne Brésilienne et Française* (2 vols., Paris, 1899), especially I, 202-223. Important source materials are to be found in *Les Frontières entre le Brésil et la Guyane Française. Mémoire présenté par les Etats-Unis du Brésil au Gouvernement de la Confederation Suisse, Arbitre choisie selon les stipulations du traité conclu à Rio de Janeiro le 10 Avril, 1897, entre le Brésil et la France* (3 vols., Paris, 1899). See especially III, 173-82. See also *Second Mémoire présenté*, etc. (3 vols., Paris, 1899), especially III, 307-322.

Brazil, and particularly of the border province of Pará, in 1835, the French government ordered the establishment of a military post in this region, far to the east of the Oyapoc, in the district known as Amapa.[21] The occupation of this district passed entirely unnoticed in the United States. It was the subject of no diplomatic representation to France, and of no appeal from Brazil. On the other hand, the British government, despite its own acquisitive tendencies in Central America, took a very real interest in the matter. It sent out a naval commander to investigate the facts in 1838, and in December Lord Palmerston addressed to the French government a mild inquiry as to its encroachment upon the territory of Brazil.[22] The diplomatic pressure exerted by the British government was not severe. But it seems to have been sufficient. The French Foreign Minister expressed his willingness to negotiate with Brazil as to the territory in dispute early in 1839.[23] For a time negotiations were delayed by the insistence of Brazil that they should be preceded by the withdrawal of France from the disputed territory, but early in 1840 this obstacle was overcome, and in July the French troops evacuated Amapa.[24] Thus the controversy was for a time closed.

[21] Da Silva, L'Oyapoc et l'Amazone., op. cit., I, 208.

[22] London, P. R. O., F. O., France, vol. 558, December 11, 1838.

[23] Paris, Min. des Aff. Etr., Corr. Pol., Brésil, vol. 18, January 18, 1839.

[24] Ibid., July 4, 1839, and vol. 19, February 22, 1840, and October 21, 1840.

The whole incident is not of great importance. Yet
it is well to remember that sixty years later similar
encroachments by Great Britain not only led to the
invocation of the Monroe Doctrine, but became the
cause of an extremely acute diplomatic controversy.
The allusion, of course, is to the Venezuelan dispute of
1895. The striking contrast between the handling of
the two questions justifies at least this brief mention of
the French encroachments of 1835.

But it is not only attempts to extend political sovereignty over New World territory that concern the
student of the Monroe Doctrine in the period 1826-41.
One must take account as well of various projects which
were intended to reestablish monarchical government,
and draw closer the ties between the New World and
the Old. Such projects were contrary to the doctrine of
the two spheres, implicit in the President's declaration.
They were contrary, too, to the spirit of his pronouncement, if not to its letter. For, although Monroe had no
general hostility to monarchy, as is proved by the recognition of Brazil in 1824, against monarchy as a cloak
for European political control American governmental
opinion had been firmly set from the beginning. Opposition to any such conception had been voiced by Galla-
tin to Chateaubriand in May, 1823; it had figured in the
instructions of Adams to the ministers sent out to the
new republics of Latin America; it had lain behind the
phrases in which Monroe declared that the extension of
" the political system " of the allied powers would be
regarded as dangerous to the " peace and safety " of the

United States; it had figured in the instructions drawn up for the American delegates to the Panama Congress in 1826.

In Mexico the monarchical idea had a more tenacious hold than in any of the countries which the revolutionary movements of the post-Napoleonic period severed from the dominions of Spain. In 1822 it seemed entirely possible that an independent monarchy under a prince of the Spanish house would be established there, and had it not been for the unshakable obstinacy of the Spanish Cortes, which rejected a treaty looking toward such a monarchy, the plan might very conceivably have been realized. In 1823 the military leader Iturbide actually proclaimed the Mexican Empire, and assumed the title of Agustín the First, and though his tenure of authority was brief enough, it affords ample evidence of the strength of royalist sentiment, and of the support which the clergy and the aristocracy were willing to accord to the establishment of a strong monarchical government. With 1824, it is true, there came a reaction. The constitution of that year was modelled upon the federative constitution of the United States, and the enemies of republicanism were for a time reduced to a feeble, and for the most part subterranean, opposition. Yet there was never a period of any considerable length between 1824 and 1840 when men, monarchist by conviction, did not hold important posts in the government, and many occasions upon which they were represented in the ministry of foreign affairs. The administration of Victoria, elected in 1824, brought to the control of Mexican foreign policy Lucas Alamán, a convinced believer in the necessity of restoring monarchical forms. The movement toward the left which temporarily installed Guerrero in the presidential chair in 1829 was soon followed by one to the right, which brought Bustamente into power, and again gave Alamán control of his country's relations with the outside world. On this occasion, indeed, the Mexican Foreign Minister sounded Pakenham, the British representative in Mexico City, on the feasibility of setting up a government under a European prince.[25] The overture was coldly received, yet it seems to have been renewed in 1834.[26] The next year, Santa Anna being President, there appears at the Foreign Office the dominant figure, one might almost call him, in the history of Mexican monarchy, Gutierrez de Estrada. This man, who pursued for a quarter of a century with inexorable tenacity the realization of the monarchical idea, does not seem to have made any direct overtures to European governments at this time. But in 1840 he published a pamphlet which produced a great sensation, calling for a Convention which should give to Mexico a royal form of government under a European prince.[27] It is not necessary here to

[25] "Humanity had induced Great Britain, France, and Russia to undertake the adjustment of the political state of Greece, and why should not a like feeling induce them to take the state of this Country into consideration, and provide a remedy for the evils which afflict it?" P. R. O., F. O., Mexico, vol. 60, no. 30, March 25, 1830.

[26] Eugène Duflot de Mofras, *Exploration du territoire de l'Orégon, des Californies, et de la Mer Vermeille, exécutée pendant les années 1840, -41, -42* (Paris, 1844, 2 vols.), I, 36.

[27] *Carta al E. S. Presidente de la República,* par Don J. M. Gutierrez de Estrada, antiguo Ministro de Relaciones interiores y exteriores (Mexico, 1840).

trace in its details the arguments by which Gutierrez sought to sustain his point of view. But what is necessary and important is to point out the clear antagonism to the United States which lay at the basis of this monarchical scheme. " I can discover," he writes, " no other means of saving our nationality, in deadly peril from the Anglo-Saxon race, which translated to this continent, prepares to invade it all, supporting itself, on the democratic principle, element of life and strength for it, but the germ of weakness and death for us." And again, " Can we flatter ourselves that we can better our deplorable situation [except by a change of political form]? If our situation grows worse from day to day, as must happen unless we have recourse to a radical and vigorous remedy, will we be able to resist this raging torrent of the North, which has already invaded our territory, and which will inundate it all with the onrush of democratic principles, which constitute the strength of that people, as they visibly constitute our weakness?" Language like this make clear that schemes of European monarchy were very definitely related to hostility to the American government. And conversely, it makes clear also that Monroe and Adams were wholly right when they conceived of European monarchy in the New World as alien to the interests of their country.

The clash of systems which Gutierrez de Estrada outlined was to express itself in dramatic form before a quarter of a century had gone by. At the time, however, Gutierrez de Estrada's appeal earned him only execration. He was compelled to flee the country, being

allowed to escape with the connivance of the government, whose chief, in his heart of hearts, perhaps, was
not unfavorable to the whole monarchical idea. Yet he
was not alone in his point of view. The French traveler, Duflot de Mofras, who travelled throughout the
length and breadth of Mexico in this period, wrote at
about the same time that " the mine-owners, the great
land-holders, the honorable merchants, the old noblesse,
all the families in which are found the Spanish virtues,
the feeling of honor and loyalty, regret the fall of the
monarchical régime, and long for its reestablishment." [28]
De Mofras was, of course, sympathetic with this point
of view, indeed he saw in the reestablishment of royal
government the only solution of the question of an independent Mexico, and believed that if it could not be
brought about, the best which could be hoped for (and
this even from the standpoint of French interests)
would be the absorption of Mexico by the United
States; but his testimony is that of a clear-eyed, if no
doubt partial, observer.[29] The course of events in the
next few years, indeed, was to furnish ample evidence
of the existence of a monarchical sentiment which would
have to be reckoned with, and would, sooner or later,
be translated into a vigorous effort for the restoration
of monarchical government and of the European con-

[28] Duflot de Mofras, op. cit., p. 30.

[29] See also on this question of monarchy L. M. del Rivero,
Méjico en 1842 (Madrid, 1844), which offers further testimony
as to the strength of monarchical sentiment, pp. 90 and 102. See
also I. Löwenstern, Le Mexique. Souvenirs d'un Voyage (Paris,
1843), which declares republicanism to be an impossible form of
government for Mexico, p. 455.

nection. The clash of systems implicit, yes, explicit, in the Monroe Doctrine, is thus to be discovered beneath the surface of international politics in these relatively uneventful years between 1826 and 1841.

Even in this period, indeed, there are some evidences of interest on the part of European governments in the monarchical idea in Mexico. The first of these emanates from the French premier, Jean de Villèle, who, in an earlier epoch, had been the partisan of Bourbon monarchies in the New World. In 1827 Villèle commissioned the Marquis Crouy-Chanel to negotiate with Ferdinand VII, in order that the Infante Francisco de Paula might be sent out to become Emperor of Mexico. As had been the case in 1824 and 1825, Ferdinand was stubbornly opposed to any such project. But the Infante himself felt very differently. He was, indeed, inclined to leave for the New World even without the consent of his brother and authorized the marquis to treat with the Mexican authorities, negotiate a loan, and attempt to win the favor of the British government by granting commercial privileges. The French king, and Villèle, were not enthusiastic over any such alteration of their original plan, but Crouy-Chanel visited London in order to seek a loan to carry the project through. His efforts were a complete failure, and the whole scheme seems to have come to an end, for the time being.[30]

---

[30] For the episode above see D. J. Hidalgo, *Apuntes para Escribir la Historia de los Proyectos de Monarquía en México desde el Reinado de Carlos III hasta la Instalación del Emperador Maximiliano* (Paris, 1868). Hidalgo was one of the lead-

during this rue

failure

In 1829, however, relying upon the reports of strong monarchical elements in the country, the Spanish government attempted the conquest of Mexico. A small force of men was landed at Tampico in the romantic expectation that a large number of Mexicans would rally to it. No such rallying took place, however, and the whole effort ended in a complete and humiliating fiasco. Yet the Spanish government does not seem to have foregone entirely the hope of an arrangement that might restore monarchy in Mexico. In 1833, at least a decade after the proposal was practicable, it cautiously sounded the Chilean minister at Paris with regard to sending out Don Carlos to rule in Mexico City.[31] The enterprise came to nothing; indeed a violent Hispanophobia settled upon Mexico after the abortive expedition of 1829. But the episode is interesting from the standpoint from which we are studying the problem, and it shows, what could be amply demonstrated, that the hope of the reestablishment of monarchical forms was never completely extinguished in Europe. At a later date, at the time of the pamphlet of Gutierrez de Estrada, both the French and British ministers in Mexico City complimented the author on the sound judgment which

ing Mexican monarchists. See also E. K. H. Freiherr von Richthofen, *Die Aüssern und Inneren Politischen Zustände der Republik Mexico seit deren Unabhängigkeit bis auf die neueste Zeit* (Berlin, 1859), pp. 72-3.

[31] See *British and Foreign State Papers*, XXII, pp. 1108-1116. See also R. Soto Mayor Valdes, *Historia de Chile bajo il Gobierno del Jeneral D. Joaquin Prieto* (4 vols., Santiago, 1900-05), I, 362-66.

lay behind his view.[32] Though nothing was attempted in practise, European judges of Mexican affairs frequently found monarchy to be the only salvation of the distracted condition of that unhappy country.

So the story runs, indeed, with regard to other states of Latin America, though not with regard to all of them. Proceeding southward from Mexico, we shall find in Central America something of the same condition of affairs, though there, during most of the period covered by this chapter, the Liberals, under their great leader, Francisco Morazan, were in more or less complete control. The conservative classes, as in Mexico, undoubtedly remained loyal to monarchy in theory, and hoped for the restoration of a European connection. They were sustained and encouraged by the British minister, Chatfield. In 1839, indeed, on the break-up of the Central American federation, the Nicaraguan minister, Soliz, appealed to Chatfield not only to ask the mediation of the British government in the struggle with Salvador, but also for a "powerful and impartial guarantor" between them.[33] His appeal was echoed by Pavón, one of the leading conservatives of Guatemala.[34] There was much hope that Costa Rica could be persuaded to join in a movement to establish a British protectorate.[35] These ideas got nowhere, for Palmerston would assume no

[32] Gutierrez de Estrada, *Méjico y el Archiduque Fernando Maximilian de Austria,* pp. 14-16 (Mexico, 1862).

[33] Lorenzo Montufar, *Reseña Histórica de Centro-America* (7 vols., Guatemala, 1881), IV, 70.

[34] *Ibid.,* p. 76.

[35] *Ibid.,* p. 78.

obligation to use armed force in Central America, but their existence and the encouragement given them by the British minister on the spot is a matter of no small interest to the student of the Monroe Doctrine.

In Colombia the question of European connection was of real importance at the beginning of the period. Bolivar, as the researches of Professor Arragon have already shown,[36] at an early period in his political career had in mind some kind of British protectorate, and we can find allusions to this conception in his correspondence as early as 1815. But the idea attained a greater importance in 1825 and 1826, and although it never took a wholly definite form, it was at least sufficiently real to form the subject of conversation with British agents, and with some of the great Colombian's associates in the war for independence. The British government would have nothing to do with any such conception, but as time went on, and the political conditions in Colombia became worse rather than better through the strife of factions, the idea of a monarchy with a European connection began to take shape in the mind of many of the conservatives. The scheme was to make Bolivar sovereign, and then to provide for the reversion of the kingdom thus established to some European prince. There are evidences of the existence of this scheme as early as 1825, when General Paez, the famous llanero who had played so great a rôle in Venezuela as the champion of independence, sent a mission

[36] R. F. Arragon, *The Congress of Panama,* doctor's thesis in Harvard University Library.

to Lima to offer the crown of Colombia to the Liberator.[37]

The idea received a very considerable impetus from the disordered state of Colombia in the years which followed, which obliged Bolivar to put aside constitutional forms, and to assume the dictatorship in the spring of 1828. It reached its climax in the course of 1829. By this time the Council of State, which was governing the country in the absence of Bolivar, was very decidedly turning toward monarchy. In the fall of the year, the Colombian minister, by instructions of September 8, 1829, was directed to sound the French government with regard to the monarchical idea, and to intimate that on the death of Bolivar a prince of the House of Orleans might be chosen as king. France was to be asked for men, money, and arms to aid in sustaining the new régime.[38] At the same time the British government was sounded as to the project, though in more general terms, and, of course, without mentioning the intended succession.[39]

It is almost certain that the French commissioner at Bogotá, Bresson, was in favor of this scheme, and that the special messenger whom he sent back to France in the fall of 1829 was charged with presenting it in a

[37] J. Humbert, *Histoire de la Colombie, et du Vénézuéla des Origines jusqu'à nos Jours* (Paris, 1921), p. 172. See also C. A. Villanueva, *El Imperio de los Andes* (Paris, 1913), p. 42.

[38] Instructions furnished by Dr. Zubieta of the Colombian Foreign Office.

[39] Instructions of September 8, 1829, to José Fernandez Madrid, Colombian minister at London. Furnished by Dr. Zubieta.

favorable light to his government.[40] The British minister was not averse to the project, since he corresponded with Bolivar with regard to it, and in a long despatch to his government set forth the case in favor of monarchy, which, even if it involved a French connection, did not seem to him to jeopardize British interests.[41] As for the Liberator, he never committed himself definitely, but there is some reason to believe, from a letter of his to Colonel Campbell, that he was not disinclined toward it, if he could have been sure that it would have obtained for his unhappy country the support of powerful European states.[42]

[40] See instructions just cited.

[41] See especially London, P. R. O., F. O., Colombia, vol. 52, September 13, 1829, and December 6, 1829.

[42] Encl. in *ibid.,* September 6. Encl. in P. R. O., F. O., Colombia, vol. 66, September 13, 1829.

" That which you are pleased to tell me concerning the new project of appointing a Successor to my authority, in the person of a European Prince, does not take me by surprize, because something of the kind had already been communicated to me with no small mystery and with a certain timidity, my way of thinking being well known. I know not what to say to you on this project, which contains within it a thousand difficulties. You must be aware that, so far as regards me, there will be none, determined as I am to resign the Government into the hands of the approaching Congress; but who shall be able to contain the ambition of our Chiefs or to assuage among the lower orders the apprehension of the destruction of equality (of rights)? Do you not think that England would feel jealous at the election of a Bourbon? What an opposition would there not be made by all the new American States? And the United States who appear destined by Providence to bring on America a plague of miseries under the name of Liberty! It seems to me that I already see a Confederacy of all the Republics of

But the difficulties in the way of any such program proved insuperable. The French government was never interested in it, and it recalled Bresson in November of 1829.[43] Lord Aberdeen, the British Foreign Secretary, was strongly opposed to the selection of a French prince, and when consulted on the matter, suggested the

America against our poor Colombia (already too much the object of invidious feelings). On all sides would the Press be put in action calling for fresh Crusade against the accomplices of Treason against Liberty, of the Partisans of the Bourbons, of the violators of the American system. In the South, the Peruvians would kindle the flame of discord, on the side of the Isthmus, Guatemala and Mexico would do the same, and throughout the Antilles, Americans and Liberals of all descriptions would follow the example. St. Domingo would not remain inactive, and would call on her brethren to make common cause against a Prince of France. All the states would be converted into enemies, without anything being done by Europe for our support; seeing that the New World is not worthy of the cares of the Holy Alliance; at least we have reason to think so, from the indifference with which have been witnessed our efforts and struggles for the emancipation of one half of the world, which will soon prove the most productive source of Prosperity to Europe.

" In short, I am very far from opposing the re-organization of Colombia, after the model of the approved institutions of enlightened Europe. On the contrary, I should be most happy and would exert myself with increased energy in favor of a work which might be entitled one of salvation; but which would be accomplished, not without difficulty, were we supported by England and France. With these potent allies we should be adequate to everything, without them we could do nothing. For this reserve my definite opinion until we shall learn what the Governments of England and of France think of the proposed change of system, and of the election of dynasties."

[43] Paris, Min. des Aff. Etr., Corr. Pol., Colombie, vol. 4, instruction of August, 1829, and November 21, 1829.

choice of a member of the Spanish royal family, a
choice utterly unacceptable to the Colombians.[44] Without any effective European backing the plan of the
Colombian conservatives was not likely to make much
headway. Bolivar himself repudiated it when it was
submitted to him by the Council, denouncing it in
unsparing terms.[45]

The incident, despite the collapse of the scheme,
has its decided interest. It well illustrates the orientation of Colombia in the late twenties. The trend in
Latin America, despite Monroe's message, was very
decidedly toward closer relations with European governments, not with the government at Washington.
Bolivar himself, though repudiating the monarchical
scheme, felt this as strongly as did others.

The collapse of the plans of the monarchists, it
may be added, did not take place until their plans had
produced a minor crisis in the relations of Colombia
with the great Republic of the North. In 1828, General
William Henry Harrison was sent by the Adams administration as minister to Bogotá. This bucolic personage
(for so at least he appeared to the Colombians) soon
identified himself with the party of the republicans.
Ordered out of the country in September, 1829, he
capped his indiscretions by a long letter to Bolivar, in
which, with an eloquence of which the word " ornate "

[44] See Madrid's despatch of December 16, 1829, furnished by
Dr. Zubieta.

[45] For further discussion, see J. M. Groot, *Historia Eclesiás-
tica y Civil de Nueva Granada, Escrita sobre Documentos
Auténticos* (5 vols., Bogotá, 1889-93), especially V, 302-15.

is a mild description, and with a wealth of classical allusion as striking as that which irked Daniel Webster at the time of Harrison's inaugural, he pleaded with the Liberator to put away ambition and to scorn a crown. His expulsion illustrates, in a measure, how little pleasing to Bogotá in 1829 was the republican idealism which, a little more than five years before, had inspired the message of Monroe.[46]

In the face of this threatened reversion to monarchy in Colombia the influence of the United States was unimportant. Moral suasion it did attempt to apply. Harrison, himself, though warned against interference in domestic politics, had been directed on " proper occasions " to express the " ardent hope " that Colombia's dissensions might "terminate in the establishment of constitutional government," and had been authorized to communicate freely and frankly the nature of our institutions and their practical operation.[47] His successor, the Jacksonian Democrat, T. P. Moore, was instructed in much the same sense. But, as has been made clear, other factors were decisive in putting an end to such projects, and shortly thereafter the death of Bolivar, and the break-up of Greater Colombia into the two states of New Granada and Venezuela dealt the monarchical idea a blow that was virtually final.

[46] For this episode, see A. C. Rivas, *Ensayos de Historia Política y Diplomática* (Madrid, 1916). *La Diplomacia de los Estados Unidos y la Monarquía en Colombia,* pp. 164 *et seq.* See also Dorothy B. Goebel, *William Henry Harrison* (Indianapolis, 1926), pp. 256 *et seq.*

[47] Washington, Dept. of State, Instructions to Ministers, Colombia., vol. XII, pp. 152-55.

4

It would be easy to exaggerate the importance of such monarchical plans as those we have been examining. Only in Mexico do they culminate in a serious threat to the republican tradition in the New World. The general trend of Latin American politics in the period which we are examining is undoubtedly toward a greater self-sufficiency and independence. In particular, in the states of South America proper, with their greater remoteness from Europe, and consequent security from interference, national individuality becomes more clearly defined, and the thought of a European connection is abandoned. Local oligarchies or dictators supply to Latin American conservatives what they might otherwise have hoped to gain from a closer association with the Old World. Monarchical projects tend to disappear. An imperial Brazil might seek, as it actually did seek in 1830, to promote the idea of constitutional kingship, and invoke the diplomatic support of Old World powers for its policy, but in general the drift was in the other direction. In the Argentine and in Uruguay one finds references to the monarchical idea in 1828, but these references seem to mark the end of an epoch. In the first of these states the picturesque, ferocious, and vigorous Rosas dominates the scene from 1829; and in the latter the convulsions of the Civil War, though they reveal factions more and less friendly to Europe, do not connect themselves with projects of kingship. In Chile a shrewd, land-holding oligarchy secures practical control of government, and asks nothing better than the perpetuation of the reactionary constitution

which it has framed; in Paraguay, landlocked and isolated, the dictator Francia dominates the scene; and in
the tangled politics of Peru and Ecuador and Bolivia
one meets often extreme conservatism and military dictatorship, but, as far as I have been able to discover
almost no traces of a desire to revive the old connection with Spain, or to cement one with any other European state. Though we shall have to treat of the abortive
monarchical plot of Flores of Ecuador in a later chapter,
and though, of course, we must analyze at length the
development of monarchical ideas in Mexico, in general
we may say that sentiment in favor of European monarchy or of a direct connection with a European state
was pretty well dissipated by 1841. This does not mean
that European influences were not still strong; it does
not mean that there was any very close political sympathy with the United States; it signifies merely that
the new-born states of Latin America were becoming
genuinely attached to their national independence.

The attempt on the part of European nations to
extend their territorial sovereignty in the New World,
and the efforts made in the Old World and in the New
to restore the connection between Latin America and
Europe involve the principles of the Monroe Doctrine
in a fairly direct and obvious manner. But it is interesting to observe that the Doctrine was actually invoked
in several instances, in which its application may be
said to be less obvious. One of these relates to the
war between La Plata and the Empire of Brazil. On
August 17, 1826, the Argentine President, Rivadavia,

had a conference with Forbes, the American minister at Buenos Ayres. He attempted to maintain the thesis that the close family connection between Brazil and the European states of Portugal and Austria made it possible to invoke the principles of 1823, which involved, as he declared, " the policy of shutting out from this Continent all European power and influence." [48] To this ingenious but not wholly convincing argument, Forbes returned a noncommittal reply. Apparently this reply diminished Argentine hopes, but did not utterly dash them. On August 24, de la Cruz, the Argentine foreign secretary, addressed a note to the American containing two questions, less related to the existing situation than Rivadavia's remarks to Forbes, but connected with the Monroe Doctrine. These questions were as follows: first, whether the principles enunciated in 1823 would apply in case Brazil were aided by a European power, and second, if it would apply in case the Emperor of Brazil attempted to draw from Portugal any kind of assistance.[49] The government at Washington made no haste to reply to the Argentine interrogatory. But finally, on January 3, 1828, Clay responded to Forbes. Following the technique of Adams on a previous occasion, he minimized the danger of European action, asserting that in the event of such action the decision would rest with Congress. He then proceeded to declare that the existing war, as a purely American affair, did not bear " the remotest analogy " to the case which

[48] For this whole episode, see W. S. Robertson, *Political Science Quarterly*, XXX, 101-04, especially p. 102.
[49] *Ibid.*, p. 103.

President Monroe's message deprecates. His action was a definite and complete rebuff.

Far more important than this case, however, are the instances of coercive action by European states against Latin American ones and of political intermeddling in the domestic affairs of these states. There are several incidents which deserve to be examined under this head. The earliest in point of time is the British blockade of the port of Cartagena, the principal harbor of the state of New Granada, in the year 1837. The occasion for this blockade was a street brawl in the city of Panama, in which one of the principal actors was the British consul Russell. On the basis of alleged indignities heaped upon the head of this individual (who, by the way, from the impartial standpoint of history, does not seem to have exhibited any very heroic self-restraint on his own part) a British squadron proclaimed the closing of the ports of New Granada, on January 21, 1837.[50] The New Granadan minister at Washington acting apparently without instructions appealed to the government of the United States on the basis of the Monroe Doctrine,[51] declaring that the British action concealed ambitions to possess the Isthmus of Panama, already beginning to be actively talked about in connection with

[50] For the documents, see *British and Foreign State Papers,* XVI (1837-38), pp. 128 *et seq.* See also in this connection, the important article by Falcke, "Die Friedensblockade," in *Zeitschrift für internationales privat-und-öffentliches Recht,* XIX, 68-175, especially pp. 96-100.

[51] Washington, Dept. of State, New Granada, Notes from, vol. 2, February 25, 1837.

an inter-oceanic canal, but Secretary Forsyth took no
action. Despite the fact that the Jackson administration had taken sufficient interest in the canal project to
despatch Colonel Biddle to the Isthmus in 1835, it
refused to permit itself to be alarmed by the fear of
British aggression. Indeed, by the time the Granadan
note had been delivered, the blockade had been lifted,
and the Secretary therefore contented himself with a
reply which really evaded the point at issue.[52] British
intentions had, no doubt, been innocent enough, and
there was no reason for Forsyth to act otherwise than
he did. ✓

The Monroe Doctrine also figured, though to a minor
degree, in the case of the French blockade of Mexico in
1837-39. This blockade had its origins in the failure
of the Mexican government, passing through a period of
domestic turmoil only too characteristic of its history, to
give the slightest satisfaction with regard to the claims
of French citizens, claims swollen to a figure worthy
of a bourgeois monarch like Louis Philippe, but not
without some justification in fact. The French government, pacific in the broad lines of its European policy,
was not averse, especially under the weak ministry of
M. Molé, to satisfying the critics of its generally cautious policy by vigorous action in defense of French
interests under circumstances where the risks can hardly
be said to have been great. At the end of 1837 the
French minister at Mexico City withdrew, and from
on board a French naval vessel in the harbor of Vera

[52] *Ibid.*, Notes to Legations, VI, March 2, 1837.

Cruz addressed to the Mexican government a vigorous demand for satisfaction, accompanied by a threat of a blockade if no answer were returned within three weeks' time. The demand was indignantly repelled, and in the summer of 1838 Captain Bazoche, of the French naval forces, instituted what was called a pacific blockade. In October an additional French squadron was sent out, under Admiral Baudin, and after a futile attempt at negotiation, the fortress of San Juan de Ulloa was bombarded and forced to surrender on November 28. A week later the city of Vera Cruz was temporarily occupied, and its guns put out of commission, after which the French forces withdrew to their ships. At the end of the year a deadlock existed between the two governments, the Mexicans refusing to treat, and the French being unable, with the forces at their command, to undertake any extensive operations on land.[53]

It would not have been surprising if these events had produced a rather unfavorable reaction in the United States. As a matter of fact, in the press comment of the time, there is a surprising lack of interest in them. Though most of the important newspapers carried descriptive accounts of what had transpired, any kind of

[53] For the documents, see *Archivo Histórico Diplomático Mexicano.*, XXVII. *La Primera Guerra entre Méjico y Francia* (Mexico, 1927). For a good secondary account see G. L. Rives, *The United States and Mexico* (2 vols., 1913, I, 433-446). There is a briefer discussion in Paul Thureau-Dangin, *Histoire de la Monarchie de Juillet* (Paris, 1884-92, 7 vols.), III, 307-8. See also the article by Falcke, *op. cit.*, in *Zeitschrift für internationales privat-und-öffentliches Recht,* XIX, especially pp. 101-111.

editorial comment is extremely rare. But before long the French action led to the introduction in Congress of a resolution in which the Monroe Doctrine was directly cited, and in which the President was asked for information as to what explanations the French government had given to the United States with regard to its blockade of the Mexican coast, and with regard to " the ulterior views and designs of the French government with regard to the Mexican Republic." [54] The mover of this resolution was Caleb Cushing of Massachusetts later to be the negotiator of the first treaty between the United States and China, and to enjoy a long, varied, and able, if somewhat inconsistent, career as politician, statesman and diplomat. On the 11th of February, that is, after considerable delay, the House accepted the Cushing proposal without a division.[55]

[54] *Cong. Globe,* 25th Cong., 3rd Sess., p. 82.

[55] *Ibid.,* p. 176. The language of the resolution was as follows:

" WHEREAS, In the message of the President of the United States at the opening of the Eighteenth Congress, it was, among other things, avowed and proclaimed as the settled policy of the United States, that ' in the wars of European Powers, in matters relating to themselves, we have never taken any part, nor does it comport with our policy to do so,' that ' with the movements in this hemisphere we are, of necessity, more immediately connected,' that ' we owe it therefore to candor, and to the amicable relations existing between the United States and those Powers, to declare that we should consider any attempt on their part to extend their system to any portion of this hemisphere as dangerous to our peace and safety '; that, ' with the existing colonies or dependencies of any European Power, we have not interfered, and shall not interfere but with Governments who have declared their independence and maintained it, and whose independence we have, on great consideration and just principles acknowledged, we could not view any interposition for the

The resolution, of course, committed to nothing; it did not imply that the United States would take action in this specific case under the Monroe message; it mentioned the message, indeed, only in a long preamble. And yet the invocation of the principles of 1823 is in itself an interesting thing; and interesting, too, is the fact that the appeal to those principles passed without question.

The action of the executive branch of the government, however, was never based on the message of Mon-

---

purpose of oppressing them, or controlling in any other manner their destiny, by any European Power, or [*sic!*] in any other light than as the manifestation of an unfriendly disposition, toward the United States,' and that ' it is impossible, therefore, that we should behold such interposition, in any form, with indifference,'

" *Resolved, therefore,* That the President of the United States be requested to inform this House, if the same be not, in his judgment, incompatible with the public interest, what explanations the King of France has rendered to the United States in relation to the recent blockade of a part of the coast of the Mexican Republic by France; the treatment of vessels of the United States, public or private, by the blockading squadron; the reduction of the castle of San Juan de Ulloa; and the ulterior views and designs of the French Government respecting the Mexican Republic. Also, to inform the House whether he has proffered to either of the contending parties the mediation of the United States in the premises, and to communicate any correspondence on the subjects aforesaid which may have passed between the Government of the United States and that of France. And that the President be in like manner requested to communicate to the House information of the same tenor in regard to the blockade of Rio de La Plata by the French, and the differences existing between the French Government and the Argentine Republic." The last clause was not included in the resolution as introduced by Cushing on December 31. See below, p. 55.

roe. Some time after the resolution just cited, President Van Buren replied to the action of the House by transmitting a whole sheaf of documents to Congress. These documents revealed that the administration had not been indifferent to what was occurring in Mexico, though its hands had been tied, at the beginning of the Franco-Mexican controversy, by the none too cordial relations then existing between the Mexican government and the United States. The American government had at this time no regularly accredited diplomatic representative at Mexico City. It had its own claims difficulties with the Mexicans. Indeed so strained were relations at the beginning of 1838 that Deffaudis, the French minister at Mexico City, recommended to Bazoche the prompt establishment of a blockade lest the United States anticipate France in such action.[56] By September 11, 1838, however, a claims convention had been negotiated at Washington.[57] On the 28th of October, 1838, the acting Secretary of State, Mr. Vail, had written to Lewis Cass, our minister to France, that the President would be glad to bring about a termination of the existing dispute, but that he abstained from a formal offer of mediation since word had come to him that the British government had already made a move to the same end. Cass was authorized to express the readiness of the United States to afford assistance " in any form in which it may appear likely to appear beneficial," and was informed that similar instructions had been given

[56] Paris, Min. des Aff. Etr., Corr. Pol., Mexique, vol. 12, January 22, 1838.

[57] See Rives, *op. cit.*, I, 417-33.

to the American minister at London. Thus, two months before the Cushing resolution was introduced, the executive department of the government had moved to put an end to the controversy.[58] It had invoked no general principles; it had not mentioned the name of Monroe; but it had taken steps to compose the difficulty.

There is nothing, however, in the correspondence of the State Department, or in the letters of Van Buren, which leads one to the conclusion that the administration was at any time fearful of ulterior designs on the part of the French in Mexico. Nor, so far as can be ascertained, did such designs exist in reality. The instructions given to the French diplomatic and naval representatives in Mexico give no hint of any project of conquest;[59] and it seems equally improbable that any dream of monarchy figured in the purposes of the ministers of Louis Philippe. It was a *conservative* régime against which the blockade of 1838 was directed; and Admiral Baudin's correspondence shows that his personal sympathies were very decidedly with the liberal faction of the Mexicans.[60] There are other reasons, too,

[58] 25th Cong. 3rd Sess., H. Ex. Doc., No. 211, p. 39.

[59] Paris, Min. des Aff. Etr., Corr. Pol., Mexique, vol. 13.

[60] *San Juan de Ulúa. Relations de l'Expédition Française au Mexique, sous les ordres de M. le Contre-amiral Baudin,* par MM. P. Blanchard et A. Dauzats. *Suivi de notes et documents, et d'un aperçu général sur l'état actuel du Texas,* par M. E. Maissin, lieutenant de vaisseau, aide-de-camp de l'amiral Baudin (Paris, 1839), p. 459. To the Liberal general Urrea Baudin wrote as follows: "In civil wars, no intervention, no aid from outside, ought to be permitted. . . . . I do not come to offer to the cause of federalism an aid which might render it less popular on the day when its banner was united to that of a

for not taking French action in Mexico too seriously. In the summer of 1838 the British Foreign Office had demanded assurances from the Quai d'Orsay as to French purposes, and these assurances had been given.[61] The action taken, moreover, had from the beginning the opposition of powerful commercial interests, and was certainly none too popular with the country at large.[62] From the military point of view, France was deeply concerned in consolidating its position in Algeria. Finally, having regard to the general temper of French policy under Louis Philippe, it is almost fantastic to assume that the bourgeois monarch meditated at any time a policy of adventure in the New World.

The caution of Van Buren and Forsyth, their failure to invoke the principles of 1823, is, therefore, not hard to understand. Their interest in the Mexican blockade was quite properly confined to solicitude with regard to American trade; nor was there any good reason why they should not content themselves with permitting the British to undertake the so often thankless task of mediation between the contending parties. The French dispute with Mexico was, therefore, composed by the skillful diplomacy of Pakenham, and brought to an end by the convention of March 8, 1839.

---

foreigner. If, *as I like to believe,* this cause is the national cause of Mexico, it will triumph and will owe its triumph only to itself."

[61] *British and Foreign State Papers,* XXVI, p. 897.

[62] See in this connection the reply to the King's speech in the Chambre des Pairs at the opening of the session of 1839, in which the hope is expressed that the "too prolonged differences" with Mexico will soon be brought to an end. *Archives Parlementaires,* CXXIII, 47-8.

Before leaving this episode, there is one other aspect of it which deserves passing attention. It is the rôle of the British government in the whole business. It acted, it will be observed, more promptly than that of the United States; it took stronger action than did the United States; and it was more influential in bringing the controversy to an end than was the United States. No less than in 1823, it recognized the existence of important interests in the New World, and far less than then, did it accord any particular deference to the point of view of the American government. The comparative weight of the two English-speaking nations in Latin America is, in a measure, at least, revealed by this diplomatic controversy to have been much what it was fifteen years before, and the contrast between the activity of the Court of St. James, and the relative restraint of the government at Washington is an interesting commentary on the respective positions of both at the time when it occurred.

It is clear, too, that British public opinion was much more concerned with the French blockade than was public opinion in the United States. Save for the Cushing resolution, which passed without debate, there is no reference to the action against Mexico in the debates in Congress, whereas on the other hand a prolonged debate took place in the House of Commons in the first months of 1839, in which the ministry was put quite decidedly upon the defensive.[63]

[63] Hansard, *Parliamentary Debates*, 3rd series, XLVI, 891-939.

This contrast in political attitude no doubt corresponds with a difference of economic interest. British capital in 1839 still dominated in Mexico. British trade was still far more important than the trade of the United States. To the economic determinist these facts will seem, no doubt, of the first, indeed of decisive, importance. Yet it is well to remember that in the case of the Monroe Doctrine, the economic argument often breaks down or recedes into the background. Though influential in connection with the evolution of the noncolonization principle, it played little part in the warning to Europe against intervention in 1823, and in later days, especially in one of the most dramatic invocations of the Doctrine, the Cleveland message with regard to Venezuela, it was to have a very limited significance. While giving due weight, therefore, to the economic facts as they stood in 1838 and 1839, something must be attributed, at least so far as the United States is concerned, to a political indifference which is not uncharacteristic of the general temper of the Van Buren administration, and which, though it may in part be explained by the fact that the country was just recovering from the disastrous panic of 1837, is also to be set down to Mr. Van Buren's whole attitude toward foreign policy. No man was less adventurous in foreign affairs (as the Texan episode may serve to demonstrate) than the shrewd successor of Old Hickory.

But the Cushing resolution of 1839, as the assiduous reader of footnotes will have noticed, alluded not only to the French intervention in Mexico, but to the French intervention in La Plata. And of the two episodes, the La Platan is by far the more important, involving as it did not only the establishment of a pacific blockade, but also the intervention, by French agents on the spot, in the domestic affairs of two Latin American governments, that of the Argentine, and that of Uruguay. The relations of France with the Argentine had been troubled as early as 1829. The original cause of the difficulty lay in the Argentine law of April 10, 1821, which required foreigners who had been domiciled more than two years within the country, to perform the same duty of military service as nationals. As early as the year 1829, this law had been the cause of a dispute between the Argentine government and the French consul. So strained, indeed, had relations become that the consul had called to his aid a vessel of the French squadron off the coast of Brazil, commanded by the Vicomte de Venancourt. De Venancourt, unable to secure satisfaction from the government, had in April of 1829 seized the Argentine vessels of war, and by this action brought the government to terms. In the course of this episode, it is worth noting, the French consul suggested to his government the sending out of a whole fleet, and the occupation of Patagonia as a measure of satisfaction for the indignities suffered by French citizens.[64] But difficulties far more serious broke out in 1838. At this time La Plata was under the domination of one of the most remarkable men in the history of Latin America. Juan Manuel de Rosas was a landholder

[64] Paris, Min. des Aff. Etr., Corr. Pol., Buenos Ayres, May 13, 1829, cited in C. A. Villanueva, *Historia de la República Argentina* (2 vols., Paris, 1914), II (Rosas), p. 58.

of good family, but of little education, who, participating in the civil wars of the period, had risen to supreme control of La Platan affairs in 1829, and who was to exercise a virtual dictatorship during most of his long rule down to his defeat and exile in 1852. In general, it may be truly said that in the field of foreign policy Rosas was something of a brawler, or, to put it more charitably, a striking representative of the sensitive national pride which is so characteristic, not only of the Spanish race, but of the people of almost any young and growing nation. But in the quarrel with France, it cannot be said that the responsibility for the rupture which occurred was by any means wholly his. It seems rather to have lain with Monsieur Aimé Roger, the young and inexperienced vice-consul of France at Buenos Ayres. This youth appears, from the beginning of his authority, to have been anxious to pick a quarrel with the Argentine government. The basis of the quarrel was again found in the Argentine law of April 10, 1821. This law, during Rosas's dictatorship, had not for the most part been enforced against the French, and was certainly not being enforced against them in 1838, but it served as an excellent pretext for making trouble. The detention in prison of several French citizens, one of them on grounds of corresponding with the enemies of the state, and the others on charges similar, but of less gravity, afforded a further basis for demands on the Argentine government. The actual situation was reported by Roger to his government in such terms as to lead straight on toward strong measures. In this case, as in that of Mexico, the weak ministry of Molé was glad to seek to counterbalance its extremely mild European policy by an appearance of strong action in the New World. Roger, therefore, acting on instructions, began a diplomatic controversy with the Argentine government which ended in his being given his passports, on March 13, 1838. Retiring to Montevideo, he there found Admiral LeBlanc, who had sailed south from Rio de Janeiro to take a hand in the business, and on the 24th the Admiral backed up the demands of the consul in a note which was a virtual ultimatum. On the 28th, since Rosas refused to yield to the threat of force, a French blockade was proclaimed, of Buenos Ayres and the adjacent litoral. And if Thiers had had his way, Thiers of the brilliant mind and aggressive temper, 6000 more troops would have been sent to La Plata to signalize still further the purpose of France to support the foes of the dictator.[65]

The dispute with the Argentine government which thus eventuated in armed action was not to be settled for more than two years. It was, in a sense, a far more serious threat to the independent action of an American state than was the blockade of the Mexican coast. For, from the very beginning of coercive action, the French

[65] For the discussion of this dispute, see Adolfo Saldías, *op. cit.*, II, 298-320. M. A. Pelliza, *La Dictadura de Rosas* (Buenos Ayres, 1917), pp. 105-7, and, more important than either, Villanueva, *Historia de la República Argentina, op. cit.*, II, (Rosas), pp. 175-201, with the principal French documents. A. de Brossard, *Considérations Historiques et Politiques sur les Républiques de La Plata dans leur Rapports avec la France et l'Angleterre* (Paris, 1850), especially pp. 217-240.

5

authorities on the spot, despite the cautious language of
their instructions under three successive ministries [66]
pursued a policy of scandalous meddling in the domestic
affairs of La Plata and of its neighbor, Uruguay.

In order to understand that policy, it is necessary to
say a word with regard to the internal situation in these
two states. In Uruguay, General Oribe had succeeded
Fructuoso Rivera as the legally elected President of the
republic in 1835. But the latter soon took arms against
him, and there began a civil war which, from the beginning, was knit up with the course of affairs in the
Argentine. For Rivera, from the beginning, gave aid
and comfort to the enemies of Rosas, amongst others
to General Lavalle, one of the most energetic and well
known leaders of the Unitarian party, as the anti-
Rosistas were called. Oribe, on the other hand, was
friendly to the existing government of the Argentine,
and his victory was naturally ardently desired at Buenos
Ayres. From this confusing situation Roger and the
French admiral, LeBlanc, attempted to make their profit
for France, or perhaps it would be almost as exact to say
that they permitted themselves to be made the tools of
the enemies of Rosas. Though the British consul offered
mediation on favorable terms at the very beginning of
the Franco-Argentine dispute, and though the attitude
of Rosas himself was conciliatory, Roger, played on by
the enemies of Rosas at Montevideo, refused to accept
any accommodation. And when the blockade was initi-

[66] F. P. Guizot, *Histoire Parlementaire de la France* (5 vols.,
1863), III, 414 *et seq.*

ated, it was followed within seven months by the occupation of the important strategic island post of Martín García, in which operation French marines fought side by side with troops of General Rivera, and the success of which virtually determined the collapse of the cause of Oribe. Not content with this, the French agents subsidized the "Argentine commission," as the central anti-Rosista body at Montevideo was called, encouraged General Berón de Astrada in the province of Corrientes to league himself with Rivera, and partially raised the blockade to facilitate his operations. General Lavalle, the hero of the Unitarian party, was also incited to revolt, and the French fleet put at the aid of his movements, while a series of attacks on various coast cities still further emphasized the sweeping designs of the French agents. In the virtual alliance of the French with the Unitarians, was to be seen that partiality for the European as distinguished from the American party. What began as a measure of coercion for redress of grievances soon developed into actual intervention, and when the aggressive Thiers ministry came in in 1840, only the opposition of the King prevented the despatch of a considerable force to aid in carrying on the struggle. There were at least some Frenchmen, some responsible Frenchmen like Thiers, who were ready to play fast and loose with revolutionary factions in the New World, and intervene in a manner which would certainly scandalize the people of the United States if it were indulged in today. And yet it cannot be said that the aims of the successive ministries which handled the La Platan question in the years 1838-40 were ever aggressive in the

sense that the permanent establishment of French power
in Latin America was in question. The instructions of
the various cabinets clearly prove the contrary.[67] The
Molé ministry, which began the La Platan business, was
in no sense a ministry of adventure. When the British
government instituted enquiries with regard to the occupation of Martín García, Molé answered that the French
government had no intention whatsoever of holding the
island permanently, and this statement was embodied in
a formal diplomatic note of March 11, 1839.[68] And as
the year 1839 wore on, the distaste of the French government for the whole adventure, and for the acts of its
agents, became increasingly apparent. Not only was the
blockade proving irritating to Great Britain, with whom
the French at this time had been cultivating particularly
friendly relations, but, even more important, a crisis was
arising in the Near East which demanded the sharp
attention of the ministry. By 1840 the French government had become thoroughly sick of the whole business.
The instructions of Marshal Soult, then foreign minister, and especially his instructions of February 26, 1840,
show that the principal object of the government was to

[67] It is also to be remarked that the French authorities on the
spot had given assurances to the Argentine faction which they
supported against Rosas that they would seek no territorial
advantages, or impair the sovereignty of La Plata. See the
letter of the French consul, Baradère at Montevideo to Dr.
Alberdi, of the anti-Rosista faction, in Florencio Varela's *Sobre
La Convención de 29 Octubre de 1840. Desarrollo y Desenlace
de la Cuestión Francesa en el Rio de La Plata* (Montevideo,
1840), Appendix, pp. xii-xiv.

[68] *British and Foreign State Papers,* XXVII, 1838-39, p. 196.

reduce its commitments as rapidly as possible, and to make peace with Rosas.[69] Though Thiers, who came to power in March, 1840, may have wished to pursue a different policy, the King, as has been said, took a pacific view of the problem, and peace was actually consummated by the Mackau-Arana convention of October 29, 1840.

In this case, as in that of the French blockade of Mexico, the striking thing is the far greater interest taken in the whole episode in England as compared with that taken in the United States. British diplomacy had, as a matter of fact, long been active and influential in this part of the world. The treaty of April 27, 1828, which brought to an end the war between La Plata and Brazil, and established the independence of Uruguay, had come about under British mediation, and gave a solid basis for later British action. And when the French blockade was established, it produced a very speedy repercussion in the House of Commons.[70] The ministry, as we have seen, instituted enquiries of France with regard to the occupation of the island of Martín García, and it was under British auspices that the negotiations were begun which culminated in the Mackau-Arana convention. In the United States, on the other hand, there is little evidence of public interest in what was going on in La Plata. Caleb Cushing's resolution, already noted, referred both to the Mexican and the Argentine blockade, but no other evidence of con-

---

[69] Quoted in Villanueva, *op cit.*, II, 203-7.
[70] Hansard, *Parliamentary Debates*, 3rd series, LIV, p. 1113.

cern appears in the debates of Congress. The administration, so far as can be discovered, remained entirely
indifferent. Even the diplomatic representative on the
spot does not seem to have been much excited at the
policy of France. Indeed, the only evidence of American activity is the effort of the American naval commander, Nicholson, to mediate between the disputants
in April of 1839. This mediation, however, took place
without instructions,[71] and was unsuccessful. In no
sense did the United States contribute to the final settlement of the difficulties between France and La Plata.
Nor did the Argentine government, on its part, seem to
value very highly the support of the United States. It
made no effort to facilitate Nicholson's attempt at mediation; and though in June, 1838, it despatched General Alvear as minister to the United States, it does not
appear that there was any thought of securing American
aid. General Alvear, in an interview with Secretary
Forsyth in October, explained the point of view of the
Argentine authorities with regard to the French blockade, but he did not solicit or suggest any kind of action
whatsoever on the part of the American administration.[72] Whatever Rosas's faults or limitations, lack of

[71] Navy Department, Letters to Officers of Ships of War
Vol. 27, May 24, 1839, to September 30, 1839, pp. 110-111.
"Your mediation in this instance is not disapproved, knowing
as you did, that it was the desire of this Government to effect a
pacification. Such interferences, however, are delicate matters
unless in accordance with express instructions, as they may
sometimes not accord with the policy of the Government." The
Secretary of the Navy to Nicholson, July 8, 1839.
[72] Washington, Dept. of State, Argentine Republic, Notes,
vol. 1, Memorandum of a Conference, October 27, 1838.

courage or tenacity was not among them, and the suspension of the French naval action in 1840 was in no small degree a victory for his diplomacy.

On the other hand, curiously enough, an incident far less important, and an interference far less gross in the affairs of a Latin American state, occurring at much the same time, led to the invocation of the Monroe Doctrine by an American diplomatic agent, though without the support or encouragement of his government. In the course of a civil war in New Granada in the years 1840-41, the legal government suspended the payment of the customs at certain ports which were in the possession of the insurgents. The British chargé, Mr. Adams, in view of the interests of the British holders of the New Granadan debt, which was secured by the customs, notified the government that he would instruct the British consuls to see to it that this suspension of payments was enforced. Such action, of course, virtually meant aid to the existing régime against the revolutionists, and was therefore thoroughly approved by the party in power. But Mr. Semple, the American diplomatic agent, did not approve it. On the contrary, he protested that this action of the British chargé constituted a precedent contrary to the policy of the United States, with regard to the intervention of European nations in the affairs of the New World. His views were not particularly well received; they never received the commendation of his own government; and they altered not a whit the existing situation; but they are interesting evidence that even in this period of quiescence, the principles of 1823 were not unknown to Americans even to those not particularly conspicuous in the affairs of their country.[73]

[73] For Semple's protest, see Washington, Dept. of State, Colombia, Despatches, vol. 9. Encl. H. with no. 33, April 29, 1841.

"On the most mature reflection I have come to the conclusion that the interference contemplated by the British Govt. . . . . is not only contrary to the settled policy of my government, in relation to the interference of European powers in the affairs of the American States, but would be a precedent dangerous to our peace and safety. I can not therefore be satisfied that I have done my duty to my country, without expressing to the Granadian Government in the name of the U. States a disapprobation of the said measures proposed to be adopted."

See also the reply to the Colombian Foreign Minister, Encl. I in *ibid.*

> REPUBLIC OF N. GRANADA
> OFFICE OF SECRY OF STATE
> BOGOTÁ 5th Jany 1841.

"The undersigned acting Secretary of State for Foreign Affairs has received the note of the Hone J. Semple Charge d'Affairs of the United States, dated the 28th Decr. last, and an account of the same having been given to the council of Government, His Excellency the President of the Republic has directed him to answer, that he sees in the note from the British Legation referred to by Mr. Semple, nothing which appears to be an interference, by England, in the internal affairs of New Granada. And that in the time of the questions concerning Barrot and Russell, in consequence of which certain vessels of the French and English Squadrons blockaded the port of Carthagena the Govt. of the U. States made no protest against the intervention of those powers.

I take this occasion to renew the expression of
with which I have the honor to be your
> most obt. servt.
> M. CHIARI

HONL J. SEMPLE &c. &c. &c."

See also Raimundo Rivas, *Relaciones Internacionales entre Colombia y los Estados Unidos* (Bogotá, 1915), pp. 86-91.

We must not think, indeed, as we turn back to
review the evolution of the Monroe Doctrine in the
period from 1826-1841 that the Doctrine had dropped
completely out of sight, or out of the public mind.
Charles Jared Ingersoll hinted at its applicability to the
Canadian revolt of 1837 in a letter to President Van
Buren;[74] William Ellery Channing sought to apply it
to his use to prove the desirability of not mixing in the
affairs of Texas;[75] and other fugitive references to it
could be cited. The vigorous partisan debate of 1825-6
had probably done much to impress the principles of
1823 upon the public mind; and the insistent enunciation
of Adams must have done much also. At any rate these
principles were not forgotten. On the other hand, a
significant point stands out. Not once in this period was
the Doctrine invoked by those responsible for the conduct of the foreign policy of the United States. As a
basis of action, the Doctrine was ignored, ignored completely and unequivocally. And for the matter of that,
the only reference to it in the debates in Congress is
that of the Cushing resolution.

In the meantime the nations of the Old World proceeded in the New in lofty disregard of Monroe's declaration. In the despatches of European foreign offices,
at London and Paris, there is not an allusion to it. And

[74] Washington, Library of Congress, Van Buren Papers. " The
British ministers, agents and authorities altogether should be
given *very* distinctly to know that we will not move a finger to
help them, that even colonial dependencies at all are not conso-
nant with our system as agreeable neighbors, and that are
soldiers marched over the disputed territory (they?) will be
repelled instanter and resented as an act of hostility."

[75] W. E. Channing, *Works* (10 vols., Boston, 1849), II, 214.

certainly the policy of Great Britain and France in
the instances which have been brought before the reader
in this chapter were flatly opposed both to its letter
and its spirit. But it is possible to say even more.
It is possible to add that the political influence of the
United States in Latin America was distinctly less
than that of either of the two European powers just
mentioned, and in especial it was less than that of
England. Consider again for a moment the activity of
Great Britain, the mediator in the Argentine-Brazilian
war, the mediator in the French dispute with Mexico,
the mediator in the French dispute with the Argentine,
the power to whom Bolivar looked in 1826, and his successors in the government of New Granada in 1841, for
protection, the power on whose views the Colombian
monarchists of 1829 set inevitable importance, the power
whose representations put a stop to French encroachments on Brazil. What was American influence, what
was the significance of the policy of the United States,
beside all this? Friendly activities there sometimes were,
such as the mediation of 1828 in the war between Peru
and Colombia; but in the long run and the broad view,
what comparison between the position of the two great
English-speaking peoples is possible?

As for the Latin American states, where, in the years
1826-41, lies the importance of the Monroe Doctrine?
No doubt Latin American politicians, no doubt so great
a figure as Rosas himself, made appeal from time to
time to the American spirit as against the spirit of
ancient Europe, and successfully capitalized sentiment
of this kind; no doubt in the strife of Latin American

political parties there is, as in the Argentine, most strikingly, to be discerned a faction more and a faction less favorable to close relations with the Old World; but where, in all this period, is the evidence that Latin American states looked to the United States to defend them from the ambitions of trans-Atlantic governments? Only two instances of appeal to the principles of 1823 are in the record, Galindo's appeal with regard to Belize in 1835, and the appeal of New Granada against the British blockade in 1837. Nor can it even be said that the relations of the United States with the republics to the south were especially close or friendly. With Mexico relations were for the most part strained, especially in the latter period, as the clouds of the Texan question began to gather on the horizon; with Central America there was maintained only a fitful contact, which may be contrasted with the ceaseless activity of the British agents; with New Granada and Venezuela, our relations were variable, but hardly close; with the Argentine they were long interrupted by the dispute over the Falkland Islands; and with the west coast states they were, in the case of Ecuador and Peru, almost nonexistent, and in the case of Chile not particularly warm. All in all, American influence was far from great. In the fifteen years which follow 1826, little can be seen which would enhance the place of the Monroe Doctrine in American foreign policy, or give to the United States that leadership in the New World to which it has often pretended. But with 1841 the period of quiescence comes to an end. The forties were to see a highly important change of view.

CHAPTER II

The Revival of the Doctrine

Second only in importance to the message of December 2, 1823, in the history of the Monroe Doctrine, stands the message of President Polk of December 2, 1845. This important pronouncement gave new life to the principles which had been promulgated twenty-two years before; and from the time when it was enunciated there begins a new period in the history of the Doctrine itself. The process by which Monroe's attractive dogmas became deeply imbedded in the American public mind was bound to take some time to complete; for some years to come after Polk's revival of them they had, in some measure, at least, a partisan rather than a truly national character; but they became progressively popular in the course of the next fifteen years, and may be said to have gained something very like general acceptance in the period of the Civil War. The year 1845, therefore, may be taken as crucial in the history of the great diplomatic shibboleth which we are here examining.

It is not to be understood, however, that the message of President Polk came like a bolt from the blue, and that it was the first sign of reviving interest in the principles of 1823. So, perhaps, it has often been treated, but there is a process of evolution behind the message which it will be necessary to examine, a process which has a two-fold explanation.

There can be little doubt that the period of the forties was in the United States a period of rising nationalism. To what causes this rather jingoistic mood is to be traced would be an interesting question, unfortunately beyond the limits of this study. It might be traced to economic factors, to the influence of the Industrial Revolution and the demand for markets, to the land-hunger of the Western farmer, now pushing forward across the Mississippi to the conquest of new empires. It might be regarded as a natural expression of the principle of action and reaction in the psychology of peoples. After the mood of peace, the mood of war, after the mood of war, that of peace. It might be thought of in connection with the personalities who presided over American foreign policy in the epoch, the militant Upshur, the still more militant Calhoun, the hard and narrow Polk himself.

But there is another reason why the Monroe Doctrine was to be revived at this particular epoch. In the earlier period, as we have seen, the intermeddling of European powers in American affairs touched, in the main, areas relatively far removed from the American sphere of interest. The French blockade of Mexico in 1838 might be thought of as an exception, but it came at a time when American sympathies with Texas and strained relations with Mexico made popular resentment against French action unlikely. British aggression in Central America might also seem an exception, but American interests in this part of the world were still inchoate, American relations only fitful, during the whole of the fifteen

years just considered. The violations of American principle did not touch very nearly national pride or national
sentiment.

It was not to be so in the period which followed on
1841. In Texas, in California, and in Oregon, the ambition or the intrigue of European nations seemed to the
dominant political generation of Americans to threaten
fundamental American interests. It was only natural
that in such circumstances a foreign policy opposed to
such ambition and such intrigues should seek to base
itself upon precedents, and what better precedent
existed than the great pronouncement of 1823? It was
easy to find in its language a justification of the policy
which it was desired to pursue.

The clash of American and European conceptions of
foreign policy which produced the Polk message of 1845
is well illustrated in the case of the republic of Texas.
For some years prior to Polk's accession to the presidency, the policy of the European powers had been
directed at thwarting annexation to the United States.
Far from recognizing the hegemony of the American
government on the North American continent, Great
Britain and France set to work to counteract its influence, and to carry over into the New World the principle of the balance of power so often invoked in the
Old. The invocation of this principle, on the one hand,
and its flat repudiation, on the other, gives to the Texan
question an interest of the first order in the history of
American foreign policy.[1]

[1] The classical work on this subject is Justin H. Smith *The
Annexation of Texas* (New York, 1911).

In the early stages of the matter, it was Great Britain which was more actively in opposition to the United States. Even before the movement for Texan independence, such a statesman as Huskisson, obeying the spirit of Canning's diplomacy,[2] had declared that the United States could not be suffered " to bring under their dominion a greater portion of the shores of the Gulf of Mexico " than already belonged to them;[3] and in August of 1836 Palmerston in dealing with the question of the Texan revolt in the House of Commons had affirmed his belief that the American government could not be allowed " to pursue a system of aggrandisement " in that quarter, and that the annexation of Texas would be a question " which ought seriously to engage the attention of that House and of the British public." [4] It is not strange, therefore, that when this question of Texan annexation entered the sphere of immediate importance, the British government should be found aligned in opposition to the United States.[5] The negotiations of the late fall of 1843, looking to the negotiation of a treaty of annexation, aroused the natural anxiety of the British Foreign Office. As early as January 9, 1844, Lord Aberdeen, then Secretary of State for Foreign Affairs, directed a despatch to Pakenham urging him to oppose the project of annexation, and three days later he sought the diplomatic support of France for

[2] See my earlier work, pp. 92-3.
[3] American Historical Review, XI, 795.
[4] Hansard, *Parliamentary Debates,* 3rd series, XXXV, 935.
[5] For this whole question, see Smith, *op. cit.,* especially pp. 76-101 and 382-413.

this policy. In the latter part of May, 1844, he proposed to the Mexican Minister at London, Tomás Murphy, that England and France should guarantee the independence of Texas as the price of its recognition by Mexico, and couched the proposal in such language that it seemed to imply that he would be ready, if necessary, to oppose the views of the United States by force of arms. Not long after this, he brought forward, this time in conversation with the Texan minister, the project of a triple guarantee of the independence of Texas, to which Great Britain, France, and the United States should all adhere.

These early projects were destined to be abortive. The very idea of imposing a settlement of the Texan question by force was one which Great Britain could hardly contemplate, if it involved war with the United States. The vast commercial interests involved and the cautious policy of the French cabinet made such a contingency extremely improbable. One even finds oneself wondering how much importance is to be attached to the few sentences in the diplomatic correspondence on which Justin H. Smith has built up the theory that in 1844, for a time at least, Lord Aberdeen was ready to put his views to the test of arms. At any rate, by the end of the year, any such danger may be said definitely to have passed. Not so, however, the diplomatic interference of Great Britain in Texas.

The elections of 1844 in the United States had, of course, turned in part on the Texan issue, and had brought the Democrats, pledged to annexation, into power. In the course of the next few months there was to be introduced and pressed to its passage the joint resolution which, so far as the American government was concerned, was definitely to consummate the annexation of Texas. Against the project of annexation, the British opposition was keen. Lord Aberdeen strove vigorously to bring about peace between Texas and Mexico, enlisting in behalf of his own aims the support of the French government. The British and French ministers to Texas secured the consent of the Texan President to a new negotiation with the former mother country. Sir Charles Elliott, the British chargé, made a special trip to Mexico City, and wrung from the Mexican government reluctant consent to recognize Texan independence. Annexation might have been prevented if it had not been for the irresistible push of public opinion in Texas itself, which rejected the settlement with Mexico, and declared for union with the United States. From the standpoint of this study it is of course superfluous to comment upon such proposals. They reveal with absolute clearness that British diplomacy in 1844, as in the earlier period which we have examined, paid not the slightest heed to any claim of special dominance which the United States had ever put forward, and that it was in fact hostile to the expansion, and in this case the peaceful expansion, of the American people.

The views of the British government were, from the beginning, well understood at Washington. Indeed, long before the diplomatic manœuvres which we have just

6

considered were under way, the American President had
issued his word of warning. President Tyler's annual
message of 1842 had " a tang of Texas and Mexico," as
Sir Charles Elliott put it. " Carefully abstaining," wrote
the President, " from all interference in questions exclusively referring themselves to the political interests of
Europe, we may be permitted to hope an equal exemption from the interference of European Governments in
what relates to the States of the American Continent." [6]

[6] J. D. Richardson, *Compilation of Messages and Papers of
the Presidents* (Washington 1896-1899, 10 vols.), IV, 197.

Elliott's comment on this to his government is racy enough
to deserve quotation. " Bolting the bran, I presume this means
that United States Politicians and financiers mislike disturbance on this little Island, forming the Continent of North and
South America. But it is possible that this pretension may not
be equally acceptable to all ' the States of the American Continent.' There is room to suspect that some of the States of the
American Continent have no particular confidence in Washington purposes, and no desire to cast off all other friendship
in peace, or alliances in War. Be that as it may, it is pleasant
to observe how considerately Mr. Tyler has blended the Civil
with the decided in this ' Bon Soir ' to European influence in
this quarter of the globe. His self permission to hope for ' an
equal exemption from the interference of European Governments in what relates to the States of the American Continent '
is a fine instance of the Multum in parvo in comprehensive
political discussion.

" Washington on the Potomac is the place of places in President Houston's emphatic language, 'A God's Earth,' for great
strokes of this kind—Washington on the Brazos has its promise
too, but we are giving and they get. When I read this announcement drumming us off all this Continent, from the Arctic
to the Antarctic, I could not but pull back to what had been
said some distance up the stream of small print. There we had
been instructed that ' the question of peace or war between the

A year and a half later, when the treaty of annexation negotiated by Upshur and Calhoun came before the Senate for consideration, British motives came in for very considerable discussion, the attitude of the Court of St. James was scored again and again, and, what is more striking, the fear that Great Britain would attain a dominant commercial and political influence in Texas led a number of Senators to invoke the Monroe Doctrine.[7] It is amusing enough to see who some of these Senators were. One was Senator Woodbury of New Hampshire, an ardent Jacksonian, and no friend of the Panama Congress or of the Monrovian principles in 1823.[8] The plaguing notion of inconsistency may account for the fact that this gentleman alluded to the non-colonization principle as " Mr. Madison's." Another was Senator Buchanan, also in opposition in 1826 and soon to become Secretary of State in the administration of James K. Polk.[9] Still a third was that brilliant McDuffie of South Carolina, the associate of Cal-

United States and Great Britain is a question of the deepest interest, not only to themselves, but to the Civilized world, since it is impossible that War could exist between them without endangering the peace of Christendom."

(London, P. R. O., F. O., Texas, vol. 4. Dec. 28, 1842.) Quoted in *British Diplomatic Correspondence Concerning the Republic of Texas.* Edited by E. D. Adams. Texas State Historical Association. Reprinted from the *Quarterly of the Texas State Historical Association,* vol. XV, nos. 4 & 5, and from the *Southwestern Historical Quarterly,* vol. XVI, nos. i-xxi, No. 2, January, 1912–October, 1917.

[7] *Cong. Globe,* 28th Cong., 1st Sess., Appendix, *passim.*

[8] *Ibid.,* p. 762.

[9] *Ibid.,* p. 721.

houn, who had pronounced an exultant valedictory in the Panama debates of 1826. " Never till now," McDuffie declared, had he " realized the truth and justice of Mr. Monroe's declaration, that no European power must ever be permitted to establish a colony on this continent. The more I reflect on this subject the more I am convinced that the interests, both of Europe and of this country require that the declaration shall be maintained." [10]

This jealousy of British influence in Texas was not unnatural. During the whole year, 1844, in fact, the villain of the Texan melodrama, from the American point of view, was Lord Aberdeen and his associates. But in the year 1845, just before the actual consummation of annexation, the views of informed Americans underwent something of a change. It was discovered that the reprehensible conduct of Great Britain was closely parallelled by the almost equally reprehensible conduct of France. For it became known that the French government had gone hand in hand with Great Britain in the Texan question, and had been hardly less eager than the cabinet of London to frustrate the designs of the United States. On June 10, 1845, the French prime minister, Guizot, had been goaded by the opposition into discussing his Texan policy. He had responded in a speech of the highest importance, the main theme of which was the application of the principle of the balance of power to the affairs of the New World. This point of view is, no doubt, to be found

[10] *Ibid.*, p. 531.

elsewhere, as for example, in the despatches of Lord Aberdeen.[11] But Guizot, with unconscious imprudence, as it would seem, trumpeted it to the world. " France," he declared, " has a lasting interest in the maintenance of independent states in America, and in the balance of forces which exists in that part of the world. There are in America three powers, the United States, England, and the states of Spanish origin. . . . . What is the interest of France? It is that the independent states remain independent, that the balance of forces between the great masses which divide America continue, that no one of them become exclusively preponderant. In America, as in Europe, by the very fact that we have political and commercial interests, we need independent states, a balance of power. This is the essential idea which ought to dominate France's American policy. It is not a question of protesting against the annexation of Texas to the United States, nor of going to war to prevent such an annexation if it should take place. . . . . France ought only to act by the use of its influence, by the expression of its opinion, on the side which appears most conformable to French interests. It is not called

11 " Her Majesty's Government are of opinion," wrote the British Foreign Secretary, " that the continuance of Texas as an Independent Power, under its own Laws and institutions, must conduce to a more even, and therefore a more permanent, balance of interests in the North American Continent, and that its interposition between the United States and Mexico offers the best chance of a preservation of friendly relations between those two Governments." London, P. R. O., F. O., Texas, vol. 21, no. 1, Jan. 23, 1845. Published in *British Diplomatic Correspondence, op. cit.*, pp. 429-30.

upon to compromise itself, to bind itself with regard to the difficulties of the future, but it ought to protect by the authority of its name the independence of states and the maintenance of the balance of the great political forces in America." [12]

It is true that nothing in the sentences just quoted implied a policy of armed intervention in the New World; it is true, indeed, that the French minister expressly disclaimed the use of force; but the theory which he propounded in this defense of his policy was a theory which could not fail to be entirely uncongenial to the public opinion of the United States. For behind the Monroe Doctrine, from the very first, had lain an antagonism to those shifting arrangements of interest on which the balance of power was based; and however innocent might be the methods employed for the moment to promote the idea of an American equilibrium, the idea itself was naturally repugnant to the people of the rising republic of North America. In an era of self-confident nationalism, it was naturally a little galling to be regarded, not as the dominant nation of the New World, but as only one element in an American balance of power.

At the time that Guizot made this extraordinary pronouncement Congress was not in session, and so a flare-up there was avoided. But the French minister's views came in for plenty of tart comment from the

---

[12] *Histoire Parlementaire de France. Receuil Complet des Discours Prononcés dans les Chambres de 1819 à 1848 par M. Guizot* (5 vols., Paris, 1864) IV, 562-4.

press. Polk's organ, the *Washington Union,* spoke with contempt of this "absurd and new-fangled doctrine." The *Democratic Review,* equally faithful to the administration, delivered itself as follows, "Away, then, with all idle French talk of balances of power, on the American continents. There is no growth in Spanish America. Whatever progress of population there may be in the British Canadas is only for their own early severance of their present colonial relation to the little island 3000 miles across the Atlantic; soon to be followed by Annexation, and destined to swell the still accumulating momentum of our progress, and whosoever may hold the balance, though there is cast into the opposing scale all the bayonets and cannon, not only of France and of England, but of Europe entire, how can it kick the beam against the simple, solid weight of 250, or 300,000,000— and American millions—destined to gather by the flutter of the Stars and Stripes in the fast hastening year of our Lord 1845." [13] Comment such as this was not improbably read by the President himself. It is not at

---

[13] *Democratic Review,* XVII, July, 1845, p. 9, in an article on "Annexation," pp. 5-10. See also an article in the September *Review* which expresses itself in the same fashion, "The balance of power is an idea purely European. It has no place in the relations of other States. Its introduction here would at once draw us into a vortex of European politics and would be resisted by the Americans as one man. We will meet the evil at the threshold. If force be necessary to prevent it, we will use force, and we will use it at the first moment of provocation. To hesitate would be to fall." (Vol. XVII, September, 1845, "British Reviews on Oregon," pp. 323-331, especially p. 330.)

all unlikely that it had its direct influence upon the framing of the message of 1845.

But neither Guizot's speech, nor even the Texan problem as a whole, accounts entirely for the revival of the Monroe Doctrine. The Oregon question assumed a large importance in the President's mind, and had much to do with his pronouncement to Congress. It is necessary for us to glance briefly at this problem in its relation to the document which we are about to examine.

Oregon, as is well known, had been for a long time in dispute between the United States and Great Britain.[14] The disposition of this territory had been for a considerable time adjourned by the treaties of 1818 and 1827 which provided for a joint occupation by the two claimant powers. But in the early forties interest in Oregon, lukewarm in the twenties and the first years of the thirties, began to become increasingly vigorous. American settlements were made in the Willamette valley, and in Congress an agitation began, despite the agreement with Great Britain, for the organization of a territory in the disputed region. This agitation crystallized in the Linn bill, introduced by Dr. Linn of Missouri, for several successive years, but first brought out and debated in 1843. In the course of these debates, so far as I can discover, the Monroe message was for the

[14] For a discussion of this question see particularly R. Greenhow, *The History of Oregon and California*. (Boston, 1845) and Schafer, Joseph, the " British Attitude toward the Oregon Question, 1815-46," in *Amer. Hist. Rev.*, XVI, 273 et seq., and Schuyler, R. L., " Polk and the Oregon Compromise," in *Pol. Sci. Quart.*, XXVI, 443 et seq.

first time invoked with regard to Oregon. It was mentioned by Sevier of Tennessee as " a sentiment to which he most cordially responded," [15] and described by Woodbury of New Hampshire as a " noble declaration " in which he thoroughly concurred.[16]

The Linn bill did not pass in 1843. But the issue which it embodied again came up before Congress in 1844. This time a Committee of the House of Representatives reported on the Oregon question. Its recommendations extended only to the establishment of military posts, and the extension of the civil and criminal jurisdiction of Iowa over the territory, but in the course of its examination of the problem it invoked the principles of 1823. Quoting, not the non-colonization clause, but a portion of the Spanish-American part of the message, the committee declared, " This declaration, it is well known, had the most important immediate effects at the time of its utterance, when certain of the European powers contemplated forcible interference in the affairs of the Spanish colonies in America. It has deservedly come to be regarded as an essential component part of the international law of the New World." [17] The claim set forward, here, that the Monroe Doctrine embodied certain definite principles of international law, has a peculiar interest. Nothing in the writings of Wheaton, to which the committee alluded in support of its viewpoint, would seem to justify this claim. Nor is

[15] *Cong. Globe,* 27th Cong., 3rd Sess., p. 154.
[16] *Ibid.,* App., p. 91.
[17] *Reports of Committees,* 28th Cong., 1st Sess., vol. 1, Report of March 12, 1844, p. 18.

there any evidence that in 1823 James Monroe regarded that part of the message which referred to Spanish America as embodying a definite legal principle. Such a claim was to come later. On the other hand, Adams no doubt thought from the beginning of the famous non-colonization clause as expressing a legal concept, and Henry Clay, in his instructions to Poinsett and Forbes in 1825 maintained that the message of 1823, in both its parts, expressed what he describes as principles of " inter-continental law." [18] The point of view put forward by the committee is not, therefore, having regard to the Monroe Doctrine, as a whole, an entirely novel one.

It was not only in the House of Representatives that the Monroe Doctrine figured in the discussion of the Oregon question in 1844. In the Senate Breese of Illinois and Atchison of Missouri, both staunch Democrats, alluded to it with approval.[19] And far more important than this, on April 23, 1844, one James K. Polk, under discussion as a candidate for the vice-presidency, asked his views with regard to Texas and Oregon, wrote a public letter in which occurred this significant sentence, " Let the fixed principle of our Government be, not to permit Great Britain, or any other foreign power, to plant a colony or hold dominion over any portion of the people or territory of either [continent]." [20]

[18] See my previous work, p. 198.

[19] *Cong. Globe,* 28th Cong., 1st Sess., pp. 328 and 306.

[20] Library of Congress, Polk Papers. Published in *Washington Globe,* May 6, 1844.

The question of Oregon stood in the forefront of American politics throughout the years 1844 and 1845. The dying administration of President Tyler made an effort to settle the problem in the summer of 1844. Calhoun, the Secretary of State, offered, in August, the division of the territory along the line of 49°, but this offer was refused. On the other hand a British suggestion of arbitration, made in November, was turned down by the United States in January, and again in March, after the political leader who wrote the letter of April 23, 1844, had become the President of the United States. The tension between the two disputants increased. Polk at first was not wholly unconciliatory. Feeling himself bound by the action of the preceding administration, in July he permitted Buchanan again to offer a settlement on the line of 49°. But when this offer was refused by Pakenham, the President refused to take any further action, declaring that the next move belonged to Great Britain. Nor did the pacific counsels of Buchanan alter his temper.[21] To the desire to rebuke the temerarious Guizot for his enunciation of the principle of the balance of power was added the desire to " look John Bull in the eye," and use the Doctrine of 1823 to justify American policy in the northwest.

A third element in the enunciation of the Monroe Doctrine by Polk in 1845 was the President's suspicion that Great Britain had designs on California. The

[21] For much of the correspondence on this question, see *British and Foreign State Papers*, XXXIV (1845-6), 14, 49 *et seq.*

acquisitive instinct of the Americans of the forties
seems frequently to have expressed itself in dismal
forebodings and dark imaginings as to the wickedness of
other powers, and of all powers that most likely to be
regarded as unscrupulous and grasping was Great
Britain. This feeling had had a rather comic expression
in the year 1842. At that time the relations between
Mexico and the United States were seriously strained,
as a result of the aggressive diplomacy of Santa Anna,
then President of Mexico. The warm exchange of
notes between Daniel Webster and Bocanegra, the
Mexican minister at Washington, on the question of
American neutrality with regard to Texas, is well
known. This correspondence, at least Bocanegra's part
of it, was received by Commodore Thomas ap. Catesby
Jones at Callao in September of 1842, together with the
observation of the American consul at Mazatlan that
war seemed " highly probable." The vigilant naval man,
already alarmed lest California should come into the
possession of Great Britain,[22] sailed promptly for the
coast of that province, and on October 20 occupied the
town of Monterey. He speedily discovered, however,
that his action had been, to put it mildly, premature; and
so sailed away again with his self-esteem entirely
undamaged by the incident. Jones's self-esteem no doubt
matters little to the historian of the Monroe Doctrine.
What is more interesting and important is that the gallant, if somewhat over-impulsive, naval officer rested
his seizure of Monterey upon the principles of 1823,

[22] 27th Cong., 3rd Sess., H. Ex. Doc. no. 166, pp. 69-70.

and had, before the taking of the town, extorted from
his subordinates a solemn oath to be faithful to these
sacred dogmas.[23] This is the first instance in history,
so far as I am aware, in which the sanctions of religion
were invoked in connection with the famous declaration
of Monroe. It must have been only fortifying to Jones's
sense of rectitude for him to discover in the Mexican
newspapers found at Monterey prophecies to the effect
that the United States would never permit the seizure of
California by Great Britain, since such an act would be
inconsistent with the Monroe Doctrine.[24]

But the Monterey episode by no means put an end to
American suspicions. The bond which united California to Mexico was, after all, but a very tenuous one;
since 1836 there had existed in the province a government which yielded only nominal allegiance to the republic, and which in 1845 drove out the Mexican troops
sent thither by Santa Anna two years before. It was not
perhaps unnatural to fear that the flimsy sovereignty of
Mexico should be replaced by that of some stronger
power. There was not infrequent comment on the subject in the press at the outset of Polk's administration,
and before very long disquieting news began to arrive
from Thomas O. Larkin, the American consul at
Monterey. Larkin reported that a British agent was
encouraging, and that British banks might finance, a
reconquest of California by the Mexicans, and at the
same time he alluded to the appearance of a British
Vice-Consul in the province who was apparently with-

[23] *Ibid.,* pp. 85-6.
[24] *Ibid.,* p. 72.

out any genuine commercial business.[25] This despatch
apparently caused considerable perturbation at Washington. It may or may not have been discussed in the
cabinet meeting of October 17; but, at any rate, on that
day Buchanan despatched to the consul an instruction of
high historic interest in its relation to the Monroe Doctrine. The President, he wrote, " could not view with
indifference the transfer of California to Great Britain
or any other European power. The system of colonization by foreign monarchies on the North American
continent must and will be resisted by the United
States. . . . . On all proper occasions, you should not
fail promptly to warn the Government and the people of
California of the danger of such an interference to their
peace and prosperity; to inspire them with a jealousy of
European dominion, and to arouse in their bosoms that
love of liberty and independence so natural to the
American Continent." [26] A few days later President
Polk told Benton that he intended in his annual message
to reassert Mr. Monroe's doctrine against permitting
foreign colonization, and that in doing this he had
California and the fine bay of San Francisco as much
in view as Oregon.[27]

For the suspicions which the administration felt with
regard to this important and coveted province, there was

[25] Washington, Dept. of State, Consular Despatches, Mexico,
July 10, 1845. This despatch is specifically referred to in Bu-
chanan's answer, in *Works of James Buchanan,* edited by J. B.
Moore (12 vols., Philadelphia, 1908-1911), VI, 276.

[26] *Ibid.*

[27] The Diary of James K. Polk, edited by M. M. Quaife
(4 vols., Chicago, 1910), I, 71.

some measure of justification, if one thinks, not of the Foreign Office, but of the British authorities on the spot.[28] Various British agents in the New World did think seriously of the acquisition of the province by England. Thus Pakenham, then minister to Mexico, wrote a despatch to his Court on August 30, 1841, in which he advocated the colonization of this fertile region in exchange for a settlement of the debt that Mexico owed to Great Britain. The colonization was to take place under Mexican sovereignty, but as the British minister observed at the time, that sovereignty " would not last forever." [29] At a later date Forbes, the British vice-consul at Monterey, reported to Barron, consul at Tepic, and his official superior, the proposal of a number of Californians that the province should be put under a British protectorate, and urged that some consideration

[28] See E. D. Adams, *British Interests and Activities in Texas 1838-46* (Baltimore, 1910) Addendum, pp. 234-64, and also *American Historical Review*, July, 1909, XIV, 744-63.

[29] London, P. R. O., F. O., Mexico, vol. 146, no. 91. " I believe there is no part of the world offering greater natural advantages for the establishment of an English colony than the provinces of Upper California; while its commanding position on the Pacific, its fine harbours, its forests of excellent timber for shipbuilding as well as for every other purpose appear to me to render it by all means desirable, in a political point of view, that California, once ceasing to belong to Mexico, should not fall into the hands of any Power but England; and the present debilitated condition of Mexico, and the gradual increase of foreign population in California render it probable that its separation from Mexico will be effected at no distant period." Certainly nothing of the spirit of the Monroe Doctrine here.

be given to it,[30] and Barron in transmitting this proposal to London expressed a similar sentiment. But the authorities in London never contemplated a policy of acquisition. The Pakenham proposal was promptly vetoed by Lord Aberdeen, and the reports of Forbes and Barron received treatment a little better, but hardly calculated to put Great Britain in possession of California. The British Foreign Secretary in a despatch of December 31, 1844, expressed himself as not unwilling to let Californian unrest take its natural course, and though signifying a distaste for seeing the region come into the possession of the United States he gave no sign that he had any positive policy in view. As a matter of fact, British diplomacy, perhaps tempted to challenge the position of the American government in the early months of 1844, had become pretty definitely cautious by the end of the year. The British Admiralty records, and the failure of the British ministry to strengthen its forces in the Pacific, even after the warnings which came to them of the agitation in the province, and the fiasco of Monterey, afford additional evidence

[30] London, P. R. O., F. O., Mexico, vol. 179. "I feel myself in duty bound to use all my influence to prevent this fine country from falling into the hands of any other foreign power than that of England. I repeat that it is impossible for Mexico to hold California for a much longer period, and if the Govt of Great Britain can with honor to itself, and without giving umbrage to Mexico, extend its protection to California, reaping those benefits which, by proper management, would infallibly attend that protection, I should presume that it would be impolitic to allow any other nation to avail itself of the present critical situation of California for obtaining a footing in this country."

of the absence of any really aggressive design on the part of the authorities in London.

Just enough was known at Washington, however, to make suspicion plausible, and the language of the American consular officers on the spot made it easy to believe the worst of Great Britain. No doubt Polk's own eager appetite for California made him ready to believe in the expansionist designs of others. At any rate, there can be no question, as already indicated, that the message of 1845 was written with California, as well as Texas and Oregon, in mind.

But there is still a fourth geographical area the events in which may have had something to do with the revival of the Monroe Doctrine. In the course of the year 1845 the French and British governments instituted first a diplomatic and then a naval interference in the affairs of the Argentine, and in the war which the ferocious Rosas was waging against Rivera in Uruguay. The details of this interesting episode, which extends over a considerable term of years, I shall leave until the next chapter. It will be sufficient to say here that as early as June, 1845, *Niles's Register* had commented unfavorably upon the action of the powers, and mournfully declared that Monroe's words had become a dead letter;[31] that Mr. William Brent, the American chargé at Buenos Ayres, had, in a long letter to his government, undertaken to remind Polk and Buchanan of the existence of the principles of 1823,[32] that the press was full

[31]*Niles's Register,* LXVIII, June 7, 1845.
[32] Washington, Dept. of State, Argentine Republic, Desp. 5, Brent to Buchanan, August 2, 1845. See also a letter of the

7

of denunciations of the French and British policy in the fall of 1845; and that the events taking place in the La Plata were the subject of interesting conversations between Buchanan and the British minister at Washington.[33] It can hardly be doubted, therefore, that the administration found in the French and British policy towards Rosas an additional, if not a controlling, reason for speaking out on the fundamentals of American foreign policy.

No man, of course, would have been more likely to take such action if the occasion at all warranted than James K. Polk. Hard, narrow, humorless, but thoroughly patriotic, and convinced of the greatness of American institutions and of America's future, Polk

---

same date published in the *Daily Union* of Washington in October, 1845, in which he wrote:

" There has long been, and now exists, a settled determination more particularly in the British Government to get a foothold in these countries. . . . . The government of the United States and the people of the United States should be aroused to the critical situation of these republics. . . . .

" Is not now the time to see what is meant by the United States in the letter of Mr. Jefferson of 24th October, 1823, to Mr. Monroe, by the message of Mr. Monroe of December, 1823, and of Mr. Tyler's message, August 11, 1842? . . . . Shall the countries of La Plata be suffered to arrange their own affairs, without the intermeddling of European powers? Or shall they be ruled by them, under a commercial vassalage certainly, or perhaps by such a rule as India, Barbary, and Greece (and China too perhaps) are now governed? . . . . The United States can at least extend some moral influence against this European intermeddling in American affairs. What they can, or will, or ought to do, is for those who are at the fountain head to determine."

[33] See below, p. 134.

perfectly reflected the militant temper of the time. He had, it is true, opposed the Panama mission in 1826, and had then had little good to say of the Monroe Doctrine. But intense partisanship was in the nature of this usually silent, yet forceful, Tennesseean and amply explains his attitude at that time. Faced with responsibility, and confronted with what seemed to him a challenge to the American point of view, he was bound to take up the gage which had been thrown down, and take his stand on what he conceived to be American principles.

A well known student of American foreign policy has propounded the theory that the revival of Monroe's principles in the message of 1845 may have been due to the Secretary of State, James Buchanan.[34] That Buchanan was impregnated with the spirit of 1823 is clear. His speech of 1844 on the Texan treaty attests the fact. So, too, do his instructions to Larkin. And if more evidence were needed it might be found in the well known despatch of November 10 to Slidell.[35] But, on the other

[34] C. R. Fish, in *Dict. of Am. Biog.*, III, 210.

[35] Buchanan, *Works*, VI, 295. " The nations on the continent of America have interests peculiar to themselves. Their free forms of Government are altogether different from the monarchical institutions of Europe. The interests and independence of the sister nations require that they should establish and maintain an American system of policy for their own protection and security, entirely distinct from that which has so long prevailed in Europe. To tolerate any interference on the part of European sovereigns with controversies in America ; to permit them to apply the worn-out dogma of the balance of power to the free States of this continent ; and above all, to suffer them to establish new Colonies of their own, intermingled with our free Republics, would be to make, to some

hand, it can be stated quite definitely that Buchanan was averse to challenging Great Britain on the Oregon question.[36] The first mention of the projected public revival of Monroe's principles in Polk's diary implies that it was the President who initiated the idea, and the Secretary who gave reluctant consent.[37] Assuredly, the sharp and public rebuke to European diplomats was more in the natural manner of the Tennesseean than of his subordinate.

At any rate, as early as October 21 the idea of the reaffirmation of the famous declaration had been discussed in the cabinet, and three days later the President mentioned the matter to Senator Benton.[38] From this time forward, it appears to have been a foregone conclusion that the forthcoming annual message would contain a reference to Monroe's principles. And when in November, Polk read his draft of that document to

---

extent, a voluntary sacrifice of our independence. These truths ought everywhere, throughout the continent of America to be impressed upon the public mind."

[36] Polk, *Diary*, I, 64.

[37] *Ibid.*, "Mr. Buchanan thought we ought not to precipitate a crisis between the two countries, and that by delay we might secure the Oregon territory, but by strong measures hastily taken we would have war and might lose it. The President said he was satisfied with the state of the negotiation as it stood; and went on to state what he proposed to communicate to Congress in his first message. He would maintain all our rights, would take bold and strong ground, and reaffirm Mr. Monroe's ground against permitting any European power to plant or establish any new colony on the North American continent."

[38] Polk, *Diary*, I, 70. Benton seems to have displayed very little enthusiasm.

the members of the cabinet, there seems to have been not a word of dissent. The declaration of 1845, unlike that of 1823, caused no prolonged debate in the meeting of the President's official advisers. Perhaps it would not have mattered if it had, for few of our Presidents have been more fixed in their purposes, once a decision had been made, than James K. Polk. A great man, in any exacting sense of the word, Polk certainly was not. But a strong man, with definite views and great tenacity in carrying them out, he certainly was. His foreign policy, it can be stated positively, was in its broad lines his own. He treated Buchanan, as his *Diary* shows, with a suspicious contempt, and in every crisis dominated this weaker will. He had made up his mind as to what ought to be done in 1845. It would have taken a very positive and vigorous current of opposition in the cabinet to have induced him to change his mind. So, on December 2, 1845, precisely twenty-two years after the original enunciation of the Monroe Doctrine, there was sent to Congress a restatement of the principles of 1823. Before proceeding to an analysis of this restatement it will be desirable to quote it in full.

" The rapid extension of our settlements over our territories heretofore unoccupied, the addition of new States to our Confederacy, the expansion of free principles, and our rising greatness as a nation are attracting the attention of the powers of Europe, and lately the doctrine has been broached in some of them of a ' balance of power ' on this continent to check our advancement. The United States, sincerely desirous of preserving relations of good understanding with all nations, can not in silence permit any European interference on the North American continent, and should any such interference be attempted will be ready to resist it at any and all hazards.

" It is well known to the American people and to all nations that this Government has never interfered with the relations subsisting between other governments. We have never made ourselves parties to their wars or their alliances; we have not sought their territories by conquest; we have not mingled with parties in their domestic struggles; and believing our own form of government to be the best, we have never attempted to propagate it by intrigues, by diplomacy, or by force. We may claim on this continent a like exemption from European interference. The nations of America are equally sovereign and independent with those of Europe. They possess the same rights, independent of all foreign interposition, to make war, to conclude peace, and to regulate their internal affairs. The people of the United States can not, therefore, view with indifference attempts of European powers to interfere with the independent action of the nations on this continent. The American system of government is entirely different from that of Europe. Jealousy among the different sovereigns of Europe, lest any one of them might become too powerful for the rest, has caused them anxiously to desire the establishment of what they term the ' balance of power.' It can not be permitted to have any application on the North American continent, and especially to the United States. We must ever maintain the principle that the people of this continent alone have the right to decide their own destiny. Should any portion of them, constituting an independent state, propose to unite themselves with our Confederacy, this will be a question for them and us to determine without any foreign interposition. We can never consent that European power shall interfere to prevent such a union because it might disturb the ' balance of power ' which they may desire to maintain upon this continent. Near a quarter of a century ago the principle was distinctly

announced to the world, in the annual message of one
of my predecessors, that

> " ' The American continents, by the free and
> independent condition which they have assumed
> and maintain, are henceforth not to be considered
> as subjects for future colonization by any Euro-
> pean powers.'

" This principle will apply with greatly increased
force should any European power attempt to establish
any new colony in North America. In the existing circumstances of the world the present is deemed a proper
occasion to reiterate and reaffirm the principle avowed
by Mr. Monroe and to state my cordial concurrence in
its wisdom and sound policy. The reassertion of this
principle, especially in reference to North America, is
at this day but the promulgation of a policy which no
European power should cherish the disposition to resist.
Existing rights of every European nation should be
respected, but it is due alike to our safety and our
interests that the efficient protection of our laws should
be extended over our whole territorial limits, and that it
should be distinctly announced to the world as our
settled policy that no future European colony or dominion shall with our consent be planted or established
on any part of the North American continent.')

This vigorous declaration was, beyond all doubt, the
most important single document intended to give renewed and greater weight to Monroe's principles
between the date of the original message, and the
despatch of Secretary of State Richard Olney of June
20, 1895. It is by a curious irony that it comes from the
pen of the man who in 1826 had been so far from enthusiastic over the implications of the declaration of '23.
Yet there always has been a difference between the critic
and the administrator, and the foreign affairs of any

great nation wear a very different aspect from the outside than they do from the post of control. This, in itself, is sufficient to explain the change in the views of the President.

But how far did the message of '45 express the thought of the earlier pronouncement? How far was it merely iteration, and in what respects was it new? This is a question of a very considerable importance.

In one aspect, at any rate, the Polk doctrine went far beyond the Monroe principles. What Monroe had forbidden was armed intervention in the New World or European colonization therein.[39] What Polk forbade was even diplomatic interposition. What he condemned quite frankly was the purely advisory policy which France and England' had pursued in Texas; he would not concede any right of interference whatsoever. Such a claim was obviously a most sweeping one. It went far beyond the bounds of ordinary diplomatic logic. It could not be justified, as could the President's original message, on the ground that the peace and safety of the United States were involved, for the right of one government to give friendly counsel to another could hardly be said to involve any question of national self-preservation. It would be entirely natural that a prin-

[39] It is true that the phrase in the Monroe message, "for the purpose of controlling them, or of influencing in any other manner their destiny" might be so construed as to pronounce a ban on all diplomatic interposition, as well as on armed action. But the sequel of events clearly shows that no such prohibition was intended. The diplomacy of 1824 and 1825 was, as I have shown, extremely cautious in its construction of the declaration of 1823.

ciple so sweeping should be challenged, and challenged
with a good deal of force, and this we shall soon see
to be the case. And yet one cannot be entirely sorry that
the statement was made. For the application of the
principle of the balance of power to America, it cannot
be denied, was filled with peril. It might begin with
mild diplomatic representations; but if the principle
took root, it would probably eventuate in armed intervention. That it should be challenged after so clear
and public an enunciation of it was probably an excellent thing. Not, as will appear, that it put an end to
European interest, sometimes a sinister European interest, in the states of the New World. But it stated
quite bluntly and frankly the point of view of the
United States; it faithfully interpreted contemporary
American public opinion; it served notice, at least, of
the attitude that the American government would assume in the future.

A second aspect of the Polk message that deserves
to be noted is the emphasis which was laid upon the
application of the Monroe Doctrine to the North American continent. It is not correct to say that Polk definitely limited the doctrine to that continent.[40] He spoke
exclusively, it is true, of applications of the doctrine
all of which involved North American, and not Central
or South American areas, and consistently used the
expression, " this continent," not " these continents," in

[40] This is, however, declared to be the case by Hector Pétin,
Les Etats-Unis et la Doctrine de Monroe (Paris, 1900), p. 102.
See also E. I. McCormac, *James K. Polk, A Political Biog-
raphy* (Berkeley, 1922), p. 693.

banning European influence. He declared that the principles of '23 would " apply with greatly increased force "
to North American territory. He sought thus adroitly
to strengthen his own position by establishing more
completely the nexus between the general theory and
the concrete instances in which he wished to apply it.
But he also explicitly declared, without qualification, his
" cordial concurrence " in the " wisdom and sound
policy " of the original pronouncement. Subsequent
events, and indeed antecedent ones, show clearly that
no absolute restriction of the scope of the earlier maxims
was contemplated. The instructions to Slidell, already
quoted,[41] make no distinction between the two continents. There is, moreover, a passage in the message
which, as Professor Cady has pointed out, probably
refers to the Anglo-French intervention in the Argentine. " The nations of America," Polk had written,
" are equally sovereign and independent with those of
Europe. They possess the same rights, independent of
all foreign interposition, to make war, to conclude peace,
and to regulate their internal affairs. The people of the
United States cannot, therefore, view with indifference
attempts of European powers to interfere with the
independent action of the nations on this continent."
Such language might have been written with Texas in
mind. But the emphasis on the right of American governments to make war makes it seem more likely that
it had reference to the meddling of the European powers in the struggle between Rosas and the Rivera fac-

[41] See above, p. 85.

tion in Uruguay. We know very well that the administration was not indifferent to what was transpiring in that part of the world. Buchanan, indeed, had expressed quite frankly to Pakenham the distrust of the administration.[42] It seems reasonable to suppose, therefore, that Polk meant to include Anglo-French action in South America in his denunciation of European policy. He knew, as his language shows, that the United States could not act on precisely the same lines in the case of a quarrel so far removed from its shores as it could in cases nearer home. As Webster had done in 1826, he drew a clear, and indeed a valuable, distinction between different geographical areas. But he never intended to limit the Monroe Doctrine to the North American continent alone.

A second aspect of the message which deserves to be noted is the manner in which the President tied together the original Monroe Doctrine and the so-called no-transfer principle, or what Herbert Kraus suggestively

[42] J. F. Cady, *Foreign Intervention in the Rio de La Plata, 1838-50* (Philadelphia, 1929), p. 185. Pakenham wrote to Lord Aberdeen, November 13, 1845, "He (Buchanan) talked of the jealousy with which the American people viewed any European interference in the affairs of this Continent, and he added that the idea began to prevail that the British and French Governments intended to retain possession of the Island of Martín García for the purpose of securing for themselves the exclusive Commercial advantages in that part of the World. . . . . No such suspicion as that . . . . was entertained by the United States Government, ... he had referred to it merely as a proof of the susceptibility of the American people on all (such) questions."

describes as the Madison doctrine.[43] The union of these two concepts is rare in the whole period covered by this book. There was not a single instance of such a union between 1826 and 1845.[44] There were numerous pronouncements of American Secretaries of State during this period with regard to the interest of the United States in the retention of Cuba by Spain.[45] There were statements by both Webster and Buchanan expressing American opposition to the acquisition of Hawaii by any European power. But none of these were related to the message in 1823. It was Polk, who, for the first time since 1826, tied together the principles of 1823 and the no-transfer idea. His use of the words " colony or dominion " in the message of 1845 clearly attests the fact, and, as has already appeared, his anxiety with regard to California explains it. And yet there is one qualification that ought to be made. Speaking broadly, the Madison doctrine has been applied to the transfer of territory by one European power to another. It was only Polk who used this doctrine to express his opposition to a cession by an *American* to a European power. The fact is one that has generally escaped the attention of the commentators.

Turning to another aspect of the message, it seems inaccurate to declare, as does Hector Pétin,[46] that the

[43] For the validity of this term, see my previous work, p. 203.

[44] For the situation previous to 1826, see my previous work, p. 202.

[45] For the more important of these statements, see Moore, *A Digest of International Law,* VI, 447-457.

[46] Pétin, *op. cit.,* p. 102.

Monroe Doctrine, in the message of 1845, became not a doctrine of self-preservation, but a doctrine of aggression. It is true that Polk was using it to condemn the interference of other powers with the designs of the United States in Texas. But the annexation of Texas came about with the free acquiescence of the Texan people themselves. It was no act of aggression, whatever may be thought of the acts which followed it. Texan independence had existed *de facto* for more than a decade. The Texans themselves wished to come into the Union. Granted that the new state had not been recognized by its former mother-country, by what process of reasoning is the United States to be stigmatized as guilty of aggression because it did not wait for such recognition before completing the act of annexation? [47] That Polk's restatement of the message opposed a veto on European opposition to the expansion of the United States is, no doubt, true. That the Monroe Doctrine has been transformed with time into a pretext (or justification, according to the point of view) for intervention in the affairs of some of the states of the New World, and for the extension of American political control, if not of American sovereignty, is also true. But this process cannot be said to have been completed, by any means, in 1845. In the case of Texas, the principles of 1823 remained essentially a warning to the Old World, not the basis of aggressive action.

The use of the Doctrine to justify extreme American claims in the Northwest, and to warn Europe not to

[47] For this whole subject, see Smith, *op. cit.*, especially pp. 468-70.

interfere in California, the other purposes of the Polk message, can no doubt be qualified as aggressive if one chooses to do so. But with regard to Oregon Polk was reasserting a claim long put forward, and with regard to California, it is not to be thought that at the beginning of December, 1845, Polk in warning others off was necessarily thinking of conquering that province for the United States. That he expected it to revert to his own country is certain; but at the time which we are considering, he was still seeking, through the Slidell mission, an accommodation with Mexico, and an accommodation of which the *cession of California was not an essential part.*[48]

So much for the analysis of the meaning of the President's pronouncement. But what of its diplomatic wisdom? What of its justification from the standpoint of sound policy? I have already stated that in one respect, despite the extreme character of its pretensions, the message was probably a warning justified by the facts, and capable at least of sounding the alarm in the United States, if not of altering the policies of Europe. The Guizot doctrine of the balance of power in the New World, (if it be not unfair to call by the name of Guizot a doctrine not uncommonly held by many others), was a doctrine dangerous to the future peace of the Ameri-

---

[48] The instructions given Slidell authorized him to make an arrangement of the claims of the United States, and of the Texan boundary controversy. The minister was to offer to purchase California, but he was not to make acceptance of this a *sine qua non* of a settlement. Buchanan, *Works,* VI, 294-306, especially 303.

can continents. It ought to have been challenged, and
so far as the United States was concerned, repudiated.
It might, of course, be argued that by his action the
President would unfavorably affect the friendly relations of the United States with France, and that at a
time when the critical status of the Oregon question
would have made French friendship highly desirable.
But in answer to this it can be pointed out that the risks
of any very serious breach with France were decidedly
not great. There existed in France a very friendly feeling indeed for the United States. The language of
Guizot himself attests this fact, and the reception of his
speech of June 10, 1845, attests it still more.[49] The
American government would have had to go much further than to dispute what was after all a theoretical
principle, however dangerous, before a genuine tension
in Franco-American relations would result. And, as a
matter of fact, the Guizot ministry, shortly after the
reception of the message, indeed, at the very time when
it was engaged in answering it, went out of its way to
declare its neutrality in the difference between the
United States and Great Britain with regard to Oregon.[50] Judged by the practical test, therefore, the message did no harm whatsoever. It must be admitted on
the other hand that, like the message of 1823, Polk's
declaration did not effect a revolution in the diplomatic
habits of European chancelleries, even of the French
chancellery itself. French policy after 1845 was not

[49] See below, p. 118.
[50] Smith, *op. cit.*, pp. 397-99.

heedful of the warning of the American President. It did not abstain, as will appear in more detail later, from intervention in the affairs of the New World, or accept the pretensions of American hegemony which were implicit in the language of the Monroe Doctrine. Indeed, it was France who was most seriously to challenge the principles of 1823 and 1845 before two decades were gone. But, none the less, balancing all considerations, I incline to believe that it was the part of wisdom not to permit to pass unchallenged the Guizot speech of June 10. If the results abroad were not extraordinarily important, it was worth while to make the issue clear at home.

It would have been possible, no doubt, to issue this challenge without reference to the message of 1823. The connection between the balance of power conception and the Monroe message is real, but not inevitable. The one might have been discussed without linking it with the other. But there was a great advantage in binding the two together. In invoking the Monroe declaration, Polk was acting with a degree of imagination that hardly seems to be generally consistent with his prosaic character. He was rallying to the support of his thesis the name of one of the most respected Presidents of the United States, and principles which had already begun to take their hold upon the public mind. This was sound strategy, and sound statesmanship.

But if the Polk message, in so far as it was a reply to Guizot, seems highly justifiable, its wisdom is less obvious with regard to the question of California or of

Oregon. In respect to the first-named, the judgment may well be a balanced one. British designs on this province were virtually a fiction, as we have seen. And yet it is to be remembered that the policy of Great Britain in the New World was not, perhaps, that spotless thing which Anglophiles of the extreme type might have pictured it. Belize and the Mosquito Coast rise up before the mind to refute a too complete belief in British stainlessness. And it is to be remembered, too, that in the summer of 1845 Pakenham had refused the offer of compromise of the Oregon question, and that to a man of Polk's temperament this might well seem evidence of a generally sinister purpose, not only with regard to Oregon, but with regard to everything else. While it must be confessed therefore that suspicion of British designs on California was unjustified, it is possible to understand the President's attitude in the light of all the circumstances.

As to Oregon, however, the justification of the enunciation of the Monroe Doctrine seems decidedly less clear. What was to be gained by the assertion of these principles? They had played no useful part whatsoever in 1823 or 1824, and had Polk cared to consult such an expert as Greenhow, the chief clerk of the State Department, or to read the book which Greenhow had written, he would have discovered as much. If the administration intended to stand upon the ground of the election crisis of 1844, and make good its claim to 54-40, it might rouse public opinion at home, perhaps, by an appeal to Monroe's declaration. But as an inter-

8

national factor, as an argument in support of the American claims, the declaration was as unconvincing as it had been twenty years before. The claim of the United States to bar Great Britain from all the northwest on the basis of the non-colonization principle was utterly illogical and illegal, in view of the British occupation of a considerable part of this region, and in view of the implied admission of the doubtfulness of American title, as recorded in the conventions for joint occupation of the region in 1818 and 1827. If, on the other hand, the object of the administration was compromise, its case could derive no strength, nor could the will of Great Britain to compromise be stimulated, by the assertion of a doctrine which had proved inacceptable to British ministers when it was first enunciated, and which was sure to prove inacceptable to them again.

To say this is not to imply, of course, that the settlement of the Oregon question was in actual fact *prejudiced* by the assertion of the Monroe Doctrine. There is nothing in the diplomatic correspondence which indicates this fact. On the contrary, the British minister at Washington hardly mentioned this part of the message in his communications to his government, and the reports of the American minister at London do not indicate that Polk's language caused any particular irritation in the British cabinet. It has seemed to be the good fortune of the American government on more than one occasion to exhibit anything but good manners in dealing with the British, and yet never to have to suffer the consequences of its own blustering tone. Again and again, the British people when matters have come to a crisis have been vigorously and vocally averse to a breach with the United States. The compromise with which the Oregon dispute was finally settled was not prevented, or even impeded, by the truculent tone of the American President.

Nor, in this instance, did Polk's appeal to the principles of 1823 alter the strength of the sentiment for compromise in the United States. Despite the tone of the message, there were, even in Polk's own party, from the beginning, strong elements looking towards conciliation. Buchanan, the Secretary of State, may have been in character what John Quincy Adams contemptuously called him, " the shadow of a shade," and yet from his very position he was bound to exert some influence. By private correspondence with McLane, the American minister at London, he strove to bring about a peaceful settlement of the whole problem. Calhoun and Benton, the towering figures of the Democratic party in Congress, were also friends of peace. The debates of 1846 in both Houses attest the strength of pacific sentiment. The bill for the termination of the joint convention of 1827, originally a rather threatening measure, was so phrased, by the time it had been enacted, as to have lost all sting, and to have hindered not a whit the settlement by compromise. Polk's message roused no aggressive national sentiment which could not be allayed.

The declaration of 1845, indeed, cannot be said to have been hailed with anything like unanimous approval. In the case of the press, the Democratic papers, as was

only natural, applauded vigorously. Such a course of
action was to be expected, and indicates very little
indeed. Occasionally, a Whig organ, such, for example,
as the *American Review,* commended the attitude of the
President, and endorsed the principles of 1823.[51] Many
other of the Whig papers, however, took a wholly different course. Some influential papers, such, for example, as the *Boston Transcript* [52] and the *Philadelphia
Inquirer* [53] and the *Washington National Intelligencer,*
ignored the Polk revival of Monroe's principles, but
spoke strongly in favor of a moderate and pacific policy
with regard to Oregon. Others, as for example, the
New York Tribune, minced no words in condemning
the language of the President. "All the gas of the Message about ' the balance of power ' on the Continent,
and our resistance to further European conquest and
colonization," wrote the irrepressible Horace Greeley,
" is the paltriest fishing for thoughtless huzzas, worthy
of a candidate for constable rather than of a President
of the United States. When Mr. Monroe declared our
opposition to European conquest on this Continent, it
was supposed that the Great Powers were meditating
the subjugation of our sister republics by their arms to

[51] *American Review,* January, 1846, " The Mission to Panama," pp. 1-20. The author of this article derived a good deal
of satisfaction, however, from contrasting Polk's attitude in
1845 with his attitude in 1826.

[52] *Boston Transcript,* December 29, 1845, quoting with approval the *New York Journal of Commerce,* and the *Sunday
Times and Messenger.*

[53] *Philadelphia Inquirer,* December 4, 1845.

the Spanish Yoke. It was right that we should regard such a procedure with jealousy and meet it with prompt remonstrance. . . . . But what is there like to this in the present attitude of Europe toward this Continent? Is any body asserting a ' right divine ' to restore revolted colonies to the parent states? Great Britain claims Oregon on just such grounds as our claim rests upon—Discovery, Exploration, Settlement, Possession. . . . . Her right to her portion of the Continent is as strong and as just as ours to what belongs to us, and we shall betray a conscious weakness in our pretensions if we resort to foolish gasconade about the ' balance of power ' and ' this continent ' as without the proper sphere of European interest or observation." [54]

In an age of partisan and personal journalism, such statements as these ought not to be taken too seriously, as indicative of the general trend of public opinion. And yet it is abundantly clear that Polk did not have the country solidly behind him in the rather provocative attitude which he was willing to take with regard to Great Britain. The course of events itself amply proves this assertion.

In Congress, too, there was no tremendous enthusiasm for the revival of the Monroe Doctrine. This will become clear if we examine the attempt of some of his supporters to secure congressional sanction for the principles Polk had laid down.,

On January 14, 1846, Senator Allen of Ohio, a strongly nationalistic Democrat, and chairman of the

[54] *New York Tribune,* December 3, 1845.

Committee on Foreign Relations, asked leave to bring
in a resolution endorsing the stand of the President.
The resolution read as follows:

" *Resolved,* By the Senate and House of Representatives of the United States of America in Congress
assembled, That recent manifestations of a disposition
by certain Powers of Europe to interfere in the political
arrangement of this continent, with a view to the
enforcement of the European principles of the ' balance
of power,' upon the independent nations of America,
having made it, in his judgment, the duty of the President of the United States to call the attention of the
Congress to this subject in his Annual Message, and to
announce, on the part of the United States, the counter-
principle of non-intervention, it is the judgment of Congress that the announcement thus made by the President was demanded by the manifest hazard to which
such interference would inevitably expose the relations
of peace now existing between the Old World and the
New.

" *Resolved,* That Congress thus concurring with the
President, and sensible that this subject has been forced
upon the attention of the United States by recent events
so significant as to make it impossible for this Government longer to remain silent, without being ready to
submit to, and even to invite, the enforcement of this
dangerous doctrine, do hereby solemnly declare to the
civilized world the unalterable resolution of the United
States to adhere to and enforce the principle, that any
effort of the Powers of Europe to interfere or meddle
in the social organization or political arrangements of
the Independent nations of America, or further to
extend the European system of Government upon this
continent by the establishment of new Colonies, would
be incompatible with the independent existence of the
nations, and dangerous to the liberties of the people of
America, and therefore would incur, as by the right of

self-preservation it would justify, the prompt resistance of the United States." [55]

The language of this resolution, it will be seen, goes considerably beyond the language of the message. It does not make, as did the President's pronouncement, any distinction whatsoever between North and South America; its language with regard to French intervention in the Texan question was distinctly more aggressive than that of Polk; and its final clause virtually implied that the United States would, under all circumstances, go to war whenever the Monroe Doctrine was violated. That propositions of so sweeping a character should arouse opposition was to be expected, all the more so since the international situation was distinctly ominous, and the relations of the United States and Great Britain over the Oregon question strained to the utmost. Without an instant's delay, therefore, John C. Calhoun began the attack upon Senator Allen's proposal. Calhoun, though a Democrat, had been ignored in the composition of Polk's cabinet, and denied the Secretariat of State to which he had so good a claim. Now an old man, no longer of the aggressive temper of the "war-hawk" of 1812, he believed it to be his preeminent public duty just at this time to prevent a breach between the two great English-speaking nations; and he saw the move of the Senator from Ohio as a threat to the pacific relations of these two peoples. Accordingly, he criticized the resolution, on the ground that it involved commitments of a far-reaching character, practically speak-

ing, a pledge to protect all the nations of the New World
against aggression. He expressed doubts as to whether
the country had arrived at that state of maturity where
it could wisely assume such obligations, and declared
that, if such a declaration were to mean anything, it
would be necessary to " concentrate the entire energies
of the country on carrying it out." As for the original
declaration of President Monroe, he declared that it had
been devoid of practical effect, and had indeed even
produced certain embarrassment. There was no necessity for reiterating it now, especially in language that
might involve the choice of " the path of error and
danger." Acting on such views, he declared that he
would oppose even leave to bring in the resolution, a
step very far from usual in dealing with matters brought
before the Senate.[56] Though Allen tried to defend
his proposal, declaring that the silence of Congress
would be a " negation of what the President has laid
down," he was unable to secure affirmative action, and
the motion for leave was laid on the table by a vote of
28 to 23. The vote, it is interesting to note, was a partisan one. Three Democrats, Calhoun and his colleague
McDuffie, and Westcott of Florida, lined up with 25
Whigs to defeat the proposal of the Senator from Ohio ;
not a single Whig voted in its support.[57] In this division
we can already see the signs of that partisan difference

[56] *Ibid.,* p. 197. Calhoun raised the question as to whether
such a resolution were in order, since it dealt with a part of
the President's message already referred to the Committee on
Foreign Relations.

[57] *Ibid.,* p. 198.

of opinion with regard to the Monroe Doctrine which was characteristic of the period extending from Polk's Presidency to the Civil War.

Senator Allen, though declaring at the time that he would consider the vote on the question of leave as final, was not content to accept defeat. On January 26 he again made an effort to bring his proposal before the Senate. This time considerable debate followed. Lewis Cass, one of the staunchest defenders of the Monroe Doctrine, made a long speech in its support. Stung by the tone of British newspaper criticism, Cass denied that the principle of the President's message was, in any sense, aggressive in character. On the contrary, respect for existing rights were expressly proclaimed. The danger of aggression existed, not from the United States, but from Great Britain. What of California? Should it be allowed to fall into British hands? What of the joint Anglo-French intervention in the affairs of Buenos Ayres, going on at the very moment? Should the United States Congress cringe before the British lion by refusing to consider the resolution of the Senator from Ohio? [58] Again Calhoun took up the cudgels on the other side, proclaiming the resolution to be futile if not dangerous, and asserting that abstract declarations would infallibly do more harm than good.[59]

The debate now assumed a partisan flavor. Allen had declared that his resolution ought to form one of the principal doctrines of the Democratic party. John

[58] *Ibid.*, pp. 240-242.
[59] *Ibid.*, p. 245.

M. Clayton of Delaware, soon to be Secretary of State, took advantage of the opening. With obvious pleasure, he called attention to the language of Polk and Buchanan and other Democrats in the Panama debates, and inquired how it was possible to reconcile their language in those debates with the tone of the President's message.[60] In reality there was no inconsistency here. But there was a talking point for a party man, and the Delaware man made the best of it, without, however, evoking any answer from the Democratic side. A series of running comments followed, and when the Senate voted, the decision of twelve days before was reversed. By a vote of 26 to 21 the Allen resolution was referred to the Committee on Foreign Relations. This time the majority mustered more of its strength; and only two Democrats, Calhoun and the faithful MacDuffie, lined up with the Whigs.[61]

It seems probable, however, that the favorable vote on this occasion was designed by Senator Allen's party colleagues rather to smooth his feelings, badly ruffled by the opposition of Calhoun, than to promote the passage of the resolution. For, once referred to the Committee, it never saw the light of day again. In the Senate the two parties were pretty equally balanced. A defection of four votes would defeat the measure. The two Senators from South Carolina were known to be opposed to it. Parliamentary reasons may easily explain the collapse of Allen's effort to secure the

[60] *Ibid.*, p. 247.
[61] *Ibid.*, p. 248.

endorsement of Congress for the Monroe Doctrine. At any rate, this is the last we hear of the project until seven years later, when it is revived by Cass.

In the House of Representatives, the President's message never became the subject of any prolonged debate. There are occasional references to it in the discussion of the bill authorizing the President to give notice to Great Britain of the termination of the treaty of 1827.[62] A militant Congressman from Illinois, the Chairman of the Committee on Territories, Stephen A. Douglas, alluded with warm approval to the " memorable declaration of Mr. Monroe," and declared magnanimously that on reading Polk's reiteration of it, he had found it possible to forgive the President from the bottom of his heart for ever having offered to compromise on Oregon.[63] Parrish of Ohio introduced a resolution affirming the principles of the President's message,[64] which, however, was never discussed. In view of the flood of oratory on the Oregon question in the winter and early spring of 1846, it is, on the whole, surprising that so few references to the President's pronouncement are to be found.[65] Interest in it does not appear to have been very long sustained.

[62] *Ibid.*, pp. 200 and 259.

[63] *Ibid.*, p. 259.

[64] *Ibid.*, p. 329.

[65] It is worth noting that, only a few days after the message, John Quincy Adams talked with George Bancroft, then Secretary of the Navy concerning it, and declared that he " approved entirely " of Polk's action. It is also interesting to learn that on this occasion Bancroft asked Adams if it were true that he [Adams] were the author of the non-colonization clause in the

We may turn, then, from the question of the reception of Polk's declaration in the United States, to the question of its reception on the other side of the Atlantic. In official British circles, as we have seen already, the reassertion of the Monroe Doctrine caused no particular fluttering in the dovecotes. It did not alter British policy in any important respect; it was not the subject of any very critical comment on the part of the British minister at Washington; and it was not debated or discussed in Parliament. In the British press, however, it did not pass unnoticed. In the discussions on the Oregon question in British periodicals, even prior to Polk's pronouncement, there had been occasional references to the Monroe Doctrine. Thus *Fraser's,* in an article on " The New Boundary Question," published in April, 1843, cited Rush's invocation of the Monroe message in 1824, and went on to declare contemptuously that " it ought to have been laughed at unless it could have been supported by force of arms." [66] And the *British and Foreign Review,* a year later, no doubt influenced by the trend of American comment, declared that it was " the moral duty of individuals, as well as of governments, to protest against doctrines, which, if acted upon, would necessarily lead to acts of violence and aggression, and the destruction of the established principles of international law." [67] Now that these doc-

---

original message. The answer was, of course, in the affirmative. *Memoirs of John Quincy Adams,* edited by Charles Francis Adams (Philadelphia, 1874-77, 12 vols.), XII, 218.

[66] *Fraser's,* April, 1843, XXVII, 484-502, especially 501.

[67] *British and Foreign Review,* July, 1844, " The Oregon Territory," pp. 560-86, especially p. 582.

trines had been re-enunciated by the President himself, there was a further outburst of indignation. " These passages of the message," wrote the *Morning Chronicle,* referring to the prohibitions on European colonization, " have created much sensation here, and are to a great extent considered as rather gratuitous. . . . . With regard to the objection to any further European colonies on the continent of North America, most people are puzzled to discover to what it immediately points. Is it particularly against England, France or Russia—that is, supposing that France or Russia should wish to colonize any portion of Mexico or elsewhere, by purchase ; and Russia besides her territory north of Oregon, has already a settlement at Bodega in California. At any rate, it is a bold assertion of a bold policy that, if carried to extremes, might prove as dangerous to peace as the Oregon question itself." [68] This was a relatively moderate statement of the case. The strongly anti-American *London Times* practised no such mildness of language. " In the old world," it declared, in its issue of December 27, " we are not accustomed to hear statesmen and rulers announce new principles of public morality, to demand an insulation from the universal laws and sympathies of their kind, and in their place to erect a convenient system of original and axiomatic claims : we only aspire to develop the old. Whoever declines to rest his cause on the ancient foundations of equity and truth, is immediately asked for his credentials, and nothing less than a heavenly sanction will

[68] *Morning Chronicle,* December 30, 1845.

satisfy us for the absence of admissible human pleas. From the beginning of time the man who promulgates a new morality, or what comes to the same thing, an exemption from the old, is solicited for a sign. We still confess our dependence on Divine authentications. When *Mr. Polk* has performed a miracle, and the Congress has attested the presence of supernatural powers, then, and then only, shall we admit it to be a mortal sin deserving the summary vengeance of the Union, to offer our mediation or advice to any North American state, to enforce ancient treaties, and defend ancient occupation in a neutral and unappropriated American territory."

Having thus vented a portion of its spleen, the *Times* proceeded to demonstrate the fallacious logic of the message in a passage not without charm, and not without cogency.

" The natural insulation of the new continents must be great indeed, which can justify so great a social, or rather anti-social independence. It must be shown not only that there is no necessity for political relations, but not even a possibility, not even a case in which such could possibly arise. The fact, however, is far otherwise. The old and the new world are separated by much less distances than those which divide the constituent nations of each. The western nations of Europe are within a fortnight's voyage of nearly the whole North American population, from the Isthmus of Darien to the shores of Lake Superior. In the same practical point of view we are far nearer to North America, we could almost add the South, than we are to Africa and Asia. If America is a world of its own, then also is each of the four conventional quarters of the globe. In fact, there is no more reason in nature why America should segregate itself from the universal system and universal code, than any other quarter. Nor does history present any contradiction to this antecedent and natural unity of the whole world; and the *President* only shows the utter groundlessness of his theory, when he affects a reference to the political facts of the question : . . . ."

The rest of this interesting editorial is too long to quote here,[69] and the paragraphs just cited may reveal the general nature of the argument; but it does not seem at all improbable that the viewpoint that the *Times* expressed found an echo of sympathy in the minds of many Europeans.

Across the Channel, indeed, Polk's message was naturally not well received by those in power. King noted that at the New Year's reception of 1846 both Louis Philippe and his prime minister seemed " unusually reserved and stately " in addressing him.[70] And not so very long after this, on January 12, Guizot made an important speech in the Chamber in which he amplified and expanded his views of American policy and his doctrine of the balance of power, and directly challenged the President's doctrine. The two great races of the New World, the Spanish and the English, he declared, must not be permitted one to absorb the other, and in particular the southern Catholic race must not be devoured by the Anglo-American. The doctrine of the balance of power, he went on, in language which sounds a little grotesque to the generation which remembers the

[69] See special note at the end of this chapter.

[70] Washington, Dept. of State, Despatches, France, January 1, 1846.

balance of power of 1914, had been the source of the development, the prosperity, the moral and social greatness of Europe, and would be equally salutary in the New World. The danger against which the enlightened friends of civilization had always contended, in the days of Charles V, or of Louis XIV, or of Napoleon, was the danger of the domination of a single power. " What was not good for Europe under the form of universal monarchy would not be good for America under the form of universal republicanism; would not be good from the standpoint of prosperity, of civilization. There is a very sound, a very practical interest in a balance of power, an interest which is no philosopher's chimæra, but which is applicable to the New World as to the Old, which can determine the happiness of nations in the New World or in the Old." Having thus restated his doctrine of the speech of June 10, Guizot went on to make frank prediction of its future : " Do not deceive yourselves; whether or not it is adopted today, this idea (*i. e.,* of the balance of power) will grow ; it will develop as the relations between the states of the Old World and those of the New develop. You will see, naturally, inevitably, by the simple progress of enlightened public opinion, that European policy will strive to maintain, between the different states of America, that same tendency to the balance of power which has, I repeat, been responsible for the greatness, the prosperity, the dignity of the states of Europe." With regard to the United States the French prime minister made his viewpoint clear. The relations of the United States with France, he declared, were entirely friendly ; France, far from looking with regret upon the rising greatness of the new republic of the West, applauded it, and found in its growth reason to hope that it would exercise its power in a manner more moral (*sic!*) and more useful than had been the case with many other great peoples. But at the same time no one had a right to complain if French policy took account of this increasing power, and views its advance with a vigilant, God forbid that he should say, a suspicious eye. The same independence of action which the President had declared that the United States had always practised toward the nations of the Old World France might reasonably practise toward the United States.

The notion that no European state should exercise any political action in the New World Guizot declared that he could not accept.

" Gentlemen, the maxim is a strange one. The United States is not the only nation of North America. There are, on the North American continent, other independent nations, other legally constituted states ; I will name only Mexico. These states have the same right to seek or to reject alliances, to form such political combinations as appear to them to accord with their interests. The proximity, the existence of the United States cannot in any degree limit their independence or their rights. Nobody in the United States, I am sure, would make any such claim.

" With these independent nations, these duly constituted states of North America we have natural and treaty relations, we have treaties of every kind; we have the same right to make and maintain these treaties that these independent nations had to conclude them with us. It is impossible to maintain that there is any-

9

thing in this to offend the susceptibilities of the United
States. There is in all this nothing that we have done,
or can do, which the nations with which we are in relations cannot do also. The language to which I allude,
if one were to interpret it in the sense which it seems to
have, would far exceed the limit of the rights which
can be recognized as existing on the part of other governments, however great they may be.

" Gentlemen, these bonds that we have with other
nations of the American continent, these relations that
we have contracted with them, that they had a right and
we had a right to make, these commercial, political, even
territorial interests will be maintained ; we will maintain
them without any feeling of hostility toward the United
States, indeed, with the same sentiments of good will
and friendship which we have long professed and practised toward them ; we will maintain them without
giving the United States any just subject of complaint, but also without yielding to any unfounded
pretension." [71]

[71] Guizot, *Histoire Parlementaire, op. cit.,* V, 20-32, especially 30.

While thus protesting against the doctrines of Polk, Guizot
made no diplomatic representations to Washington. On the
contrary, he instructed the French minister there as follows :
" You will not add any official demonstration to that which I
have already made. You will take care simply to regulate your
conduct according to the principles which I have laid down in
my communications to the two Chambers.

" We address ourselves to the public opinion of the United
States themselves. We respect, we love, this new, already great
people which France aided in bringing into being, but we intend
to maintain our entire independence in relation to them as in
relation to everyone else. We refuse to admit those distinctions
between American and European governments, between monarchies and republics. All civilized nations exist on the same
legal basis, and are equally obliged to respect one another."
Paris, Min. des Aff. Etr., Corr. Pol., Etats-Unis, vol. 102,
January 29, 1846.

The language of the French prime minister deserves the closest attention on the part of the student of American diplomacy. In the speech of January 12, the Monroe Doctrine was for the first time definitely challenged by a responsible European statesman in a public address. George Canning, in 1824, had made clear to Rush his opposition to the more important of its principles, that of non-colonization; Prince de Polignac had lectured the American minister on the danger of such maxims; in a formal protocol the British negotiators of 1824 had expressed their determination not to recognize the doctrine of the President. But no public act transpired to make this view clear to the world. It was Guizot, in 1846, who, first of all European statesmen, denounced the pretension of the United States to the hegemony of the New World in a public address. And the views which he expressed on January 12 were reiterated in a speech of January 21, in which, replying to the criticisms of Thiers, he again declared that France could not admit that it accorded with her interests to leave to the United States the domination of the American continents.[72]

None the less, his defense of his policy, and his excoriation of the Doctrine, came in for serious criticism in the Chamber. The foremost rival of the French prime minister, a rival in whom personal and party bitterness often prevailed over reasons of state, and who could never resist a chance to harry the ministry, arose on January 20 to attack the diplomacy of the govern-

[72] Guizot, V, 43-59.

ment. In a long speech Adolphe Thiers denounced
French interposition in the affairs of Texas, eulogized
the United States, and even defended the attitude of
the American President. The theory of the balance of
power as proclaimed by Guizot he pronounced to the
interest only of England. The American government,
he admitted, showed a jealous susceptibility, and sometimes even expressed itself in a manner somewhat
wounding to French pride. But, on the other hand, it
was, he declared, " the only nation except France to
which I wish greatness," [73] and its declaration of principle with regard to European colonization was fundamentally sound. "America does not belong to the first
occupier, for her territories are already occupied." [74]
No French interest, Thiers went on to assert was threatened by the development of the great nation across the
seas.

The language of Thiers was dictated in no small
degree by partisan antagonism to Guizot. With light-
hearted inconsistency, the brilliant opponent of the
ministry was a few years later to favor a vigorous
policy of force in the Argentine, oblivious of the relation of such an enterprise to the views of the United
States, and his observations in the speech just noticed
must not therefore be taken entirely without reserve.
There is plenty of evidence, moreover, that the idea of
the balance of power in the New World was no doctrine peculiar to Guizot, and that it found root in many

[73] L. A. Thiers, *Discours sur les rélations de la France avec
les Etats-Unis d'Amerique, prononcé dans la séance de la
Chambre des députés du 20 janvier 1846* (Paris, 1846), p. 16.
[74] *Ibid.*, p. 19.

French minds, and was, to a degree, expressed in French policy. Yet Thiers was in a measure sincere, and he did not stand alone. King thought that his views were listened to with obvious approbation by a majority of the Chamber.[75] And whether this be true or not, they were certainly echoed in the French press. The *Quotidienne,* in commenting on Polk's message, spoke sneeringly of " the doctrinaire policy " of the prime minister, and of the " scholastic theory of the balance of power " which had made France hated and scorned.[76] " M. Guizot and his theory of the European balance of power applied to America," wrote *Le National,* " will have a good deal of difficulty in vindicating themselves against the principles which Mr. Polk has maintained." [79] *Le Siècle* spoke approvingly of the " just declaration " of the President,[78] and *Le Constitutionnel* took much the same tone. Only the semi-official *Journal des Débats* took up the cudgels in behalf of the government, and declared the theory of Mr. Polk to be " entirely inadmissible." [79] Like the *London Times,* the *Débats* found

[75] Washington, Dept. of State, Despatches, France, January 30, 1846.

[76] *Quotidienne,* December 26, 1845.

[77] *Le National,* December 25, 1845.

[78] *Le Siècle,* December 26, 1845.

[79] *Journal des Débats,* December 26, 1845. The *Débats* argued at some length on the matter. " Sixty years ago," it declared, " it possessed the totality of America, and it has still retained there possessions which it will not renounce. We have Guiana, from which we hope to gain some advantage some day soon; England retains Canada with its vast dependencies, Belize, and its own Guiana; Russia and Holland have important domains on the Continent. All the archipelago of the Antilles belongs

the revival of the Monroe Doctrine nothing else than the cover for American expansion. The notion that the principles of 1823 were merely a cover for aggression and imperialism thus appears for the first, but very distinctly not for the last, time in the judgments of European publicists.

In the Old World, and in the New, then, the message of 1845 was the subject of very considerable discussion. It cannot be said that it altered very materially the course of diplomatic events, any more than had the message of 1823; with regard to the problems which stimulated it, it is worth noting that one, Texas, had been settled; that another, California, existed only in the President's imagination, and in the imagination of other Anglophobe Americans; and that the third, Oregon, was finally composed without reference to what Polk had to say. It is also to be remembered that the support which was accorded it was very largely a partisan support. The Democrats (and the Democrats were, of course, the larger and more influential party at the time) hailed it with the usual applause; the Whigs were distinctly not enthusiastic; all in all it cannot be asserted

---

to Europe. The European powers are therefore at the same time American powers; that is why they have the right to wish for a balance of power in the New World. The claim of Mr. Polk on this point would do him honor, ill-founded as it is, if it were disinterested; but he takes care to warn us expressly to the contrary. He is the enemy of the doctrine of the American balance of power because he wishes those states who wish to join the United States to have the right to do so. At least this is franker than the protestations of sympathy for Mexico which he has had the effrontery to insert in another part of the message; but it is a little more honest."

that the mere fact of the restatement of the Monroe principles immediately elevated those principles to the position of a national dogma which it would be treason to deny and folly to dispute.

And yet Polk's action marks a very decided step forward in the evolution of the Monroe Doctrine. Partisanship might depreciate the value or the propriety of the President's utterances; prudence might dictate that the foreign policy of the United States be bottomed on concrete necessities and interests, and not on vague formulas, not very easily enforceable in all circumstances; but, none the less, the power of simple generalizations over the minds of men is a thing not to be disregarded. The iteration and reiteration of a formula almost inevitably secures its acceptance by a very large number of men, and in this case the formula was a very attractive one, and, in a sense, a very sensible one. For, whatever may be said of the perversion of the Monroe Doctrine, the instinct of the American people, in mistrusting European meddling in the New World, has been by no means fundamentally unreasonable; and, whatever the views of the critics, the condemnation of such meddling was likely in the long run to enlist popular sympathy. The history of the period after 1845 will show that the Democratic party, which Polk had pledged to the principles of Monroe, was never obliged to withdraw its allegiance to them, and that the general trend of opinion was distinctly in their favor. By his pronouncement the President no doubt powerfully contributed to imbed in the public mind the memory of and the belief in the Monroe Doctrine.

SPECIAL NOTE—CHAPTER II

Citing Polk's theory, the editorial goes on,

"As a matter of fact nothing can be more untrue. By the proof of history America is inextricably mixed up with European politics. In the last European war the Union sympathized with our continental foes, and took advantage of our embarrassments to assert its claims. In so doing it only followed the instinct of all contending parties, who, whatever be the nature of the quarrel, or the principles on which they maintain it, do in fact select the season of their adversary's weakness as the best opportunity of striking a blow, and cannot help feeling a common cause with other hostile parties. France sympathized with the States, and rendered them most important service in the war of independence; and that sympathy was long after returned. We cannot express the fact better than in the words of Governor *Strong,* addressed to the Legislature of Massachusetts on January 12, 1814:

"'The friends of peace (says the Governor) are accused of being under British influence; but their accusers ought to reflect whether partialities of an opposite kind have not produced the evils we suffer, and whether if our conduct to both belligerents had been impartial, a war with either would have been thought necessary. We had assumed the character of a neutral nation, but had we not violated the duties imposed by that character? Had not every subject of complaint against one belligerent been amply displayed, and those against the other been concealed or palliated? It has indeed been suggested that we have no connexion with France in regard to the war, *but when France and England were engaged in a most arduous struggle and we interfered and assaulted one of them, will any man doubt our intention to assist the other?'*

"But, as it happens, and as every one moderately read in the popular Anglo-American literature knows full well, our republican kinsmen do feel a more generous, more expansive, more universal, and, we may even say, a more humane and social ambition, than President *Polk* would give them credit for. They do not cut down their prospects to the compass and policy of a Presidential address. Like all other nations of the earth, they aim at exercising what they consider a beneficial influence on all their brotherhood of the human kind. They feel the universally innate desire to regenerate all the world after the image and type of self. To extend the principles of 'self-government,' and 'free institutions,' to extinguish tyrants and aristocrats, to level all social irregularities, all over the world, especially where reform is most needed, and the change will be the greatest, are objects ever on their lips and deep in their bosoms. They only bide their time to fulfill their great 'mission,' and execute a glorious deliverance from class legislation and territorial bondage for every nation of the earth. That golden vision is circumscribed by no continental bounds. Old and new are all alike to the American philanthropist, and philanthropy in that country is the theory and profession of every citizen. Any substantial and resolute resistance offered by any considerable portion of Europe to the dominion of the altar and the throne may almost reckon on the certainty of Anglo-American co-operation.

"The classical reader will find in this theory of political insulation a most exact counterpart of one advanced with much plausibility and eloquence, though without either truth or effect, by an ancient state, in many respects the prototype of the Anglo-American commonwealth. It was a people of great enterprise, daring, and power; famous in those days, the America of Greece, though of no great consideration now. It was the little island of Corfu; once the 'far west' of civilization, now absorbed into its most central recess and innermost bosom. When the mother country of that colony, long after the actual independence of the latter, had some occasion to resent the arrogance of its offspring, the ambassadors of Corcyra pleaded in the Athenian assembly their distance and separation from all the old world, and independence of interests, and their habitual 'practise' of non-interference, in lines which the American President might almost be supposed to have borrowed for his purpose. We will not enter into the arguments adduced on the Corinthian side of the controversy. The facts of the case were certainly against the Corcyreans, who do not appear to have made the best use of their insulation, and their theory of being, as Mr. *Polk* says, 'the best judge' in their own cause. However, they were now forced to solicit Athenian aid, and soon became the focus of a most dreadful and disastrous war, which ended in the utter disruption of the community, and ruin of their state. Such was the end of *their* theory of a political and moral insulation."

See also the editorial of January 1.

"Mr. *Polk* declares in the most explicit language, that so far as the continent of North America extends the United States are determined to warn off all intruders. The *President* at Washington is lord of the manor; all the other American Powers are copy-holders under him, and whenever a fresh enclosure bill is passed, the sovereign republic is to receive the lion's share—or, rather, these other Powers are mere tenants by sufferance, whose claims will be quashed upon the first dispute, and who will infalliby be ejected in the end.

"We reply, without hesitation, that all the Powers of the civilized world are bound to protest against such a doctrine, as they did protest against a similar declaration when it was made by Mr. *Monroe;* for those which have no territorial rights to defend, are equally interested in the maintenance of the plain principle that rights of sovereignty are limited by the frontier of every state, and that to claim the exercise of a power of exclusion, or to assert a prospective dominion over territories beyond those frontiers, is to confuse and overthrow all the barriers of power, and to hasten the return of universal war and confusion. . . . . Mr. *Polk* denies (at least as far as the American continent is concerned) the restraint which these eternal laws have imposed upon every civilized Government. He denounces as 'the diplomatic arts and intrigues' of foreign states, the attempt to vindicate the public law of nations; and in the severe language which he applies to France, he forgets that that nation never swerved from the traditional policy which prescribed a firm alliance with the United States of America, until the United States had embarked in a career of aggression and injustice in which no wise or honest Government could follow them. At the time we live in, acts like these are not only degrading to the Government which commits them, but they are dangerous to all nations; and they will infallibly provoke from all nations first censure—then opposition—finally resistance. Is the whole continent of Europe, teeming with a superabundant population, to be told that the vast regions of the Western World are henceforward closed against them, unless they cast off their national character and adopt the social institutions and the political ascendancy of the United States? Is emigration to become expatriation, and is no State to plant its colours on the American coast, without abjuring all that its subjects or citizens hold dear? Nay, we must even infer from the language of the *President* that existing rights and settlements are held by a questionable tenure; and that all the various dependencies of Britain, Russia, Spain, France, Holland, Belguim, and the Baltic Powers, in and about the soil of North America await the application of the grand principle of absorption, whilst the independent Governments of a purely American character, such as Mexico and Guatemala, are already condemned to aggressive spoliation. We are not pleading our own cause in the question of Oregon, or writing with reference to the encroachments which must, ere long, be directed against the oldest British settlements in America, if such a principle as this be allowed to prevail. For the maintenance of those rights we look confidently to the strength of England, which inspires a secret dread even to those who have ceased to acknowledge the obligations of good faith and justice. If we are ourselves, after Mexico, the most open to these attacks, we are also by far the best to repel them. But it cannot be too often repeated that, be the issue of this controversy what it may, all Europe is more or less interested in the duty of moral and political resistance to this assumption of universal dominion on the part of the United States, which can only be compared to the arrogant pretensions of a successful conqueror when, his triumph over, the independence of the world is all but complete. If such principles as these are to regulate the policy of America, and the relations of States on that continent, how long will they be excluded from Europe? The fashion of attacking the weak and plundering the helpless, and exalting dubious claims into absolute right, would soon find its application here. It is the spirit of the factious minority which deblaterates about war and national honour in the French Chambers; it is the motive of unscrupulous politicians all over the world. In Europe we see it happily crushed and imprisoned; but in the United States it speaks with the voice of the Executive Government, and threatens to wield the power of a nation."

CHAPTER III

New Interpretations, 1845-1848

The message of 1845, as we have seen in the preceding chapter, was brought about by events in the North American continent, and had to do largely with that particular geographical area. But in the four years of the Polk administration, more than one issue was to arise involving the principles which the President had invoked. Anglo-French intervention in the Argentine, intrigue to establish monarchy in Mexico and in Ecuador, an American Congress at Lima, the question of the Isthmus of Panama, new British aggression in Central America, and possible American intervention in Yucatan, all these have a direct connection with the Monroe Doctrine. All of them are to be examined in this chapter, but solely from this restricted point of view, with reference to the light they throw on the development and interpretation of the principles of 1823.

It is worth while to say at the outset, however, that two striking facts especially stand out. The one is the invocation of the Monroe Doctrine by a not small number of Latin American states, by Argentina, by Peru, by Ecuador, by New Granada, by Nicaragua and Honduras, and by Yucatan. It has sometimes been assumed that the Mexican War was the ruin of American influence in Latin America. The facts do not bear out this point of view. Never in a single administration were the appeals to the Doctrine more numerous than in the administration of James K. Polk.

The second fact that deserves to be underlined, even at the beginning, is that in the main the President and his Secretary of State limited themselves to a platonic restatement of the principles of 1823. Lip-service to the revived dogma of Monroe they often gave; but action to uphold it they never took. No doubt the Mexican War had much to do with their caution in this regard; and in some of the cases already cited as involving the Doctrine, the crisis was dissipated before any important decision could have been made. None the less, there is an interesting contrast between the bold pronouncement of 1845, and the restrained policy of the years that follow.

Amongst the various episodes that must be examined in this chapter, the first in point of time is the Anglo-French intervention in the Argentine. To this I have already made passing allusion in the previous chapter. It is necessary, however, at this point, to examine it in more detail, with a view to determining the motives of the participants, and the rôle which was played in the whole business by the United States. The French intervention in 1838-40 in La Plata, though it did secure greater consideration for French citizens, was certainly not successful in producing a stable political situation in that part of the world. Don Manuel de Rosas remained supreme, and his determination to reinstate Oribe in the presidency of Uruguay was as firm as ever. An equivocal article in the Mackau-Arana convention bound the

dictator to respect the independence of his neighbor-
state, but as it expressly declared that nothing in its
terms was to be construed to limit the right of the
Argentine to defend its "natural rights," whenever
" justice, honor, or security " should make it necessary,
there was no difficulty whatsoever in brushing it aside
so far as the war with the partisans of Rivera was concerned. The struggle along the banks of the Paraná,
therefore, continued; and indeed the tide of victory
began to flow strongly in the direction of Buenos Ayres.
Both Great Britain and France did their best to bring
the conflict to an end; the British offered their good
offices in 1841, France and Great Britain together in
1842, but Rosas obstinately refused to consider terms
which did not make Oribe once more President. More
and more confident of victory, he saw his troops over-
run Uruguay, and in February, 1843, begin the siege of
Montevideo, the last stronghold of the opposing Uruguayan faction. The heroic defense of this city deserves
to rank with that of Sebastopol, or of Candia, and it
gave time for the forces of opposition to the Argentine
dictator to form once more, and to attain consistency.
In the fall of 1844, Brazil, more and more uneasy at the
march of Rosas's power, sent the Viscount de Abrantes
as a special commissioner to Europe to urge the interposition of France and England in the struggle. Accepting the Brazilian invitation, though refusing to associate Brazil itself with their action, Lord Aberdeen and

¹ For an account of this mission, and numerous documents,
see Anon., A *Missão Especial do Visconde de Abrantes de
Outubro de 1844 a Outubro de 1846* (Rio de Janeiro, 1853).

Guizot began a new effort at mediation in the first months of 1845, designating respectively Mr. Ousely, and the Baron Deffaudis, the latter French minister in Mexico during the events of 1838, as their special representatives to La Plata, the principal object of their mission being stated as the preservation of the independence of Uruguay, and as a necessary condition thereof the withdrawal, by Rosas, of the aid which he persisted in giving to the forces of General Oribe. The commissioners were to attempt an amicable mediation, but they were authorized, in case their efforts at such mediation should prove a failure, to resort to a blockade of the Argentine ports in order to arrive at their end.[2]

The efforts of Ouseley and Deffaudis at a peaceful solution of the question of Uruguay were doomed to failure from the beginning, as was perhaps to be expected. After a considerable period of futile negotiation, the commissioners were compelled to proceed, first, to the blockade of the ports in possession of Oribe, and later, on September 22, to the blockade of Buenos Ayres itself. Moreover, as had been the case in 1838, the initial measures that were taken naturally led to others. The Argentine naval force was seized; the island of Martín García was reoccupied; a loan was floated in behalf of the struggling government at Montevideo; an English and French squadron sailed triumphantly up the Paraná; and an attempt was made to

[2] For a more detailed study of this period, see Cady, *op. cit.,* pp. 93 *et seq.,* Saldías, *op. cit.,* IV, 135-357, and V, 1-33, and 141-208; also Villanueva, *op. cit.,* II, 237-265.

rouse resistance to Rosas in the province of Corrientes, and to enlist the aid of Paraguay against Rosas.

Even in its inception, to say nothing of the measures to which it led, the Anglo-French intervention in the Argentine may be regarded as an infringement of the Monroe Doctrine. It is not, of course, that anything like conquest was intended; neither the British nor the French foreign ministers were men to embark upon any such policy, and the instructions of both the one and the other strictly limited the sphere of coercive action to naval pressure.[3] But the action of the powers constituted from the beginning a noxious interference with the political balance of South America. The motives behind it were not those of the redress of grievances (as had been the case, in a measure, with the French blockade of 1838); they were strictly political, and of precisely the character that offered dangerous precedents for the future. They really involved the support in Uruguay of a government which, if it survived at all, would owe its existence to European powers, and would be, in a measure, at any rate, dependent upon them. Already, as early as 1841, the Uruguayan faction opposed to Oribe had broached the question of

[3] For the instructions to Ouseley, see *British and Foreign State Papers*, XXXIII (1844-45), 930 *et seq.*, "It is the hope of Her Majesty's Government that neither a continued refusal on the part of General Rosas to come to terms, nor the still more improbable event of active resistance on his part, may make it necessary to have recourse to a blockade of the port of Buenos Ayres." For the instructions to Deffaudis, see Min. des Aff. Entr., Corr. Pol., Buenos Ayres, vol. 24, March 22, 1845.

a British protectorate,[4] and while the proposal was rejected, it illustrates well enough the danger that there might be established too close a political connection between a European and an American state. The menacing possibilities of such an intervention were, in fact, made clear as the intervention itself developed. The British government, it is true, though it had taken the initiative in the business, soon grew cautious, and with the fall of the Peel ministry, and the accession of Palmerston, directed its policy toward a new understanding with Rosas. But in the case of France, the course of events was entirely different. Left alone to pursue a policy of coercion and itself by no means bellicose, the French government found itself subjected to much pressure in favor of a truly aggressive policy. Thus, Count Waleski, who had been sent out by Guizot to negotiate a settlement in 1847, came back to Paris demanding a force of 6000 men to raise the siege of Montevideo.[5] He brought with him a Frenchman who had, with 250 of his fellow-nationals, been held as hostages at the town of Durazno since 1843, and who was ardent for a strong policy.[6] The closing days of the July Monarchy saw the Guizot ministry subjected to a savage attack for its emollient policy in the La Plata, and the clamor for vigorous action was renewed in 1849. At this time appeared an interesting work by one

[4] London, P. R. O., F. O., Buenos Ayres, vol. 78, March 17, 1841.

[5] Washington, Dept. of State, Despatches, Argentine Republic, Harris-Buchanan, September 16, 1847.

[6] Benjamin Poucel, *Les otages de Durazno,* Paris, 1864.

Eugène Guillemot,[7] who had been chargé d'affaires at
Rio de Janeiro, and had thus had an opportunity of
familiarizing himself with the course of the intervention. Guillemot, it is interesting to observe, was strongly
anti-American. He writes of the United States, which
" have already in their own eyes absorbed Mexico,"
advancing " with giant strides on the rest of America." [8]
He seems, quite without reason, to fear an American
protectorate over Montevideo.[9] He calls for the despatch of an expeditionary force to the Argentine to
uphold the prestige and the policy of France. Nor did
he stand alone. Weak as was the Second Republic, and
reluctant as were the ministers of the Prince-President
to undertake any further adventures in the La Plata,
strong pressure was applied in the Chambers in favor
of further chastisement of the Argentine dictator and
further support of Montevideo. Adolphe Thiers led a
vigorous movement of opposition to the government,
and it was only by close votes that a policy of conciliation prevailed. The appearance of a new work on La
Plata by Brossard,[10] a virtual plea in favor of France's
establishing a protectorate in Uruguay, furnishes additional evidence of the strength of interventionist sentiment. What began in 1845 as a well-intentioned effort

[7] Eugène Guillemot, *Affaires de la Plata. Extrait de la Cor-
respondance de M. Eugène Guillemot pendant sa mission dans
l'Amérique du Sud* (Paris, 1849).

[8] Guillemot, *op. cit.,* p. 21.

[9] *Ibid.,* p. 29.

[10] A. Brossard, *Considérations historiques et politiques sur
les républiques de La Plata dans leurs rapports avec la France
et l'Angleterre* (Paris, 1850).

to bring peace to a troubled part of Latin America came dangerously near to developing into a movement of aggression that would have run entirely counter to the principles of the Monroe Doctrine. Discount, as one may, the element of domestic politics which led the opposition to Louis Philippe and to the government of Prince Louis Napoleon to press for a vigorous policy in the Argentine, the very fact that it was willing to raise and press the issue is a fact of high significance.

In the debates on La Plata in the French Chambers there is little reference to the views of the United States. Thiers, who had been so quick to condemn the policy of Guizot in Texas, as distasteful to a friendly power, never seems to have suspected that intervention in the Argentine might not be particularly popular in Washington. Nor did the spokesmen for the government ever offer in defense of a policy of conciliation the necessity of conciliating American opinion. The famous doctrine of 1823 and 1845 does not appear, by this time, at any rate, to have penetrated very deeply into the French mind. There was, perhaps, no reason why it should be otherwise. For the Polk administration, and its successor, remained for the most part extraordinarily indifferent to what was going on in La Plata.

We have already seen that the Anglo-French intervention did not pass entirely unnoticed in the United States.[11] In December, a meeting of protest was held in New York, at which resolutions were introduced con-

[11] See above, p. 43.

demning the action of the European powers and affirming the Monroe Doctrine. The Allen resolution, already
alluded to, brought within its scope interventions in
both South and North America. A slashing article in
the *Democratic Review* for January, 1846,[12] from the
pen of Caleb Cushing, sharply criticized the policy of
France, and, still more of Great Britain. But the administration from the beginning to the end pursued a moderate course. In October Buchanan assured Pakenham
that " the Government of the United States had no intention of interfering with or opposing in any way the
efforts of Her Majesty's Government and the Government of France for the pacification of the two South
American Republics." [13] Though, a month later, the Secretary made a mild reference to " the jealousy with
which the American people viewed any European interference in the affairs of this Continent," and alluded to
the fear which " began to prevail " that France and
Great Britain intended to retain the island of Martín
García for the purpose of securing exclusive commercial
advantages in that part of the world, he added that no
such suspicions were entertained by the American government.[14] The administration also gave a more practical proof of its conciliatory policy. The United States
was represented at Buenos Ayres by a veteran Democrat
of the name of William Brent. Without any instructions
to do so, Brent interfered officiously in the negotiations

[12] *Democratic Review,* January, 1846, p. 163 *et seq.*

[13] London, P. R. O., F. O., America, vol. 429, October 13,
1845.

[14] *Ibid.,* November 13, 1845.

at the outset, and he had protested against the Anglo-French blockade. When Pakenham complained of this meddling activity, the American Secretary of State indicated that it was the intention of the administration to recall the over-zealous chargé, and the protest against the blockade was disavowed.[15]

The administration very obviously had no desire to pursue a vigorous policy in La Plata. The language of Polk's message demonstrates that the President made a distinction, though not an absolute one, between European activity in North and in South America. As for Buchanan, he was certainly not the man to pursue an aggressive course. Such a course, indeed, at the end of 1845, would have been the most demonstrable kind of folly. Our relations with England were still strained over a question far more important; and it was obviously desirable not to increase the tension, that is, if peace and not war was the object of the administration. To antagonize France, at this precise moment, was also something well worth avoiding, though it must be admitted that with regard to the "balance of power" principle Polk had not been very careful to spare French susceptibilities. And there was also the question of our relations with Mexico. It is true that the mission of Slidell had not yet failed, and there seems no reason to doubt that the administration was making in good faith an effort to settle outstanding difficulties; yet the result of that mission was distinctly problematical, and furnished another reason for caution in dealing with the problems

[15] *Ibid.,* and also December 13, 1845.

of more remote parts of the American continents. The case against picking one quarrel more when two already were brewing was naturally a strong one.

When Buchanan instructed Mr. Harris, Mr. Brent's successor in the mission to Buenos Ayres, the reasons for moderation had become stronger than ever. For these instructions bear the date of March 30, 1846. By this time the Slidell mission had been a proven failure; Zachary Taylor had been ordered to advance beyond the Nueces; and war with Mexico was an extreme probability. Thus it is that the American Secretary of State confined his observations on the intervention in La Plata to a rather academic statement of principle, and to an assurance with regard to the nonrecognition of the republic of Paraguay, over which the government at Buenos Ayres still claimed sovereignty. " The late annual message of the President to Congress," wrote Buchanan, " has so clearly presented the great American doctrines in opposition to the interference of European Governments in the internal concerns of the nations of this continent, that it is deemed unnecessary to add another word upon the subject. That Great Britain and France have flagrantly violated this principle by their intervention in La Plata is manifest to the whole world." But, reluctantly confessed the Secretary, " existing circumstances render it impossible for the United States to take a part in the present war." On the other hand, continued Buchanan, " the President desires that the whole moral influence of this Republic should be cast into the scale of the injured party. We cordially wish the Argentine Republic success in its struggle against internal interference. It is for these reasons, that although the Government of the United States never did authorize your predecessor Mr. Brent to offer his mediation in the affairs of Great Britain, France, and the Argentine Republic, this act has not been publickly disavowed." [16] With regard to Paraguay, it appears that General Alvear, the Argentine minister at Washington, had earnestly solicited the American government to abstain from recognition. This state had, of course, been for a long time independent under the dictatorship of the famous Dr. Francia, but had practised a policy of rigorous isolation. The death of Francia offered hopes that it might now be opened up to the commerce of the world. Behind the Anglo-French intervention in La Plata, indeed, lay as one of the motives a hope that the Paraná and the Uruguay, closed by the government of Rosas, might be opened up to international trade. And the American government, too, was interested in this opportunity of trade expansion. But, in the circumstances of 1846, out of respect for the Argentine, it held its hand, all the more so since the Lopez régime in Paraguay had speedily aligned itself with the enemies of Rosas, and thus, as Buchanan wrote to Harris, " become in fact an ally of Great Britain and France." [17]

The outbreak of the war with Mexico confirmed the administration in its cautious policy. The withdrawal of Britain from the intervention in July, 1847, diminished still further the reasons for action. Officially, that is,

[16] Buchanan, *Works,* VI, 445.
[17] *Ibid.*

so far as Washington is concerned, there is little or no evidence of interest in the affairs of the Argentine from this time forward.

Before taking leave of this whole episode, it is desirable to consider for a moment the very different attitude displayed by some of the American agents in South America. The attitude of Brent has already been described. His successor, Harris, was a far abler and more discreet man. Yet he too was to protest against Anglo-French action, and even directly to invoke the principles of 1823. The circumstances of his action are rather peculiar, and merit explanation. In the spring of 1847, new commissioners from France and Great Britain had arrived in La Plata. The British commissioner, Lord Howden, was only too anxious to terminate the intervention, was, indeed, seeking for a pretext to do so. It was at his instigation that Harris, on July 1, 1847, delivered a formal protest to the two Commissioners in which he made direct appeal to the policy of noninterference which had become traditional with the United States.[18] Thus, by a curious irony, it was a British diplomatic agent who led to the invocation of the Monroe Doctrine. Harris's note met with a conciliatory reply from Howden, as was to be expected, and with an argumentative one from Waleski.[19] Neither diplomat made any reference to the developing American dogma. With the former, the action of the American became a pretext

[18] Washington, Dept. of State, Despatches, Argentine Republic.
[19] Paris, Min. des Aff. Etr., Corr. Pol., Buenos Ayres, July 3, 1847.

for the lifting of the blockade. With the latter, it was wholly ineffective. Though it may have served to raise American prestige in the Argentine, it cannot be said to have demonstrated that the policy of the United States carried great weight. It is interesting, however, as an episode, if nothing more.

On the periphery of our subject there lies one other aspect of the intervention. This concerns the efforts of American diplomatic agents to counteract the activities of the European powers, and to limit the scope of the intervention. Thus, Henry A. Wise, our minister to Brazil, sought in July, 1845, to persuade the Brazilian government to act to forestall European intermeddling.[20] A little later, Wise seized upon the mission of Edward A. Hopkins, dispatched by the Polk administration to negotiate with the government of Paraguay for the navigation of the Paraná, to urge neutrality upon the authorities at Asunción in the impending struggle. He instructed Hopkins, who stopped at Rio, to strain every nerve to accomplish this end. Thus, diplomatically, at any rate, an effort was made to lighten Rosas's difficulties. If it failed, through the obstinacy of the dictator (who refused to recognize the independence of Paraguay), and through the monumental ineptitude of Hopkins, it was none the less an effort to counterbalance European influence with that of the United States.[21] That it met with no encouragement from Washington is

[20] *Ibid.*, Brazil, July 31, 1845.
[21] For the details of this episode, see Cady, *op. cit.*, pp. 169-182.

additional evidence of the relative indifference of Polk and Buchanan to the events in the Argentine. In this whole episode, indeed, the United States appears in no very impressive rôle. Nor can it be said that its opinions influenced in any respect whatever the action of the states of the Old World.

In other spheres, besides La Plata, there is additional evidence at this time of the disregard by European powers of the pretensions of the American government. The monarchist intrigues in Mexico and Ecuador in 1846 afford further examples of the same temper, and attract the attention of the student of the Monroe Doctrine.

With regard to Mexico, the existence of monarchical sentiment has been already noted. For a long time such sentiment was in eclipse, nor does the troubled history of Mexico afford any clear example of the rise of a monarchist to the presidency till 1846. Monarchists there were in public office, and plenty of them, men like Alamán, one of the best educated, subtlest, and ablest minds in Mexico. But the dominant figure of most of the period is Santa Anna, an extraordinarily clever military and political adventurer, untroubled by principles of any kind, even of the most tenuous description. In the play of factions in Mexico, Santa Anna was more than once borne to the presidency, and he held that office from 1841 to 1844. But then came revolution, and after the weak régime of the mild and bewhiskered Herrera, the advent to power of Paredes y Arrillaga. As early as 1832 Paredes had confessed to the Mexican historian

Arrangoiz that he was a partisan of monarchy,[22] and no sooner was he in the saddle than there began an intrigue for the establishment of a Bourbon prince upon the throne of Mexico. A monarchist paper, *El Tiempo*, was established at Mexico City to disseminate the principles upon which the government wished to act, and a call was issued for a convention to revise the Constitution.[23] But the difficulties in the way of the success of the monarchist movement were very great, from the beginning. The tide of public opinion in favor of republicanism was still strong, and Bankhead, the British minister at Mexico City, noticed that though *El Tiempo* began bravely enough in its advocacy of a change of system it very early began to moderate its tone.[24] Moreover, the monarchists themselves were not united upon a candidate for the throne. There was a very influential Spanish party, headed by the Minister of Foreign Affairs, and supported by a not inconsiderable section of the clergy, including the Minister of Justice, the Bishop of Chiapas.[25] But Paredes himself was apparently in favor of some English connection, no doubt seeing in it a protection against the United States.[26] He tried to get a trusted agent to carry proposals of this nature to London, but failed in the effort. And, indeed, as time went on, he

[22] F. deP. Arrangoiz, *Historia de Méjico desde 1808 hasta 1867* (4 vols., Madrid, 1872), II, 269.

[23] *Ibid.*, p. 271.

[24] London, P. R. O., F. O., Mexico, vol. 196, no. 22, February 27, 1846.

[25] *Ibid.*, no. 57, April 29, 1846.

[26] *Ibid.*, "You do not mean to let us be eaten up," was the President's observation to Bankhead one night at dinner. *Ibid.*, no. 28, February 27, 1846.

was compelled more and more to hedge with regard to the whole matter, until the outbreak of war with the United States soon gave the rulers of Mexico other matters to think of than monarchy or republicanism.

It is probable, indeed, that monarchical sentiment was in 1846 as it had been earlier by no means the majority sentiment of that small body of Mexicans who were interested in politics at all, though Bankhead, the British minister, did not regard schemes of the monarchists as entirely impracticable.[27] But the monarchist faction was sustained and encouraged by European elements, and the advent of Paredes may have been brought about by, and certainly synchronizes with, the initiation by Spain of a rather extraordinary effort to reestablish by indirection her old ascendancy in Mexico. The scheme may seem to have been a romantic one, and it would be easy to take it too seriously, but its very existence throws no inconsiderable light upon the attitude of Europeans toward the problems of the New World.[28] In the fall of 1845 General Narváez was the ruler of Spain. A quarter of a century after it was truly practicable, his government took up with zest the idea of a Bourbon monarchy in

[27] "If they can continue to count upon the Army, and possess energy enough to carry out the principles embodied in the 'Plan of San Luis' (for a strong centralized government), they may well hope to succeed in preparing the way for a radical change in the Government of the country." *Ibid.*, vol. 195, no. 15, January 30, 1846.

[28] For this episode see Antonio Pirala, *Historia Contemporánea de la España. Anales desde 1843 hasta la Conclusión de la Actual Guerra Civil* (6 vols., Madrid, 1875-79), especially I, 432-33.

Mexico, under the rule of Don Henrique, the son of the Infante Francisco de Paula, who had himself had ambitions for an American crown at an earlier period. In pursuance of this idea Señor Bermudez de Castro was sent to Mexico City as the Spanish minister, well supplied with funds with which to promote the cause of monarchy. More than a half million dollars, so it would appear, was expended by this individual in the course of his activities,[29] and in the spring of 1846, with an exuberant optimism that no doubt went beyond the facts, he wrote that the President and his Council were with him, that 10,000 or 12,000 troops were at the disposal of the monarchists, and that a meeting of distinguished Mexicans had been held at his house to sign a declaration in favor of the calling of a Spanish Prince to the throne. More than this, the Spanish government attempted to enlist the support of France and England in the enterprize, and to give to it a European character. In a memorandum transmitted to the British government, and dated February 7, 1846, an attempt was made to set forth the merits of the project in some detail. Emphasis was naturally laid upon the strength of the monarchical elements in Mexico for a long time past, but what is fully as interesting is the importance attached to the ambitions of the United States, and the putting forward of the monarchical idea as the only counter-agent to the republican ambition of the North Americans. In the language of this memorandum, indeed, is a suggestion of a direct

[29] London, P. R. O., F. O., Mexico, vol. 196, no. 57, April 29, 1846.

reaction to the Polk message of 1845. Beginning with
an allusion to the plan "which the Republic of the United
States has begun to develop, and which is only the prelude of others more vast of aggrandizement and domination," which it "audaciously announces" to the world,
the Spanish communication goes on, "The recent annexation of Texas, the like means now employing with
respect to California, the proposals which it would seem
have been made to the Government of Mexico of pur-
chasing that entire territory, without prejudice to taking
it by other means should the former expedient fail, and
the solicitude with which public opinion in the United
States is operated upon by announcing the annexation of
Mexico to the territory of the Union as probable and
convenient, *proclaiming that the U. S. Flag is to be the
only one which is shortly to float over that Continent;*
these and other similar announcements combined with
the policy which it would appear has been adopted in that
country have the effect that in Mexico the opinion is
gaining ground that, if she continue in her present
plight, she must sooner or later see herself incorporated
with the United States, without possessing either the
courage or the strength to prevent it." Only in monarchy, so the Mexicans have come to believe, according
to the Court of Madrid, is safety to be found from "gigantic plans" to "sweep away the Spanish race and
swallow it up in the gulf of the Union." The question,
if it presents itself, if indeed a Spanish Prince is called
to the throne of the Montezumas, will be European, not
Spanish. "All monarchies have a great interest that the
Brazilian throne should not stand isolated in the midst

of the American Continent, and that on the contrary, another should be raised, to become in process of time great and powerful. All nations, and much more those that found their power and greatness in the development of their marine and commerce have a great interest in not allowing the American territory to be subject to the influence of a single Power, especially if this Power be animated by a spirit of rivalry toward the ancient Continent, proclaiming as the basis of its policy to exclude all European nations from any participation in the rule of, or influence upon, the New World." It is to be hoped, therefore, concludes this interesting paper, that the British Government will see the question from the same point of view.[30]

The temper of this memorandum for the Court of St. James is matched by a similar document which was sent to Paris. There were, in all this business, the makings of a very pretty diplomatic intrigue, and the foreshadowings of more remote events to come, when a Prince of the House of Austria should seek in Mexico to sustain a tottering throne. But in 1846 the Spanish proposals received a cool reception in both London and Paris. Lord Aberdeen would have nothing to do with the project, and when Bankhead wrote him from Mexico City that Bermudez de Castro was hinting at the possibility of common action, he was instructed to maintain a complete reserve with regard to the whole scheme.[31] Guizot, too, was not enthusiastic, and Louis Philippe told King that

[30] London, P. R. O., F. O., Spain, vol. 711.
[31] *Ibid.*, Mexico, vol. 194, no. 2, July 16, 1846.

he wished to have nothing to do with any such project.[32]
Even in Spain difficulties arose. For the Queen-mother,
Christina, once apprised that crowns were in prospect,
wished that of Mexico to be given to one of her sons, and
not to Don Henrique, and Narváez was not particularly
enthusiastic about this idea. Yet the project simmered
for some time, even after the American declaration of
war with Mexico had altered the aspect of affairs, and
made the establishment of monarchy in Mexico a matter
of a direct challenge to the rising republic of the West.

But what of the reaction of the United States to projects of the kind just described? That rumors of monarchical projects were in the air is certain. Such a leading Southern newspaper as the *New Orleans Picayune*
began to comment upon them with frank hostility as
early as January of 1846. And Slidell, whose mission
to Mexico did not terminate till March, transmitted to
the State Department the news of what was in the
wind.[33] The message of 1845 had had nothing to say on
this subject. But Buchanan's instructions of March 12
to the American envoy to Mexico were more explicit.
" Should Great Britain and France attempt to place a
Spanish or any other European Prince upon the throne
of Mexico, this would be resisted by all the power of the

[32] Washington, Dept. of State, Despatches, France, vol. 30,
January 30, 1846.

[33] Washington, Dept. of State, Despatches, Mexico, March
18, 1846. Slidell's advices were that the public mind was excited by the idea of an " alien monarchy " " to a degree of
which I had not considered it capable." He mentions, too,
Paredes's intimacy with the British minister. But it is clear
that he does not believe the project very popular.

United States," wrote the Secretary of State.[34] Such an attempt, in his judgment, would cause party distinctions to vanish in the opposition that it would arouse among the American people.

With regard to monarchical schemes, it will be observed, it was England and France, in Buchanan's judgment, who were to be feared. There is at this time no hint of any knowledge of the intrigues of the Spanish monarchy.[35] There is, also, in the language used, a clear indication that it was a *forcible* intervention which Buchanan had in mind. What would have been his position if a convention of the Mexican people, regularly constituted, had invited a Spanish Prince to assume the Mexican throne, we can only surmise. But it is fairly certain that even such a project would have been received with considerable hostility in Washington, and that every effort would have been made to prevent its consummation. And yet, despite the monarchist leanings of Paredes, it was suggested to Slidell that he offer to relieve the administration from financial embarrassment, on condition that the differences outstanding with the United States might be satisfactorily liquidated.[36] The fears of a change of republican institutions could not therefore have been a very powerful factor in the policy of the State Department.

[34] Buchanan, *Works,* VI, 405.

[35] The liberal deputy Olózaga was to allude to them in a speech in the Cortes delivered December 1, 1847. (*Diario de las Cortes,* 1847-48, p. 200.) This speech came to the attention of Senator Dix of New York, and mention of it is appended to a speech which he made in the Senate January 26, 1848. (*Cong. Globe,* 30th Cong., 1st Sess., p. 252.)

[36] Buchanan, *Works,* VI, 403.

After the war came, the whole subject of monarchy seems to have dropped into the background. A monarchist faction, of course, remained, and Paredes, who was driven into exile in August, came back from Europe in the latter part of 1847, attended by new rumors of the aid of European powers in the setting up of a monarchical régime. Yet it cannot be said that the fear of monarchy had any influence upon the peace negotiations which terminated the Mexican war. On this subject we are tolerably fully informed. In the summer of 1847, as is well known, President Polk sent to Mexico to negotiate for peace the chief clerk of the State Department, Nicholas P. Trist. The story of how, after he had been recalled, Trist had the courage to negotiate a settlement which was finally accepted and which ended the war, has been often told. And the details of his exchanges with the Mexican government, together with a mass of information on the state of parties in Mexico, are contained in his despatches, amongst the most voluminous in the annals of American diplomacy. It is clear that Trist did not fear the monarchists. He speaks of them as a faction altogether impotent, and of General Paredes as having utterly failed in his efforts to secure European support for any monarchical schemes. He took little account of them in his negotiations. Mexico, in his judgment, was preponderantly republican and would remain so.[37]

The whole monarchical movement of 1846 might, indeed, seem rather ridiculous if it were not for the events

[37] The British minister at Mexico City, Doyle, wrote to his government that Trist feared the monarchists greatly, and was

which followed within twenty years, and if it were not for the illustration which it affords of how very far from ruptured, as yet, were the bonds between the Old World and the New. The separation of the two hemispheres, with regard to which Pozzo di Borgo and Metternich had waxed so melancholy in 1823 and 1824, was by no means accomplished well nigh a quarter of a century later. European statesmen, it is clear, still found in America a field for intrigue of the old type, and Latin American political leaders, equally clearly, could still envisage a connection between their own states and Europe. There are, in the whole Mexican business, other evidences of this same general temper besides the monarchical intrigue of 1846. The Mexican government, then, as earlier, in the affairs of Texas, was anxious to secure some European guarantee of its territorial integrity, and this idea appears again and again in the negotiations, while on the other hand, though it is true that the European chancelleries observed an exemplary caution in the war between Mexico and the United States, the European press abounded in hostile references to this country, and even in allusions to the desirability of an armed intervention on the part of England and France to put an end to the onward march of what, to innocent Europeans, was regarded as American imperialism. Ob-

---

ready to extend the American occupation for a period of five years to frustrate their designs. (London, P. R. O., F. O., Mexico, Nov. 10, 1848.)

But no trace of any such proposal is to be found in any of Trist's despatches in the form in which Doyle alludes to it. I find it impossible to credit the statement.

viously, the hegemony of the United States in the New World was not yet attained.

Nor was Mexico the only focus of European intrigue in 1846. A project which, though it seems fantastic, aroused tremendous excitement in Latin America, was the effort of General Flores, one-time President of Ecuador, to attempt to reconquer his ancient dominion, with the aid of Spain, and so, at least the rumor ran, to reestablish a member of the House of Bourbon upon a new throne.

General Juan José Flores, a perennial figure in the politics of Ecuador, had been driven from the country in 1845. He first sought refuge in Madrid, and there he enlisted the support of the Queen-mother in a fantastic project for the reestablishment of monarchy in the country of which he had been President.[38] Queen Christina's son by a second marriage, young Don Juan, was to be the sovereign of the new state, and Flores was to be regent. The Spanish ministry of the epoch does not seem to have been deeply involved in this project. Yet it permitted soldiers in the Spanish army to be given leaves to enlist with Flores.[39] As for Christina herself she supplied, it is said, two millions of pesos to the Ecuadorian for the promotion of his plans.[40] Thus supported, the

[38] For the best account of this episode see C. Destruge, *La Expedición Flores—Proyecto de Monarquía Americana, 1846-47*, Guayaquil, 1906. There is a shorter account in J. Becker, *Historia de las Relaciones Exteriores de España durante El Siglo XIX* (3 vols., Madrid, 1924), II, 102.

[39] Washington, *Dept. of State,* Despatches, Guayaquil, October 27, 1846.

[40] Destruge, *op. cit.,* p. 18. For confirmation of this see London, P. R. O., F. O., Spain, vol. 719, January 30, 1847.

former President set about raising an armed force both in Spain and in Great Britain, and bought ships in the latter country to transport the expedition to the New World. In the fall of 1846 the states of South America contiguous to Ecuador were much excited at the possibility of a new effort at reconquest. But fate, in the form of the British government, soon intervened, to check the plans of the ambitious adventurer. The ships which he had bought were forbidden to sail by the British authorities, on the ground that the neutrality laws would be violated, and the 1400 men whom he had collected at Santander soon melted away.[41] By the late spring of 1847 the enterprise was completely dead. The Spanish government, faced with hostile criticism, had disavowed all sympathy with the expedition, and even published a decree forbidding the giving of aid to Flores himself.

In the United States this curious enterprise never seems to have awakened much interest. The Ecuadorian minister at Washington submitted a protest to Buchanan, under date of November 26, 1846.[42] Declaring the plans of Flores to be " offensive to the independence of the new Continents," and " deeply injurious to the honor of the American Governments," and reminding the Secretary of " the solemn protests which have at all times, and particularly at the present, been made by the cabinet of Washington, against all European intervention in the political affairs of America," he expressed the hope of " the effective cooperation and aid of the illustrious Republic of the United States." A little later, Cas-

[41] Destruge, *op. cit.,* p. 31.
[42] Washington, Dept. of State, Notes to, Ecuador.

tillo, the President of Peru, sounded Prevost, the American consul at Lima, as to the possibility of securing two large steamers in the United States which might be used in the giving of Peruvian aid to Ecuador, if the Flores expedition should actually sail, and Prevost transmitted this request with the comment that to grant it would be "a service to Republicanism and Humanity, as the United States have proclaimed long since to Europe that all attempts to interfere in the domestic affairs of these and subvert their institutions would be viewed as an act of hostility toward the American people." [43] But the appeal of the Ecuadorian, and the despatch of Prevost, both were received after the British government had stepped in to prevent the departure of the vessels which Flores had chartered, and the American government was not under the necessity of taking any action. In principle Buchanan naturally condemned the schemes of the Ecuadorian, and in his instructions to the outgoing minister at Quito in May, 1848, he made this fact perfectly clear.[44] But it is hard to believe that much would

[43] Washington, Consular Letters, Lima, December 9, 1846.

[44] Buchanan-Livingston, May 13, 1848, Instructions to Ministers, Ecuador, I, 3. Quoted in Moore, *A Digest of International Law*, VI, 473.

" The military and naval expedition which General Flores, formerly President of Ecuador, organized a year or two since in Europe for the supposed purpose of recovering his authority, connived at as it was believed to have been by some of the monarchical governments of that quarter, created great alarm, not only in Ecuador itself but in the neighboring republics, from the apprehension that its exterior was more extensive and important than its ostensible designs. It was fortunately arrested, however, before its departure. Senor Don Manuel Busta-

have been done by the American government in any case, while the United States was still in a state of war with Mexico. The real interest of this episode lies in the fact that an appeal was made to the United States by two Latin American states, and not unsympathetically received by an American diplomatic agent on the ground. At a time when it has been generally assumed that the Washington government was profoundly unpopular in

---

mente, the minister for foreign affairs of Ecuador, addressed to this Department an interesting communication upon the subject under date the 26th November 1846, which was received about the same time that intelligence of the failure of the expedition reached this city. Owing to this circumstance, the note was not formally answered, as any proceedings of this Government with reference to the expedition was rendered unnecessary. General Castillo, the President of Peru, also made an informal application in regard to it to Mr. Prevost, the consul of the United States at Lima. The accompanying extract from a letter of this Department to Mr. Prevost embodies the views of the President relative to the expedition, and you may at a proper time communicate the same to the Ecuadorian minister for foreign affairs. You will also assure him that the intervention or dictation, direct or indirect, of European governments in the affairs of the independent states of the American Hemisphere, will never be viewed with indifference by the Government of the United States. On the contrary all the moral means at least, within their power, shall upon every occasion be employed to discourage and arrest such interference."

See also his instructions to Bidlack, March 25, 1847. (Washington, Dept. of State, Despatches, Colombia.) " I heartily rejoice that the expedition of General Flores has exploded," he wrote. " May this ever be the fate of all attempts to interfere with the independence of any of the American republics ! " Buchanan goes on to say that the government watched it with intense anxiety, and then, rather inconsistently, that no action was taken, because " we never apprehended serious danger."

the countries to the southward, as a result of its spoliation of Mexico, the governors of two of these countries
were not averse to making appeal to it upon the basis
of the revived principles of 1823.

There are other evidences of a friendly attitude
toward the United States on the part of Latin American
governments during the Polk administration. The so-
called American Congress which met at Lima in the late
fall of 1847 was a favorite project of the government of
Peru.[45] Plans for such a Congress sprang from the so-
called menace of Flores, and as early as February, 1847,
Prevost reported that President Castillo wished the
United States to send a representative. The time had
arrived, the Peruvian declared, " to do something to
convince the Governments of Europe that all America,
north and south, will unite to oppose and put down any
attempt at conquest or subversion of American institutions with a view to the introduction in their stead of
monarchical ones." [46] The appeal thus made strongly
suggests the efforts of twenty years before to convert
the glittering generalities of the Monroe message into a
definite pledge of support. At the same time the Foreign
Minister of New Granada expressed a similar hope that
the American government would lend its favor to the
projected Congress. When the Congress actually met,

[45] For this subject, see especially Ricardo Aranda, *Congre-
sos y Conferencias Internacionales en que ha tomado parte el
Peru* (Lima, 1909-13, 4 vols.), I, 84-204, and J. M. Torres
Caicedo, *Unión Latino-America* (Paris, 1865), pp. 44-48, and
111-239.

[46] Washington, Consular Letters, Lima, February 1, 1847.

with five states present, it passed, partly at the instance of the newly arrived American minister, J. Randolph Clay, resolutions reaffirming the non-colonization principle, and denying the right of European powers to intervene in the affairs of the states of the New World.[47] The New Granadan minister in one of its sessions emphasized the desirability of closer relations with the United States, and brought forward a proposal for the maintenance at Washington of legations of all of the states represented to the end that " in this great American center there might be formed a diplomatic gathering of America to facilitate means of communication and accord for emergencies and other extraordinary circumstances," and suggested that a protocol be drawn up to this effect.[48] At a later session he proposed that the agreements reached at Lima should be submitted to the United States for its possible adhesion.[49] The opposition of Chile prevented the acceptance of either of these propositions.[50] But it is interesting to observe the fact that they were made. Like the events already treated, they give one a little different conception of the position of the United States in Latin America in 1846 than that commonly held.

The Polk administration, however, was singularly indifferent to the Congress at Lima. There is not a word on the subject in Polk's Diary, and more important still,

[47] Washington, Dept. of State, Peru, Despatches, January 12, 1848.

[48] Aranda, *op. cit.*, p. 149.

[49] *Ibid.*, p. 161.

[50] *Ibid.*, pp. 149 and 162.

not a word in the instructions of Buchanan to the consular or diplomatic authorities of the United States in
either Peru or New Grenada. The message of 1845 had
been enunciated for reasons having little to do with
Latin America ; and the interest of those who enunciated
it in Pan-Americanism was as lukewarm as it was in
any effective action in the Argentine.

There is, however, one extraordinary instance, contemporary with the events which we have been describing, in which Polk and his advisers took action which
went beyond anything ever before done in assuming
definite pledges of support in connection with a Latin
American state. This is the famous treaty of 1846 with
New Granada, having to do with the right of transit
across the Isthmus of Panama, and guaranteeing the
neutrality of this territory. The connection of this compact with the Monroe Doctrine is fairly obvious. At a
later date the whole question of the control of an inter-
oceanic canal became a burning international issue, and
later secretaries of state were to invoke the principles
of 1823 in support of the claim of the American government to the exclusive control of any route that might
be opened up. More important still (for the point
just made, it may be conceded, concerns primarily the
period after 1876), the guarantee of American territory
against external aggression is directly related to, and
is indeed an extension of, the doctrines of Monroe's
message. The single instance in which the United
States, the self-appointed protector of the Latin American states, translated its general principle into a bind-

ing pledge, into a treaty of guarantee, is an episode of obvious significance. And the negotiations with regard to this treaty throw light, not only on the attitude of the Polk administration, but also on the attitude of a Latin American state toward the United States.

The project of a trans-isthmian canal, as is well known, is very old. Even in the days of Spanish rule it was mooted. And as early as the Congress of Panama, the idea began to take a more definite shape, even figuring in the instructions of Henry Clay to the plenipotentiaries sent to that meeting. At this early date, however, and for some time to come, there is no evidence to show that the American government desired to control any canal that might be built, or even to exclude European capital, or European governments, from a share in the undertaking. With regard to a Dutch project, for example, in 1829, there seems to have been not the slightest hostility, the only interest of the United States being in the principle of absolute equality of treatment for the vessels using the canal.[51] The Senate resolution of March 3, 1835,[52] and the House resolution of March 4, 1839,[53] do not assume that the canal is to be built by American capital, or that it is to

[51] John B. Henderson, in his *American Diplomatic Questions* (New York, 1901), p. 70, erroneously states that the Monroe Doctrine was invoked in connection with this Dutch concession. I cannot find, however, in the archives of the State Department any evidence in support of this view. Indeed the language of the despatches would seem flatly to prove the contrary.

[52] *Cong. Globe,* 25th Cong., 3rd Sess., p. 241.

[53] *Cong. Globe,* 32nd Cong., 3rd Sess., p. 251.

be subject to American control. Nor does the idea of a guaranty appear in either the one or the other. Furthermore still, the instructions given to Colonel Charles Biddle, the brother of the more famous Nicholas, President of the Bank of the United States, and a special envoy to New Granada in 1835, do not indicate that the Jackson administration had any projects of an exclusive nature in view. Indeed, Biddle's mission was only one of information. The canal question was, of course, still of relatively slight importance in our politics, and no one dreamed at this early date that there was any connection between it and the Monroe Doctrine.

The government of New Granada was equally indifferent to any "American" treatment of the question of the canal. In 1834 a concession was awarded to Baron Charles de Thierry, and though this concession came to nothing, it indicates the point of view of the government at Bogotá. French capital was again sought in connection with the enterprise in 1838. In the latter part of 1839, moreover, began to be put forward the idea of a general guarantee, not of the territory, but of the neutrality of the canal. Mosquera, the New Granadan minister at London, discussed some such project with Palmerston, only to be told that the British government regarded it as entirely impracticable to guarantee a part of the territory of another state. But the idea of enlisting European support in the project was by no means scotched, and in 1842 the New Granadan government sponsored another proposal, which provided for the construction of the canal by the *governments* of Great

Britain, France, and the United States,[54] and a guarantee of the neutrality of the canal, of the territory through which it passed, and of the fulfilment of the privileges granted to the company undertaking its construction. To this proposal, the British again gave a chilly reception, and though it was repeatedly brought forward, the response was always the same. M. Guizot seemed to think well of the canal project in general, and even sent out an investigating commission, but he was not enthusiastic, indeed was extremely reserved when the question of guarantee of the territory of New Granada was brought into the discussion. Disgusted with the temper of the European governments, the authorities at Bogotá turned to the United States. In some respects the situation was highly favorable to success in this quarter. Its representative at Bogotá, Mr. Benjamin Bidlack, was on the friendliest terms with the New Granadan authorities. The Polk message had restated the policy of American leadership in the New World. By the year 1846, though it seemed probable that a new French company would undertake some kind of communication across the isthmus, it seemed even more certain that nothing was for the time being to be hoped from the good will of European governments, so far as a treaty of guarantee was concerned. Don Manuel Mallarino, the Minister of Foreign Affairs, was therefore given power to treat with the American minister. Mr. Bidlack was absolutely without instructions with

[54] R. Rivas. *Colombia y los Estados Unidos,* 1810-1850 (Bogotá, 1915), p. 107.

regard to the matter which the government had so much
at heart. But the circumstances were not unfavorable
to inducing him to go beyond his authority, and put his
signature to a treaty of guarantee. For it was one of
the objects of his mission to negotiate a treaty of commerce with the New Granadan authorities, which should
give to the United States the rights of the most favored
nation in New Granadan ports. As the price of this concession, it was easy for Señor Mallarino to suggest the
assurance by the United States of New Granadan sovereignty over the Isthmus of Panama. It was easy, too, of
course, to raise the scarecrow of British ambition,
" ruinous for the commerce of the United States, ruinous for the nationality of the Spanish-American Republics, fatal to the cause of democracy in the New World,
and decidedly disturbing to the public peace in this
hemisphere."

Finally, the appeal both to the letter and to the spirit
of Polk's message of 1845 was made by the New
Granadan minister.[55] And as a consequence of his representations, Bidlack on December 12, 1846, signed *sub
spe rati* a treaty which gave to the United States the
rights of the most-favored nation on the one hand, and
secured from the United States a guarantee of the neutrality and territorial integrity of the isthmus on the
other. This treaty was transmitted to the Senate with a
special message urging ratification on February 10,
1847.[56]

[55] Washington, Dept. of State, Despatches, Colombia, September 12, 1846. See also Encl. A., Mallarino's memoir.
[56] For the message see Richardson, *op. cit.*, IV, 511 *et seq.*

The attitude of Mr. Polk with regard to this interesting compact is in many respects remarkable. One might have expected, particularly in view of his attitude many years before, that the President would have declined to enter into " an entangling alliance " of the kind proposed, and it is, as a matter of fact, true that this point was discussed in the cabinet,[57] and that a large part of Polk's message is devoted to proving the inapplicability of the isolationist doctrine to this particular engagement; but what is more surprising than the abandonment of the dogmas of the Farewell Address is the complacency with which the idea of a European guarantee, supplementary to that of the United States, is regarded. In strict theory, no doubt, such a guarantee could not be considered contrary to the principles of 1823, but that the interposition of European powers in American matters, even for the maintenance of the *status quo* and the protection of common international rights, should be willingly acquiesced in by James K. Polk is a little extraordinary. From so uncompromising a nationalist, one would hardly expect precisely this point of view. The President's stand lends additional emphasis to the fact that the whole question of trans-Isthmian communications had not yet been linked in the popular mind with the Monroe Doctrine. " If the United States, as the chief of the nations, should first become a party to this guaranty, it cannot be doubted — indeed it is confidently expected by the Government of

[57] M. M. Quaife, ed. *Diary of James K. Polk* (4 vols., Chicago, 1910) II, 373.

New Granada—that similar guarantees will be given
to that Republic by Great Britain and France. Should
the proposition thus tendered be rejected we may deprive
the United States of the just influence which its acceptance might secure to them and confer the glory and
benefits of being the first among the nations in concluding such an arrangement upon the Government of either
Great Britain or France. That either of these governments would embrace the offer cannot be doubted."[58]

The ratification of the treaty of 1846 was attended
with considerable difficulties. A special mission was
sent to Washington from Bogotá to exert what pressure it could in favor of its acceptance. In the discussions which the New Granadan Emissary, General
Herran, held with various members of the Senate, and
with the Secretary of State, one of the powerful arguments which was brought forward in favor of the
compact was to be found in the march of British aggression on the coast of Central America. The New
Granadan treaty thus leads most naturally and directly
to a discusion of the question of the Mosquito coast.

Of the tendency of Great Britain to assert an increasing control over this region, I have already spoken. But
this tendency became decidedly more marked after 1842,
and was a matter of concern, not only to the government of Nicaragua, but also to the government of New
Granada, which had a claim to territorial sovereignty
over the Mosquitoes based on a Spanish royal cedula of
1803. In the year 1841, as we have seen, the enterprising

[58] Richardson, *Messages,* V, 512-13.

superintendent of Belize attempted to take possession of the little town of San Juan, at the mouth of the river of that name. But this was not all. The British corvette, the " Tweed," active before San Juan, sailed southward with the Mosquito King as far as Boca del Toro, in the territory of New Granada, and there that functionary was landed, took possession of his assumed domains and named public officers to represent him. Such conduct seemed to foreshadow far-reaching designs on Central America. It is true that these designs were the designs of the imaginative Macdonald, but there was reason to believe that they were shared by the Foreign Office at London. At any rate, in 1844, a British resident was appointed for the shore, and, on the initiative of Macdonald, his private secretary, Patrick Walker, was given the position. The territory was rechristened Mosquitia, and provided with a flag which bore a striking resemblance to the Union Jack. Very naturally neither the New Granadan or the Nicaraguan governments were precisely gratified at this evidence of British acquisitiveness. Both undertook to protest against such action, and the protests of both have a direct relation to the Monroe Doctrine.

To deal first with the case of New Granada, as early as 1843 its minister at London was instructed to make his views known, and the tension with regard to the question naturally increased when not only was the answer to this protest long delayed, but a British agent sent out to the shore, and warning given at Bogotá that no meddling on the part of New Granada would be per-

mitted. In January of 1845 the New Granadan Secretary of Foreign Affairs, Colonel Joaquín Acosta, directed to all the members of the diplomatic corps a long
argument with regard to his government's claim to the
Shore, and made a special appeal to the chargé d'affaires
of the United States.[59] In this appeal, interestingly
enough, though the Monroe Doctrine is not cited by
name, there is evident an intention to base the case upon
the principles of 1823. A change of administration at
Bogotá was followed by a period of relative indifference,
but the crowning of a new Mosquito King by the Bishop
of Jamaica in May of 1846, the propaganda carried on
by Pedro Fernandez Madrid, an able official of the New
Granadan Foreign Office, and the indifference of Great
Britain to the matter of a guarantee of the Isthmus,
caused a new burst of resentment against British interference, in the midst of which was signed the famous
treaty with the United States which we have already
examined. There followed, as we have seen, General
Herran's mission to the United States. And here enters
once again, this time very definitely, the Monroe Doctrine. For Herran's instructions called attention to the
repeated declarations of American statesmen with
regard to European intervention or colonization in the
New World, and even expressed the hope that the
United States would send a representative to the Pan-
American Congress which was planned to meet at Lima,
would assume the leadership of an American confederation, opposing to the avaricious proposals of Europe,

[59] Rivas, *op. cit.*, p. 119.

the humane and disinterested principles of the young democracies of the New World. On the question of sending a delegate to Lima, as we have seen, the Polk administration seems to have been extremely lukewarm, but so far as the Monroe Doctrine was concerned, Buchanan assured the New Granadan minister that the Doctrine would be maintained. Even if the Bidlack-Mallarino treaty should fail, declared the American Secretary of State, the United States would energetically oppose the usurpation of Great Britain.[60]

In the meantime, it became clear that the extreme pretensions put forward by the British authorities in Mosquitia were not acquiesced in or supported by the Foreign Office in London. With a noble moderation Lord Palmerston contented himself with claiming for the savages over whom the British exercised so tender a regard territorial rights extending only as far as the San Juan River, and thus not directly threatening the New Granadan control of the Isthmus. Though the government at Bogotá did not on this account cease to interest itself in the matter, the aspect of the problem was, of course, distinctly changed. It was henceforward Nicaragua alone which, from a practical point of view, was threatened by the acquisitive instincts of the British authorities in Mosquitia.

So far as the Nicaraguan government is concerned, it was sometime before it appealed to the United States. The attempted seizure of San Juan in 1841 was described to Murphy, the American agent sent out in

[60] Rivas, *op. cit.*, p. 205.

that year, but no appeal for protection was made. The sending of a British agent to the Shore in 1843 called forth a general protest from Castellon, the Nicaraguan minister at Brussels, in 1844, but no special petition was addressed to the American minister. It was not till after the Polk revival of the Monroe Doctrine, and not till the end of 1847 that the government at Washington began to be earnestly besought by the authorities at Leon. Then notes came in rapid succession, an appeal from the Supreme Director, dated December 15, 1847, an appeal from the Foreign Minister, dated March 17, 1848, and an appeal from Castellon (who stopped in Washington on his way from Europe), dated May 11, 1848. And in all these notes the Monroe Doctrine figured. Nicaragua had learned to quote the American scripture. It did so with touching evidences of faith.

But the President and his advisers were not, at any rate when the first notes were received, in a position to take any very positive action. With all their attachments to the principles of 1823, they seem not to have taken very seriously the question of Central America. The British title to Belize had not been questioned; indeed a consul had been sent thither, and had received his exequatur from the British authorities there. The question of the Bay Islands, though there the aggression of the British was as recent as 1841, was never made a subject of discussion with the government at London. And the extension and the reinvigoration of the Mosquito protectorate seems also to have produced no effect upon Polk or Buchanan. Indeed, during the greater part of Polk's term of office, the United States had no minister there, and very unimportant economic interests. Buchanan, mild-mannered man that he was, left the appeals of Buitrago and his foreign minister unanswered. In the message of 1847, the President reasserted the principles of 1845, but the reference was to California, and not to the Mosquito Shore. There is not the slightest sign that at this time he had any interest whatsoever in the latter territory. In Congress, too, there had been no sign of excitement. Senator Dix of New York, furnished by the New Granadan minister Herran with the requisite data,[61] had twice called attention to the Mosquito protectorate in speeches of 1847 and 1848, but his remarks awakened, so far as can be seen, no general interest. In the Senate debates on Yucatan, to be noted later, despite frequent commentary on the wickedness of Great Britain, the Mosquito Shore came in for almost no attention at all.

In the meantime the skies grew still more threatening. For on January 1, 1848, the British had seized, with a view to permanent possession, the little town of San Juan, or Greytown, at the mouth of the San Juan River, and this act was no mere aggression of a local agent, but the act of the British Foreign Office itself. Clearly, the British activities in Central America needed watching, whether the American people yet realized the fact or not. It was under such circumstances that it was determined to send a special agent to study the situation. Elijah J. Hise was the man selected, and on June 8 Buchanan penned for him instructions with regard to

[61] Rivas, *op. cit.*, p. 208.

his course of action. The remarkable thing about these instructions is their mild tone. When the Secretary of State was left to himself, he was commonly most inoffensive in his language. It was only when prodded by the President that he assumed the manner which Polk considered the most effective way of dealing with Great Britain. And in this case the prodding seems to have been absent, for Buchanan's tone was almost plaintive. He commented with melancholy upon the internecine strife of Central America, and upon its relation to the Monroe Doctrine. " The independence as well as the interests of the nations on this continent require that they should maintain an American system of policy entirely distinct from that which prevails in Europe," he wrote. " To suffer any interference on the part of the European Governments with the domestic concerns of the American Republics and to permit them to establish new colonies upon this continent would be to jeopard their independence and to ruin their interests. These truths ought everywhere throughout this continent to be impressed upon the public mind. But what," added the Secretary of State in his forcible-feeble way, " can the United States do to resist such European interference whilst the Spanish American Republics continue to weaken themselves by division and civil war and deprive themselves of the ability of doing anything for their own protection? " [62] These words accurately express the state of mind of Buchanan, and the temper in which he despatched Elijah Hise to the countries of Central America.

[62] Buchanan, *Works,* VIII, 81.

The Secretary was later to justify this masterly inactivity. Much perturbed (Buchanan was frequently perturbed) because the *New York Tribune* and the *New York Herald* had accused the Polk administration of not upholding the Monroe Doctrine, he stated his views at some length to Grund in a letter of April 13, 1850. It would have been " madness," he declared, to start a quarrel with Great Britain, " whilst the Mexican war was still raging." " Besides, we could have accomplished nothing. Mexico was situated between us & the Isthmus; & we could not have reached it by sea. Wisdom & policy alike required that we should wait for a more convenient season." The states of Central America, he continued, were in a state of almost indescribable distraction, and their union (which Hise was urgently enjoined to encourage) was the indispensable preliminary to the taking of action by the United States. " These states must first be willing to unite and help themselves before calling upon Hercules for assistance; and if Hercules did all he could to place them in this position, he performed his preliminary duty." [63]

Now there was some force in this point of view. It is hardly true that the Mexican war " was still raging " when Hise set out for Central America, for the treaty of peace with Mexico had been signed and ratified by the American Senate; but amendments had been attached to it, of the acceptance of which by the Mexican government the administration was not to be finally informed until June 9. There was still a bare chance

[63] *Ibid.,* pp. 377-81.

that new difficulties might intervene. The disorder which existed in Central America might also serve in a measure as an argument for inactivity; at least it would be more convenient to have a strong Central American government with which to deal in challenging British aggression. But such extreme caution hardly seems characteristic of the Polk administration. It had not counted the cost of irritating Great Britain in 1845 when the Oregon question was still unliquidated, and our dispute with Mexico brewing; it had not counted the cost in the midst of the war when it reasserted the Monroe Doctrine with regard to California, in the message of 1847; and it did not count the cost when, as we shall see, it again put forward the Doctrine with regard to Yucatan in April, 1848. Why was there, then, not even the most casual public allusion to the British encroachments in Mosquitia? Why was there not the slightest notice paid to the entreaties of the Nicaraguan government? Why this complete inertia in a concrete case, the only concrete case, in which the Monroe Doctrine was directly and flatly violated during the whole Polk administration?

The answer lies, no doubt, in the complete torpor of American public opinion at this time. It may lie in part, too, in the distraction of the pending presidential election, in the probable ignorance of Polk with regard to the whole matter, and in the natural timidity of Buchanan.

In striking contrast with the cautious attitude of the administration, however, was the conduct of Elijah J. Hise when, after many difficulties and much sickness, described with neurasthenic detail in his despatches to the State Department, he finally reached Nicaragua and began his negotiations. With an ardor for the principle of America for the Americans which outran that of his chiefs, Hise negotiated a treaty giving to the government of the United States or its citizens the exclusive right to construct an inter-oceanic canal, and in exchange he pledged the United States to guarantee the territorial integrity of Nicaragua. But this compact was not signed and transmitted to Washington until after the Polk administration had left office, and we may therefore postpone consideration of it until the next chapter. It is necessary to turn from the affairs of Central America to one other episode in the history of the Polk régime which concerns the Monroe Doctrine.

The province of Yucatan had not been free from the civil conflicts which were characteristic of the history of Mexico. Behind these conflicts, as not infrequently, a difference of political ideals was to be detected, the difference in this case being the question of Yucatan's relation to the Mexican confederacy. In the years which particularly concern us there existed an autonomist party, under the leadership of Santiago Mendez, and a party in favor of closer relations with Mexico, dominated by Miguel Barbachano. At the end of 1846 the first of these two parties managed to attain power. But before long it found its authority challenged, not so much by its political opponents, as by a formidable rising of the indigenous Mayan population. Ever since 1840 the contending factions in Yucatan had played with fire by appealing to the Indians for support, and the hour of retribution came in the spring of 1847. A gigantic conspiracy was formed, and though the government discovered what was in the wind and attempted by drastic measures of repression to ward off the danger, it was too late. The horrors of a race war were unfolded in Yucatan; and a truly desperate situation arose in consequence.[64] The result was an appeal to the government of the United States for aid.

At the moment of its entry into power, the autonomist party had proclaimed the neutrality of Yucatan in the war which was waging between the United States and Mexico, and had sent a commissioner, Don José Robira, to Washington. Robira, on his own initiative, sounded Buchanan with regard to the annexation of the province to the United States, but received from him the decided reply that not a single vote could be obtained in favor of the proposition in either House of Congress, in view of the distance of the territory from the United States.[65] Buchanan's language could not have afforded much encouragement to the Mendez régime, but as the Indian situation grew more and more desperate, the necessity of external aid became increasingly apparent. Don Justo Sierra, Mendez's son-in-law, appeared in Washington, and he, too, began to talk of annexation and protection.[66] On March 25, 1848, he received from his government for transmission to the President the

[64] For this situation see Eligio Ancona, *Historia de Yucatan desde la Epoca más Remota hasta Nuestros Días* (Merida, (Mexico) 4 vols., 1878-80). See also Joaquin Baranda, *Recordaciones Históricas* (Mexico, 2 vols., 1913), especially II, 1-84.

[65] Baranda, *op. cit.*, II, 23.

[66] *British and Foreign State Papers*, 1860-61, LI, 1202-04.

text of an appeal to outside powers for aid, an appeal which offered " dominion and sovereignty " over Yucatan in exchange for succor, and which was made, interestingly enough, at the same time to the United States, to Great Britain, and to Spain. The Mendez faction despite its neutrality in the war, was evidently not at all concerned as to who protected it and maintained it in power, provided that someone would do so. There is here no hint of that exclusive Americanism which is at the heart of the Monroe Doctrine, and, of course, no mention of the principle. But Sierra, before this document was received, had already made an appeal on his own account, and in making his own appeal for American aid, acted far otherwise. He based his request, of course, on the special situation which existed in Yucatan, but he based it also on the general foreign policy of the United States. He called the specific attention of the President to the Monroe message of 1823, citing the non-colonization principle with all the zeal of a votary, and he went on to argue that the very fact that an appeal for aid had also been addressed to the governments of Spain and Great Britain imposed upon the United States a special obligation in the circumstances, since, as he sententiously put it, " though the doctrines of Mr. Monroe and Mr. Polk may be a declaration of principles of the United States, the other Powers may or may not accept it, according to their own political views and objects." [67] An appeal of this kind was just the sort which would impress the then President of the

[67] *Ibid.*, p. 1222.

United States, for the British bogey was always in
Polk's mind, and powerfully affected his action. On
the other hand, not at all improbably, Buchanan stood
where he had stood not long before in his interview with
Robira, and in addition to this the treaty of peace with
Mexico, which had now reached Washington, contained
a clause expressly forbidding the annexation of more
Mexican territory. Under the circumstances the message of April 19, 1848, in which Polk laid the Yucatan
question before Congress, lacked that definiteness of
tone which was usually characteristic of the President.
The specific policy to which the administration committed itself went no further than the use of the American navy in the Gulf to afford what relief it could to
the inhabitants of the devastated province; annexation
was not directly recommended; but it is clear that Polk
was decidedly uneasy at the offer which had been made
by the Mendez government to England and Spain.
According to our established policy, he wrote, we could
not consent to a transfer of this " dominion and sovereignty either to Spain, Great Britain, or any other
European power. In the language of President Monroe
in his message of December, 1823, ' we should consider any attempt on their part to extend their system
to any portion of this hemisphere as dangerous to our
peace and safety.'" Proceeding further to quote from
his message of 1845, with its endorsement of the non-
colonization principle, Polk declared that Yucatan would
be " dangerous to our security " in the hands of a European power, and added that he had authentic information that if the United States did not grant aid, " such

aid will probably be obtained from some European power, which may hereafter assert a claim to ' dominion and sovereignty ' over Yucatan." It is clear that the President was deeply troubled by the situation, was determined to utter a new warning to Europe, and while not anxious for immediate annexation, would have regarded such action as unavoidable if there were danger of either Spain or Great Britain fixing its grasp upon the distracted province.[68]

But what are we to think of his application of the Monroe Doctrine to this situation? Was there here a *bona fide* case which Monroe and Adams would have recognized? An argument can certainly be made out in the negative. Assuming, what in itself is not to be taken for granted, that that part of the message of 1823 which laid down the policy of the United States with regard to Latin America, and European intervention therein, was intended to be expressive of general principles of lasting value, it would seem that there is no real comparison between the conquest of the former Spanish colonies by the Holy Alliance, and the voluntary offer of sovereignty by an American government to a state of the Old World. The first ran frankly counter to the fundamental principles of self-government on which the American republic was founded ; the second, in broad theory, at least, was an expression, not a denial, of those democratic principles. Applying the Monroe Doctrine to Yucatan, it might be maintained, was essentially a perversion of the original meaning of

[68] Richardson, *Messages,* IV, 582.

the message of 1823. It was the beginning of that historic process by which a principle of non-intervention
has been transformed into a principle of intervention.
It implied, not the protectorship of Latin American
states in the exercise of their own sovereign rights, but
the limitation of those rights to suit the interests and the
dictates of the United States. Nor could the language
of the non-colonization clause justify the President's
action. It is only by a gross perversion of language that
the word " colonization " can be applied to the voluntary
transfer of sovereignty by one people to another. In the
original language of the Doctrine, it is easy to argue,
there is not much support for the position which the
President assumed.

Yet let us do Polk the justice of stating his position
as favorably as possible. " The peace and security of
the United States," he declared, were involved. The
motive of self-preservation was invoked. As to whether
it was logically invoked or not was soon to be the
theme of debate in Congress, and of very different
opinions. But the President might well have argued
that the offer of sovereignty by a faction, and after all
that was what the offer amounted to, was a very different thing from, say, a spontaneous and general movement for annexation to another nation. Such an offer as
that of the Mendez régime, if permitted to be accepted
by a European power, would almost certainly mean
armed intervention in fact. With a European power
once fairly established in Yucatan, the theatre of intrigue might shift to Mexico itself, and the march of
European influence become more and more rapid. The

year 1848 had already afforded a dramatic example of
the acquisitive instincts of one European power in the
British seizure of Greytown, and the exclusion of European influence from Yucatan might properly be regarded as necessary for the protection of the United
States from the steady onward movement of the sinister
forces of Old World imperialism.

I do not put forward this argument, the reader will
understand, with the view of endorsing it. I put it forward as a possible explanation of the point of view expressed in the Polk message of April 19, 1848. " Security " is a word susceptible of many interpretations, de-
pending very largely upon the activity of the imagination
of him who uses it. Polk was naturally hard and suspicious. It is not curious that he saw a question of
security involved in the problem of Yucatan, or that he
should seek to buttress his position with the language
of the Monroe Doctrine. For, if by a strict interpretation, the Doctrine could not be said to apply, implicit
in its words was a distrust of all European intermeddling in American affairs, and this distrust had grown
and waxed great, in the years of Polk's administration.
There is, therefore, nothing strange in his invocation
of the shades of the statesmen of 1823 to justify his
point of view.

The logic of the message of April 29 has often been
said to rest upon the no-transfer principle. But it is a
little hard to see that such a point of view is sound.
What was at issue here was not the transfer of sovereignty from one European power to another, without
the consent of the inhabitants concerned. What was at

issue, at least in theory, was the right of the Yucatecos to dispose of themselves as they would. The distinction between the two cases is obvious.

Acting on the spur of Polk's message the Committee on Foreign Relations in the Senate reported a measure for the temporary occupation of Yucatan. The debate on this measure naturally led to many expressions of opinion with regard to the Monroe Doctrine. Once again, as in 1845, the tendency to party division in connection with Polk's reassertion of the principles of 1823, was very decidedly apparent. But, once again, also, there were deserters from the Democratic ranks, and the most powerful speech made in opposition to the extension of Monroe's message to the case in point came from John C. Calhoun.

Calhoun had never been an ardent supporter of the Mexican War. He had, indeed, advocated purely defensive operations, and had expressed himself vigorously against the acquisition of territory inhabited by large numbers of Mexicans. His attitude on the Yucatan bill was to have been expected, and his position on the Monroe Doctrine hardly less so. In brief comments made in the course of debate on the day the message was received, the venerable Senator from South Carolina denounced the language of the President's message. It went, he declared, " far beyond Mr. Monroe's declaration," it was " a broad and dangerous principle, truly," it was " difficult to say what limits can be fixed to it, or to what it would carry us, if reduced to practise." [69] But these observations were only preliminary

[69] *Cong. Globe,* 30th Cong., 1st Sess., 712.

to a much more careful consideration of the question. In a long speech of May 15 Calhoun lent the weight of his authority, all the greater because he had been a witness at first-hand of the momentous events of 1823, to reducing to the smallest proportions the scope of the Monroe Doctrine. His utterance at this time deserves to rank among the most powerful criticisms of the Doctrine as a national shibboleth that have ever been delivered.

Calhoun began by tracing the circumstances which gave rise to Monroe's warning to Europe in 1823. His account is exceedingly accurate, considering the lapse of a quarter of a century, and interestingly enough, it gives full credit to the activities of Great Britain, in preventing the interposition of the Holy Alliance in the New World. But, continues the speaker, the Holy Alliance has passed away, and with it the need for Monroe's declaration has passed. " And yet the President has quoted that very declaration (that is, a part of it referring to Spanish America), but in a manner changing entirely its meaning, by separating it from the context as it stood in the message, and which referred it to the allied powers ; and placing it in connection with a portion of his message which made it refer to Great Britain, Spain, or other European powers. The change has made the declaration so inconsistent and absurd that, had it been made by Mr. Monroe, as it stands in the President's message, it would have been the subject of the severest animadversion and ridicule, instead of receiving, as it did, the approbation and applause of the whole country. It would have placed England in the

false position of acting against us and with the Holy
Alliance in reference to the Spanish-American republics; and it would also have placed us in the position of
opposing Spain in her efforts to recover her dominion
over those states; and, finally, it would have involved
the absurdity of asserting that the attempt of any European state to extend its system of government to this
continent, the smallest as well as the greatest, would
endanger the peace and safety of our country."

In these vigorous words Calhoun utterly repudiated
the idea of a general and permanent principle of universal application embodied in the words of Monroe
with regard to the extension of the political system of
the Allied powers. His view was the same with regard
to the declaration that we should " regard the interposition of any European power, with the purpose of oppressing them, or of controlling in any other manner
their destiny as the manifestation of an unfriendly disposition towards the United States." The need for any
such principle has passed, and there was not in the circumstances of Yucatan, in any case, the remotest simi-
larity to the conditions which existed in 1823. The offer
of voluntary sovereignty could not possibly come within
the language of Monroe.

The non-colonization principle also, Calhoun contended, was wholly inapplicable. The word " colonization " had a definite meaning. It means " the establishment of a settlement by emigrants from the parent
country in a territory either uninhabited or from which
the inhabitants have been partially or wholly expelled."
" This is not a case of that character."

With these words Calhoun proceeded to enter upon an account of the origin of the non-colonization clause. His purpose, of course, was to discredit it, and accordingly, he laid down the proposition that it had not been discussed in the cabinet, and insinuated (which was false) that it had been smuggled into the message by the Secretary of State without the approval of the President. " If that declaration had come before that cautious cabinet," he declared, " for Mr. Monroe was among the wisest and most cautious men I have ever known — it would have been modified, and expressed with a far greater degree of precision, and with much more delicacy in reference to the feelings of the British Government."

Taken altogether, he went on, Monroe's declarations were " declarations—nothing more. . . . . Not one word in any one of them in reference to resistance. There is nothing said of it; and with great propriety was it omitted. Resistance belonged to us—to Congress; it is for us to say whether we shall resist or not, and to what extent." The President " tells you that these declarations have become the settled policy of this country. What, the declarations? Declarations are not policy, and cannot become settled policy. He must mean that it has become the settled policy of this country to resist what these declarations refer to; and to resist, if need be, by an appeal to arms. Is this the fact? Has there been one instance in which these declarations have been carried into effect by resistance? If there be, let it be pointed out. Have there not been innumerable instances in which they have not been applied? Certainly. Still

stronger; these declarations, under their broad interpretation, were disavowed entirely three years afterward
by the vote of the Republican party, when the administration of Mr. Adams endeavored to carry them out
practically, by sending ministers to the Congress at
Panama." Moreover, contended Calhoun, Polk's mis-
conception of Monroe's declaration is positively dangerous. " The principle which lies at the bottom of his
recommendation is—that when any power on this continent becomes involved in internal warfare, and the
weaker side chooses to make application to us for its
support, we are bound to give them support for fear
the offer of the sovereignty of the country may be made
to some other power and accepted. It puts it in the
power of other countries on this continent to make us a
party to all their wars; and hence I say, if this broad
interpretation be given to these declarations, we shall
forever be involved in wars."

This language was rather sweeping, and goes beyond
the bounds of convincing argument, but the Senator
from South Carolina proceeded to state his positive
opinions with regard to the Monroe Doctrine in language
that deserves to be remembered. His principle of action
was simple. It was not that the Monroe Doctrine should
be repudiated. It was certainly not that it should be
unqualifiedly endorsed or extended. It was that it should
be applied in each case on its merits, invoked when national interest demanded, neglected when no such interest existed, and applied " by negotiation, remonstrance,
or some intermediate measure, or by a resort to arms,"

as the circumstances of the case might warrant. In other words, circumstances were to determine its application.

Calhoun's speech of May 15, 1848, is one of the most powerful assaults on the Monroe Doctrine as a general and immutable rule of action that have ever been delivered. And what is more important, at the time of which we are speaking, his view assuredly had a far greater influence and acceptance than it would have today. For, though in recent years bold voices have been raised to criticize the Monroe Doctrine, it can hardly be doubted that as a symbol, as a phrase, as a rallying cry, the words have a greater force that ever before, as is clearly indicated by the fact that in the discussions of the League of Nations the League's own friends conceded to the principles of 1823 a special place in a general covenant of peace.

It was not thus in 1848. The opinion expressed by Calhoun found support in both Houses of Congress, and may well have been the majority view. " Mr. Monroe had committed us," exclaimed Root of Ohio, in the House of Representatives. " Aye! and what authority had Mr. Monroe to do any such thing? None at all. But it was sometimes very convenient, when gentlemen had a point to carry to resort to some of Mr. Monroe's musty old letters (*sic!*). [70] " And in the Senate Niles of Connecticut and Miller of New Jersey and Davis of Massachusetts made strong speeches denouncing the President's policy. They called attention to the fact that

[70] *Ibid.*

Monroe's original pronouncement laid down a principle of noninterference, not of interference; and naturally cited against Polk (as partisans seem ever to delight in twitting their opponents with inconsistency) the language which he had used in the Panama debates of 1826.[71] With much vigor and power Niles pointed out that in the course of a quarter of a century the United States had taken no action under the Doctrine in several different cases, in the case of Belize, in the case of British Guiana, in the case of La Plata, and declared that it had been engaged in " carrying out the great doctrine of Mr. Monroe by a quiet acquiescence." [72] It was easy, too, for a Whig, at any rate, to bring up the case of Oregon. There, as it seemed, the administration had pronounced for the Doctrine with a magnificent blare of trumpets, and had later beat a signal retreat; and in this case the claims of the United States had been pronounced by those who invoked the principles of 1823 as " clear and unquestionable." More important still are the allusions of the Whig orators to the Monroe Doctrine as interpreted by Polk as a Doctrine of war and conquest. Calhoun had made this point, as has been seen, and had mournfully alluded to the days when the great Democratic party was the party of peace; but the Senate orators across the aisle drove home the point with increasing force. " It is too late in the day," exclaimed Niles, " to take ground quite so high as this

[71] For Niles's speech, see *ibid.*, App., pp. 608-613; for Davis's, pp. 620-25; and for Miller's, pp. 625-630. For comments on Polk's inconsistency, see especially pp. 610 and 624.

[72] *Ibid.*, p. 611.

put forth by my honorable friend from Indiana (that is, Hannegan, in charge of the bill). It is too late in the day, and it is a ground which ought never to have been taken, because it was one that we could never have maintained. It would have led to perpetual war with the world, or at least with England, the mightiest power in it." [73] The declaration of 1823, exclaimed Davis of Massachusetts, " has become, in the minds of such as adopt it, an authority justifying any and all schemes of aggression or ambition, under the assumed pretension that we have a right so far to regulate the affairs of this continent, as to determine who shall hold sovereignty here, and under what form of government. . . . . We who traffic in nations, and when we cannot buy, conquer them to make acquisitions, have a monopoly, a patent right to this particular trade, and hold the right to restrain others from engaging in it." [74]

Under such assaults the friends of the administration do not seem to have been entirely easy, for there were Democrats, not a few, who sought entirely to separate the question of the military occupation of Yucatan from the Monroe Doctrine. Jefferson Davis, Senator from Mississippi, admitted in the course of the debate that the principles of 1823 were not involved (though he added that he was ready to maintain them).[75] Cass sought to qualify the too broad interpretation of the Monroe declaration by declaring that it did not forbid

[73] *Ibid.*
[74] *Ibid.*, p. 624.
[75] *Ibid.*, p. 599.

a European nation to wage war against an American
nation (as in the case of La Plata), or prevent the
holding of territory already acquired,[76] and declared
that the principle was involved only in the sense that,
if we did not act, we could not legitimately complain
if Spain or England did.[77] Dix of New York, later to
be famous as Buchanan's Secretary of War in the last
trying days of that President's administration, thought
that the application of the President's theory was "a
question of prudence," and Bagby of Alabama and
Houston of Texas declared that they did not think that
Monroe's message had much to do with the question
before the Senate.[78] The former of these men, in a
speech which is a splendid example of the politician's
ability to get on both sides of a public question with
immense conviction, declared that the message of 1823
proclaimed "a true policy, but not a fighting policy,"
and that, "with the exception of a case that might involve our self-preservation, the United States would not
be justified in carrying out to extreme results the policy
of Monroe's declaration." [79]

Some voices, there were, of course, raised in defense
of Polk's message of April 29. In the main Cass, though
not assuming the most extreme position, endorsed the
President's stand. In his view, the Monroe Doctrine was
an expression of American determination to exclude
European influence from the American continents for

[76] Ibid., p. 615.
[77] Ibid.
[78] Cong. Globe, 30th Cong., 1st Sess., pp. 738 and 773.
[79] Ibid., p. 773.

all future time, and foreshadowed the entire political
separation of the Old World from the New. Failure to
enforce this principle would expose the country to "eternal self-reproach and to the contumely of the world." [80]
Much the same were the views of Westcott of Florida
and Foote of Mississippi. And Hannegan, in charge of
the measure, and its ardent supporter, at the beginning,
declared that the principles of 1823 had never been so
important as they were at that moment, that they were
among the " cardinal doctrines of the American political
creed," and that Polk, so far from extending them had
actually made them more modest in their scope by restricting them to the North American Continent (a contention, which, as we have seen, was of a very doubtful
validity).[81] But for all these bold words, the friends of
the military occupation of Yucatan were very obviously
on the defensive, and so, too, were the supporters of the
Polk version of the Monroe Doctrine. Indeed, perhaps
on no other occasion was the Doctrine so roundly condemned as it was in the debates of 1848. It was probably with some relief that Hannegan and his associates
soon found a way out of the whole matter. For after
about two weeks' debate, the chairman of the Foreign
Relations Committee took advantage of the news of an
armistice in Yucatan to withdraw the bill, and the celerity
with which this action was accomplished seems ample
evidence of the bad reception which the measure, and
the arguments by which it was supported, had met with
in the forum of public opinion.

[80] *Ibid.*, App., p. 615.
[81] *Ibid.*, p. 729.

But what of the bogey which Polk and his supporters conjured up of British designs on Yucatan? Would Britain have accepted the sovereignty of the province had the United States refused? And were the British, as was more than once charged in the Senate debates, aiding the Indian insurrection with sinister purposes of their own? With regard to the first of these questions, the answer is not difficult. The British government held entirely aloof. It is true that its minister at Mexico City, to whom the Mendez appeal of March 25 was addressed, declared that he would transmit it to his government, and that in his opinion it would be favorably acted upon. But he spoke for no one but himself. In London there was no desire to earn the ill-will of Mexico by accepting the invitation of a faction to assume the sovereignty of one of its provinces, and even had the British government been willing, events would soon have prevented any such step. For early in April, Mendez found it no longer possible to remain in power, and handed over his authority to his rival, Don Miguel Barbachano. And Barbachano, on April 19, withdrew the offer which had been made in the note of March 25.

As for the question of British aid to the Indians, there was most certainly carried on a contraband traffic which proved most distressing to the rulers of Yucatan. Belize, of course, was directly contiguous to the distracted province, and the opportunities of profit in an illicit trade were not likely to be neglected. In February of 1848, a commissioner was sent to Belize to urge the suppression of this commerce, and returned, so says the Yucateco historian Ancona, very much pleased with

the result of his mission.[82] After the seizure of the
frontier post of Bacalar, April 19, 1848, there seems to
be little doubt that the Indians were recognized as possessing belligerent rights, and the traffic in arms with
them redoubled.[83] In 1849, Colonel Fancourt, the superintendent of Belize, offered his mediation to the Mexican government with the object of bringing about a
peace on the basis of a cession of territory to the insurgents, and the recognition of their independence. This
proposal, though not frowned upon at Mexico City, was
bitterly opposed by the Yucatecos, and it got nowhere.[84]
It is possible to see in it a subtle plan for the extension
of British influence in Central America. Indeed, the
authorities on the spot probably put it forward in a
spirit not entirely disinterested. Taking all these facts
together, the suspicions of the American Senators who
denounced Great Britain do not seem altogether fantastic. It was, it is true, the local authorities, and not
the British government, which were responsible for the
position assumed. At London the interest in Yucatan
appears to have been lukewarm, if not positively nonexistent. But in answer to this plea of nonresponsibil-
ity, so far as the Foreign Office itself is concerned, it
may reasonably be answered that the process by which
the British empire has been built up is very largely one,
not of conscious direction from the government itself,
but of the ambition and energy of British agents or

[82] Ancona, *op. cit.,* IV, 229.
[83] *Ibid.,* p. 233.
[84] *Ibid.,* pp. 277-78.

British individuals whose acts have been later ratified
by the authorities at home. In view of this, it seems
possible to sympathize in some measure with the Anglo-
phobes in the Senate of the United States. They had
good reason to distrust Great Britain in 1848. On the
other hand, it is to be admitted that some of the arguments that they brought forward were flimsy in the extreme. The fact that muskets with the Tower mark upon
them had been found in the hands of the Indians proved,
of course, nothing at all except what hardly needed to be
proved, the existence of a contraband traffic, and there
is hardly a word in the speeches in Congress which can
be said to substantiate the general assertions of British
intrigue which were put forward. The attacks on British
policy were based on the fear-psychology, not on anything else, and were easily demolished by the eloquence
of Calhoun.

But what of the third power to whom the desperate
Yucatecos had offered their "dominion and sovereignty," what of Spain? The Spanish had offered aid
to the Yucatecos long before the appeal of March 25
was made, and arms and other resources had been sent
to the struggling government by the captain-general of
Cuba at Havana.[85] But the matter does not seem to
have gone any farther. Barbachano, when he came into
power in April, 1848, though withdrawing the offer
made by the Mendez régime, with charming inconsistency, so far as Spain was concerned, sent special commissioners to Cuba to plead for further aid, and, if

[85] *Ibid.*, p. 106.

necessary, to offer the cession of the province as the price thereof, but the captain-general responded that he was without authority to undertake any such engagement.[86] The commissioners then proceeded to Mexico City, and there were able to enlist the aid of the central government. With the granting of such aid, indeed, this curious chapter in the history of Yucatan comes to an end.

Of very little practical consequence, the episode which has just been related is one of the most interesting in the history of the Monroe Doctrine. For the Senate debate of 1848 is one of the very few occasions on which the question of the validity and expediency of the Doctrine has been generally debated. In general, all parties and groups today do lip-service, at least, to the principles of 1823. And this fact prevents many questions of American foreign policy from being debated upon their merits. Only cry out, " Monroe Doctrine," and the door to reasonable and orderly discussion is already half-closed. It was not so in the period we are examining. There was as yet no such blind acceptance of a shibboleth. Polk had carried Monroe's principles to great lengths, and there were those ready to tell him so. The Doctrine, far from being absolutely accepted, had as yet acquired only a party authority. It was possible to denounce it, as did Calhoun, without being regarded as un-American. This is not to say that there was a disposition flatly and completely to deny the truth

[86] For this episode, see *ibid.*, pp. 161-164, and Baranda, *op. cit.*, II, 66-71.

of the maxims of which the message of 1823 was an expression. There was merely a tendency to consider each case involving those maxims upon its individual merits, as it arose. Was this, after all, not a wholly tenable point of view; was it not only tenable in 1848, but is there not much to be said for it today?

CHAPTER IV

The Central American Question and the Doctrine, 1849-1863.

The question of Central America, bequeathed by the Polk administration to its successor, was for more than a decade to vex the relations between the United States and Great Britain. It involved, as has already become clear, a definite challenge to the principles of the Monroe Doctrine. It has, therefore, a very high interest for the student of the principles of 1823.[1]

To trace its evolution in all its details, however, would be to pass beyond the limits which I have set for this study. I shall confine my examination of the problem to those points which may serve to clarify the attitude of American and European statesmen and of American and European public opinion toward the dogmas which were by now indelibly connected with the name of Monroe.

It may, perhaps, be observed at the very outset of this chapter that two points of view are apparent in the evolution of the Central American controversy. The one

[1] The important work on this period is that of Mary Wilhelmine Williams, *Anglo-American Isthmian Diplomacy,* already cited. See also, for a somewhat different interpretation, Ira D. Travis, *British Rule in Central America: or a sketch of Mosquito History,* no. 5 in *Publications,* Michigan Political Science Association, and also *The History of the Clayton-Bulwer Treaty,* no. 8 in *ibid.*

may, for convenience, be called the Whig point of view;
the other, the Democratic point of view. The difference
between them did not, of course, amount to an absolute
antithesis, the Democrats completely championing the
principles of 1823, and the Whigs as vehemently repudiating them; it was a difference, partly of degree, and
partly of method. With regard to European encroachments the Whig doctrine, speaking broadly, was the
doctrine laid down by Calhoun in 1848, that such encroachments were in every individual case to be considered on the facts of that specific case, and not with
regard to some general principle. In negotiating with
regard to them the emphasis was to be laid upon the
concrete circumstances involved, and there was to be no
mention of Monroe's message, or any appeal to the
doctrines of 1823. The Democrats, on the other hand,
were inclined to lay down a broader theory, to seek to
establish Monroe's declaration as of universal application, and even to put it forward as an international
argument in an international controversy.

The Polk administration, as has been seen, did little
with regard to the encroachments of the British government on Nicaragua. It did not even answer the fervid
appeals of the Nicaraguan President and the Nicaraguan Secretary of State. Preoccupied with other problems, facing a presidential election, and perhaps not as
yet fully alive to all the implications of the matter, it
bequeathed the whole matter unliquidated to its successor. But the administration of Zachary Taylor was,
from the first, deeply conerned with the question. The
cession of California to the United States had im-

mensely increased the importance of the question of inter-oceanic communication. It had led American capital to think seriously of a Nicaraguan canal, and to the organization of a company for the construction of the same. And this company, formed in March, 1849, speedily discovered that the British occupation of San Juan put important obstacles in its way. For shortly after it had signed a contract with the Nicaraguan government, Chatfield, the British minister in Central America, caused notice to be served upon the Nicaraguan authorities that the whole of the San Juan River from its mouth to the Machuca Rapids belonged to the Mosquito kingdom and could not be disposed of without reference to the tinsel sovereign of that region, and his protector, the government of Great Britain.[2] A little later the Foreign Office directed Barclay, the British consul at New York, to serve notice on the grantees not to begin work on the canal, as the territory of Mosquitia would be bisected by it.[3]

[2] London, P. R. O., F. O., Guatemala, vol. 57, April 2, 1849, and April 14, 1849.

[3] *Ibid.*, America, vol. 497, June 28, 1849. Encl.

" If the United States Sec'y of State should in conversation with you advert to the Subject of the Existence and Rights of the Mosquito State," Lord Palmerson added in a later despatch, " you will observe that in the first place the British Government has not acknowledged and never can acknowledge the Doctrine or Principle laid down by President Madison [sic!] with regard to the formation of any new European Settlement in North America, but that such Principle has no bearing whatever upon the relations of Great Britain with the Mosquito State inasmuch as those Relations existed nearly a Century before the United States became politically separate from the British Crown." *Ibid.*, America, vol. 497, July 13, 1849.

The American company, of course, lost no time in seeking the support of the State Department. Over the Department presided at this time John M. Clayton of Delaware. To us today Clayton is only a minor figure, yet to his contemporaries he seemed a considerable figure, an orator and debater of distinction, with a mind that was subtle and ingenious, and a geniality that won him many friends. Clayton's appointment, moreover, if not as popular, perhaps, as would have been that of Webster, was in the Whig tradition. He upheld those conservative views of foreign policy which contrasted strikingly with the more noisy patriotism of the Democrats. He was not an ardent expansionist, and he was an advocate of friendly relations with England, in fact, altogether such a man as a Whig President would be likely to call to take charge. There were, as it happened, striking weaknesses in his character, a certain indecisiveness, a certain indirection, which limited undoubtedly high abilities, but these weaknesses were not apparent when the Secretary took office, nor were they demonstrated by the way in which he first took hold of the thorny question of Central America. The government of Nicaragua was informed that the United States would look after its interests in the Mosquito controversy,[4] and a new commissioner, Ephraim George Squier, a young man of twenty-nine with a taste for diplomacy—and archaeology—was sent out to Central America, with instructions which declared that the American government would employ any moral means

[4] 31st Cong., 1st Sess., No. 75, H. Exec. Doc. p. 132.

in its power to frustrate British ambition on the Mosquito Coast.[5] At the same time instructions were sent out to George Bancroft, American minister at London, which directed him with courtesy and moderation to press upon the British government the objections to the exclusive control of the port of San Juan by any single nation, and if mild representations failed, to direct a formal written protest to the British government.[6] Thus began negotiations which were to produce, after a year of crowded diplomacy, the famous document known as the Clayton-Bulwer treaty.

The American and British governments were, on the whole, to display a fairly conciliatory spirit from the beginning, neither one, in all probability, being ready to risk a war over the matter, and neither one, it would appear, having any intention at this time of monopolizing an inter-oceanic canal route across Central America; but this moderation was hardly matched by the representatives of the two governments in the very theatre of the controversy. Chatfield and Squier, in the course of 1849 and early 1850, were to engage in a diplomatic duel which might have had unfortunate consequences if their governments had not, on the whole, been intent on maintaining peace. Chatfield had been no retiring person, as has already been seen. He had sought all along to build up British influence in Central America. He had undoubtedly taken part in domestic politics, and done what he could to strengthen the faction which was more sympathetic to Britain. At the time which we are

[5] *Ibid.*, p. 119.
[6] *Ibid.*, p. 232.

now considering, he was on the friendliest terms with the government of Guatemala, and with that of Costa Rica, for in each of these states the party of the Serviles, commonly pro-British, was in control. In the case of Costa Rica, indeed, friendship might not inconceivably have been changed into tutelage, had different counsels prevailed in London. In December of 1848, the Costa Rican government, doubtless instigated by Chatfield, had actually appealed to Great Britain to take it under its protection.[7] The appeal was denied, just when it is not easy to determine,[8] but disquieting rumors with regard to a possible British protectorate of this little state continued during 1849, and had their part in the negotiations which culminated in the Clayton-Bulwer treaty.[9]

Friendly with Guatemala and Costa Rica, the British minister was on terms distinctly less cordial with Nicaragua, Honduras, and San Salvador. This feeling he displayed in a striking fashion in the course of the year

[7] London, P. R. O., F. O., Costa Rica, vol. 1, December 23, 1848.

[8] *Ibid.*, vol. 3, March 23, 1850, Molines-Palmerston.

[9] Buchanan, writing in 1850, declared that but for the determination to resist European colonization on the North American continent, expressed by Polk's administration, this offer would have been accepted. (Buchanan, *Works*, VIII, 379.) But Buchanan, in making this statement, was defending himself against the charge of inaction, and the observation must be discounted on this ground. Furthermore, the assumption of any such protectorate would have served no real interest and would have been contrary to the general policy of Britain in the New World. See the interesting observations of Miss Williams, *op. cit.*, pp. 71-2.

1849. On the pretext of nonpayment of claims due to the British government, an ultimatum was despatched to San Salvador, demanding payment within twenty-four hours, and, when satisfaction was not given, the whole coast was ordered blockaded. Similar claims were pressed against Honduras, and in January, 1849, a lien was laid upon the island of Tigre, in the gulf of Fonseca. At a later date, when Squier, in order to check aggression in this quarter, secured a temporary cession of the island from the Honduran government, Chatfield ordered a British man-of-war to take possession of it in the name of the British Crown, and it was only given up after a formal protest to Great Britain on the part of the United States.[10] As for Nicaragua, Chatfield made no secret of his intention to treat it with little regard for its claims, and in December of 1849 he notified the Nicaraguan government, without authority in fact, that it must not challenge the rights of Costa Rica south of the San Juan, and that that state was under British protection.[11] But Squier, on his own part, was not behindhand in vigorous action; indeed his ardor far outran the cool moderation of the administration at Washington. The steps which he took to forestall British possession of the island of Tigre have already been described. They did not stand alone. Squier not only bent his efforts to bringing about a union of the Central American States,[12] but he secured from Nicara-

[10] For this episode, see Williams, *op. cit.*, pp. 64-66.

[11] London, P. R. O., F. O., Guatemala, vol. 60, no. 21, December 1, 1849.

[12] Washington, Dept. of State, Despatches, Guatemala, vol. 2, August 20, 1849.

gua and Honduras declarations which affirmed their
intention to live up to the Monroe Doctrine, striking
examples of the adoption of the language of that doctrine by the agencies of Latin American governments.[13]

[13] See the declaration adopted by the Nicaraguan Legislature in 1849, and unanimously accepted by the Congresses of
San Salvador and Honduras as well, declaring " their adhesion
to the principle of the total exclusion of European interference
from the domestic and international affairs of the Republican
American States, as necessary to their peace and independence,"
and " that the extension of monarchical institutions by conquest,
colonization or by a support of savage chiefs to sovereignty, or
savage tribes to national existence, or by other means upon the
American continent, is in opposition to the interests of the Republican American States, dangerous to their peace and safety,
and an encroachment upon their individual and collective
rights." (London, P. R. O., F. O., Guatemala, vol. 60, October
25, 1849.) Squier's answer to this resolution is worth quoting.
" I need not assure you, sir, of the concurrence of my Government in the principles thus forcibly set forth to the world.
They are of vital importance to the American Republics, and
were early asserted by the United States. They were proclaimed
when the Spanish American provinces threw off the dominion
of Spain, and in the very year when the States of Central
America perfected their independence (1823), the President of
the United States declared to that most Unholy Alliance, which
then threatened the subversion of liberty thoughout the world,
that ' the United States would consider any attempt on their
part to extend their system to any portion of the American
Continent, as dangerous to their peace and safety.' He declared
also, with equal frankness and decision, that ' the United
States would consider an interposition for the purpose of oppressing, or in any manner controlling' the destinies of the free
American States, whose independence she had, on great consideration and just principles acknowledged, as the manifestation of an unfriendly disposition against herself.
" These principles have been often re-affirmed by the United
States, by her public declarations and by her acts. When the

Squier managed too to secure the consent of Nicaragua to a treaty providing for the construction of the long-projected canal, and a new concession to the American company for such construction.

Despite these activities of Squier and Chatfield, the threatened breach between the British and American governments never came. The seizure of Tigre Island was disavowed by the British Foreign Office. In London Abbott Lawrence, the American minister, was conciliatory in the extreme, and in Washington, to which city, after a time, the discussions were transferred, the Secretary of State was moderation itself. The country was in the midst of a great debate over slavery, perhaps the greatest in our history, and, even had Clayton's general

---

celebrated French armament of 1825 approached the American Coasts, the Government of the United States informed that of France, as also that of England that the 'armament was disproportioned to any ordinary purposes of peaceful commerce,' and that if it was its intention to occupy any portions of the continent, or the West Indies, 'the United States would not consent thereto, under any circumstances whatsoever.' At a later period, in 1843, the same principle was avowed in respect to the Sandwich Islands.

"With these declarations and historical facts before you, you will perceive, sir, how earnestly the United States have sustained the great principle set forth so eloquently in the declaration of the Legislature of Nicaragua, and I feel warranted in saying that, under no circumstances, will my Government recede from the position which it has so deliberately taken, and in which she will be supported by every truly American State. I shall take great pleasure in transmitting the Declaration to my Government." (*Democratic Review,* October, 1852, p. 351, in "Our Foreign Relations. Central America. The Crampton and Webster Projet." pp. 337-352).

temper not been pacific, the circumstances of the case were highly favorable to a pacific policy.

In dealing with the problem before him the American Secretary of State was certainly not actuated by any dogmatic attachment to the Monroe Doctrine. He did, it is true, at the begining of the negotiations which were to result in the Clayton-Bulwer treaty, put forward the demand for the surrender of the port of Greytown,[14] but this demand was to be permitted to drop before the end of the negotiation. Instead of insisting upon the relinquishment of British control where it existed at the time of his entry into the State Department, Clayton determined to content himself with a British disclaimer against further colonization, and in an agreement for mutuality of rights with regard to the projected canal, in the belief that if this latter point could be satisfactorily fixed upon, the question of Mosquitia would lose all practical importance. He was very distinctly interested first and foremost in the question of inter-oceanic communication, on terms of equality for all nations in accordance with the then declared policy of the United States, and only secondarily in the question of the extension of British control in the region of Central America. But Clayton was not able to make his view prevail in the cabinet without opposition. In early March it apeared as if a serious situation were about to result. Acting under the pressure of his colleagues and public opinion, on March 1 the Secretary of State wrote the American

[14] 31st Cong., 1st Sess., H. Exec. Doc. No. 75, p. 232, and 32nd Cong., 2nd Sess., Exec. Doc. No. 27, p. 51.

consul at Belize, withdrawing his exequatur, on the ground that the appointment had been made " without full consideration of the territorial rights of Great Britain in that quarter," [15] and on March 19 he transmitted to the Senate the treaty which Squier had sent back from Nicaragua, clear notice of an intention to proceed without waiting for Great Britain. But in the course of the next few weeks he seems to have been able to proceed in a more conciliatory way. Satisfactory explanations, or at any rate explanations which might be accepted as satisfactory, were received from Palmerston with regard to the Mosquito question, and fears which had cropped up with regard to Costa Rica were laid to rest by the express declaration of the British government that it had no intention of establishing a protectorate over that little state. The negotiations, therefore, proceeded, and on the 19th of April Clayton and Bulwer Lytton, the special representative sent out from London, signed the famous document which has ever since been known as the Clayton-Bulwer treaty.

It is the first article of the treaty which particularly concerns the historian of the Monroe Doctrine. I have said that the Secretary of State was not dogmatically attached to that doctrine, and the observation is a true one. Indeed, he actually told Crampton, the British minister, that the Taylor administration " in no way adopted these principles." [16] But, despite this fact, it is not to

[15] *Ibid.*, 32nd Cong., 2nd Sess., Doc. No. 12, p. 2, Clayton-Hempstead. March 1, 1850.

[16] *British Parliamentary Papers*, 1856, LX, 5.

be believed that Clayton was wholly indifferent to the advance of British dominion in the New World, and especially in Central America. On the contrary, as early as the date of his instructions to Abbott Lawrence, he had directed that minister to inquire of Palmerston as to the purposes of the British government in that part of the world, and Lawrence, on November 8, 1849, had directed a note to the British Foreign Secretary inquiring as to whether Great Britain intended to " occupy or colonize Nicaragua, Costa Rica, the Mosquito Coast, or any part of Central America." [17] To this note Palmerston replied with a positive disclaimer of any such purpose on November 13.[18] When it came to the final drafting of the Clayton-Bulwer treaty, the assurances thus given were incorporated into the famous first article, and present the first, and indeed the only formal, treaty assurance in history by a European state with regard to colonizing activities in the New World. " The Governments of Great Britain and the United States," read this article, " hereby declare that neither the one nor the other will ever obtain for itself any exclusive control over the said Ship-Canal; agreeing that neither will ever erect or maintain any fortifications commanding the same, or in the vicinity thereof, or occupy, fortify, or colonize, or assume or exercise any dominion over Nicaragua, Costa Rica, the Mosquito Coast, or any part of Central America; nor will either make use of any protection which either affords or may afford, or any

[17] 32nd Cong., 2nd Sess., Exec. Doc. No. 27, p. 45, November 8, 1849.
[18] *Ibid.*, p. 46.

alliance which either has or may have, to, or with any
State or people, for the purpose of erecting or maintaining any such fortifications, or of occupying, fortifying or colonizing Nicaragua, Costa Rica, the Mosquito
Coast, or any part of Central America, or of assuming
or exercising dominion over the same.") This article
was to cause much difficulty later, and the interpretation
of the term " Central America " apparently seemed a
little doubtful even to the negotiators. After its ratification an exchange of notes took place between Clayton
and Bulwer, by which it was expressly declared that the
treaty did not apply to the Belize, or, in the phraseology
of the American Secretary of State, to "the small islands
in the neighborhood which may be known as its dependencies." But here, again, was another ambiguity. For
whether the Bay Islands were included in this disclaimer was by no means certain, and was, as a matter
of fact, to be the cause of a very warm dispute in the
not far distant future.

All in all, the course of Clayton in connection with
the negotiation of this famous treaty is not free from
indirection. The definition, by exchange of notes, of the
terms of an international engagement requiring the
consent of the Senate was a proceeding which, if not
exactly partaking of bad faith, was likely to give rise to
difficulties later, and, though it appears that Mr. William
R. King, the Democratic chairman of the Foreign Relations Committee, assured Clayton that it was perfectly
understood that the treaty did not apply to the Belize,
it was perilous, indeed, to take the assurance of one man
as the combined judgment of all the Senators where a

question of interpretation was concerned.[19] The exchange of notes itself evaded the question of the Bay
Islands, instead of facing it. In his anxiety for an
accommodation, Clayton had left certain questions in
the shadow.

In the Senate, too, very obviously, these same questions were no more frankly faced. The Clayton-Bulwer
treaty was ratified by the decisive vote of 42 to 12. The
debates on it were in executive session, and have never
been reported. But from such information as can be
pieced together from later speeches in Congress, it does
not appear that the question of the Belize was ever raised
in the debates on ratification. At a later date, in 1853,
Senators in some number were to arise and protest at
the idea that this region was not included, and solemnly
to vow that they would never have voted for the treaty,
if they had not believed that it applied to Belize; but not
one of these same gentlemen had the temerity to declare
that he had raised the question when the treaty was
actually before the Senate. The only evidence, indeed,
that this territory figured in any way is to be found in a
statement of Lewis Cass, made in March, 1853. At this
time Cass quoted W. R. King as saying in 1850 he had
assured Clayton that, if Bulwer's declaration declaring
the treaty inapplicable to British Honduras had been
known to the Senate, the agreement would not have
received a single vote.[20] But Cass was speaking as a
partisan; the interview which he had had with King

[19] *Cong. Globe,* 32nd Cong., 2nd Sess., App., p. 248.
[20] *Ibid.*

ran directly counter to the tone of the latter's communication to Clayton; and at the time of the interview King was lying on a bed of sickness from which he was never to arise again. It is much to be doubted, therefore, whether this bit of evidence is of great value.

At any rate, this much may certainly be said. The ratification of the Clayton-Bulwer treaty was not followed by any movement in Congress for the British evacuation of Belize. Nor does it appear from an examination of a variety of newspapers and periodicals for the latter half of 1850 that the Belize question figured at all prominently in the public mind.

At a later date, however, a great to-do was to be made about the Clayton-Bulwer treaty as violative of the Monroe Doctrine, and the question whether or not any such criticism was justified is one that certainly ought to be examined here. In discussing it, it will be possible, however, from the beginning, to exclude the idea that the principle of a canal, free and open to the commerce of all nations, and under the protection of the United States and Great Britain, was in itself a violation of the principles of 1823. Of course, this charge was to be made, and made by those in authority in the discussions with regard to the canal question in the eighties. But it is pellucidly clear that nothing in Monroe's original declaration supports any such view. That declaration was aimed at three things, intervention by European powers in the domestic concerns of Latin American states, the extension of European institutions to the New World, and colonization by European powers. It could not possibly have been construed to forbid con-

certed action by the United States with another nation
to keep open a channel of international communication.
This fact seems too obvious to argue, on the basis even
of a broad interpretation of the message of 1823. Indeed, when the Polk administration, with all its devotion to the principles of Monroe, was willing to acquiesce
in, even to encourage, an international guarantee of the
projected canal, there can be no doubt whatsoever that
in 1850 American public opinion did not regard such a
guarantee, much less a concert of action with regard to
such a canal, as a violation of the fundamental principles of American diplomacy. And though, no doubt,
it is possible to extend, some persons would say, to per-
vert, the spirit of the Monroe Doctrine to the point
where any association with European powers in matters
relating to the New World is regarded as beyond the
pale, it is certain that no such extension was meditated,
even by its chief supporters, at the time when John M.
Clayton put his signature to the famous treaty with
Great Britain.

A question which this treaty presents, however, for
more careful consideration is as to whether its provisions with regard to Central America were or were not
a violation of the principles of 1823. Such a charge was
more than once to be directed against the instrument.
According to this charge, it was Clayton's business in
1850 to drive the British out of Central America, for
every one of their settlements there was contrary to the
Monroe message. Take, for example, the case of Belize.
In this territory certain limited rights might be recognized as belonging to Great Britain under her treaties

with Spain.[21] But the transformation of these rights into actual possessions was clearly contrary to the Monroe Doctrine. Such a transformation may by 1850 be said to have taken place *de facto*, if not *de iure*. The principles of 1823 had thus been egregiously violated.

When it comes to the Bay Islands, the case is even stronger. British *de facto* possession, in this case, dates from 1838. Such possession was clearly contrary to both the letter and the spirit of Monroe's principles. Finally, in the case of Mosquitia, though it is possible to argue that the assertion of a protectorate was not that extension of dominion which was implied in the famous message, the activities of the British in the seizure of Greytown, and the real control which was exercised under the fiction of Mosquito sovereignty, were acts which might legitimately be brought within the scope of the declaration of 1823. Marshal all these facts together, and we have a strong case for the theory that the famous Doctrine had been contemptuously ignored by the British, and that a treaty which did not put an end to all these violations ran counter to the pronouncement of Monroe.

But there is a good deal to be said on the other side of the question. In the first place, if the Clayton-Bulwer treaty was to be held up to scorn because it did not provide for an end of British sovereignty in Central America, it could at least be replied that there were ample precedents for such laxity. Preceding administrations had shown no particular interest in the matter,

[21] See above, p. 10.

and even Polk and Buchanan turned a deaf ear to the appeals of Nicaragua, and failed to answer the letters which the rulers of that distracted country sent to Washington. Clayton himself was to point out three years later, when he rose to defend the treaty in the Senate debate of 1853, that it was not particularly logical of his party foes to assail him, on the ground of violating the Doctrine, when he had been the first Secretary of State to raise the Central American question into true international importance, and to attempt to put a check on British encroachments in this part of the world.[22]

Moreover, let it be noted, the Clayton-Bulwer treaty did not *recognize* British sovereignty in any part of Central America. It left open the question of the Belize, and the question of the Bay Islands, but it did no more. There was no acquiescence in British pretensions in that quarter. To have so acquiesced in territorial arrangements which dated from a period after 1823 would have been one thing. But it is difficult to see how a mere failure to deal with the problem can properly be described as a surrender of principle. The principle, clearly enough, was left intact, to be bartered away, as events were to prove, by a later administration, and by one which had the Monroe Doctrine perpetually on the tip of its tongue.

But this is not all. In one sense, the Clayton-Bulwer treaty was the first acceptance by another nation of the dogmas of 1823. It certainly opposed a barrier to British aggression in the future. It was Clayton's expecta-

22 *Ibid,* p. 255.

tion, too, that it would, by the limitations which it imposed upon the exercise of the British protectorate over
the Mosquitoes, render that protectorate practically
worthless. And though that expectation was not to be
immediately realized, it was, in the course of time, to
come true. All in all then, the compact seems rather to
have been an important affirmation of the Monroe declaration, rather than a denial of its validity. Indeed, as
already stated, it represents the only occasion upon which
a European nation bound itself by solemn agreement
to abstain from doing those things which Monroe's
message forbade. The language was not as clear as it
should be, it is true. But it was clear enough, in the long
run, to form the basis of American claims which were,
after long negotiations with which we shall have to
concern ourselves, to be settled, broadly speaking, in accordance with the wishes of the United States and with
its prepossessions in regard to European exercise of
sovereignty in the New World.

There is one other aspect of this matter, however,
which we should, for a moment, examine. The Clayton-
Bulwer treaty, it will have been observed, forbade not
only Great Britain, but also the United States, to colonize Central America. For this reason James Buchanan,
one of the most caustic of its opponents, declared that
it "reversed the Monroe Doctrine," and applied it
"against the United States." [23] The observation is an
interesting one, quite consistent with the expansionist
spirit so prevalent at the time, and which we have already

[23] *American Historical Review*, V, 101, "Letters of Bancroft
and Buchanan on the Clayton-Bulwer Treaty 1849-50."

15

seen in the discussions on Yucatan. According to this viewpoint, the object of the famous declaration was to reserve to the United States the sole privilege of conquest or acquisition in the New World, and to clear the path of European rivalries. In other words, the declaration was to be the instrument and the weapon of American imperialism, to use a dangerous word without prejudice as to the issues involved in it.[24]

In connection with this question, by the way, it is interesting to observe that the way would have been open for Clayton to pursue a more exclusive policy. The neurasthenic but enterprising Hise, who had been sent out to Central America, it will be remembered, by the Polk administration, had, without instructions and after Taylor had become President, secured from Nicaragua a treaty by which the United States should assume a protectorate of that state, and by which there was conceded to the American government or its citizens exclusive control of any canal that might be undertaken in this region. In refusing to press this treaty, in seeking conciliation with Great Britain, rather than in challenging the British government, the Secretary of State acted with sagacity, and in all probability in full accord with the dominant opinion of the time.

The general principles of the Clayton-Bulwer treaty, indeed, judged from the year 1850, were not unwise, nor

[24] The views of Buchanan were not the views of a single individual. Stephen A. Douglas, to cite only one example, obviously felt much the same, and voted against the treaty on this precise ground. But the vote in the Senate clearly shows that no such opinions were at this time generally held.

did they represent a policy of ignoble surrender. The principle of an international waterway was in line with the frequently declared policy of the United States. The disclaimer of aggressive purpose secured from Great Britain was by no means worthless, and it could not have been secured without a like disclaimer on the part of the American government. The agreement averted serious difficulties at no very great cost. Where Clayton erred was in not facing frankly some of the questions on which the treaty turned, in leaving the future of Mosquitia and of the Bay Islands uncertain, due to the ambiguity or obscurity of the instrument which he had in part drafted and which he had signed, and in making necessary long and sometimes vexing negotiations over a matter which ought to have been, and probably could have been, settled then and there once for all.

The Mosquito question was not to be finally liquidated till 1860. Soon after the ratification of the Clayton-Bulwer treaty President Taylor died, and his death ended the career of John Middleton Clayton at the Department of State. In his place stood the " god-like " Webster, a very clayey divinity, with a distinct penchant for letting Great Britain off easily. It is not necessary to follow here in their details the discussions of the Mosquito question in 1851 and 1852; it will suffice to say that if Webster could have had his way the settlement arrived at would have left the Mosquito protectorate almost intact, though erecting Greytown into a free port.[25] But Nicaragua, by this time distinctly peevish

[25] See the Webster-Crampton project in *British Parliamentary Papers*, 1856, LX, 155-158.

at the not too militant attitude of the United States, refused to have anything to do with any such arrangement, and it was left for the administration of Franklin Pierce to take up the whole question anew.

Before turning to the Pierce administration, and its handling of the Central American question, there is another phase of the problem in the days of Whig ascendancy which demands consideration. This is the discussion raised by the proclamation of the Bay Islands colony by Great Britain in March, 1852.

Since the year 1838, when the Bay Islands had first been permanently occupied by Great Britain, no steps had been taken to transform *de facto* possession into legal sovereignty. Indeed, the British government seems actually to have discouraged settlement there.[26] But petitions from the inhabitants thereof, praying for a more regular status, frequently reached London, and the Derby ministry which came into office in 1852, found it expedient to pay heed to these petitions. So mild and forbearing had been the attitude of Mr. Clayton and still more of Mr. Webster, that it probably seemed clear to the British ministry that no great opposition would arise in the United States to any action that might be taken. Moreover, a case could be easily made out for the theory that the Bay Islands were not included in the terms of the Clayton-Bulwer treaty. The exchange of notes between the two negotiators, it will be remembered, had exempted Belize and its dependencies (" the

[26] London, P. R. O., C. O., Honduras, vol. 78, no. 111, April 14, 1851.

small islands which may be called its dependencies," in Clayton's language), from the operation of the treaty. The Bay Islands had been governed from Belize. Why did they not come within the meaning of the interpretative clause just referred to? And might not the possession of these islands be useful in the future, in case a canal were actually constructed? Acting, in all probability, on such considerations, the Derby ministry, by a royal proclamation of March 20, 1852, declared that Ruatan, Bonacca, and four neighboring islands were erected into the British " Colony of the Bay Islands." At first, this step does not seem to have been noticed in the United States. In the press I can find no reference to the matter until the end of 1852, nor is there any evidence that it was brought up in the first session of the 32nd Congress. A presidential election was impending, and the thoughts of the American people were apparently centered upon matters nearer home. But once the election was over, the aspect of affairs began to change. The Democrats, the friends of the Monroe Doctrine, and the party less favorably disposed toward Great Britain, had been swept into power. And before the actual advent, before the inauguration of Franklin Pierce, they opened fire upon what was doubtless considered as the emollient foreign policy of the Whig administration.[27]

[27] In the *Democratic Review,* in December, 1852, appeared a truly ferocious article on the subject of the Bay Islands, written by (Shall we call him the apostate?) Ephraim George Squier, who may be assumed to have been far from happy at the policy of the administration which had sent him to Central America, and permitted him to combine ethnology and diplomacy in his

The first move was a call for information with regard to the " new British colony in Central America," along with a request to know what measures, if any, had been taken by the Executive to prevent the violation of that provision of the Clayton-Bulwer treaty which forbade either party to colonize any part of Central America.[28] The President, replying, declared that the State Department had no information on the subject, but sent to the Senate the Palmerston declaration concerning Belize, and the Clayton-Bulwer notes exchanged with regard to it. At once a debate arose with regard to the whole question of British dominion in Central America. Lewis Cass, the introducer of the resolution, and not a few other Democrats, now declared that they would never have voted for the Clayton-Bulwer treaty if they had not believed that its effect would be to banish all British influence from Central America.[29] On the other hand, more than one Senator on the Whig side flatly denied that it had ever been understood that the treaty included British Honduras, and Hale of New Hampshire went so far as to say that the subject was never mentioned.[30] In this debate the Monroe Doctrine hardly came in for explicit mention at all, but it is obvious that its principles, broadly interpreted, if you will, lay behind the complaints and criticisms of the Democrats.

---

activities. Squier naturally found that the Monroe Doctrine had been egregiously violated. His article was the signal for further attacks in the Democratic press. When Congress met, the opposition to the inactivity of the administration naturally found voice there.

[28] *Cong. Globe,* 32nd Cong., 2nd Sess., p. 158.

[29] *Ibid.,* p. 237. See as well Downs's speech, p. 268.

[30] See *ibid.,* pp. 248, 270.

And before long this was to be made abundantly clear. For contemporaneously with the debate on the treaty went another discussion on the resolution introduced by Cass on January 3, calling upon the Senate to affirm the pronouncement of 1823. This resolution, unlike that of Senator Allen, six years before, got squarely before the Senate, and on it there took place one of the most notable discussions which has ever taken place in Congress on the subject of Monroe's famous declaration.[31]

The most important speech made in favor of the resolution was undoubtedly that made by Lewis Cass himself. He began by the citation of the Monroe message, and the Polk reaffirmation of it. He quoted Monroe's message of 1824 as declaring that European powers had appeared to acquiesce in the principles laid down the year before.[32] He called attention to the recent

[31] Cass's motion read as follows: (*Ibid.*, App., p. 90).

"Be it resolved: That the United States do hereby declare that the 'American continents by the free and independent condition which they have assumed and maintained are henceforth not to be considered as subjects for further colonization by any European Power.' And while 'existing rights should be respected' and will be by the United States they owe it to their own 'safety and interest' 'to announce as they now do, that no further European colony or dominion shall with their consent be placed or established on any part of the North American continent.' And should the attempt be made they thus deliberately declare that it will be viewed as an act originating in motives regardless of 'their interests and safety' and which will leave them free to adopt such measures as an independent nation may justly adopt in defense of its rights and its honor."

[32] There was no real foundation for this statement, unless Canning's views with regard to intervention in Latin America may be so regarded. See my earlier work, pp. 225-227.

instances in which those principles had been violated, and to the Guizot balance of power speech of 1845. The nations of the Old World, he contended, needed to be reminded of the doctrines which had been laid down nearly thirty years before, and which they had lately shown evidences of disregarding. The British action in the case of the Bay Islands, the intrigues of the French in Mexico (of which more later), demonstrated that the time had come to reiterate a point of view which public sentiment, " with almost unequaled unanimity," approved. And to give final authority to that point of view, it was not enough that it should have been enunciated and reiterated by the Executive. It was necessary that the representatives of the people should announce their adhesion to it. No one could doubt that the principles laid down by Monroe were valid. They were increasingly valid, as time had developed the strength of the United States, and increased the disparity between its interests and those of Europe. The moment had come to assume the full responsibility for such principles in the face of the world.[33]

The point of view thus expressed by Cass was naturally challenged. In general the arguments which the opponents of the resolution presented had to do, as was the case in the Yucatan debate, with the inexpediency of asserting general principles of action, and with the wisdom of judging each specific case on its merits. Such, for example, was the view of Senator Butler of South Carolina, the follower of the now deceased Cal-

[33] *Cong. Globe,* 32nd Cong., 2nd Sess., App. 90-95.

houn,[34] of Mason of Virginia,[35] and of Dawson of Georgia.[36] But the most striking speech voicing this objection was made by a relative newcomer in the Senate, on the Whig side, and by one who, a decade later, was as Secretary of State to be confronted by the most palpable and dangerous violation of the Monroe Doctrine in all American history. The point of view of William H. Seward in this great debate of 1853 deserves more than a merely passing mention. Seward began by relating the principles of the Cass resolution to the career of John Quincy Adams, whom he had long admired, and whose follower, in a sense, he was. He declared that out of respect to the memory of that illustrious man he would vote for the proposals. But he deplored the manner in which they had been brought into the debate, and declared that the issue had been raised at the wrong time, toward the close of a crowded short session, and in the wrong way, since it might embarrass the administration soon to come into office. He declared, too, that the resolutions not only had been advanced without reference to the Foreign Relations Committee, but were in opposition to its " deliberate judgment," and that they could not possibly secure a majority " either in the Senate, or in the Congress, or in the country." " The principles involved," he went on, " have become a tradition among the American people, and on acknowledged occasions they would act upon them vigorously and with unanimity. On the other

34 *Ibid.*, p. 96.
35 *Ibid.*, p. 100.
36 *Ibid.*, p. 134.

hand, the Americans are a practical people, engrossed with actual business affairs; and they will not act upon abstract principles, however approved, unless there be a necessity, or at least an occasion." No such occasion, he maintained, existed at the time. The case of the Bay Islands came under the Clayton-Bulwer treaty, and ought to be argued on the basis of the treaty. The danger from France existed only in the newspapers. " The alarms raised by the Senator from Michigan pass by me like the idle winds. The Monroe Doctrine was a right one—the policy was a right one, not because it would require to be enforced by arms, but because it was well-timed. It was the result of a sagacious discovery of the tendency of the age. It will prevail if you affirm it. It will equally prevail if you neglect to affirm it hereafter as you have refused to do here-to-fore. As a practical question it has ceased to be. It is obsolete. You are already the great Continental Power of America." [37] Language such as this shows clearly that though Seward was ready to vote for the Cass resolution, he had no faith in the efficacy of asserting an abstract principle. This view, by no means original with him, he was to reiterate in later debates, and to carry into the State Department in 1861.

A point much discussed in the Senate debate on the Cass resolution was as to whether or not President Monroe intended to lay down principles of universal application. This question, though not of much practical importance, ought certainly to interest the historian.

[37] *Ibid.,* p. 126.

The case in favor of such a view was stated by Cass, and amplified by others. The Senator from Michigan called attention in particular to the general language of the non-colonization clause, and to the words which it contained, " as a principle in which the rights of the United States are involved." He called attention to the reiteration of the non-intervention paragraphs in the warning against European intervention in the message of 1824, at a time when the danger had passed.[38] He cited the general language used by Jefferson in his famous letter of October 24, 1823, to the President. He pointed out the instructions of Clay to Poinsett,[39] urging the validity of the principles of the original declaration. To all these Soulé of Louisiana added the Adams message to Congress of March 15, 1826, stating the full case for the non-colonization principle. But there were those who took a contrary view, and who even denied the right and the purpose of President Monroe to lay down principles of universal application. " I have yet to learn," exclaimed Badger of North Carolina, " that Mr. Monroe was anything more than a President of the United States. Mr. Monroe was not what Louis XIV or Napoleon claimed for themselves with regard to France—the State. He was not the embodiment or representative of the whole powers of the American people. He was not the nation. I know of no authority that he had, by any declaration of his, to bind us and our posterity to maintain a particular course of policy

[38] *Ibid.*, p. 124.
[39] See my earlier work, p. 198.

forever, or for any length of time." [40]   And Butler of
South Carolina, in an able speech, as well as Mason of
Virginia, set forth the view earlier stated by Calhoun
that the Monroe message had reference to a specific contingency, and was not intended to lay down general
principles.

As to the question which of these views is the more
accurate one, I have already had something to say in
another place. So far as Monroe was concerned, it
would seem as if he were thinking, in both the messages
of 1823 and 1824, of an immediate danger; the whole
phraseology of the documents strongly enforces that
view. But Adams, practical statesman, but also much
attached, in his thinking, to general principles, intended
something different, when he enunciated the non-colonization doctrine, and sought to establish general formulae. His point of view was not accepted; the dogmas
for which he contended gained no immediate and certainly no general acceptance, but dogmas they were
meant to be. Cass and his supporters could rightly cite
some of the statesmen of the past as believing in the
general principles which they were sponsoring. It does
seem true, moreover, that by 1852 these principles had
been gaining in their hold on the popular mind. They
were not as yet by any means accepted without demur,
but the tone of the debate reveals far less opposition to
them than was the case in 1848. Even those who opposed the Cass resolution were inclined to pay lip-service to the general conception involved. Butler, for

[40] *Cong. Globe,* 32nd Cong., 2nd Sess., App. p. 176.

example, spoke of " doctrines which we ought to maintain, perhaps, without admonishing the world as to them." [41] Badger cautiously declared that he might " go for the Monroe Doctrine altogether," but " not because it is the Monroe Doctrine, but because, upon examination of it, I believe it to be right, proper, and expedient," [42] and Seward, as we have seen, for all his criticism, affirmed his willingness to vote in the affirmative.

There is another aspect of the debate on the Cass resolution which is well worth noting. In it we hear for the first time of the *Monroe Doctrine*. In earlier discussions the references are invariably to the " principles " of Mr. Monroe, or to " the Monroe declaration." " The dignified appellation" now given to the great pronouncement of 1823 was, so Douglas states in a speech of this period, one only very recently brought forward.[43] Whence it came it appears impossible to say. It appears in the newspaper comment on the Cass resolution, as well as in the discussions in the Senate. Whatever its origins, the phrase stuck. It becomes not only common, but practically universal, from this time forward, as the term by which to describe the growing American dogma.

The indignation at British action in the Bay Islands, expressed in Congress and in the press, was no mere ebullition of feeling. For the responsible committee of the Senate, that on Foreign Relations, and the new administration itself reflected precisely the same view. The Senate committee, as a result of the communications

[41] *Ibid.*, p. 97.
[42] *Ibid.*, p. 176.
[43] *Ibid.*, p. 170.

of President Fillmore in January, 1853, took the whole subject under consideration. It came not only to the conclusion that the proclamation of the Bay Islands colony was a distinct breach of the Clayton-Bulwer treaty, but it also declared with regard to Belize that, while it was not prepared to say that the United States could challenge the rights acquired by Great Britain under the treaties with Spain, there could be no justification whatsoever for the extension of the limits of the settlements therein provided for, or for any enlargement or change in the character of those settlements. And it added that any permanent establishments by Great Britain must necessarily excite concern, and if persisted in, "lead to consequences of the most unpleasant character." [44] As for the Pierce administration, it assumed from the beginning a stand consistent with the Democratic point of view, if it may be so called, on the matters in dispute. The incoming President's inaugural alluded to European colonial establishments, though only in a single sentence, and the first message to Congress took the same view. [45] The instructions drawn up by Marcy for Buchanan, July 2, 1853, who was now to proceed as ambassador to London, proceeded on the distinct assumption that the object to be attained was the withdrawal of the Mosquito protectorate, and the re-

[44] S. Reports, 32nd Cong., 2nd Sess., Doc. No. 407, p. 17.

[45] "The rights, security, and repose of this Confederacy reject the idea of interference or colonization on this side of the ocean by any foreign power beyond present jurisdiction as utterly inadmissible." Richardson *Messages*, v, 200.

striction of British rights in Belize.[46] An issue had thus been posed between the government at Washington and the government of London on the line of the principles of 1823.

There followed long negotiations, extending over the course of the administration of President Pierce, and indeed even further. Into these negotiations, in their details, it is not necessary to go. I shall call attention only to those aspects of them which have a direct relationship to the Monroe Doctrine, ignoring the ingenious and complicated arguments brought forward by both sides in attempting to construe the Clayton-Bulwer treaty, and to fit it to their own view of the situation. Broadly speaking, it may be said that the attitude of the British government was not wholly unyielding. It was faced with an increasingly difficult situation in Europe, for the Crimean War was impending, during 1853, and

[46] 34th Cong., 1st Sess., H. Exec. Doc. No. 1, p. 44. Instructions of July 2, 1853.

" The object which it is to be hoped you may be able to accomplish is to induce Great Britain to withdraw from all control over the territories and islands of Central America, and, if possible, over the Belize also, and to abstain from intermeddling with the political affairs of the governments in that region of the world. This object is the more earnestly desired by the United States, as it is apparent that the tendency of events in that quarter is to give a foothold to British power there, in contravention of the policy which this government is resolved to sustain."

In instructions two months later, Marcy declared further that any assertion by the British of full sovereignty over Belize would be contested by the United States as " an infringement of the Monroe Doctrine—a doctrine which it is the policy of the President to maintain." (*Ibid.*, p. 50.)

actually broke out before the close of the year. The British policy was rather to let the negotiations drag, than sharply to reply to American insistence; at the same time there was never a moment, so far as can be ascertained from the correspondence, when there was any possibility of a complete acceptance of the American demands. The Bay Islands and the Mosquito Coast were debatable matters; but in view of the Clayton-Bulwer exchange of notes with regard to Belize, it was hardly to be expected that the British government would permit its rights in Belize to be called into question under the treaty, and still less likely that it would permit a vague general principle held by the United States to determine its course of action.

Yet an attempt was made by Buchanan to inject the Monroe Doctrine directly into the negotiations. In an able memorandum of January 6, 1854, a memorandum, for the most part, devoted to close historical argument, and not to loose assertion, he penned the following sentences, " Mr. Monroe, one of our wisest and most discreet Presidents, announced in a public message to Congress, in December, 1823, that ' the American continents, by the free and independent condition which they have assumed and maintained, are henceforth not to be considered subjects for future colonization by any European powers.' This declaration has since been known throughout the world as the ' Monroe Doctrine,' and has received the public and official sanction of subsequent Presidents as well as of a very large majority of the American people. Whilst this doctrine will be maintained," he continued, " whenever in the opinion of

Congress the peace and safety of the United States shall require it, yet, to have acted upon it in Central America might have brought us into collision with Great Britain, an event always to be deprecated, and, if possible, avoided." [47]

Buchanan's statement is the first time that the Monroe Doctrine under its own name had ever been introduced into a diplomatic controversy. As a diplomatic principle, it had been brought forward by Richard Rush in the Oregon negotiations of 1824, and on that occasion flatly challenged by Great Britain.[48] And now, cited by its new name, it was to be challenged again. In an answering memorandum, long delayed, and dated May 2, 1854, Lord Clarendon, the British Foreign Secretary, declared that " with regard to the doctrine laid down by President Monroe in 1823, concerning future colonization of the American continent by European states, it could be viewed only as the dictum of the distinguished personage who announced it, and not as an international axiom which ought to regulate the conduct of European states." [49] This flat denial of the validity of the Monroe dogma as of binding force in international relations was one which the American minister could hardly refute. But, in a new and extremely careful

[47] *Ibid.,* p. 63. See also Moore's *Digest,* III, 159.

It does not appear that in thus introducing the President's message into the negotiations Buchanan acted upon instructions, the only reference to the Monroe Doctrine in Marcy's communications to the minister being that cited above.

[48] See my earlier work, p. 38.

[49] 34th Cong., 1st Sess., H. Exec. Doc. No. 1, p. 83, and see also Moore, *Digest,* III, 162.

16

memorandum of July 22, 1854, Buchanan made such answer as he could to the observation of Lord Clarendon. He declared that, though the message had not been formally sanctioned by Congress, it was certainly not " a mere dictum of its distinguished author." It was greeted with enthusiastic approbation, when first announced, and had, when reiterated, been hailed on every occasion " with unmistakable indications of public approbation." " If the occasion required," he added, " Mr. Buchanan would cheerfully undertake the task of justifying the wisdom and sound policy of the Monroe doctrine, in reference to the nations of Europe, as well as to those of the American Continent." Finally, the fact that the United States rested its case, in the main, on the Clayton-Bulwer treaty, must not be taken as an indication that it did not regard the principles of 1823 as valid, or would not eventually have interfered, in obedience to them.[50]

With this interesting exchange of views, which, however, advanced not a whit the solution of the Central American question, the Monroe Doctrine disappears for some time from the negotiations. However popular as a rallying cry in the United States, however sound as a principle of American diplomatic action, the time had very obviously not yet come when it could be brought forward as a tenet which other powers were bound to accept as the basis of an international discussion. This was clearly realized both at Washington and by Buchanan in London, to judge from the silence with

[50] 34th Cong., 1st Sess., H. Exec. Doc. No. 1, p. 109, and Buchanan, *Works,* IX, 236.

regard to the principles of 1823 which was observed from this time on, for some years to come.

Despite the insistence of the administration, in theory, on the withdrawal of the British from Central America, its actual policy was certainly not as vigorous as might have been expected from the representatives of the militant democracy. Internationally speaking, the posture of affairs was distinctly favorable to putting pressure on Great Britain while she was engaged in the Crimean War, but no such pressure was applied. It may well be that Pierce and his advisors were more concerned with the disastrous controversy aroused by the Kansas-Nebraska bill and the events which followed it; at any rate, unqualified devotion to the principles of 1823 seems to have been lacking. And yet, at the same time, relations with Great Britain grew distinctly worse as 1854 dragged on, and as 1855 went by. In Central America American intrigues irritated British susceptibilities. The American minister, Borland, was aiming at bringing the whole region under American dominion, and Squier, now a private citizen, appeared upon the scene, with objects in view which could hardly fail to appear sinister to the British government. The bombardment of Greytown by the American captain, Hollins, as a result of a quarrel that had arisen between the municipality and the Accessory Transit Company, the American concern engaged in transportation across Nicaragua, was an act of violence that awakened widespread condemnation in Great Britain, and led to a demand for its disavowal which was refused by President Pierce, and left the situation still more tense. These years, moreover,

were the years of the filibusters. In 1854, a movement
organized by Colonel Kinney of Philadelphia for " the
colonization " of Nicaragua aroused natural suspicions
of sinister intent. In 1855 came the famous expedition
of William Walker, the most audacious piece of unofficial imperialism in the history of American foreign
politics. In the meantime the conciliatory Aberdeen had
been succeeded as Prime Minister of Great Britain by
the not temperamentally conciliatory Palmerston; and
an attempt to reopen the discussions with Great Britain
in August, 1855, appeared to offer very little hope of a
favorable settlement. New difficulties appeared in the
way of amicable relations between the two countries.
The British minister, Crampton, in violation of international law, had encouraged enlistments in the British
forces for the Crimean War within the limits of the
United States, and British naval armaments had been
increased in the American waters. All in all, the situation was becoming " distinctly squally," as Buchanan put
it, in the last months of 1855.[51]

And now broke out, both at Washington and London,
new debates on the Central American question, after
more than two years of quietude. The President's message of December, 1855, again threw the whole matter
into the field of public discussion, alluding as it did to
the differences of viewpoint which still existed between
the two governments, and the dangers which those differences might breed. In the Senate the whole subject
was gone over in great detail. There was, by now, how-

[51] *Ibid.*, p. 446.

ever, a very distinct unanimity of opinion with regard to the matter. The partisan tone which is to be remarked in the debates of 1853 was wholly absent. With one voice Senators denounced the ambition of Britain and demanded the application of the Clayton-Bulwer treaty.

The application of the Clayton-Bulwer treaty! The emphasis should be put upon this phrase, for the debates of the turn of the year 1855-56 find the Monroe Doctrine figuring in a distinctly subordinate place. There was something like general recognition of the fact that it was far easier to invoke a solemn diplomatic instrument, even an ambiguous instrument, in the support of the viewpoint of the United States than it was to recur to general principles. This attitude had its practical expression, not only in the subordinate place given to the message of 1823, but in the slight attention that was paid to Belize in the debates themselves. The Bay Islands and the Mosquito Coast came within the scope of the Convention of 1850, but the expulsion of the British from Belize could only be argued on general grounds. For the most part, therefore, it was not argued at all.

But it must not be imagined that, because the Monroe Doctrine was relegated to a secondary place, it was barely mentioned. Lewis Cass, as devoted as ever to the viewpoint he had expressed nearly three years before, still maintained that it ought to be given the sanction of a congressional declaration, and even made all over again a good part of the speech which he had then delivered.[52] He even claimed, preposterously enough,

[52] *Cong. Globe,* 34th Cong., 1st Sess., App., pp. 69-70.

that the principle of the Doctrine had never been challenged, and that Lord Clarendon, in the communication to Buchanan already quoted, made " no attempt to avoid " it. Clayton and Seward, who had both spoken in the debates of '53, declared their willingness to accept the Doctrine in this instance, if the attempt to base American rights on the treaty should fail, though Clayton added what he had said more than once before, that he did not believe a majority could be secured for any such declaration in that or any other Congress.[53]

[53] *Cong. Globe,* 34th Cong., 1st Sess., p. 108.

" In reference to this particular territory, I would not hesitate as one Senator to assert the Monroe Doctrine, and to maintain it by my votes; but do I expect to be sustained in that, or does any other man here expect to be sustained in such a vote by both branches of Congress? Whenever the attempt has been made to assert the Monroe Doctrine in either branch of Congress it has failed. The present Democratic party came into power after the debate on the Panama mission on the utter abnegation of the whole doctrine, and stood upon Washington's doctrine of non-intervention. It is a principle which, whether it be right or wrong, and I am not standing here today to discuss its propriety—you cannot prevail on a majority, and I will venture to say you cannot prevail on a third of either House of Congress to sustain."

Clayton's statement that the Democratic attitude in the Panama debates was the abnegation of the Doctrine is, of course, a partisan exaggeration. In reality, foes of the administration argued and voted merely against the transformation of Monroe's principles into an alliance with Latin American states. But the Delawarean's statement that not a third of either house of Congress would vote to accept the Doctrine in terms is decidedly interesting. Clayton's explanation of his statement is to be found in *ibid.,* App., p. 441. He denied being an advocate of the Doctrine, and declared that he meant only that, *in this*

There was, however, still much distrust of the wisdom of basing American foreign policy upon general principles. Wilson of Massachusetts, an old Whig, after announcing his willingness to vote for the Doctrine, declared that until such action was taken, " the less our statesmen at home and diplomats abroad say about it, the better." [54] Butler of South Carolina, who had figured in the debates of 1853, again declared against a commitment to a formula. " Woe! woe! to the coward, That ever he was born, Who seized not the sword, Before he blew the horn." [55] And Bell of Tennessee, in a powerful speech, declared that it was useless to make a struggle for " exclusive dominion " in the New World, and that the time had certainly not come to " coerce England into submission " to the principles of 1823.[56] He also called attention to the transformation that was taking place in the spirit behind Monroe's utterance. Originally a shield of defense to the republics of Spanish America, it was becoming the means by which the way was prepared for the onward march of American imperialism, and, as Bell declared, this " perversion " of it had lost us the confidence of the republics of the New World.

The debates of 1855 called forth one of the most interesting efforts ever made to check the growing popu-

specific case, as applied to Central America, he would vote for the Doctrine, rather than see a wrong go unredressed.

For Seward's view, see Cong. Globe, 34th Cong., 1st Sess., p. 110.

[54] Ibid., App., p. 87.

[55] Cong. Globe, 34th Cong., 1st Sess., p. 395.

[56] Ibid., App., p. 113.

larity of the new American dogma. In the April number of the *North American Review* in 1856, appeared
anonymously the first article in any American periodical
to bear the title, " The Monroe Doctrine," and one of
the ablest attempts to minimize the importance of the
great American shibboleth.[57] Beginning with an interesting summary of the circumstances which produced
the message of 1823, the author passes on to indicate
the temporary and restricted character of the propositions therein laid down. He points out that they had
never been sanctioned by Congress; he maintains, as
had some members of the Senate in the debates of '26,
that the paragraphs on Spanish America were directed
against an immediate danger, and " ceased to be of any
force, even as a presidential recommendation, so soon
as the crisis which called it forth had passed." [58] In
proof of the similarly restricted character of the non-
colonization principle he quotes the language of Adams
at the time of the Panama mission, when it was proposed
that each nation should " guard, by its own means,"
against the establishment of European colonies within
its borders. He calls the attention of his readers to the
significant statement in Clay's instructions to Poinsett,
that of all countries which have an interest in the principle, " that of the United States has probably the
least." He declares, quoting from the same source, that
the non-colonization dogma applied to the establishment
of new settlements " founded on priority of discovery
or occupation," but not " to purchase, treaty, or lawful

[57] *North American Review,* vol. 82, pp. 478ff.
[58] *Ibid.,* p. 489.

conquest," cites the Buchanan resolution of 1826 as an additional proof of the little enthusiasm of the people of the United States at the time for the maintenance of the general conception laid down by Monroe, and declares, in this case erroneously, that the principle was not insisted on by Rush at the time.[59] He closes by declaring that the principles now advocated in the name of the Monroe Doctrine " are wholly unhistorical, and without foundation in any legitimate interpretation of his guarded language. It is therefore unjust to the memory of that distinguished man to associate his honored name with principles which he never approved, and from which his cautious nature would have been among the first to shrink." [60]

This able argument against the Monroe Doctrine contains much that is worth considering. It is, as I have already observed, true that the purpose of Monroe was in all probability immediate rather than otherwise, and it is true, too, that the language of Clay and Adams in 1825 and 1826 seemed to restrict the purport of the non-colonization principle. Yet Adams himself had given his approval to Polk's reenunciation of the dogma in 1845, and this effectually explodes the notion that that pronouncement was contrary to his own conceptions of policy. He had declared at the time that " the rights and interests of the United States were involved." He

[59] *Ibid.*, pp. 507-8. The fact is that, while Rush did not press the principle immediately after its enunciation, he did formally declare it in the negotiations of the summer of 1824. See my previous work, p. 22.

[60] *North American Review*, vol. 82, p. 512.

might, or might not, have defended the use of the Doctrine in the case of Yucatan, but he could hardly have denied its strict applicability to the case of the Bay Islands. Though the Monroe Doctrine was, in the period we are discussing, undoubtedly undergoing transformation and expansion, though it was sustained by many, as we shall soon see, as a principle which kept the way open for the unhampered intervention of the United States in Latin American affairs, and for the march of American "imperialism," it must be freely admitted that, in the controversy which we are now examining, it was distinctly applicable, even by a conservative interpretation. The assailant of the Doctrine in the *North American Review* attempts to prove a little too much. At the same time, the warning that he sounds against the invocation of the principles of 1823 to cover cases which they were never intended to cover was not entirely superfluous, and is certainly, from his own point of view, vindicated by the developments of the years. It is sober truth to declare today that under the authority of Monroe many things have been done which neither he nor Adams would have sanctioned, and controversies started which they might have avoided.

But to return to the Central American controversy. The debates of '55, one might perhaps have expected, would have only increased the tension of an already strained situation. As a matter of fact, they produced an exactly contrary effect. With the turn of the year a distinct popular reaction in Great Britain made the situation favorable to the United States. As has so often happened in the history of Anglo-American relations, a considerable body of British public opinion rallied in behalf of a policy that would leave uninterrupted the friendly relationship of the two nations. In the debates which followed on the opening of Parliament in 1856, the strong trend of the sentiments expressed was in favor of a reasonable settlement of the questions of Central America. In the main these debates have no special interest for the student of the Monroe Doctrine, and they turned very little on the principles of 1823. But it is interesting to note that, in the course of them, one very important political personage, who added his voice to that of other speakers in behalf of amicable relations, did challenge the Monroe Doctrine in explicit terms. This personage was none other than Benjamin Disraeli. Alluding to the introduction of the subject by Buchanan, the future premier continued as follows, " Now, sir, the Monroe Doctrine is one which, with great respect to the Government of the United States, is not, in my opinion, suited to the age in which we live. The increase in the means of communication between Europe and America have made one great family of the countries of the world; and that system of government, which, instead of enlarging would restrict the relations between those two quarters of the globe, is a system which is not adapted to this age." The British government, Disraeli declared, should seek to impress upon the United States that " instead of vaunting that they will build their greatness on the Monroe Doctrine, which is the doctrine of isolation, they should seek to attain it by deferring to the public law of Europe, and by allowing their destiny to be regulated by the same high principles of policy which all the European communities that have a political system have invariably recognized."[61] Thus to Canning and Chateaubriand, Metternich and Alexander, Guizot and Lord Clarendon, may be added one more distinguished European who in terms repudiated the principles connected with the name of Monroe.

In view, however, of the trend of British sentiment, the year 1856 saw a very earnest effort to settle the outstanding difficulties with the United States. Buchanan had by this time been succeeded by Dallas, and the result of new negotiations bears the name of the Dallas-Clarendon convention, signed October 17, 1856. This convention provided for the settlement of the boundaries of Belize by direct agreement between Guatemala and Great Britain, for the incorporation of the Mosquito territory within the limits of Nicaragua, for the establishment of Greytown as a free port, with indemnity to the Indians, and for the recognition of the Bay Islands as a part of the republic of Honduras, in conformity with a treaty just negotiated by Clarendon with Herran, the Honduranean minister.

These terms fell short of what the most ardent Monrovians might have desired or demanded. They fell short of the terms first put forward by the United States, which demanded the withdrawal of the British from that part of Belize south of the Sarstoon. But they were satisfactory enough to meet the approval of

[61] Hansard, *Parliamentary Debates,* 3rd Series, CXLII, cols. 1511 and 1513, June 16, 1856.

President Pierce, who recommended them to the favorable consideration of the Senate in his message of December, 1856. It may be that the passing of the Presidential campaign had something to do with this noble restraint. Cynics have sometimes suggested that the imminence of an election does not make for a conciliatory tone in matters diplomatic, and Pierce had, earlier in the year, obviously been anxious for renomination. But his own relative mildness was not echoed without reserve in the Senate. That body amended the instrument. Its chief disapproval was expressed with regard to the stipulations of the Bay Islands. There was strong feeling against any reference, in a treaty with Great Britain, to the agreement for their restoration, and this provision was struck out, and another substituted by which the two parties agreed to recognize and respect those islands, as part of the republic of Honduras. With regard to Belize, however, no objection was made, so that, despite its pitching its tone a little higher than President Pierce, the Senate cannot be said to have shown an unadulterated devotion to Monroeism, but rather adhered to the safe ground of the Clayton-Bulwer treaty.

But its action, taken early in Buchanan's administration, threw the whole problem back for negotiation, and the new President and his Secretary of State, none other than Lewis Cass, were warm Monrovians. The question of Belize was again introduced into the discussion, and the British-Honduranean treaty, which made the Bay Islands a free state under Honduranean sovereignty, was declared entirely unacceptable. Indeed the new administration showed a strong desire for the abrogation of the Clayton-Bulwer treaty, a step which would free its hands with regard to the acquisition of territory in Central America, dissolve the partnership with regard to an inter-oceanic canal, and amount to a direct challenge to Britain to compete for exclusive influence in that part of the world with the United States.

This attitude only made the British government more anxious for a settlement, and at the end of 1857, it sent out Sir William Gore Ouseley, of La Platan fame, to settle the whole matter by direct negotiation with the various states concerned. Ouseley proved, however, but a maladroit diplomat, as he had twelve years before at Buenos Ayres, and, as the months dragged on, the Central American question still remained unliquidated. It is not necessary here to follow the course of the negotiations nor of those which were conducted contemporaneously at Washington. As time went on, the American government began to gravitate toward a settlement, rather than abrogation, especially after it learned that in the case of the latter the British intended to retain Honduras and the Bay Islands. The mission confided to the incompetent Ouseley was handed over to Wyke, the British minister, and pushed to a satisfactory conclusion. By a series of treaties the various disputes were liquidated, the frontiers of Belize defined in accordance with the actual facts of the situation, leaving the British the territory as far south as the Sarstoon, the Bay Islands handed back to Honduras without inadmissible conditions, and the Mosquito Indians recognized as under the sovereignty of Nicaragua and Honduras, and a small annuity assured to them, and Greytown made a free port. This settlement received the approval of the American government, and in his message of 1860 President Buchanan declared his complete satisfaction at the outcome of the Central American question.[62]

Though further negotiations with regard to the Mosquito question were to take place, at a much later period, and though the final incorporation of the Indian territory into the republic of Nicaragua was not to be consummated until 1894, the negotiation of the treaty of 1860 may be said to mark the end of the matter, as a vexing subject of dispute between Great Britain and the United States.

How shall we sum up the part played by the Monroe Doctrine in the diplomatic controversy which we have just analyzed? In one sense, that part was considerable. There can be no question that the sensitiveness of the American people to encroachments or expansion by European powers in the New World had greatly increased in the period which we have had under review, and that the appeal to Monroe's principles had a considerable effect in arousing public interest with regard to the whole matter. Equally true is it that the very prolongation of this discussion increased the popularity of the Doctrine, and made it more widely known. And, furthermore, it is worth recalling that the Central American controversy is the first diplomatic contro-

<hr>

[62] Richardson, *Messages,* V. p. 639-640.

versy in which the famous declaration of 1823 was appealed to by name by those in authority, and in which
its principles were directly put forward in negotiation
as binding on another nation.

But, on the other hand, certain facts diminishing the
importance of the Doctrine are equally clear. In the
first place, it is to be noted that, speaking broadly,
in the actual negotiations as distinguished from political
debate, appeal was made, not to the Doctrine itself, but
to the Clayton-Bulwer treaty. The extension of British
territorial rights in Belize was surely as much a violation
of the American dogma, as the seizure of the Bay Islands or the protectorate over the Mosquitoes. It could
not, however, be challenged under the Clayton-Bulwer
treaty. It played, therefore, a wholly subordinate rôle
in the discussion, and the whole controversy was liquidated on terms which left the British secure for the
future. A postal convention of 1860 with Great Britain,
having regard to the territory in question, describes it
as a British colony.[63] And it may not be amiss here to
observe that in 1862 the British government formally
fixed its status as such, without a word of protest, or
even of notice, on the part of the government of the
United States.[64] The appeal to dogma, though occasionally made, in the long controversy with Great Britain
with regard to Central America, was recognized to be
futile. The single attempt to introduce the Monroe Doctrine into the negotiations was a feeble one, as made by
Buchanan, and it was not based upon instructions from

[63] M. W. Williams, *op. cit.*, p. 284.
[64] *Ibid.*, p. 272.

Washington. Moreover, this appeal was flatly repudiated by Great Britain. British diplomatic opinion condemned the Doctrine as unjustifiable from every point of view. It repudiated it as an expression of binding principles of international law. It yielded, not to the general theory, but to the American interpretation of an international treaty.

But it might be thought, perhaps, that if the assertion of the Monroe Doctrine was of little utility in our negotiations with Great Britain, it at least enhanced the prestige of the United States in Central America. There is, however, only a measure of support for this view. Guatemala and Costa Rica were, at every stage of the negotiations which we have been examining, rather inclined toward Great Britain than the United States. Though both might have been expected to appeal to the government at Washington against British encroachments, in the one case in Belize, in the other case on the San Juan river, neither ever did so. The reactionary and clerical elements in control in the first of these two states could hardly be expected, perhaps, to view with favor the democratic republic of the North; the dread of America was far greater than the dread of Britain,[65] and Costa Rica, as we have seen, was even ready to discuss the notion of a British protectorate. The alignment of the United States with Nicaragua in the dispute over Greytown only deepened the preference of the Costa Ricans for the Anglo-Saxons on the other side of the

[65] London, P. R. O., F. O., Central America, vol. 82, no. 9, March 13, 1854, and Washington, Dept. of State, Despatches, Nicaragua, vol. 1, no. 11, December 10, 1853.

17

sea, for the Costa Rican government had a boundary dispute with Nicaragua, it will be remembered, as to the San Juan river.

As for the three other little states of Central America, Honduras, hopeful of American influence in the question of the Bay Islands, remained on friendly terms with the government at Washington throughout the period. An anti-American faction gained control in Salvador in 1853. In Nicaragua, which yielded its support so cheerfully to the Monroe Doctrine in the days of George Squier, a change was not long in making itself felt. The Clayton-Bulwer treaty somewhat cooled its enthusiasm. The Webster-Crampton project of 1852, by which an American Secretary of State attempted to prescribe to Nicaragua a settlement agreed upon with the very power against whom aid had been invoked, was still more chilling.[66] In 1853 the Nicaraguan government attempted to settle the Mosquito question directly with Great Britain, a clear sign that it had come to put little faith in the disinterestedness of the American government, and then in 1855 came the filibustering expedition of William Walker. Already, sometime before it took place, statesmen like Douglas had been interpreting the Monroe Doctrine in a sense which implied the future hegemony and the future expansion of the United States in the New World. Now to words were added deeds, and such deeds. It is well enough to say that the activities of William Walker were unofficial. But the power-

[66] Washington, Dept. of State, Nicaragua, vol. 1., no. 5, September 20, 1853. 34th Cong., 1st and 2nd Sess., Exec. Doc. No. 25, pp. 100-101.

lessness or the unwillingness of the American authorities
to prevent the first of his expeditions, and the shameless
recognition of the government which he set up by the
Pierce administration, were not easily excused. The
activities of Walker were nothing less than the ruin of
American influence in Central America. Perhaps the
best illustration of this fact is to be seen, not in the field
of Anglo-American relations, but in the extraordinary
episode connected with the name of Félix Belly.

Belly was a French newspaper man who as early as
1855 became interested in the question of an American
canal.[67] He believed that such a canal might be constructed by private enterprise, and that it ought to be
free and open to the commerce of the world. The principal menace to the building of such a canal on sound
principles he discovered in the aggressive attitude of the
United States, and in the Monroe Doctrine. In a scholarly analysis of the political situation in Central America, published in the *Revue Contemporaine*, June 15,
1856, and entitled " De L'Equilibre du Nouveau
Monde," after alluding to the existing controversy between Great Britain and the United States, he expressed
himself as follows: " For the first time the Monroe
Doctrine is translated into formal acts in opposition to
Europe; the sovereignty of all the New World is
claimed by a conquering republic; pretensions are put
forward which menace at once the independence of
neighboring republics, the autonomy of the Spanish

[67] For a note on his career, see the preface by Ch. Potvin *in*
Félix Belly, *L'Isthme Americain. Notes d'un premier voyage,*
(Bruxelles, 1889), pp. vi-xlii.

race, and the commercial liberty of the globe." [68] Citing
recent diplomatic history, and making great play of the
outrageous activities of William Walker, Belly went on
to declare that the United States " were advancing to
the complete absorption of the New World," and that
Europe must take prompt action to save the little countries of Central America from the " brutally material-
ist " nation of the North.

There is not the slightest sign in the archives of the
Ministère des Affaires Etrangères that Belly received
encouragement from the government of Louis Napoleon; but a person so energetic as he did not need such
encouragement. Not content with verbal denunciation,
in the winter of 1858, he set out upon a purely private
mission to Central America.[69] His success there was
nothing short of phenomenal. Playing upon the fears
of American filibustering, capitalizing the growing dread
of the United States, he proceeded to score a remarkable
diplomatic triumph. He persuaded the Nicaraguan dictator of the moment to set aside the so-called Cass-
Irisarri treaty, which provided for a neutral transit
across the isthmus, and gave the United States the
right to land troops to protect it; he reconciled the Nicaraguan and Costa Rican governments, and brought

[68] Reprinted in Félix Belly. *Percement de L'Isthme de
Panama par le Canal de Nicaragua. Exposé de la Question,*
(Paris, 1858), pp. 121-57, especially p. 122.

[69] Félix Belly. *A travers L'Amérique Centrale. Le Nicaragua
et le Canal Inter-Océanique,* (2 vols., Paris, 1867), vol. II, 117.
See also Belly's articles in *Revue des Deux Mondes* (1860)
XXVIII, 328-68, 597-633, and 865-902.

about a settlement of the long agitated boundary dispute between them; and he signed a contract for the construction of a canal by himself and his associates in Paris. Contemporaneously with the signing of this contract, the Presidents of Costa Rica and Nicaragua, and the Foreign Minister of the latter state, issued to the world an extraordinary manifesto, complaining of the aggressive intentions of the United States, and of the aid which its government lent to filibustering, and ending with a request for the protection of France, Great Britain, and Sardinia.[70]

Very naturally Belly's success and the manifesto by which it was accompanied were received with very little enthusiasm in Washington. Very naturally, too, Lewis Cass sought an immediate explanation from the Comte de Sartiges, and discovered, no doubt to his profound satisfaction, that the French government had had nothing to do with Belly's extraordinary activities in Central America.[71] The enterprising journalist was disavowed by his government, and the episode was virtually closed. Its only aftermath was an interesting despatch from Cass to Lamar, American minister to Nicaragua, in which the traditional principles of American policy in the New World were effectively asserted.[72]

[70] This manifesto is to be found in 35th Cong., 2nd Sess., Exec. Doc. No. 2, pp. 62 *et seq.*

[71] Washington, Dept. of State, Central America, Instructions, June 16, 1858. See also Instructions, Great Britain, November 26, 1858.

[72] 35th Cong., 2nd Sess., Exec. Doc. No. 2, p. 56.

" But the establishment of a political protectorate by any of the powers of Europe, over any of the independent States of this

The Belly incident, as I have already said, is a revealing evidence of the collapse of American influence in
Central America. No such success as was temporarily
his could have been won, except in an atmosphere suf-
fused with apprehension. The United States, at the end
of the fifties, was feared and hated by those whom it
assumed at times to protect.

What was true of Central America, it may be remarked before bringing this chapter to an end was true
of other Latin American nations. The case of Mexico is
so important that I shall deal with it at length in another

---

continent, or in other words, the introduction of a scheme or
policy which would carry with it a right to interfere in their
concerns, is a measure to which the United States have long
since avowed their opposition, and which, should the attempt be
made, they will resist by all the means in their power.

"The reasons for the attitude they have assumed have been
fully promulgated, and are every where well-known. There is
no need upon this occasion to recapitulate them. They are
founded on the political circumstances of the American continent which has interests of its own, disconnected from many of
the questions which are continually presenting themselves in
Europe, concerning the balance of power, and other subjects of
controversy, arising out of the condition of its States, and which
often find their solution or their postponement in war. It is of
paramount importance to the States of this hemisphere that they
should have no entangling union with the powers of the old
world; a connexion which would almost necessarily make them
parties to wars having no interest in them, and which would
often involve them in hostilities with the other American States
contiguous or remote. The years which have passed by since
this principle of separation was first announced by the United
States, have served still more to satisfy the people of this country
of its wisdom and to fortify their resolution to maintain it,
happen what may."

place. But one may briefly note here other evidences of anti-Americanism. The state of New Granada, as we have had occasion to see, had been throughout most of the preceding period distinctly friendly to the government of Washington. Its policy, however, is altered with the late fifties; it ceases to look toward the United States.[73] This was due in part to the aggressive stand taken by the United States at the time of the Panama riots of 1856,[74] and when the Pan-American conception is revived in the sixties, New Granada is found opposing (not advocating, as in 1847) the participation of the United States.[75] More striking still is the attitude of the states further south. In Ecuador the period closes with an effort on the part of that extraordinary figure, Garciá Moreno, to establish a connection with France.[76] The writings of Peruvian and Chilean publi-

[73] J. A. Hoyos, *Les Etats-Unis et la Colombie,* (Paris, 1918), p. 35.

[74] *Ibid.,* pp. 31-34.

[75] E. Quesada, *La Evolución del Panamericanismo,* (Buenos Ayres, 1919), p. 23.

[76] This episode deserves a footnote. Garciá Moreno, poet, professor, journalist, and statesman, was the leader of the Conservative party in Ecuador. As early as 1859, while still out of power, he had made overtures to the French minister, La Trinite, but these overtures had never been received by the government at home. (Paris, Min. des Aff. Etr., Corr. Pol., Ecuador, vol. 5, June 27, 1861. For the account which follows see *ibid.,* and *passim.*) Becoming President in 1861 he sought once more to consolidate his position by an appeal for aid from some European state. He appears first of all to have made overtures simultaneously to both France and Spain, but from the representative of the latter country at Quito he received little encouragement. The French chargé, on the other hand, became

cists bear witness to the fear inspired by the Colossus of the North,[77] and the views that they put forward may have found political expression in the so-called treaty of guarantee of September 15, 1856, by which Chile, Ecua-

---

increasingly enthusiastic. In a series of interviews with the President, and with the precious Flores, who had now returned to Ecuador, and was General-in-Chief, a plan was roughly sketched out. French troops, ostensibly on the way to Tahiti, were to be landed at Guayaquil. The Constitution was to be revised, under their protection, and the people invited to accept the overlordship of the Emperor of the French. To this interesting project, however, the government of Louis Napoleon turned a deaf ear. The isolation and poverty of the country made the idea appear far from exciting. The opposition of Spain or Great Britain was apprehended. The suspicion that the offer to France was the work of a faction, and not of the whole Ecuadorian people, was clearly entertained at Paris. The instructions sent to Fabre, therefore, were distinctly cool in tone. If the nation should declare for France, the " Emperor would take account of this fact to the degree compatible with his interests." (*Ibid.*, October 10, 1861). But it would not be consistent with French dignity " to provoke a demonstration, the outcome of which is uncertain." Projects of territorial acquisition would inspire doubts as to French disinterestedness, and might involve the Emperor in internal quarrels. (*Ibid.*, February 28, 1862.) Such language seems to have put an end of Moreno's solicitations, and indeed, as he became more firmly seated in power, he in all probability became also less desirous of buttressing his position by accepting European tutelage.

[77] Quesada, pp. 16-7. The Chilean Bilbao, writing in 1856, expresses himself as follows: " Look at the empires which pretend to resuscitate the old idea of the domination of the globe: Russia and the United States, the first is very far away; the second is very near; Russia is limiting her warlike operations; the United States are extending theirs every day, in this ' partida de caza ' which they have undertaken against the south; we already see fragments of America fall into the clutches of the Anglo-Saxon boa constrictor, and involved in its coils; yester-

dor, and Peru bound themselves to unite against " expeditions or aggressions with land or naval forces proceeding from abroad," [78] though the sole purpose of this
treaty was certainly not protection against the United
States.[79] At the same time the Argentine jurist Alberdi,
the friend of Pan-Americanism, was pronouncing the
exclusion of the United States from the counsels of

day Texas, after that northern Mexico and the Pacific salute
a new lover; today the advance guard of guerillas scour the
isthmus, and we see Panama, that future Constantinople of
America, hang in suspense, view its destiny in the abyss, and
ask, ' Will there be a south, will there be a north? '.....We
commence to follow the steps of the Colossus, which steadily
advances without fearing anyone, with its diplomacy, with its
spreading cloud of adventurers, with its influence and its growing power, which attracts its neighbors as with a magnet; with
the complications which it creates between our peoples, with
anticipatory treaties, with mediations and protectorates, with its
industry, its marine, its industrial enterprises, lying in wait for
our faults and weariness, taking advantage of our divisions; we
understand this collossus always more impetuous and audacious,
which believes in its right to rule as did imperial Rome, and
which, already infatuated with the long roll of its felicities,
advances like a tide to discharge its waters like a cataract over
the south; we see that this nation, which had always been our
star, menaces the autonomy of America; the Saxon of the North
gathers his forces, unites his efforts, harmonizes the hetero-
geneous elements of his nation to attain the possession of
Olympus, which is the absolute dominion of America."

[78] The text is in Torres Caicedo, *op. cit.*, pp. 242-50. The
relevant article is Article 15.

[79] Anon., *Cuadro Histórico de la Administración Montt*
(Valparaiso, 1861) p. 268. This author declares that it was
nothing more nor less than a pact on the part of the three
governments concerned to maintain themselves in power, and
to prevent revolutionary interests from being set on foot in their
territories.

Latin America.[80] The prestige of the United States, despite the development of the Monroe Doctrine, was, perhaps, never lower in the republics of the South than it was in the decade of the fifties.

[80] For Alberdi's views see W. W. Pierson, "Alberdi's Views on the Monroe Doctrine" *in Hispanic American Historical Review*, III, 362-74, especially 373.

CHAPTER V

The Question of Santo Domingo, 1849-1865

In the negotiations between the British and American governments with regard to Central America, the advantage has been seen to lie quite definitely with the United States. Though Great Britain at no time admitted the principle of the Monroe Doctrine, it must be conceded that in practise her policy was based upon a considerable regard for American susceptibilities. In this instance the principles of 1823 were in a measure applied and consolidated during the period which we have been reviewing.

But the years from 1849 to 1860 are not, in general, years in which the rising American dogma was honored by European governments or by European public opinion. On the contrary, they are years in which European intrigue in the New World was on the increase, and they culminated in the most serious threats to the Monroe Doctrine which have been levelled against it. How far from dead was the spirit of interference may easily be discovered by examining the question of Mexico or the question of Santo Domingo. In both the one case and the other, European diplomacy was constantly active, almost steadily hostile to the United States, and aiming at objects contrary to American interests and American principles; and in both the one case and the other a decade of intrigue is followed by armed intervention with a view to the reestablishment of European influence. The case of Mexico is doubtless the more important, as it is certainly that which has attracted the greater degree of attention from historians; but the relative novelty involved in the study of French and Spanish relations with the Dominican republic gives to this part of the story a peculiar interest.[1]

It was Spain which was, in the sixties, to reassert European sovereignty over the western half of the island of Santo Domingo; but before the designs of that power crystallized, there is a long period of intrigue by the agents of France, which may well engage the attention of the student of the Monroe Doctrine. It is but fair to say at the outset that at no time were the responsible authorities at the Quai d'Orsay anxious to add the Dominican republic to the French colonial responsibilities; but it is also to be noticed that the French agents on the spot thought very differently, and that there are interesting signs of an annexationist propaganda in France itself.

The relations of France with the Haitian republic had, of course, always rested upon a special footing, since they were those of the former mother country. It is interesting to observe that French recognition of

[1] There has recently appeared an excellent general work in English on the history of Santo Domingo. See Sumner Welles, *Naboth's Vineyard. The Dominican Republic,* 1844-1924 (2 vols., paged continuously, New York, 1928). See also the works of the Dominican historian, José Gabriel García, especially *Compendio de la Historia de Santo Domingo* (3 vols., Santo Domingo, 1896).

Haitian independence in 1825 took the form of a royal decree of Charles X, and that it was accompanied by a demonstration by a French fleet which compelled the Haitian republic to bind itself to the payment of a large indemnity to France. This indemnity, it goes without saying, could not be paid, and in 1838 there came a new demonstration, and a new treaty which modified that of 1825, but still left the Haitian republic with heavy responsibilities toward its exacting creditor.[2] There were, before long, new lapses in the payment of the sums that had been stipulated for; and the situation was not improved when in 1843 there came a rising which hurled from power President Boyer, who had successfully dominated the whole island since 1822, and which brought about as well the beginnings of a movement for independence in the eastern half of Santo Domingo, where a Spanish-speaking and, as it believed itself to be, white population had for a generation groaned under the rule of the negro dictator.

One might have thought that French interests would hardly have viewed with favor a movement of revolution which, by splitting the island into two distinct states, would diminish France's hopes of securing from Haiti the discharge of the financial obligations contracted for in the treaties of 1825 and 1838. But the French agents on the spot looked at things differently. They aimed at the effective assertion of French influence over the eastern part of Santo Domingo, and seem to have be-

[2] H. Handelmann, *Geschichte der Insel Haiti* (Kiel, 1860), pp. 121-3.

lieved that the creation of a French protectorate there would more than compensate for the crippling of Haitian finances. From an early period they were in touch with the revolutionists, and especially with that extraordinary if not admirable Dominican politician, Buenaventura Baez, who for a quarter of a century plays a leading rôle in the politics of his country. As early as 1841 Levasseur, the consul-general at Port-au-Prince, recommended to his government the seizure of Samaná Bay as a recompense for the nonfulfillment by Haiti of the terms of her engagements; [3] and from an early period he took a hand in the plottings of the Dominicans, and encouraged them to believe that they might secure the protection of France. At the same time he urged on his own government the acceptance of such a protectorate.[4] In these activities, moreover, the consul-general was undoubtedly encouraged by M. Adolphe Barrot, special commissioner to the Haitian republic, by the consular agent at Santo Domingo City, M. Juchereau de Saint-Denis, and by the commander of the French fleet in the Antilles, the Admiral Des Moges. By the end of the year 1843 this group was hand in glove with the revolutionaries, and was actively negotiating for the creation of the special connection with France on which their hearts were set. Levasseur as their spokesman redoubled his entreaties to the home government to intervene actively in the island. Des Moges, in the meantime, went so far as to participate in the struggle be-

[3] Paris, Min. des Aff. Etr., Corr. Pol., St. Domingue, vol. 2, Rapport de M. Levasseur, undated.
[4] *Ibid.*, p. 27.

tween the Haitians and the Dominicans, and force a
Haitian warship to give up two Dominican vessels which
it had captured.[5]

That some of the most influential Dominican leaders
were at this time in favor of a French protectorate is
undoubted. The two men whose personalities bulk largest in Dominican history for a political generation after
the revolution, Buenaventura Baez and Pedro Santana,
were certainly ready to accept this solution of their
situation, and Baez as a member of the Haitian Assembly in 1843, had early entered into relations with the
French agents. In March, 1844, the revolutionary Junta
then in charge of affairs proposed to Juchereau de Saint-
Denis a formal treaty of friendship and alliance, asking
for naval, military, and financial aid, in exchange for
the cession of Samaná Bay, and the conceding of commercial advantages.[6] At the same time Juchereau reported that there was a strong desire to hoist the French
flag without waiting for the action of the French government. There is little reason to doubt that the Dominican
pear was ripe for the picking, if the French government
could only make up its mind to pick it. But the Guizot
ministry had no mind for any such policy; it was well
aware that the acceptance of a protectorate would alien-

---

[5] *Ibid.* See also A. de St. Mérant, *Samaná et ses Projets de
Cession,* 1844-91 (Paris, 1896), especially pp. 10-12. There is a
garbled account in B. C. Clark's *Remarks upon the United
States Intervention in Haiti, with Comments upon the Cor-
respondence Connected with It* (Boston, 1853), and in 33rd
Cong., 1st Sess., Exec. Doc. No. 12, pp. 12-15.

[6] Paris, Min. des Aff. Etr., Corr. Pol., St. Domingue., vol.
I, p. 44.

ate Great Britain; and it was concerned with regard to the Haitian debt. The French consul-general was informed, therefore, that France would have nothing to do with the notion of a protectorate.[7] This attitude was consistently maintained during the years which followed.

Yet the idea of a French protectorate showed a quite remarkable vitality. It by no means expires with the hostile reception given it by the French government; indeed new soundings were made in Paris through M. Levasseur in 1845.[8] Rebuffed once more, the Dominicans, as we shall see, began a flirtation with Spain; but in 1849 the idea of a French connection again enters into the picture, and into the foreground of the picture, at that. External danger was responsible for the new appeal to Paris. In 1848 an extraordinary person by the name of Soulouque had become President of Haiti. Illiterate, brutal, and barbarous, this picturesque savage had certain broad, if rather juvenile, conceptions of his rôle as leader. At home he was, within a few years, to transform the Haitian republic into an empire, assuming the gaudy title of Faustin the First. Abroad his policy was directed toward the reconquest of the eastern part of the island, which his predecessors had neglected. In the spring of 1849 he launched a terrific campaign— terrific, at any rate, for this part of the world. He defeated the Dominicans at Azua, and seemed to have opened the road to the capital itself. The fear at Santo Domingo City amounted to panic, and the Dominican

[7] *Ibid.*, Instructions, November 20, 1844.
[8] *Ibid.*, vol. 2, Rapport de M. Levasseur.

leaders hastened, in their extremity, to turn to France,[9] raising the question of a protectorate. The French consul at Santo Domingo City at this time, Place, by name, was obviously friendly to the idea; indeed he had urged it upon his government as early as February 10.[10] The President of the Chambers at the moment was Buenaventura Baez, always a friend of the French connection, and more influential in Dominican politics than the wobbly individual named Jímenez who occupied the presidency. On April 4, not improbably encouraged by Place,[11] Baez came to the consul and requested that the French flag be hoisted. The request was refused, for such a step was, of course, far beyond the authority of the man to whom it was proposed. But on the 19th Baez managed to jam through the terror-stricken Congress a resolution earnestly requesting the French government to assume a protectorate over the republic. This resolution Place received, and set out posthaste for Port-au-Prince to consult with the consul-general, Raybaud, as to the future. At the same time the proposal of the Congress was forwarded to the government in Paris. The régime of the Second Republic under Louis Napoleon had other fish to fry much nearer home than the Caribbean, and a deaf ear was turned to the urgings of the consuls, and the appeals of Baez; but the project was further discussed in the course of the year, new proposi-

[9] *Ibid.,* April 4, 1849.
[10] *Ibid.,* February 10, 1849.
[11] On this see also London, P. R. O., F. O., Dominican Republic, vol. 3, May 22, 1849, in which M. Place is described as " clamorous for a French protectorate."

18

tions made in October, when Baez had become President, and a personal letter addressed by the Dominican leader to the chief of the French Republic urging a protectorate.

One naturally asks oneself the question in connection with these interesting episodes as to how far, if at all, respect for the views of the United States influenced the course of action decided upon at Paris? The answer, beyond all question, is, " Very little indeed." Neither in 1844 nor in 1849 can the attitude of Washington be thought to have much to do with the matter. M. Guizot, as we have seen, was no ardent admirer of the Monroe Doctrine, nor was he, in 1844, pursuing a policy very respectful of American interests. He was, on the contrary, anxious to be on good terms with England, and French expansion in the Caribbean would hardly serve to advance such a policy. He did not view with favor a revolutionary movement which seemed to make impossible by Haiti the payment of the indemnities provided for by the treaties of 1838. The documents in the Ministère des Affaires Etrangères make it obvious that these were the considerations which prompted French action in 1844, and that the position of the United States was hardly taken into account.[12] Not quite the same thing can be said with regard to 1849. The same arguments that we have just indicated were again brought forward then, but the author of an interesting memorandum which apparently served as the basis of French policy in 1849 did mention, amongst other objections

[12] *Ibid.*, vol 1, Instructions of November 11, 1844.

to the protectorate the attitude of the American government, " which always regard with extreme distrust attempts made by European governments to regain their footing in America." [13] It is worth noting, however, that the emphasis in the latter as in the former case was placed very decidedly on other factors. Certainly there is not the slightest reason to assume that the position of the American government was of decisive influence.

The slender respect paid to the United States is still better illustrated when one examines such works as those of Pelletier de Saint Rémy and Gaston d'Alaux, which deal with the Dominican question. The first of these individuals was a governmental official attached to the Council of State. In 1846 he published a book entitled *Etude et Solution Nouvelle de la Question Haitienne,* in which he proposed the cession of Samaná Bay to France, to be brought about by the common consent of Haiti (which still claimed it), and of the Dominican republic. There is not a word in his discussion of the matter which remotely suggests that such a project might be distasteful to the United States. Only a few months after President Polk had penned his solemn warning, this well informed and highly intelligent Frenchman writes as if he had never heard of it, or of anything like it. The same comment is to be made with regard to the articles published five years later in the *Revue des Deux Mondes* under the pen name of Gaston d'Alaux, but believed to have been written by M. Maxime Raybaud,

[13] Ibid., vol. 2, *Mémoire sur les conséquences de l'acceptation du protectorat,* p. 233, undated.

the French consul general at Port-au-Prince. These
articles, like the work of Pelletier de Saint Rémy, suggest the acquisition of Samaná Bay by France. The
only allusion to the United States is in a single sentence.
" Should the American government intervene in Dominican affairs," wrote d'Alaux, " half of the American
continent would rise to whistle down the Yankee, casu-
istical pirate that he has become." [14] Nothing in this
suggests exaggerated respect for the views of the
United States.

French policy and French opinion with regard to
Santo Domingo in the late forties, then, were little influenced by the revival of the Monroe Doctrine. And
if the project of the protectorate was abandoned, if it
scarcely appears except for fugitive references after
1850, this does not mean that the French government
took no interest whatsoever in the affairs of the Dominican republic. On the contrary, it was very much concerned with them, and sometimes in a way by no means
favorable to the interests of the United States. It certainly did not practise that abstention from interference
in New World affairs which Polk had attempted to
deduce as a natural corollary from the principles of
1823. And on at least one occasion, the course of action
which it pursued led directly to the invocation by the
American agent on the spot of the famous presidential
declaration.

Before examining this aspect of the matter, however,
we must turn back to speak of American policy with

[14] *Revue des Deux Mondes,* XIX, 211-224, and 459-501.

regard to Santo Domingo. At first the attitude of the
United States seems to have been that of very mild interest. In 1844, a Dominican agent having arrived at
Washington to plead for recognition, Calhoun, the Secretary of State, despatched one John M. Hogan to the
island on a mission of information. This person spent
money upon his mission with a truly Celtic liberality;
but he seems never to have suspected the danger of a
European protectorate, and his reports apparently
slumbered unnoticed in the State Department after
they had been received.[15] The Polk administration, with
its quick suspicions of European purposes, interested
itself very little in this newborn republic of the Caribbean. It did send out a commercial agent, first Mr.
Francis Harrison, and after his death, Mr. Jonathan
Elliott, but neither of these men had power to negotiate a treaty nor was the recognition of the new state
involved in sending them. It was only with the advent
of the Whigs to power that diplomatic interest in the
affairs of the Dominican republic began to develop.
Curiously enough, though it was French intrigue which
was most dangerous, it was fear of Britain which
prompted the Taylor administration to send a special
agent to the island. In January, 1849, Sir Robert
Schomburgk had arrived in Santo Domingo to serve as
British consul. Elliott wrote that he had instructions
looking to the acquisition of Samaná Bay. Accordingly,
Secretary Clayton decided to despatch Benjamin E.
Green, the son of Duff Green of Texan fame, to the

[15] The essential data on this mission are in 41st Cong., 3rd
Sess., H. Exec. Doc. No. 42.

island to prevent any such cession, if possible, by " strenuous representations," and, if possible, to secure a coaling station for the United States in the same region.[16] This Green mission was the beginning of a very active policy, as we shall see, and indicates that the Whig régime, although it talked little of the Monroe Doctrine, was thoroughly alive to the necessity of upholding American influence in the Caribbean. When the American agent arrived in Santo Domingo he soon learned of the French intrigues, and of the movement for a French protectorate.[17] He also discovered that the Dominicans were catholic enough in their taste for foreign support not to be opposed to American protection, or even annexation, if the French government turned a deaf ear to their petitions. He soon became the partisan of a policy which would commit the United States to the support of the new republic against the Haitians, and urged such a policy upon the government at Washington. Powerless, however, to make any commitments in default of instructions, he was unable to prevent renewed appeals to France, after he had replied in a noncommittal manner to the overtures of Baez and of Del Monte, the foreign minister.[18] In the ardor with which he pressed a vigorous policy upon the administration,

[16] Washington, Dept. of State, Special Agents, I, June 13, 1849.

[17] Washington, Dept. of State, Secret Service, August 27, 1849.

[18] *Ibid.*, September 27, 1849. In this interview with Del Monte Green declared that a French protectorate might not be pleasing to the United States.

however, is to be seen a hostility to European influence not altogether unconnected with the principles of 1823.

Nor were Green's urgings wholly without practical results. The Taylor administration, and its successor, the Fillmore administration, soon went a step farther along the path of diplomatic intervention in the affairs of the island of Santo Domingo. It took part in a tripartite intervention, one of the few examples, in the period with which we are here dealing, of departure from the rule of isolated action which generally governed the policy of the United States. This interesting episode deserves a brief examination.

In January of 1850 the Baez régime made a special appeal to Green for the intervention of the " powerful Anglo-American nation " in the struggle between the Dominican republic and Haiti.[19] This move aroused the natural jealousy of the consuls of France and of Great Britain, nor was the American commissioner able to respond to it favorably. On February 22, therefore, the Dominican foreign minister addressed identic notes to the representatives of all three powers requesting that they use their best efforts to bring the destructive conflict with Haiti to a close. Secretary Clayton agreed to this proposal, as did Webster, when he entered the State Department in the summer of 1850. Though Green was recalled, a new agent, R. J. Walsh, was sent out in January, 1851, with instructions to cooperate with the representatives of France and England, and conjointly with his colleagues to " require the Emperor to conclude a permanent peace with the Dominican

[19] *Ibid.*, January 24, 1850.

government, upon the basis which you may jointly prescribe to him, or to consent to a truce with that government of not less that two years." [20] Walsh arrived in
Port-au-Prince in February, 1851, and before long the
negotiations commenced. It cannot be said that they
were brilliantly successful. The Haitian monarch refused to assent to the terms proposed by the commissioners of the three powers. The possibility of coercive action against Faustin was rejected by Walsh as
outside his instructions, though he did not discourage
the possibility of such a course by the other two powers.
In May the American's mission expired, and he returned
to the United States with very little accomplished.
After his departure, by virtue of a threat of blockade,
the representatives of France and England extracted
from the Haitian potentate the promise of a truce for
one year.[21] It was European, not American, action
which in the end proved to be most effective.

The common action of European powers with the
United States in composing a dispute between American
states would be considered as contrary to the Monroe
Doctrine only by those who give to those principles
their very widest extension. But the threat of the use
of force by European powers involves a wholly different question. For the making of any such threat involves
the possibility of having to make the threat good by
action. And the armed action of European governments
in American controversies would be filled with dangerous implications. It would have consequences that

[20] 32nd Cong., 1st Sess., S. Exec. Doc. no. 113, p. 4.

[21] Paris, Min. des Aff. Etr., Corr., Pol., St. Domingue, vol.
4, October 24, 1851.

might be far-reaching. The complacency, therefore, with which the Whig administration not only looked on, but encouraged, the action of France and Great Britain in Santo Domingo, shows how little devoted it was, in any abstract sense, to the principles of 1823.

The episode, of course, was a small one at best. Yet it did not pass unnoticed in the American press or in Congress. The *Democratic Review*, always faithful to the great Doctrine, had its word of scathing criticism of the policy pursued by the Whigs.[22] Democratic Senators, in the debates on the Cass resolution, made free to condemn the inaction of Fillmore and Webster in the name of the principles of 1823.[23] The relation of the intervention to the Monroe Doctrine, in other words, was not completely ignored, and the Pierce administration, when it entered into power in March, 1853, proceeded to interest itself without delay in the question of Santo Domingo. This brings us to the mission of General William L. Cazneau.

This individual, not the most savory of our diplomatic agents, was appointed early in 1854.[24] It may well be that rumors of European action, transmitted by Jonathan Elliott, still commercial agent in Santo Domingo

[22] *Democratic Review,* February, 1853, p. 185, "Rumored Occupation of Santo Domingo." " Let France and England stand aside and let the people of America manage their own affairs in their own way. Why draw on two jealous rivals to mix themselves in negotiations vital to the integrity of our system? "

[23] *Cong. Globe,* 32nd Cong., 2nd Sess., App., p. 102, speech by Senator Dixon.

[24] Washington, Dept. of State, Special Missions, vol. 3., William L. Cazneau. Cazneau's instructions are dated June 17, 1854.

City, had disquieted the administration. It may be that the new administration was merely illustrating its freedom from "timid forebodings of expansion" so proudly proclaimed by Pierce in his inaugural. But at any rate General Cazneau was instructed to offer the recognition of the republic in exchange for the cession of Samaná Bay, and at the same time, with a jaunty confidence in the outcome of the negotiation, an American army officer, whose name chanced to be George B. McClellan, was despatched to the island to make soundings and to render a report as to the desirability of this harbor as a naval base of the United States. The Dominican government, in 1854, as formerly, was always ready for a deal with a strong power. Its leaders, though they might have mild prejudices in favor of this or that particular state, were never so blinded by these prejudices as to be unwilling to consolidate their own position by a compact with some other government. When General Cazneau arrived in Santo Domingo, General Santana, the military hero of the liberation, was President of the Republic. He proved entirely hospitable to the advances of the American. A draft treaty was drawn up providing for the cession of the desired tract of territory, brought back to the United States by Cazneau and approved by the administration, and taken back again by the agent to Santo Domingo. The way seemed clear for favorable action upon it. But now the consuls of France and Great Britain aroused themselves.[25] The

[25] Schomburgk was instructed to oppose American machinations. See London, P. R. O., F. O., Dominican Republic, vol. 19, September 29, 1854.

treaty was ready for formal signing on September 7. On the 8th Sir Robert Schomburgk at the tropical hour of 7 A. M. sought out President Santana to tell him what he thought of it. At noon he called again with his French colleague. The French and British governments, Santana was reminded, had extended their protection to the Dominican government. They could do so no longer if the republic were to subinfeudate itself to the United States. The provision with regard to Samaná Bay must be stricken from the treaty. The hard pressed Chief Executive yielded to the pressure. A new treaty was drawn up, and signed (by the Vice-President, not by Santana, who had prudently withdrawn to his estates), on October 5. But even so the hostility of the consuls was not averted. On October 27 M. Raybaud arrived from Port-au-Prince to use his influence against the new compact. On the 28th Schomburgk, acting on instructions, protested against the Dominican negotiation with the United States.[26] Both the one and the other proceeded shamelessly to lobby and agitate against the ratification. Cazneau, naturally somewhat put out at all that had occurred, had recourse, also quite naturally, perhaps, to the Monroe Doctrine. On the 17th of November he addressed to the consuls a strong note, in which he took occasion to remind them very pointedly of the principles of 1823.[27] But the consuls seem to have

[26] *Ibid.,* November 23, 1854.

[27] *Ibid.,* Encl. William L. Cazneau, Santo Domingo, November 17, 1854. " The undersigned Commissioner Plenipotentiary of the United States of America near this Government having good reason to know that the Agents of France and England

have by various means—aided by the menacing display of an armed force before this Capital—over-awed and controlled the free action of the Dominican Republic in its relations with the United States, hereby protests in the name of his country, against this breach of honorable faith towards his Government and against this unwarranted encroachment upon the sovereign rights of an independent American power.

"Every enlightened government in amity with the United States is perfectly informed of their determined purpose, as a nation to oppose whatever measure may be intended to subject the independent nationality of an American people to the arbitrary will of a foreign power, or make its action—and even existence—dependent on the dicta of a foreign policy; and none of those nations have taken exception to this immutable principle of the American Systim (*sic*).

"The United States makes no difference in the application of this rule between the strong and the weak of their Sister republics and they have a just right to expect the powerful and magnanimous nations of Europe will follow their example.

"These facts being so well understood I must call your particular attention Sir—to this inconsiderate violation of the relations of Amity and Commerce now subsisting between our respective countries in the trust that you, as the responsible representative (*sic*) of your government at this Capital, will use the necessary precautions to guard those relations from further disturbance.

"If this due care should be omitted, the government and people of the United States may conceive they have just cause to distrust the sincerity and good faith of any Government whose Agents in these waters are thus permitted to interfere in affairs and negociations belonging entirely and exclusively to the interests of the United States and the Dominican Republic— I am confident that you Sir—would regret equally with myself the consequences which might result from this unauthorized inter-meddling with the sanctity and freedom of inter-American relations."

Yours Respectfully
WILLIAM L. CAZNEAU.

been unconvinced by this appeal to dogma.[28] Discouraged and thwarted, the American agent on the 24th notified the Dominican foreign minister that he withdrew the treaty from consideration. It was submitted, none the less, and ratified with offensive mutilations,[29] but it was, of course, never accepted by the United States. In the meantime Santana was compelled to give assurances to the French and British agents that under no circumstances would the republic sell, lease, or alienate any portion of Dominican territory to any foreign state, or give to any state special privileges within its borders. The diplomacy of the Pierce administration had been thoroughly outmanoeuvered; a more thoroughgoing assertion of diplomatic influence and diplomatic pressure by European powers in the affairs of an American state

[28] The British consul responded that the language of the note "permits me but to acknowledge it out of courtesy. I shall transmit that document to Her Majesty's Secretary of State for Foreign Affairs, to which I am the more inclined as I am of opinion that it belongs exclusively to Her Majesty's government to pass on those international principles which your note presumes to establish." (Encl. in Paris, Min. des Aff. Etr., Corr. Pol., vol. 5, St. Domingue, p. 317.)

The French consul replied merely that "the purpose which you are pleased to assign to the presence in this roadstead of three vessels belonging to the naval station of the Antilles; the conjectures which you hazard, and the tone which you adopt do not permit me to answer your letter of yesterday. I shall confine myself to transmitting it to my government." (*Ibid.*)

Schomburgk, however, had mentioned the "Monroe principle" in his earlier despatches. London, P. R. O., F. O., Dominican Republic, vol. 14, July 20, 1852, and vol. 16, December 31, 1853.

[29] Washington, Dept. of State, Special Agents, vol. 19, William L. Cazneau, December 6, 1854.

is not to be recorded. The policy of France and Great Britain in the case of Texas is mild by comparison.

It might be contended that the action taken by France and Great Britain in this case was contrary to the explicit language of the original Monroe Doctrine. Monroe, it will be remembered, had protested against European action against American states, " for the purpose of oppressing them, or controlling in any other manner their destiny." But if it seems a forced construction of these words to apply them to the episode just cited, certain it is that the French and British action was contrary to the Polk Doctrine of 1845. It was certainly clear evidence of the fact that the balance of power in the New World was still a matter of solicitude to European diplomats in 1854, and that European diplomacy was still a long way from abdicating the field to the United States, or of watching with complacency any step toward American aggrandizement.

Having regard to all these facts, it is curious that the Pierce administration never gave vent to the resentment which it must have felt at the policy of France and England in the Dominican republic. There were, of course, more important matters in train; but even this can hardly adequately explain why the Dominican business is virtually completely neglected in the correspondence with London and with Paris. The whole affair, of course, was a secret from the American public; it was of secondary importance, and to have brought it forward would have been to confess defeat; but one might expect at least a reference or two to the matter in Secretary Marcy's correspondence. As a matter of fact, there is nothing at all. Indeed, when the French government protested to Washington at the language of Cazneau (the first diplomatic protest, by the way, based upon the claims of the Monroe Doctrine), Secretary Marcy refused to justify that gentleman, but responded instead that both the spirit and the form of the General's communication had been indefensible. He even went so far as to declare that his agent misunderstood the limits and the nature of his mission. Nothing could have been more disarming than this, certainly.

It is to be noticed, however, that the American government, though it did not exhibit the slightest indignation at the attitude of France and Great Britain, continued to press for a commercial treaty at Santo Domingo City. In May, 1855, Jonathan Elliott, the commercial agent, reported that negotiations might be reopened with some hope of success. In December President Santana's position was strengthened by the decisive defeat of a Haitian invasion. By March the treaty had been signed, ratified by the Dominican Senate, and was on its way to Washington.[30] In the meantime amiable efforts were made by the European powers to compose the dispute between Haiti and the Dominican Republic; but they did not prevent the invasion of Dominican territory by Soulouque at the end of 1855. It was only after his decisive defeat by Santana that the Haitian potentate finally consented to the negotiation of a two-year truce, eventually consummated in 1857. When he fell from

[30] Welles, *op. cit.*, p. 172.

power in 1859, to be succeeded by one of the most capable of the Haitian Presidents, Geffrard, negotiations were entered into spontaneously by the government at Port-au-Prince. In the friendly support given these negotiations by the French and British ministers in both capitals there was nothing that could run counter to the interests of the United States, or involve a challenge to the principles of the Monroe Doctrine.

It is, indeed, not France or Great Britain, but Spain which must fix our attention as the story of Santo Domingo proceeds. The protectorate of 1861, a direct challenge to the principles of 1823, has its origins in the events of the previous fifteen years, and these origins we must now briefly examine.[31]

It has already been indicated that from the very beginning the Dominicans showed a real catholicity of taste in their appeals for foreign aid. They were as perplexed and as shifting in their offers of alliance as the gentleman in " The Beggar's Opera " who complained of how happy he could be with either were " t'other dear charmer away." The beginnings of relations with Spain go back to the period of the revolution itself. In the spring of 1843, for example, certain Dominican leaders got in touch with the Spanish vice-consul at Jamaica, in an attempt to secure aid for a revolutionary movement. Their propositions were transmitted by the consul to the Governor-General of Cuba, who wisely

---

[31] The best secondary account, rigorously based on the sources, is El General Gándara, *Anexión y Guerra de Santo Domingo* (2 vols., Madrid, 1884).

decided to have nothing to do with them.[32] In 1844 negotiations were set on foot by none other than the versatile Baez with the Governor-General of Porto Rico, and this functionary reported very favorably with regard to the project to Madrid.[33] The government itself seems to have been not averse to a protectorate, and sounded both France and Great Britain with a view to ascertaining whether they would oppose the project.[34] It may be as a result of these soundings a Spanish fleet was despatched to the island in the winter of 1846, but for some reason, which remains obscure, no understanding was arrived at, and a special mission was appointed by the President to proceed to Madrid, probably to discuss the question of a protectorate. Arrived there in May of the same year, it found the domestic situation much unsettled, and Spanish dilatoriness even more extraordinary than usual. Even so, there was a moment at which it seemed possible that success would attend the mission. The Cortaza ministry which held office in the fall of 1847 was willing to sign a treaty of alliance, and to give a promise of protection, but just when matters looked brightest, it fell from power, and the Dominican emissaries found themselves as badly off as ever.[35] No wonder that they left in disgust, to try their luck at Paris, where they met with no better fortune.

[32] *Documentos Relativos à la Cuestión de Santo Domingo. Sometidos al Congreso de los Diputados,* Ministerio del Estado, p. 4 (Madrid, 1865).

[33] *Ibid.,* pp. 9 and 11.

[34] *Ibid.,* p. 14.

[35] Welles, *op. cit.,* I, 82.

19

After the negotiations of 1847, the idea of a Spanish protectorate seems to have lapsed for some time. But in 1852 a Spanish agent, named Mariano Torrente, visited the island, and on his return published a remarkable book, *Política Ultramarina*,[36] in which he frankly argued for the protectorate. To Torrente the carrying out of such a policy seemed not only in accordance with the interests of Spain, but invulnerable against criticism. The United States, he thought, could not legitimately protest, since what would be involved would be a mere reassumption of a previous political relationship, and this with the consent of the Dominicans themselves;[37] while the establishment of Spanish control would put an end to projects of American colonization, and prevent the danger of the new republic becoming a base for new filibustering expeditions against Cuba.[38] As for the Monroe Doctrine, Torrente seems never to have heard of it. In a sketch of the political relations of Spain and the United States, he describes the period between 1819 and 1848 as one in which there is nothing really worth mentioning![39] The vital interest of the American government in Dominican independence seems entirely to have escaped this by no means unintelligent observer.

In the interval between Torrente's visit in 1852 and the publication of his book in 1854 a new attempt to realize the idea of the protectorate seems to have been

[36] M. Torrente, *Política Ultramarina* (Madrid, 1854).
[37] *Ibid.*, p. 343.
[38] *Ibid.*, p. 337.
[39] *Ibid.*, pp. 69 and 78.

made at Madrid. President Santana despatched General Ramón Mella to the Spanish court to negotiate along such lines, but the government in power turned a deaf ear to the pleadings of this emissary. It is not at all improbable, though the fact cannot be definitely proved, that Spanish relations with the United States had something to do with this decision. The period which Mella spent at Madrid was the period of the Black Warrior episode, when war between the United States and Spain seemed amongst the possibilities; circumstances were hardly propitious for a bold policy in Santo Domingo. Whether in any case the Spanish government could have nerved itself to such a policy is a fair question. Domestic politics were in confusion; a series of weak ministries distinguishes the period, along with revolutionary movements in 1854 and 1856; a feeble foreign policy was perhaps an inevitable concomitant of such conditions. Yet Madrid continued to take an interest in the affairs of the island; a special agent was maintained there; and through this man Spanish opposition was united to that of France and Britain against the American treaty of 1854. And early in 1855, the danger from this source having been averted for the time, Spain recognized by solemn treaty the independence of the new republic.

There follows on the treaty of 1855 an intrigue looking toward Spanish control of the island which seems to have been conducted by the Spanish agent in Santo Domingo rather than the Spanish government. The name of this agent was Segovia, and from the moment

of his arrival he was obviously much excited at the negotiations which had been reopened between the Dominican republic and Jonathan Elliott, looking to a
commercial treaty. He proceeded to set on foot a campaign against the United States as furious as that
of the French and British agents two years before.
Taking advantage of an article in the treaty of 1855
permitting Spaniards who had adopted Dominican nationality to recover their former allegiance, he proceeded to matriculate upon the registers of the con-
sulate a large number of persons as subjects of
Isabel II, and at the same time, convinced that Santana
was the friend of the United States, and eager for
the American connection, he plunged into domestic
politics. Faced with the hostility of the Spanish
minister, Santana withdrew from office, General Regla
Mota succeeding to the presidency. But Regla Mota,
too, was a friend of the United States; in fact in
July, 1856, he requested Elliott to make representations
to Washington looking toward the cession of a naval
base, and active support of the existing régime. Segovia,
nothing daunted, and shamelessly interfering in Dominican politics, forced Regla Mota to summon the electoral colleges, and see to it that Buenaventura Baez was
hoisted into the vice-presidency. In due time the President was forced to resign, and Baez succeeded to the
office of chief executive. Segovia, as he hoped, had
found a Dominican leader whom he could control. His
campaign against American influence had signally succeeded. The cup of his satisfaction must have been filled

by the news that the commercial treaty with the United States had been turned down by the American Senate.[40]

But Segovia's intrigues, as I have said, were never approved by the government at home. Spain was still hesitant to go forward in Santo Domingo, and its over-enterprising representative was recalled in 1857. The very régime which he created was soon involved in the most serious complications, and in January of 1858 the wheel of Dominican politics returned Santana to the presidency.

As had been the case three years before, Santana was not averse to a closer connection with the United States, and the cession of Samaná Bay to the American government. But experience had taught him how little trust was to be put in Washington; the Democratic administrations of Pierce and Buchanan had not allowed their devotion to the Monroe Doctrine to lead them to take an active part against European intrigue in Santo Domingo. Concerned with weightier matters, and aware of the fact that Santo Domingo meant little to the citizens of the United States, they had passed by on the other side. The time had come, apparently, to seek another protector, and Santana, magnanimously putting behind him the memories of Segovia, turned to Spain. Through Spanish aid the republic might gain security— and, hardly less important, Santana himself, now rapidly aging, be maintained in power.

In October of 1858, while still Provisional President, Santana had asked the Spanish government if it would

[40] For this episode, see Welles, *op. cit.*, vol. 1, pp. 163-78. Also Washington, Dept. of State, Consular Correspondence, Santo Domingo, *passim*.

preserve the Dominican republic against Haitian aggression. The reply was not encouraging. But, none the less in May the President commissioned General Felipe Alfau to the Court of Madrid to negotiate a close economic, military, and political understanding. The government of Marshal O'Donnell, the strongest government which Spain had had in years, was now in power. But it was occupied with the war in Morocco; and it was not ready for an aggressive policy across the seas. None the less, it was willing to give clandestine aid. War supplies and some money were given to General Alfau, and Spanish officers and drill-sergeants sent out to aid in the organization of the Dominican army.[41] Support of this kind became more and more obvious in the summer of 1860, attracting the vigilant attention of Cazneau, who, ever active, had once more inveigled the American government into appointing him a special agent. The tide was running more and more rapidly toward annexation.

In the events which were now to unfold themselves the captain-general of Cuba, Francisco Serrano, was now to play a prominent, perhaps a decisive, part. From the beginnings of Dominican independence the Spanish authorities in Cuba had taken active interest in the island, even when they were the advocates of a cautious policy. But Serrano, it would seem, was the first of them to become the pronounced partisan of action. A member of the Liberal Union then in power in Spain, the right arm of O'Donnell, as he was often called, he

[41] Becker, *op. cit.,* II, 567, and *Documentos, op. cit.,* pp. 22-24.

had been compelled by his absence in the Antilles to forego the honors of the African campaign. Ardent for distinction, he now saw in the question of Santo Domingo an excellent opportunity to achieve it. Impetuous by temperament, he pressed forward not a little faster than the timid and tentative authorities at Madrid. In July he sent his second-in-command, General Rubalcava, to the republic on a secret mission, to sound out sentiment. Like many another envoy, the Spaniard saw what he wished to see, and what he was shown; and his conclusions were that there was a positive ardor for annexation.[42] The Rubalcava mission, inevitably encouraging, was followed by another, that of Pelaez Campomanes, this time with more definite objects in view.[43] On November 12 Serrano transmitted to Madrid definite terms, looking either toward annexation or the protectorate.[44] A memoir by Pelaez himself with a glowing account of the Spanish sympathies of the Dominicans accompanied these proposals.

The Spanish government was not yet ready, however, to make its decision. On December 8 O'Donnell replied to Serrano in a despatch in which covetousness and caution were commingled. The captain-general was authorized to facilitate a loan to the Dominican agent then in Havana. Arms and supplies might be furnished the Dominicans to use against the Haitians. The reannexation of Santo Domingo was approved in prin-

[42] *Documentos*, pp. 26-7.
[43] *Ibid.*, pp. 30-33.
[44] *Ibid.*, p. 29.

ciple, and was described as a " noble enterprise." In
case any other power should seem to be about to act,
the offer of the Dominicans might be accepted, though
the decision taken must appear as " completely spontaneous." But Spain would prefer to delay. A year
later would be better. The time for action had not
arrived.[45]

The despatch of December 8 disclosed at bottom a
clear desire to reenter Santo Domingo. So at any rate
Serrano seems to have taken it, and in such terms, perhaps, he interpreted it to Ricart, the Dominican agent
now at Havana. On February 21, frankly avowing his
own desire for annexation, he wrote to Santana asking
him what preparations should be made for the occupation of the island when the time for decisive action
arrived.[46] He could hardly have gone further under the
circumstances to encourage the Dominican President to
press forward on his own account, and present the
Spanish government with a *fait accompli.* And this was
precisely the way in which the thing worked out in practise. Convinced that he could force the hands of the
authorities in Madrid Santana, on March 18, proclaimed
the reannexation of Santo Domingo to Spain ; as soon as
the news was carried to Cuba, without waiting for instructions, Serrano proceeded to throw troops into the
island ; and the hesitant O'Donnell and his equally hesitant foreign minister, Calderon Collantes, were put in

[45] Ministerio del Estado, Negociación 171, Legajo 2. An
abridged version is in *Documentos, op. cit.,* pp. 33-5.

[46] Gándara, *op. cit.,* I, 152.

a position from which it was difficult to retreat.[47] For a time they still seemed to hope to negotiate further with the Dominicans before coming to a decision; the instructions of April 24 were drawn up in this sense; but the next day a memorandum was sent to the representatives of foreign powers declaring that Spain could not repulse the wishes of the Dominicans if it was clearly established that they desired to return to their former mother country; and as Spanish public opinion became more and more pronounced in favor of action, the government moved in the same direction. On May 19, 1861, it acted decisively, and by royal decree without waiting for further news from the island declared Santo Domingo to be once more Spanish territory. The die had been cast at last, after much tremulous shaking of the dice box.

In casting it, the Spanish government acted, it would seem clear, with due regard to events in America. Indeed, the correspondence with regard to the Dominican question reveals a very active interest in the attitude of the United States. Jealousy and fear of American action were present from the beginning of the actual negotiations. The rearrival of General Cazneau was naturally taken as a possible threat to Dominican independence. The exploitation of the little guano island of Alto Vela, claimed by Santo Domingo, by American commercial interests in the spring of 1860, convinced Serrano, impatient from the beginning, that the

[47] For Serrano's description of these events, see Transcript, Ministerio del Estado, Legación de S.M. en Washington, Legajo 445 (13) (Anejo I).

time had come to act, even at the risk of war.[48] In
Madrid, also, this same jealousy undoubtedly prevailed,
as the instructions of O'Donnell, with their reference
to early action in case of threatened aggression by any
other power, clearly show. But in Madrid jealousy was
tempered with caution. The instructions of December
8, to which we have already alluded, contain an interesting paragraph on the United States. Alluding to the
possibility of " foreign complications," and declaring
that Spain must exercise a positive influence in Latin
America, the Spanish prime minister continued, " To
attain this object, it is necessary that the Northern Republic. . . . . lose, by virtue of the events which have
begun to take place there and which at no distant time
will acquire all the gravity implicit in them, the immense
prestige which derives from the example of a country
which, without suffering the slightest reverse, has triumphantly survived the first eighty years of its existence
as an independent nation. The question of time, therefore, is of immense importance for Spain. Its means of
action increase from day to day, and it will soon be able
to dispose of a respectable squadron ; while the moment
is coming in which the North American Confederation
will divide into two states of opposing interests, one of
which will be the natural ally of Spain in all the efforts
which it may be obliged to make in America. The re-
union of Santo Domingo brought about in such a man-

---

[48] The Dominicans sent several vessels to oust the Ameri-
cans, and this was accomplished without the slightest clash in
September or October, 1860. For this episode see Ministerio del
Estado, Negociación 171, Legajo 1, (22).

ner as would give rise to suspicions not destitute of foundation, would not only turn the gaze of the terrified states of Latin America towards the United States, thus destroying the basis of our policy in America, the unity of our race, but also perhaps making the contending parties in America forget their internal discords, might lead them to group themselves under the Monroe Doctrine, a principle accepted without reserve by the slave states no less than by those where free labor prevails." [49] Such a statement leaves little to be said with regard to the importance of the American attitude in the views of the Spanish cabinet; the Monroe Doctrine was clearly understood at Madrid, and not only understood but taken into account.

In the climax of the Dominican question, of course, other motives played their part. The hand of the Spanish government, as we have seen, was really forced; it was almost driven to its final decision; and even if the outbreak of the Civil War had not offered every encouragement to action, it would probably have had to back up the acts of its agents, and pay heed to the trend of public opinion. Yet it is obvious, also, that the progress of the secessionist movement operated as a very distinct encouragement to the Spanish ministry.

[49] Ministerio del Estado, Negociación 171, Legajo 2.
This paragraph is probably based upon a despatch from Tassara, the Spanish minister at Washington, November 20, in which he predicted that the annexation would cause a war with the United States, and that the domestic crisis would only accentuate the natural tendency of many Americans to seek a diversion from domestic difficulties in a foreign war. (In *Ibid.*)

Indeed, O'Donnell said as much as this in a conversation with the British chargé, Edwards, in April of 1861.[50] The coming of the Civil War seemed to offer the best of opportunities to Spanish, as to other European, statesmen to redress the balance of power in the New World.

It is not to be supposed, of course, that the significance of this challenge escaped the attention of the shrewd politician who entered the State Department as its chief while the events just described were coming to a head. William H. Seward had, as we have already seen, in a speech of 1853, deprecated the invocation, in terms, of the Monroe Doctrine. But this did not mean that he was hostile to its spirit, by any manner of means. And in the critical days when the Lincoln administration was rather fumblingly advancing toward Civil War, Seward, as is well known, held to the view that the menace of secession might be diminished, if not scotched, by a bold foreign policy. With an optimism that was constitutional, and a provincialism that is only too common among American politicians, he believed that the grievances of the South would fall into a secondary place if the government created an external crisis to swallow up the internal one. The idea was fantastic; it was reckless and ill-advised; but the very fact that it could be held and held by one, after all, not wholly without practical political experience is, perhaps, some measure of the extent to which the doctrine of the two spheres had taken root in the American public mind.

[50] London, P. R. O., F. O., Spain, vol. 1005, April 22, 1861.

Seward's *Thoughts for the Consideration of the President,* submitted, not inappropriately, on April 1, 1861, are well known.[51] They breathed fire and fury against the wicked powers of the Old World. They spoke of " categorical explanations " from Spain and France, and of convening Congress and declaring war against them if these explanations were not received. They were based on the idea of rousing " a vigorous spirit of independence on this continent against European intervention." It was clear, of course, from their tenor that Seward wished virtually to be given a free hand by the President to direct the foreign policy of the United States.

What is not so well known is that Seward, on the Dominican question, proceeded to act in much the same spirit as that which guided his advice to the President. On April 2, Seward addressed to Tassara, the Spanish minister at Washington, a note framed in the most menacing terms. It recounted, as having been gleaned from the press and from the reports of American agents in Santo Domingo and at Havana, the news of the transport of Spanish troops to the island, and the reinforcement of the Spanish fleet in the Antilles; it mentioned the hoisting of the Spanish flag by " Spanish subjects. . . . . in pursuance of a previous plot ; " it declared that " such an attempt to introduce Spanish authority within the territory of Dominica. . . . . cannot fail to be taken as the first step in a policy of armed intervention by the

[51] Frederic Bancroft, *Life of William H. Seward* (New York, 1900, 2 vols.), II, 132-3.

Spanish Government in the American countries which once constituted Spanish America, but have since achieved their independence ; and as it cannot be known where the next demonstration of the ambition it would imply would take place, it must be regarded as threatening Haiti, Mexico, the seven States on the Spanish Main, and even those once Spanish-American states, which having been peacefully acquired and admitted into the American Union, now constitute a part of this republic."

This was strong and sweeping language, but intoxicated by his own rhetoric, Seward went on to utter insinuations and threats with entire recklessness. The islands of Cuba and Porto Rico were, he declared, " on many accounts very attractive to the American People." The forbearance exercised with regard to these tempting territories was based upon the assumption that Spain would not be " an inquiet or aggressive neighbor."

" The President will not willingly believe that these proceedings have been authorized by the Government of Her Catholic Majesty, or that they can receive its approval. But I am directed to inform you, and also the Government of Her Catholic Majesty, that if they shall be found to have received at any time the sanction of that Government, the President will be obliged to regard them as manifesting an unfriendly disposition toward the United States, and to meet the further prosecution of enterprises of that kind in respect to either the Dominican Republic or any part of the American Continent or islands with a prompt, persistent, and, if possible, effective resistance."

" Before communicating these views directly to the Government of Her Catholic Majesty," the note concluded, " I am instructed to submit the subject to you in the hope that your undoubted accurate knowledge of the policy and intentions of Her Catholic Majesty's Government in that quarter may enable you to remove the inquietude which I have described." [52]

The last paragraph of this document does, it is true, rather temper the whole. After much strong language, Seward ends with nothing more than a request for information. One wonders if in this there is to be seen the moderating and stabilizing influence of Mr. Lincoln. But however this may be, the note, if taken seriously at all, virtually committed the United States to war. Nor had Seward apparently learned a great deal better when he drew up instructions to Carl Schurz on April 27, or when he finally learned of the annexation of the island in May. The instructions to Schurz repeat the threats with regard to the future of Cuba and Porto Rico, and conclude with the comment that " the President will regard any attempt of Her Catholic Majesty's Government to retain the territory of the late Dominican Republic as a matter claiming very serious attention on the part of the United States." [53]

The same intensity of feeling, it is interesting to observe, was felt by the representative of the United States in Madrid. William Preston, who discharged that post, was ere long to come back to America at his

[52] Washington, Dept. of State, Spain, Notes to.
[53] *Ibid.*, Instructions., Spain.

own request to espouse the cause of the Confederacy. His own position during the fateful April of 1861 must have been a painful one. Yet as early as April 12, having learned from the papers of what was happening in Santo Domingo, and in advance of any word from Washington, Preston addressed a note to Calderon Collantes which was nothing more nor less than an exposition of the principles of the Monroe Doctrine.[54] Re-

[54] Washington, Dept of State, Spain, Despatches, vol. 42.

LEGATION OF THE UNITED STATES

MADRID, 12th April 1861.

To His Excellency
Dn. Saturnino Calderon- Collantes
First Secretary of State, &c &c.
Palace

SIR,

It is announced today in the telegraphic dispatches that a revolution has occurred in the island of So. Domingo, and that the Republic of Dominica having determined to annex itself to the Crown of Spain, the Captain General of Cuba, Señor Serrano, sent to the island three vessels of war, with troops, to take possession of the country in the name of the Queen. In the London Times of the 9th instant, it is stated that the Spanish Flag was hoisted at So. Domingo on the 16th ultimo.

It has long been the settled policy of the United States, not to interpose in any of the political conflicts which might agitate Europe, and even to remain strictly neutral in all of the struggles affecting the governments of America where its own security and rights were not immediately involved. In the memorable events which separated her American Colonies from Spain, the course of my government was distinctly announced and faithfully observed.

We then declared that it was not our policy to take part in the wars of European powers in questions relating to themselves, and that as the political systems of Europe differed essentially from our own republican form of government, that we would consider any attempt on their part to extend their system to any portion of our hemisphere, as dangerous to our peace and safety. The independence of those colonies was subsequently recognized by Spain, and there is no doctrine in which my government is more fixed than in its determination to resist any attempt of an European power to interfere for the purpose of controlling the destiny of the American republics or reestablishing over them monarchical power; and to regard any such endeavour as the manifestation of an unfriendly disposition towards the United States.

The government of the United States wish to offer no impediment to any people who desire freely and voluntarily to adopt any form of government which they may deem suited to their social wants, interests and happiness, but neither will they consent, that European monarchs shall avail themselves of every tumult or intestine struggle to establish monarchical governments in the Western Hemisphere. Any endeavour on the part of my government to foster, encourage, or support democratic revolts in Europe, would assuredly be regarded by its kings as intolerable injury, and the government of the United States cannot but look upon the effort of any European Sovereign to supplant a neighbouring republic by converting it into the dependency of an European monarchy, as equally offensive.

Declaring these settled views of my government with frankness, I trust that your Excellency will readily appreciate the surprise and solicitude with which I have received the information to which I have alluded. I cannot deem it credible, that the Captain General Serrano has sent vessels of war and Spanish troops to take possession in the name of the Queen; as such haste would convey the impression irresistibly, that the Spanish authorities were the instigators of the Revolution.

Under the circumstances and from the grave importance of the events to which I have referred, I trust that your Excellency will, at the earliest moment, inform me if it be true that the Republic of Dominica has annexed itself to the Crown of Spain, and whether the Captain General of Cuba, Señor Serrano, has sent vessels of war or troops to take possession of the island in the name of the Queen; and, in that event, whether the government of Her Catholic Majesty has authorized, or disavows the act.

I have the honour to renew to your Excellency the assurances of my distinguished consideration.

W. Preston.

20

ceiving an unsatisfactory reply from the Spanish minister, he returned to the charge in a communication of April 23. Alluding once again to the " general policy of the United States. . . . . first announced in 1823," he remarked, " Your Excellency can well appreciate the conflict which the annexation of Santo Domingo and the destruction of that policy will inevitably produce between our governments. For the past thirty-eight years it has preserved peace and friendship between our countries, and has shielded Cuba and Puerto Rico from the hopes or ambition of Europe. Her Majesty's Government as you inform me now meditate its violation, and her Ministry may well pause before it ventures upon the perilous experiment." The spontaneity of Dominican action Preston strenuously denied. The change was effected, he declared, " by means which bore none of the marks of popular deliberation, but resembled rather the celerity of a military strategem. . . . . The United States cannot permit Spain, or any other European power, to espouse the cause of parties in Mexico or the island of the Gulf. To acquiesce in such a baneful course would be to open an endless source of discord between the monarchs of Europe and the republics of America and to array them as rivals coming under the mask of friendship, but in reality to domineer over feebler governments." " The United States are now involved in misfortune," Preston concluded, " but in my belief, its time-honored policy will be maintained as long as its Government remembers the wisdom of its Statesmen and the dignity of the Republic." [55]

[55] *Ibid.*, Encl. in No. 44, April 23, 1861.

This remarkable state paper should hold an important place in the evolution of the Monroe Doctrine. Constantly invoked at home, more and more deeply rooted in the popular mind, the principles of 1823 had been up to 1860 rarely used by the diplomats of the United States in their intercourse with the representatives of other nations. Buchanan, as we have seen, had sought to give strength to his argument by citing the Monroe declaration in the negotiations with regard to Central America in 1854. But Preston's note makes no incidental allusion to the great American dogma; it is based squarely upon it. And this, let it be remembered, in the case of an envoy of Southern sympathies who was, before long, to be fighting in the armies of the Confederacy. Is there not here some measure of the vitality of the principles of 1823?

Nor was it only Preston who cited the Doctrine to the Spanish ministers. Horatio J. Perry, the very able chargé left in control when Preston quitted Madrid, received in June the positive instructions of Seward to protest against the re-annexation of Santo Domingo. In discharging this duty, Perry rested his case, like Preston, on the Monroe Doctrine. His note is so important that I give it in full.

> LEGATION OF THE U. S.
> MADRID, JUNE 19/61
>
> SIR.
>
> As soon as the first intelligence reached Madrid of the recent revolutionary proceedings in the Island of S. Domingo my predecessor, Mr. Preston, lost no time in making known to Y. E. that the annexation of that Republic by Spain would not be regarded by the U. S.

with indifference; and the tenour of his notes on this subject might well be considered by the govt. of H. C. M. in the nature of a protest against that act than not yet accomplished. I have now to inform Y. E. that this prompt & energetic action of Mr. Preston has been fully approved by the President of the U. S.

The act then deprecated has since been carried into effect in spite of the remonstrances of this Legation, and with a precipitation which forbade the return of instructions from Washington in reply to Y. El.'s note of April 25.

But the govt. of H. C. M. was not ignorant of the settled policy of the U. S. well known to all nations having any interest in the Western Hemisphere.

It was precisely in reference to the possible future of the Republics formed from the ancient colonies of Spain in America that this policy was first announced by President Monroe in 1823 and has since been strictly adhered to by the U. S. and respected by Europe.

We had established a form of Government distinct from the monarchical or aristocratical governments of Europe. The greater part of the European colonies in America had already become independent states without our aid or intervention, and had also of their own accord decided to constitute themselves as Republics. Though we had no part or intervention in this decision it was naturally a motive for sympathy and satisfaction on our part.

We were the first and the most considerable of the American Republics. It became us therefore to take resolute ground against the projects then attributed to the Allied Powers, and to say to the nations of Europe with all respect but with firmness and dignity that we would not see with indifference the condition of things thus established, changed or put in peril by the intervention of any monarchical or aristocratic government. We could not permit any new colony to be planted by Europe in America though with such as already existed and had not obtained their independence we had no intention to interfere. The whole territory of that continent was already appropriated either by the independent states of America or by the existing colonies.

The U.S. declared at the same time their purpose not to take any part in the international politics of Europe, nor to meddle with the interior concerns of European states. The political systems of the two Continents had come to be radically distinct, and whilst we would ourselves refrain from all interference with the governments of Europe, reciprocally we claimed the right to say, we would not suffer patiently the intervention of any European power in the internal affairs of the nations of America.

The U. S. have faithfully adhered to the line of conduct they thus imposed upon themselves. We have neither been the allies nor the enemies of any European nation in its relations with the rest.

Many governments of Europe have since been put in peril by the efforts of parties in their interior, striving to establish democratic or republican institutions instead of such as before existed. But the government of the U. S. has not taken part in any way with these efforts. It has never undertaken the propagation of its own political system. So far as the knowledge of the undersigned extends, (and as to Spain I speak with full knowledge), it has never contributed a dollar or a musket in aid of the revolutionary movements which have from time to time occurred.

This conduct and this policy it has steadily maintained towards the governments of Europe in spite of the most urgent instigations to depart from it, and some times at the expense of hearing itself denounced as egotistical and indifferent by parties who merited and received the best sympathies of our people.

The relations of the government of the U. S. with the colonies still existing in America have been alike free from every suspicion of reproach.)

Not many years since the inhabitants of Cuba were generally supposed to be desirous to sever their connection with Spain and join themselves to the U. S. They certainly expended their money freely in the effort, and secretly recruited forces within the territories of the U. S. to aid in the enterprise.

A Spanish general at the head of about 400 men of five different nationalities succeeded in leaving our shores and landing in Cuba. But his reinforcements were cut off by the government of the U. S., which loyally and constantly discountenanced all such enterprises, impeded in most instances the departure of war material and recruits, and abandoned such persons as succeeded in escaping its vigilance to the responsibility of their own acts, declaring them alienated from its protection.

It is true that, for reasons connected with the existence of African slavery at the same time in a part of the Union and in Cuba, the enterprises referred to were favoured by a party within our limits, which party has since gone into open rebellion and war against the government of the U. S. itself. But the fact that there was some difficulty at home in the execution of its measures does not lessen but increases the proof of the faithful adherence of the government to the policy it had adopted, at a time when the dominion of Spain in her own chief colony was seriously in question.

I might have cited the conduct of my government towards the English colony of Canada a little earlier ; and a little later in 1854-55, Y. E. will remember that the more dangerous conspiracy again set on foot by Mr. Jefferson Davis and others against the peace of Spain in Cuba was made powerless by the conservative and loyal sentiments of the vast majority of the American people.

And here it may be well to say that, in the opinion of the undersigned, the material interest of the U. S. in the change which has been attempted in the island of S. Domingo is as small as it could well be. Perhaps in no other part of America would the overthrow of a republican government and substitution of the power of a

European state in its stead really affect the interests of the U. S. so little as the introduction of the Spanish jurisdiction in the Island of San Domingo.

It is the moral and political significance of the act of Spain which gives it importance, and because this is the first instance since the foreign policy of the U. S. was announced to the Allied Powers of Europe in 1823, that any nation has failed to see its own clear interests in the maintenance of that policy on the one side and on the other.

Spain alone and for the first time has chosen not to respect it. It must be supposed that she has calculated the value to herself of the precedent she has thus set up in America, but the undersigned confesses he has not been able to perceive it.

Indeed I have failed to see what considerable advantage of any kind Spain expects to reap from the occupation of S. Domingo; and may be permitted to doubt whether such an acquisition could in any case compensate her for the loss of her right to expect from the U. S. in future as heretofore the observance of a conduct so distinct from her own.

The Undersigned is not instructed what will be the ulterior action of the President in these circumstances; nor do I know whether he will think proper to depart from the settled policy of the nation towards Europe on account of this event. I do not propose to announce in any sense his future policy towards Spain.

But I call on the government of Spain itself to recognize, that the reciprocal obligations which the U. S. had imposed upon themselves and proclaimed to Europe have been annulled so far as Spain is concerned by her own failure to respect them.

By the act of Spain the U. S. are no longer bound to that policy which up to this time has been faithfully observed on their part, as well as in their relations with the people of the different nations of Europe as with their colonies.

Whether the U. S. will decide still to adhere to their time honoured policy or to depart from it in the case of this nation must depend hereafter upon their own appreciation of their duty and interest without reference to the wishes or interests of Spain.

Filled with profound regret at this unhappy state of affairs, the undersigned has now to fulfill the duty imposed upon him by the President, and in the name of the government of the U. S. of America solemnly protests against the assumption or exercise of Spanish authority in the Island of San Domingo; and this protest the U. S. in every case will expect to maintain.

The undersigned takes etc., etc.

HORATIO J. PERRY.

HIS EXCELLENCY
L. CALDERON COLLANTES [56]

The bluster of Seward and the note writing of Preston and Perry seem to have made very little impression upon the authorities at Madrid. The tone of the Spanish foreign secretary, Calderon Collantes, took little account of the great American dogma. In responding to Preston, indeed, on April 25, Collantes dwelt chiefly upon the spontaneity of the action of the Dominicans, and alluded not at all to the " general policy " of the United States.[57] The decision of Spain had not been taken, he declared. When it was taken, it would be made " without reference to interest or advantage, and mindful alone of what is demanded by its [Spain's] dignity and the power it represents." Seward's note of April 2, transmitted by Tassara, was passed contemptuously by without any reply from Madrid.[58] Then came Perry's

[56] Washington, Dept. of State, Despatches, Spain, vol. 43.

[57] Washington, Dept. of State, Spain, Despatches, vol. 42, Encl. A in No. 45, April 25, 1861.

[58] Tassara had written that it was written principally " with a view to presenting it to Congress," and that public opinion

protest, delivered in accordance with instructions early
in June, and followed by the note of June 19. To the
challenge contained in these documents, it was obviously
necessary to make reply. To Perry Seward had written
that the United States expected " to make its protest
effective." What, demanded Calderon Collantes in an
instruction of June 13 to Tassara, was the meaning of a
phrase of this kind? Was it the intention of the American government to menace that of Spain? Such a menace might oblige the Spanish government to prepare for
the worst eventualities. "Your Excellency will make
Mr. Seward understand," the instruction went on, " that
the reincorporation of Santo Domingo with Spain, precisely because it has been unanimous and spontaneous,
and on this basis accepted by Her Majesty the Queen,
is a *fait accompli*, which Spain will maintain by all the
means in her power." [59]

This instruction of June 13 was destined to cause the
American Secretary of State a good deal of embarrassment, and to teach him a needed lesson. He had blust-
ered a good deal too much, and now he was to be taken
down. In an interview with Tassara on July 8, confronted with the Spanish challenge, he said rather
weakly that he could not answer, having had no word
from Perry, but that he was free to say that the United
States sincerely desired to preserve intact its good rela-

was rather indifferent to the question of Santo Domingo. Ministerio del Estado, Negociación 171, Legajo 4 (10), April 5,
1861.

[59] Ministerio del Estado, Legación de S. M. en Washington,
Legajo 445 (21).

tions with Spain.[60]   In a later interview, held on July
29, he showed himself more adroit. He could hardly retreat with dignity from the position that he had assumed,
and so he began by declaring that Perry's protest had
been made under instructions, and that the United
States was obliged to consider the conduct of Spain as
" unfriendly and injurious to the interests of this
country." But there was not much reason, he added, for
the Spanish government to ask if a menace was intended. The United States was not accustomed to utter
threats, and it belonged to Congress alone to take action.
It seemed certain, he went on, that the Congress just
called in extraordinary session would not concern itself
with regard to Santo Domingo. As to the regular session in December, matters might be different, but the
Executive could not anticipate the action which might
then be taken.[61] With this not wholly dignified evasion
of the question propounded by the Spanish government,
the interview of Seward and Tassara came to an end.

But Calderon Collantes did not rest content with representations to Washington; he also made clear the
views of Spain to the American representative in Madrid. On the 9th of July he answered the note which
Perry had sent on June 19, and administered a sharp
rebuke to the chargé. " In this connection," (that is, in
connection with the Monroe Doctrine), he wrote, " I
ought to say, in regard to the government of Her Majesty, that this is the first time that the existence of such

[60] *Ibid.,* Negociación 171, Legajo 4 (22), July 8, 1861.
[61] *Ibid.,* (23) Anejo.

a policy has been officially & directly communicated to it. The Government of the Queen neither accepts nor declines this policy, it limits itself to saying that it does not think this an opportune time to discuss it, because it does not see the usefulness or the convenience of entering at present into such an examination." Collantes then went on again to emphasize the spontaneity of the action of the Dominicans. " It is not easy to comprehend," he remarked, " how the United States, which recognize as the fundamental principle of their political existence that of universal suffrage—that of popular sovereignty in all its extent & followed out to the last consequences, can deny to other peoples constituted in a manner analogous to their own the right to exercise their sovereignty in accepting the form of Government which they may think most convenient, or in reconstituting themselves in the way which they may judge most advantageous to their interests and their future well-being." [62]

[62] Washington, Dept. of State, Spain, Despatches.
The note of July 9 awakened the enthusiastic praise of Tassara, who had already expressed his delight at the defiance of the Monroe Doctrine. (Ministerio del Estado, Negociación 171, Legajo 4 (17), May 26, 1861.) His views on the Doctrine are worth citing. Originally enunciated against the Holy Alliance, " Europe did not pay to the Doctrine the attention which it deserved, and this Government was erected into a veritable arbiter of the public law of this continent. Matters did not go so far, however, as the exclusion of Europe and monarchical forms from this continent, but with the passage of time, and the launching of the United States upon a career of annexation, that Doctrine came to cover its own acquisitions, and with the complement of another no less celebrated phrase, ' manifest destiny,' began to furnish the formula for the general annexation of all

The technique of the diplomatic interchange which
we have just analyzed has an importance beyond that
of the question with which it deals. For the assertion,
in terms, of the Monroe Doctrine as a principle had led
only to its being challenged. At a later date, when the
government of Louis Napoleon set up a foreign monarchy in Mexico, and it fell to Seward to shape American policy in opposition thereto, the American Secretary in his despatches carefully avoided any specific appeal to the pronouncement of 1823. He had, perhaps,
always been opposed to so doing; but if he read the
despatches from Madrid in the spring of 1861 he must
have had ample confirmation of his prejudices. As a
popular dogma, the Monroe Doctrine was becoming of
fundamental importance; as a diplomatic weapon it was
still very far from potent. The significance of this con-

America. The present revolution tends to restore it in its political and anti-monarchical significance, and there are many signs
that this Government intends to arrogate to itself the exclusive
right to represent democracy in the world.

"Your Excellency understands the advantage we can gain
from the refutation of such doctrine. The ridiculous prurience
involved in not considering us as an American power, the
non-recognition of the former Dominican republic by this
government, the annexation of Texas, which to so many circumstances added that of its NOT BEING a people of the same race
which was involved [sic!], the circumstance that this was not
an annexation but a re-incorporation, which makes a great
difference from every point of view, are other indisputable
arguments to give a good lesson to the United States, above all
when Spain again attains a position equal to theirs in the balance of the influences of the world." (*Ibid.,* (24) August 5,
1861.)

trast will appear hereafter more fully when we turn to the French intervention in Mexico.

On the other hand, European statesmen had here used for the first time what might be conceived as a foil and useful counteragent to the Doctrine. Collantes had appealed in the note of July 9 to the doctrine of popular sovereignty! How could the United States answer an argument of this kind? How could they assume to fly in the face of the will of the people to determine its own destiny? How, then, could they oppose the reestablishment of European influence in the New World in accordance with democratic formulae?

In abstract logic there might seem to be no answer to this question. If a New World state by genuinely democratic methods resolved to reunite with an Old World monarchy, or by genuinely democratic methods called a European prince to rule over it, it would be very difficult to deny the validity of its choice. But fortunately for the United States, and unhappily for Europeans, no such situation existed in 1861 or indeed could exist. The action of the Dominicans, however much it might be made to appear democratic by pronunciamientos in this town and in that, was in reality determined by Santana and by none other; and the speedy development of armed opposition soon bore witness to how far it was from representing that spontaneous yearning for Spanish rule which Calderon Collantes described with so much pathos in his diplomatic papers. The sentiment of national independence was stronger than any Old World tie. The Spaniards, despite their phrase-making, were soon to learn to their cost how great a task was the reestablishment of European sovereignty in any part of the New World.

Yet, despite the difficulties that lay ahead, and which I must soon describe, there was apparently almost no one in Spain who, in 1861, was willing to oppose the glamorous opportunity to add to the dominions of Isabella II this new pearl of the Antilles. Newspapers of every political complexion hastened to approve the action of the government, without a thought of internal complications or of foreign opposition. In the press comments of the day, as they have been collected by Señor Nuñez de Arce,[63] one finds occasional reference to the aggressive views of the United States as justifying the annexation, but not one word of the Monroe Doctrine. In the same way, of the two pamphlets on Santo Domingo published in 1861 which have come under my notice, one ignores the point of view of the United States altogether, and the other dismisses the principles of 1823 light-heartedly in a single sentence, declaring them " wholly inapplicable." [64] In the Cortes a single voice, that of Olózaga, the leader of the Liberals, was raised in criticism, and this on the ground of possible future friction with the United States;[65] and in all other quarters silent acquiescence or enthusiastic support was the good fortune of the ministry of Marshal O'Donnell.

[63] Nuñez de Arce, *Santo Domingo* (Madrid, 1865), pp. 142-58.
[64] These are S. Ferrer de Couto, *Reincorporación de Santo Domingo à España. Breves consideraciones sobre esto acontecimiento* (Madrid. 1861), and Bona, Felix de. *Cuba, Santo Domingo, y Puerto Rico* (Madrid, 1861.)
[65] *Diario de las Cortes,* December 11, 1861.

The history of the next four years was to reveal a truth, not always realized in politics, that the size of the majority in favor of a given course does not necessarily bear any proportional relationship to its essential wisdom. Spanish rule in Santo Domingo, so light-heartedly assumed, was from the first, a failure, almost incredibly tactless and shortsighted. Santana himself, the genius of reannexation, was alienated within a year. Dominicans were replaced by Spaniards in the most lucrative offices, civilian and military. The pledge of the Spanish government to redeem Dominican paper in gold was again and again postponed, and finally violated. Increased taxes were levied. Rigorous and oppressive laws constrained the freedom of the people. The Governor-General sent out in July of 1862, General Felipe Rivero y Lemoyne, was a narrow-minded martinet of small abilities, with an infinite capacity for stirring popular irritation. It is no wonder that revolt flared up, to be repressed at first, but to attain serious proportions by the fall of 1863, and to be accompanied by the setting up of a Provisional Republican Government before the end of the year.[66]

The result was a military situation which became increasingly serious. Up to July, 1863, there were only about 3000 Spanish troops in the island.[67] But with guerilla warfare breaking out in every part of the coun-

[66] For these events, and on this subject, see Welles, *op. cit.*, pp. 231 *et seq.* Also General Gándara, *Anexión y Guerra de Santo Domingo* (Madrid, 1884, 2 vols.), especially I, 253 *et seq.*

[67] Washington, Dept. of State, Consular Despatches, Santo Domingo, August 31, 1863.

try it became necessary to bring in large reinforcements. By the end of the year nearly 13,000 Spaniards were busy persuading the Dominicans to be loyal to the flag which they had spontaneously welcomed in 1861.[68] Throughout the year 1864 there were reinforcements, and by the beginning of 1865 more than 25,000 soldiers had been sent to the island.[69] General Gándara, who assumed the supreme command in the spring of 1864 was an able and energetic officer. But it was impossible for him to prevail in the field against the guerilla warfare of the revolutionists, which had, as he himself confessed, assumed the proportions of a general rebellion.[70] The suffering from disease was frightful. Yellow fever took its heavy toll, and in December, 1864, had reduced by 50% the number of Spanish effectives.[71] The costs of the whole enterprise were becoming staggering.[72] Even the Spanish commander himself was ready to admit by the end of the year that there was no utility in trying to hold the island, though with the pride of his caste and of his race he wished to evacuate only after the insurrection had been put down.[73]

Some time before the end of the American Civil War, therefore, a change had begun to take place in Spanish

[68] Documentos Relativos a la Cuestión de Santo Domingo, remitidos al Congreso de los Diputados por el Ministerio de la Guerra (Madrid, 1865), p. 37.

[69] Ibid., p. 109.

[70] Gándara, op. cit., II, 291.

[71] Ibid., p. 112.

[72] The total costs are stated by Pirala to be 300,000,000 reals. Pirala, Historia Contemporánea., op. cit., III, 258.

[73] Gándara, op. cit., II, 473.

opinion. As early as October 24, 1863, Horatio Perry
reported that the intervention in Santo Domingo was
now almost universally condemned.[74] A few months
later he sent word that the Spanish newspapers were now
beginning to advocate withdrawal, and added once more
that hardly a Spaniard but regretted this unhappy enterprise. What was needed was a minister sufficiently
courageous to face the facts, and to face, not only the
facts, but the Queen, for Isabella II was obstinately
opposed to any reversal of policy. Such a statesman
was found in the cabinet crisis of September, 1864.
There was not much of democratic liberalism about General Narváez. But Narváez, unlike most politicians,
was not afraid of an unpleasant task. He took office
on the express condition that an end should be made to
Spanish rule in Santo Domingo. One of his first acts
was to announce to General Gándara that the Spanish
troops should be concentrated on the seaboard, and that
the question of Santo Domingo would be brought
before the Cortes when it convened at the beginning
of the year. At the same time he dissolved the Spanish
Parliament. The new elections strengthened his hand,
and the way was now clear, except for the opposition
of the sovereign. Isabella II, though she had accepted
Narváez with a clear understanding as to what was implied, still sought to avoid the inevitable. In December
took place a personal struggle between the minister and
the Queen. Narváez resigned; O'Donnell was sent for;
but the manoeuver failed. O'Donnell could not form

[74] Washington, Dept. of State, Despatches, Spain.

21

a ministry. Narváez came back into power with the policy of withdrawal more certain than ever. In January the debates in the Spanish Parliament began in earnest. In May the withdrawal was determined. The dream of a Spanish Santo Domingo had come to an unlovely end.

But what, during these years of trial for Spain in Santo Domingo, was the attitude of the United States? And may it not be that the decision that was taken in 1865 was in part due to the fact that victory had perched upon the banners of the North in the American Civil War, and that the ministers of Spain feared that the threats of Seward in 1861 might be made good? These are, of course, the central questions with regard to the whole Dominican episode from the viewpoint of the Monroe Doctrine, and to them we must now turn.

The blustering tone of Seward in the first months of his incumbency at the State Department had contributed nothing at all, as we have seen, to any solution of the question of Santo Domingo. Its failure may, on the other hand, have contributed to the political education of the Secretary himself. The easy optimism with which, at the beginning, he faced the issue of civil war, was soon sobered by the outcome of Bull Run. The rash utterances of the spring of 1861 were followed by an exemplary caution. The demagogue, if the word " demagogue " be not too harsh a term, was submerged in the statesman. In full recognition of the unwisdom of challenging foreign powers in the midst of a desperate internecine struggle, Seward abstained from any further forcing of the issue with regard to Santo Domingo. Not a word that is menacing or even highly critical is to be found in his instructions to those who represented the United States in Madrid in 1862 and 1863. When Gustavus Koerner, who was minister to Spain in the latter year, wrote a letter to Serrano which was critical of French policy in Mexico, and which invoked the Monroe Doctrine against French intervention there, Seward was prompt to despatch a rebuke, and to request the minister to withdraw the comments which he made.[75] In many respects this cautious policy was continued into 1864. In answer to Spanish complaints of unneutral conduct, Seward declared in March of that year that he had held no relations, even unofficial relations, with the Dominican revolutionists. And in May, while predicting to Koerner that the Spanish effort to establish its sovereignty in Santo Domingo would surely " end in disappointment," he suavely added, that this disappointment might " be delayed until the successful close of our troubles will allow the prestige of the United States to be restored.[76]

Yet the year 1864 must have afforded evidence to Spain that the policy of the United States was based on caution rather than indifference. In another quarter of the New World events occurred which led Seward to use, even in the midst of the dark days of the Wilderness campaign, language extremely direct and candid toward the Court of Madrid.

[75] Washington, Dept. of State, Instructions, Spain, February 28, 1863.
[76] Ibid., May 4, 1864.

The controversy between Spain and Peru which resulted in the seizure of the Chincha Islands by the Spanish admiral Pinzón need not long detain the student of
the Monroe Doctrine.[77] A diplomatic controversy between the two governments had arisen in August of
1863, when some Spanish workers on a plantation had
been brutally attacked and shot by the overseer. The
incident was a small one, but Spanish pride and Peruvian dilatoriness and obstinacy aggravated it into something important. At first the matter dragged its way
through the Peruvian courts; but finally the Spanish
government sent out an agent, Salazar, to press a settlement upon the government at Lima. The instructions of
this agent did, indeed, authorize the use of force, but
their general tenor was by no means unconciliatory.[78]

[77] For this episode, see especially Becker, *op. cit.*, II, 709-739,
and for a fuller account, P. de Novo y Colsón, *Historia de la
Guerra de España en el Pacifico* (Madrid, 1882), with important
source materials.

[78] See Novo y Colsón, *op. cit.*, p. 168, and Becker, II, 714.
" The mission confided to you is one of peace; the Government
wishes peace and good understanding, and by this means, rather
than by any other, the just reparation to which it aspires, and if
without its fault, it should be necessary to resort to demonstrations of force, the reasons which determine such action, taken in
concert with the commander of the squadron, ought to be such
that the Spanish government, by simply stating them, will be
justified before the nations of Europe and the rest of the civilized
world." If repulsed *in limine* Salazar was to withdraw, but he
was to negotiate if any hopeful result might be attained by negotiation. If all efforts at negotiation failed, an ultimatum was to
be despatched, demanding satisfaction within thirty hours, and if
no response were given, the matter was to be referred to Admiral
Pinzón. Even under these circumstances, however, Salazar was
to accept the mediation of the foreign Ministers in Lima, if this
mediation were offered.

But Salazar was already in a state of conflagration with regard to the sins of the Peruvian government, and his attitude was naturally not made more moderate by the refusal of the authorities at Lima to receive him, by the title of special commissioner, with which he had been invested by the Ministerio del Estado in Madrid. Sailing for the Chincha Islands, he there made rendez-vous with Admiral Pinzón. In defiance of their instructions, which required the submission of an ultimatum to the Peruvian government, the hot-headed diplomat and the bold naval man, having come together, proceeded to seize the islands and to justify their action in a manifesto in which, amongst other things, they promulgated the interesting theory that since Queen Isabella II had never recognized the independence of Peru, Spain might recover her property rights in the Chinchas.[79] Thus, having with brilliant success raised the maximum amount of suspicion in Latin America as to Spain's purposes, Salazar and Pinzón proceeded with ridiculous inconsistency to leave undisturbed the trade in guano which was the principal activity in the islands. A more inept piece of diplomacy (if the word " diplomacy " can even be used in connection with this episode) it would be impossible to imagine.

The news of these interesting events reached Washington on May 17, 1864. From the beginning of the Spanish-Peruvian controversy, Seward had taken a certain interest in what was going on ; and the good offices of the American government had been proffered at

[79] The manifesto is in Novo y Colsón, *op. cit.*, pp. 179-81.

Madrid and at Lima alike.[80] The danger of serious
trouble had not seemed great ; indeed the day before
word came of the seizure, the Secretary had written a
most optimistic despatch with regard to the whole matter to Madrid.[81] But now his tone changed. On the
19th he instructed Koerner, the American minister, to
" make it known to Her Catholic Majesty that the
United States cannot yield their assent to the positions
thus assumed in the name of Spain ; or regard with indifference an attempt to reduce Peru by conquest and
re-annex its territory to the kingdom of Spain." [82]

This interesting sentence did not stand alone. Seward seized the Chincha Islands episode for a franker
and more inclusive expression of policy. He alluded
to the French in Mexico, and the Spaniards in Santo
Domingo. The states of Latin America, he declared,
" allege that several of the European states, which once
had colonies here, are now seeking to reduce them again
to the condition of dependencies. These apprehensions
are not unlikely to be entertained by the whole people
of the United States. The proceedings of Spain in Peru
give them a color which is deeply to be regretted. Indeed, a general discontent with the forbearance of the
government is already manifest. Should the sentiment
of this country demand a reconsideration of the policy
of neutrality which this government has hitherto maintained, it is much to be feared that new complications
might arise, which would not merely disturb the exist-

[80] *Diplomatic Correspondence,* 1864, part 4, pp. 16-7, 23.
[81] *Ibid.,* p. 21.
[82] *Ibid.,* p. 24.

ing systems of commerce, but might endanger the general peace of nations. . . . . "

This language was the measure of a genuine irritation, but of an irritation really quite superfluous. The Spanish government had never cherished designs of territorial aggrandizement in the Pacific. It was pursuing a policy of prestige, as weak governments are prone to do, but it had already had its fill of conquest. Almost as soon as the news of the seizure of the Chinchas reached Madrid, the prime minister, Señor Mon, assured Koerner that Spain had no intention of retaining possession of the islands,[83] and on June 21 the Foreign Secretary, Llorente, addressed a circular to the diplomatic corps in which he expressly disavowed all thought on the part of Spain of recovering any part of her ancient colonial dominion in Latin America.[84] Two months later, Llorente declared to Perry that he could assure him, " without any hesitation, that the Monroe Doctrine of the United States would not be called in question, by any proceeding of Spain in or against Peru. If President Monroe were alive and on the spot, he should see nothing running counter to his famous declaration." [85] This must have been sweet consolation for Calderon Collantes's note of July 9, 1861. The tone was certainly more respectful in 1864 than it had been three years before.

The seizure of the Chinchas was to be the prelude to a long diplomatic controversy between Peru and Spain.

[83] *Ibid.,* p. 30.
[84] Novo y Colsón, *op. cit.,* pp. 203-6.
[85] *Diplomatic Correspondence,* 1864, part 4, p. 100.

But the islands themselves were given up in January of 1865, and it is not necessary for us here to follow the episode any further. What is interesting and important with regard to it, is the firmness of the tone assumed by Seward, and the reference to the Monroe Doctrine by the Spanish minister.

In the light, indeed, of Llorente's language to Koerner, it seems wholly probable that in Santo Domingo, as in dealing with the Chinchas, the Narváez ministry knew that it might have to reckon with the American government. There were numerous other factors involved, of course; indeed the effort to retake the island was, by the fall of 1864, most clearly a fiasco; but an additional argument for " cutting the painter " could undoubtedly be found in the trend of events in the United States.

In the debates in the Cortes, the Monroe Doctrine and the attitude of the United States were occasionally alluded to. In the Camera de los Diputados, Benavides, a member of the cabinet, called attention to the language of the New York newspapers, declaring that American ambitions no longer were limited to the fulfilment of the principles of James Monroe, but looked to the total expulsion of Europe from the New World,[86] and adduced the desirability of good relations with the government at Washington as one of the many reasons justifying withdrawal. In the Senado, Señor Lozano, the minister in charge of Spain's overseas dominions, brought forward a similar argument.[87] In neither the

[86] *Diario de las Cortes,* 1864-65, p. 1338.
[87] *Ibid.,* p. 797.

one case nor the other, however, was the point heavily stressed. Nor, indeed, would one expect otherwise. Spanish pride in itself would dictate that no great emphasis be placed on any fears that might be felt as to the attitude of another power.

The enemies of the government, however, made on occasion great play of American ambitions to support their own point of view. Canovas del Castillo declared that the island must be retained, since it was impossible not to fear a clash with " a military, proud and aggressive nation like the United States," [88] and another deputy drew a lurid picture of a clash of civilizations, of another Salamis in which Europe would, of course, play the rôle of Greece, and America that of the barbarians.[89]

It will be interesting to add to these denunciations the tirade of a Spanish pamphleteer. Of four Spanish pamphlets on the question of Santo Domingo, written in 1864 and 1865, two make no mention of the principles of 1823, and one only a passing allusion to it.[90] But a fourth work, written by one Cayetano Martín y Oñate, expresses itself as follows:

" The Monroe Doctrine summed up amounts to this, that all the European nations should abandon the great

[88] *Ibid.*, p. 1317.

[89] *Ibid.*, p. 1303.

[90] These pamphlets are as follows: Don Joaquín Francisco Campuzano, *Remedio Radical para su Situación, La de Cuba y Puerto Rico.* (Madrid, 1865) J. Lopez de la Vega, *La Cuestión de Santo Domingo.* (Madrid, 1865) Anon. *De la Cuestión de Santo Domingo. Nueve Interesantes Artículos que Publicó el Independiente.* (Madrid, 1865) In this last, there is an allusion to monarchy as the best system, " in opposition to the exclusive system of Monroe." p. 5.

and legitimate interests which they have acquired in America during more than three centuries at the cost of blood and immense sacrifices, leaving to the inhabitants of those countries liberty to constitute themselves anew, as if a lacerated and debilitated body could thus attain health.

" On the same principle it should be permitted still to the barbarians, to attack the merchant vessels of all peoples, whose tribulations were the victims of their cruelty, and whose wealth was the prize of their avarice. On the same principle the Mexican should have been permitted to adore his idols, the Chinese to continue to sacrifice their children, and to remain like the Japanese cut off from the commerce of the world; the cannibals should be permitted to devour their prisoners, and lastly, all the savages should be abandoned to the grossest errors, to the most repugnant moral practises, to the most ferocious instincts." [91]

The reasoning of Señor Martín y Oñate in this remarkable passage may not seem entirely convincing to an American. Yet however grotesquely, however excitably, phrased, the theme was not in its essence an absurd one. What this writer saw, what other Spaniards saw, what Disraeli had seen a decade before, was a tendency which in its day had terrified Pozzo and Alexander, and was to be the subject of frequent comment long after the Dominican episode itself had been fully liquidated. Could there exist, ought there to exist, a differentiation, a differentiation both broad and deep, between the Old World and the New? Was the doctrine of the two spheres a sound one? This was, after all, no slight question, and it would not be answered by Ameri-

[91] Martín y Oñate, *España y Santo Domingo*, (Toledo, 1864), pp. 17-18.

cans today as it would have been answered in 1864. The assumption implicit in the Monroe Doctrine that two alien systems of government and statesmanship confront each other across the Atlantic, would no longer be regarded as sound. The separation of the United States from Europe is today less of a fact than it has been in generations.

At the moment, however, when Martín y Oñate penned the words we have just quoted, the prestige of the principles of 1823 was about to be reestablished. Those principles had been challenged in Santo Domingo. They were now to be vindicated. They had been challenged, too, in Mexico. There, too, they were to be vindicated. To an examination of this weighty question of Mexico, perhaps the most important in the whole history of the Monroe Doctrine, we must now turn.

CHAPTER VI

The Clash of Systems in Mexico

If Santo Domingo was to some extent the theater of a diplomatic conflict between the Old World and the New in the period from 1850 to 1865, and a sharp challenge to the Monroe Doctrine, it was not, as has been said, the most important area in which the clash of systems expressed itself. The most striking episode, perhaps, in the whole history of the Doctrine is the French intervention in Mexico. To understand this intervention fully it is necessary to trace the relations of the Mexican republic with Europe and with the United States from the end of the Mexican War. In the events of this interesting period is to be seen revealed a clear-cut rivalry between two conceptions of foreign policy, as well as the inevitable tendency which made of the principles of 1823 a justification of American expansion. One finds also interesting evidence of the increasing desire of Mexican leaders themselves to summon Europe to their aid against the Colossus of the North. A growing American imperialism, a growing suspicion and jealousy of American purposes on the part of European statesmen, a growing dependence on European aid on the part of Mexican conservatives, this is the summation of the story which we must now examine in some detail.

Of the period immediately following the war, however, it is necessary to say comparatively little. When the American troops evacuated Mexico City they left in control as President the conciliatory and liberal Herrera, a man whose views were far indeed from reaction, and during his administration a brave effort was made under republican forms to introduce order and progress into the affairs of the distracted state. The monarchical faction which had backed Paredes was by no means stamped out; the most influential papers in Mexico City supported, openly or covertly, the monarchist cause, and the *ayuntamiento* of the capital was in the hands of its partisans; but there could be no possibility of action of any kind as long as the Liberal party remained in power, and for a time even the Mexican appetite for revolution seems to have been satiated. Herrera was able to pass on his office to his regularly elected successor, General Arista, in 1851. But soon the violence of Mexican factionalism was resumed; local revolts in 1852 soon widened into party uprising, and early in 1853 the notorious Santa Anna again assumed the presidency. There can be no question whatsoever that the monarchists were behind this change of government, and one of the first moves of the new President was to appoint as his minister of foreign affairs Lucas Alamán, one of the very ablest members of the monarchist group in Mexico City.

It cannot be maintained that the reentry of the Mexican conservatives into power was directly caused by the attitude of the United States. Yet the story of the

relations between the two countries during the years of
the Liberal régime makes it easy to understand why
anti-American policy should thrive in Mexico, and why
the supporters of Santa Anna soon began to look to
Europe for aid.[1] An ample number of causes for friction existed during the years following the signature
of the peace treaty. The United States proved impotent
to restrain the Indians on the northern borders of Mexico. Filibustering raids were set on foot on the American side of the boundary. A boundary dispute quickly
arose with regard to the terms of the treaty of Guada-
lupe Hidalgo. The claim to a right of intervention on
the Isthmus of Tehuantepec put forward by Webster
in the negotiations with regard to the establishment of
communications by an American company in that region, and the attitude of the company itself, gave ground
for suspicion on the part of the Mexican government,
and for accusations of imperialism on the part of the
Mexican press. And finally, the victory of the Democratic party in 1852 carried with it the implications of
an expansionist policy, and gave to the large party in
Mexico which distrusted the United States new food
for agitation. The most influential conservative paper
in Mexico was steadily anti-American at the end of
1852 and the beginning of 1853.

It is, then, not difficult to understand why the régime
of Santa Anna, which assumed power on April 20, 1853,
should turn its gaze toward Europe from the very

[1] For a good discussion of this period, see J. F. Rippy, *The
United States and Mexico* (New York, 1926), pp. 42-105.

moment of its coming into existence. Don Lucas Alamán had apparently been promised something of a free
hand. Only ten days after the triumphant entry of the
new President into the capital, Alamán entered into a
most interesting conversation with Levasseur, the
French minister at Mexico City. He dwelt with emphasis on the hopes which Mexico placed in the power of
France; he declared that what was most desirable for
his distracted country was an hereditary monarchy,
which did not seem possible at the moment; he spoke
feelingly of the menace from the United States, and
declared that it was incumbent upon Europe to establish
a balance of power in the New World as it had established a balance of power in the Old. He suggested that
France take the lead in a triple negotiation with Great
Britain and with Spain for the protection of Mexico
from the Colossus of the North.[2] This interesting proposal, so contrary to the spirit of American policy, and
to the principles of the Monroe Doctrine, found no very
cordial response in Paris. The year 1853 was a year
of impending crisis in the Near East, and so the French
government instructed its minister that while it might
be willing to lend its good offices to a settlement of the
disputes outstanding between Mexico and the United
States, it found the views of Alamán too vague to permit it to undertake the initiative in the triple negotiation
proposed. Most obviously, Louis Napoleon, now Emperor of the French, could not enter upon any ambitious

[2] Paris, Min. des Aff. Etr., Corr. Pol., Mexique, vol. 41, April
30, 1853.

program in Mexico at the time when war clouds were looming in Europe. The language of the Quai d'Orsay at this time was uniformly cautious and noncommittal in dealing with the problems of the New World.

The overture of Alamán to Levasseur, however, does not stand alone as an indication of Mexican interest in the possibility of French assistance. In the archives of the Ministère des Affaires Etrangères at Paris is also to be found a Mexican memoir of October 24, 1853. In this memoir the familiar anti-Americanism finds vigorous expression. The pretension of the United States to exclude Europe from the New World is denounced as a mere cover for aggression, which can only be checked by the action of France and of Great Britain. If the " new Vandals and Goths " are to invade the territories of their helpless neighbor, why should France stand helplessly aside? Why should it not declare that it will not permit any such action? Why should it not guarantee Mexico against spoliation? More concretely, why should it not guarantee Mexican possession of the Isthmus? Why should it not (and this is rather hinted than positively expressed) ally itself with the struggling republic which bars the way to Anglo-Saxon imperialism? [3]

It is needless to say that this second appeal to the French government fell upon deaf ears. More than ever, in the fall of 1853, Louis Napoleon was preoccupied with the affairs of the Near East. War had actually been declared between Russia and Turkey, and

[3] *Ibid.*, October 10, 1853.

the intervention of France and Great Britain in the struggle appeared more and more imminent. Mexico, very decidedly, must wait. Its appeals to Europe were ill-timed and futile. But the very existence of such appeals, is a fact of considerable interest, and the basis of that appeal of an interest greater still. For the essence of the matter is clearly this; that the Mexican drift toward Europe and the Mexican monarchical movement derived their sustenance in no small degree from fear of the United States; and that, moreover, dread of the growing domination of the Anglo-Saxon race in the New World was the argument that was deemed most decisive and most potent in securing support from the great power across the Atlantic. In the numerous discussions of the question which crop up in the years ahead this point becomes increasingly and overwhelmingly clear; and its relation to the Monroe Doctrine and to the American pretension of excluding Europe from the affairs of the American continents is obvious. The existence of a genuine " doctrine," as has already been seen, was now becoming well known both in the lands to the south and on the other side of the Atlantic; the possibilities of aggression implicit in such a " doctrine " were more and more definitely understood; the memoir of 1853 expresses a point of view which is to be iterated and reiterated in the years to come.

Nor was the appeal to France in 1853 the only evidence of effort to enlist European assistance during the régime of Santa Anna. In May Santa Anna sounded the Prussian minister with regard to the possibility of

22

securing a corps of 5000 or 6000 men from the Prussian government, and was given some assurances of support for this project,[4] only to find that the government at Berlin did not share the view of its representative at Mexico City.[5]

On July 1, Gutierrez de Estrada was invested with full powers " that he might enter into negotiations with the governments of London, Paris, Madrid, and Vienna, and make whatever offers were necessary to obtain from all these governments or from any one of them, the establishment of a monarchy derived from one of the dynastic houses of these powers." [6]

At the end of the year, almost certainly impelled by the fears aroused by the first of the filibustering expe-

[4] Washington, Dept. of State, Mexico, Despatches, vol. 16, May 14, 1853.

[5] Paris, Min. des. Aff. Etr., Corr. Pol. Mexique. vol. 41, May 4, 1853.

[6] *Circulares y Otras Publicaciones hechas por la Legación Mexicana en Washington durante la Guerra de Intervención* (Mexico, 1868), p. 232.

Gutierrez de Estrada, as we have seen, had fled from Mexico in 1840 after seeking in vain to promote the cause of monarchy. Faithful to his principles and prejudices, De Estrada had been dreaming of Mexican monarchy in the safe luxury of European capitals; he had presented a long memoir on Mexico to the Austrian Chancellor Prince Metternich, in which the familiar arguments of American ambition and the menace to the Old World system were duly rehearsed with a prolixity and turgid eloquence worthy of the author. (Vienna. Staatsarchiv. March 28, 1846, in a communication to Prince Richard Metternich, July 4, 1861, cited in Egon Cesar Count Corti. *Maximilian and Charlotte of Mexico*. (New York, 1928, 2 vols), I, 30-2.) His appeal had, of course, produced no effect upon the most realistic of reactionaries.

ditions of William Walker, who invaded Lower California in November, the Mexican government addressed its diplomatic agents in England, France, and Spain, soliciting the aid of these states against the northern Colossus, and followed this document by another in January of 1854.[7] Santa Anna even assured Doyle, the British minister, that he would resign his position to any foreign prince whom the European powers would engage to support upon the throne of Mexico.[8] He made a vigorous effort to enlist British sympathy, but was met with a blank refusal upon the part of the Foreign Office in London.[9]

When this effort failed, the Mexican dictator turned to Spain, toward which court Gutierrez de Estrada set out early in 1854, accompanied by José Hidalgo, whose name, as we shall see, bulks large in the history of Mexican monarchy. The situation at the Spanish court seemed not unfavorable; the government was in the hands of a rigidly conservative and clerical group which might have been expected to prove somewhat sympathetic; Queen Isabella, then as later, had romantic hopes of placing one of her family upon a New World throne; and Gutierrez afterwards claimed that he had received definite assurances of support for a plan to install the Infante Don Juan of Bourbon in Mexico. It seems, as

[7] See H. E. Bolton, *Materials for the History of the United States in the Archives of Mexico* (Washington, 1913), pp. 229-30.

[8] London, P. R. O., F. O., Mexico, vol. 261, no. 117, December 3, 1853.

[9] *Ibid.*, vol. 265, no. 9, January 16, 1854.

a matter of fact, not improbable that high personalities
in Madrid would have supported such a project. In
Mexico itself, the American minister reported to his
government that Spanish officers and men were being
daily admitted into the army, and the way prepared for
the success of a monarchical intrigue.[10] The existence of
some understanding between the two governments is
not in the least unlikely. But, most unfortunately for
all such designs, revolution broke out in the Spanish
capital; a ministry less reactionary—and less romantic—
came into power, and the negotiations collapsed.[11]

It is interesting to note that some suspicion of this
intrigue penetrated to the government at Washington,
and that the notion of a struggle between the republican
and monarchical systems is clearly expressed in the
despatches of the American minister in Mexico City
during the period of Santa Anna's rule. This minister
was James Gadsden of South Carolina, the negotiator
of the Gadsden treaty for the cession of the Mesilla
valley. Gadsden was very obviously a strong Monroe
Doctrine man. Very early in the negotiation of the
important compact that bears his name, we find him
writing to the Secretary of State that he has read to
Bonilla, the Mexican Secretary of Foreign Affairs, " a
chapter from Mr. Monroe's manifesto," a chapter,
which, on perusal, affords incidental illustration of the

[10] Washington, Dept. of State, Despatches, Mexico, vol. 18,
No. 38, September 2, 1854.

[11] J. M. Hidalgo, *Proyectos de Monarquía en México*
(Mexico, 1904), p. 58. See also F. deP. de Arrangoiz, *Méjico
desde 1808-1867* (Madrid, 1892, 4 vols.), II, 341-42.

way in which the famous message of 1823 had more and more become the Bible and sacred oracle of expansionism. Gadsden learned of the Spanish project in May of 1854. He was desperately concerned with regard to it, and anxious for American intervention on the side of the liberals in a conflict that might " shake another continent to its center." [12] And he continued to sound the alarmist note throughout 1855 reporting rumors of new overtures on the part of Santa Anna to the European powers, and repeating his plea for the active intervention of the American government.[13]

At Washington Gadsden's views do not seem to have been taken very seriously. The relations of the American minister with Secretary of State Marcy during the greater part of his mission were very far from cordial; the policy of the Pierce administration under Marcy's direction was the well-considered one of nonintervention in the strife of Mexican parties; and no hint of agitation at the monarchical projects of the Mexican régime appears in the volumes of instructions in the State Department. Certainly, so far as France and England were concerned, there could be no reason for any other feeling than tranquility while the Crimean War was raging in Europe, nor was very much danger to be anticipated from impotent Spain, so far as the application of armed force in the affairs of the New World might be concerned.

[12] Washington, Dept. of State, Mexico, Despatches, vol. 18, September 2, 1854.

[13] *Ibid.,* vol. 19, May 18, 1855 and November 17, 1855. For Gadsden's views on intervention, see particularly the former despatch.

Yet if there was no truly aggressive design on the part of any European government there was certainly a very deep-seated fear of the United States on the part of the European diplomats in Mexico City. Throughout the negotiation of Gadsden the British and French ministers were very decidedly apprehensive. Doyle, the British representative, was in constant touch with what was going on, and throughout most of the period of the dictatorship, gave constant advice to Santa Anna with regard to his relations with the American government.[14] His suspicions of the United States only deepened with time. In 1854 he urged Santa Anna to reject the Gadsden treaty, fearing that the amendments attached thereto by the United States Senate would give to the United States a right of intervention in the domestic politics of Mexico.[15] And in 1855 he suggested to the Mexican dictator that the Mexican minister at Washington be instructed to act in concert with the representatives of France and Great Britain, a step which clearly shows his dread of the design of the American government.[16] His attitude, it is not too much to say, was consistently anti-American. So, too, was the attitude of his French colleague. The despatches of M. Levasseur, a diplomat already known to us through his activities in Santo

[14] London, P. R. O., F. O., Mexico, vol. 261, December 18, 1853, cited in P. N. Garber, *The Gadsden Treaty* (Philadelphia, 1923), p. 99.

[15] *Ibid.*, July 3, 1854. The so-called Sloo amendment attached to this treaty of cession gave to the United States the right to intervene to protect the work of Sloo grantees, who had a concession for a railroad across the Isthmus of Tehuantepec.

[16] *Ibid.*, January 2, 1855.

Domingo, are filled with jealous references to the United States, and appeals to his government to intervene in Mexico. " Only Europe can save Mexico," he wrote as early as August, 1853.[17] " Mexico has become the avowed object of the conquering ambition of the United States," thus runs another despatch. " If it finishes by falling into their hands, it would be difficult to arrest the march of their domination in the New World. Masters of this immense territory, will they not be able to lay down the law to Europe?" [18] A little later, the French minister sent to his government, no doubt as expressing his own views, a clipping from the conservative Mexican newspaper, *El Universal*. In this clipping is instituted an interesting comparison between decadent Mexico and decadent Turkey, between Constantinople, the focus of the commerce of the East, and Tehuantepec, the focus of the commerce of the West, between the aggressive designs of Russian despotism, and those of American republicanism. " Ambition, the abuse of strength, and aspirations toward universal domination are the distinctive traits of " the national policy of both, the writer declared. " Russia aspires to dominate in Europe in the name of despotism, and the United States to dominate in America in the name of liberty. The principle of monarchy, imposed with all its exaggerations and abuses by the sabre of the Tsar, and the lance of the Cossacks, and the democratic principle, imposed by the rifle of Yankee adventurers end in the same results, absolutism

[17] Paris, Min. des Aff. Etr., Corr. Pol., Mexique, August 1, 1853.
[18] *Ibid.*, vol. 43, January 1, 1855.

and tyranny." [19] The language of Levasseur's own despatches indicates that he fully sympathized with the views herein expressed.

The mistrust of the French minister with regard to the United States is also indicated in his attitude toward the various projects of the Mexican government for introducing into Sonora bands of colonists who might serve as a barrier against the Apaches, and possibly against American hostility. In the winter of 1852, the notorious Raousset de Boulbon appeared in Mexico City.[20] This extraordinary soldier of fortune, a broken man, had drifted to San Francisco in 1850. There he had formed a connection with the French consul, M. Patrice Dillon, who encouraged him to visit the Mexican capital, with a view to leading an expedition into Sonora, and exploiting the rich mines of Arizona. M. Levasseur welcomed the adventurer, and not only facilitated for him an agreement with the Mexican government, and the formation of a mining company, La Restauradora, but actually took stock in the company himself! [21] When Raousset's first expedition into Mexico collapsed, owing to the hostility of the local authorities, it was Levasseur who initiated new efforts to bring him into contact with the Mexican government. When Santa Anna came into power in April of 1853, the

[19] Encl. in *ibid.,* May 15, 1855.

[20] For the best brief account of Raousset's exploits, see W. O. Scroggs, *Filibusters and Financiers* (New York, 1916), pp. 23-30 and 52-66.

[21] E. Vigneaux, *Souvenirs d'un Prisonnier de Guerre au Mexique* (Paris, 1863), p. 193.

French minister urged him to send for the Count, and a meeting was again arranged in Mexico City in June.[22] Nor did the collapse of the negotiations then undertaken end the matter. Negotiations, then renewed, broke down, and the French soldier of fortune returned to San Francisco, to lead into Mexico a filibustering expedition in 1854 in which he met his death. But the visit of De Boulbon to Mexico City did not end the projects of colonization in Sonora. The Walker expedition of the fall of 1853 only increased the anxiety of the Mexican government to take some kind of action looking to that end. In the spring of 1854 the Mexican consul at San Francisco was instructed to send 3000 Frenchmen to Guaymas. His efforts, though aided secretly by M. Dillon, were not brilliantly successful, and ran afoul of the neutrality laws of the United States. But in this, as in previous episodes, M. Levasseur gave his entire support. While not committing his government, the French minister was always to be found encouraging the anti-American measures of the dictator.

The attitude of the European ministers in Mexico City was, no doubt, much more apprehensive, and their hostility to the government of the United States much more active, than that of the foreign offices at home. Lord Clarendon throughout the period of his administration of the Foreign Office was extremely cautious in the expression of his views to Doyle. There is almost no evidence of anti-American sentiment in his despatches, and Drouyn de l'Huys, the Foreign Minister

[22] *Ibid.*, p. 198.

of Napoleon, pursued a rather similar policy. There is
no reason to believe that the projects of Raousset de
Boulbon, for example, received any support from the
Quai d'Orsay. On the contrary, enterprises of this
kind were systematically discouraged, and the French
ambassador at Washington doubtless expressed the
view of his government in describing the last of Raousset's expeditions with the cutting epithet of " mauvaise
plaisanterie." [23] Despite the alarmist tone of Levasseur,
De l'Huys remained very cautious in the expression of
his viewpoint during all of 1854 and the first part of
1855; the only exception to this generalization is to be
found in the instructions of May 15, 1855, in which
the French representative at Mexico City was invited
to make it clear to the American minister that France
" attached the greatest interest to the independence of
Mexico in its existing limits," and that " any aggression
which should menace them would not fail to command
serious attention." [24] While this one phrase might seem
at first blush to announce a stronger and more definite
policy, it was not followed up in any degree for a long
time to come, and cannot therefore be taken extremely
seriously. Occasional references to American ambition
creep into the correspondence of the French Foreign
Office, but that there was any serious consideration of
anti-American policy in the course of the years 1853-
55 cannot be maintained. It is possible, of course, that

[23] Washington, Dept. of State, Instructions, France, December 17, 1852.
[24] Paris, Min. des Aff. Etr., Corr. Pol., May 15, 1855.

had the Santanista régime not coincided with a great European war there might have been a different story to tell.

In August of 1855, however, even the faintest hope of the establishment of monarchy was dashed by the revolution which unseated the Mexican dictator. The pendulum in Mexico began to swing back toward liberalism; the ultra-conservative groups who were always the strongest supporters of the monarchical idea were deprived of governmental influence; and the orientation of Mexican foreign affairs seemed to be rather toward the United States than toward the powers of the Old World. By Gadsden, of course, this change of system was hailed with enthusiasm, and in the course of the next year and a half both he, and his successor Forsyth, aimed at liquidating the differences which still existed between the Mexican and American governments, and bringing the disordered republic into closer relations with its greater and stabler neighbor. It is not necessary here to follow the efforts of either one or the other of these ministers in their details; as a matter of fact, very little was actually accomplished and the various agreements negotiated by Forsyth, going far beyond his instructions, were repudiated by the Buchanan administration.[25] But what is interesting and important with regard to these negotiations is the point of view from

[25] These treaties included a reciprocity treaty, a postal convention, a compact for the settlement of commercial claims, and a convention providing for a $15,000,000 loan, partly secured by the customs duties. (See Washington, Dept. of State, Despatches, Mexico, February 2 and February 10, 1857.)

which both Gadsden and his successor regarded them. They thought of what they were doing as involving the opposition of American and European systems. " The Europeanizing of all Mexico, of all South America," wrote Gadsden to Marcy, November 25, 1855, " in opposition to Anglo-American vandalism North of the Rio Grande has to be fought here." Still more striking is the language of Forsyth, writing early in 1857, when the conventions which he negotiated had been rejected by the Buchanan administration. " It is not safe," he declared, " for statesmen of the United States to ignore the fact that other nations besides our own have their eager gaze fixed upon this rich and superb country. Whether Mexico maintains her personality or falls to pieces, we have a deep interest in her future, and should secure an influence in her counsels. If she cannot stand without the aid of some friendly power, and the late appeal to our country is a confession of it, what Power. . . . should occupy the commanding position of benefactor and friend? If the United States refuse some other must. What if it comes in the form of a French Prince supported by ten thousand French bayonets? Or of British gold, effecting that floating mortgage on her territories which we decline? Believe me, Sir, we cannot afford to play the ' dog in the manger ' with our Monroe Doctrine. Mexico cannot afford to perish for the want of a Medical interventor, because we choose not to be the physician. She must lean upon some power. Shall it be Europe or the United States? I answer unhesitatingly the United States, by every consideration of humanity, good neighborhood and sound policy. For if it be Europe, I can see a multitude of contingencies that will make Mexico the battle ground for the maintenance of American supremacy in America; the theater for the practical illustration of the value and virtue of the Monroe Doctrine." [26] Language such as this clearly reveals the clash of systems which was to lead straight toward the intervention of European powers in the New World.

It was hardly to be expected that European diplomats would view with equanimity the activities of Gadsden and of Forsyth. If, to American eyes, there seemed danger of European intermeddling in the affairs of Mexico, to European eyes the danger of the absorption of Mexico by the United States was equally clear. In the period from the fall of Santa Anna to the actual landing of European troops on Mexican soil, the growing antagonism of viewpoint was nourished by the aggressiveness of American policy on the one hand, and by the fears of European intermeddling on the other.

The administration of James Buchanan began, as has been said, with the rejection of the special treaties negotiated by John Forsyth. At the outset the new President apparently desired no policy of interference in the affairs of the distracted republic to the South. Though President Pierce had in his last annual message alluded to the mounting claims of our citizens

[26] Washington, Dept. of State, Despatches, Mexico, April 4, 1857.

against the Mexican government for the various indignities which they had been made to suffer, and though the situation was becoming worse rather than better throughout 1857, there is no allusion to Mexican affairs in Buchanan's communication to Congress in December, 1857. The existence of a liberal government is a partial explanation of this self-restraint. But far more important is the persistent land hunger of the administration. The student of the premature imperialism which precedes the Civil War will wish to fix his attention sharply upon the yearning for Mexican territory which characterizes the later fifties. The province of Lower California and a right of way across the Isthmus of Tehuantepec were the objects of American acquisitiveness. So, too, was much of Sonora and Chihuahua. Secretary Cass, only a few months after his assumption of his duties in the State Department, instructed Forsyth to seek a cession of these territories in exchange for the payment of twelve to fifteen million dollars, and the mutual settlement of claims.[27] While there seemed some hope that Mexican complacency might be persuaded to agree to such an arrangement, the tone of the Buchanan administration was one of pious moderation.

In Congress, however, a different spirit early asserted itself. As early as January, 1858, Senator Houston of Texas had introduced into the Senate a resolution calling upon the Committee on Foreign Relations to investigate and report as to the advisability of establishing a protectorate over Central America and Mexico, and

[27] Washington, Dept. of State, Instructions, Mexico, July 17, 1857.

three months later he had spoken on the subject in a discourse filled with references to the Monroe Doctrine.[28] The efforts of the Texan Senator to secure support for his resolution were fruitless; it was defeated by a vote of 32 to 16 on June 2. Congressional sentiment seems to have been opposed to any aggressive policy in Mexico, a fact, connected, no doubt, with the increasing sectionalization of our politics, and the consequent northern reaction against ambitious programs of expansion to the southward.

The defeat of the Houston resolution might have conceivably led the administration to a policy of moderation; but, as a matter of fact, the general trend of events in 1858 produced exactly the opposite effect. Early in the year new political upheavals took place in Mexico. President Comonfort, the successor of Alvarez, after an unsuccessful attempt at a *coup d'etat,* resigned, leaving Benito Juarez as his successor, and his resignation was followed by a reactionary coup which brought the conservatives into power in Mexico City under the leadership of General Zuloaga. Though in possession of the capital, the new government was not able to put down the Liberal faction under Juarez, and Mexico was, for the next three years, embarked upon the bitterest internecine strife which it had yet known. The ensuing

[28] Houston declared himself to be the last surviving member of the Congress of 1823, to which Monroe's message was addressed. He spoke at length of "the continental policy which they (*i. e.,* the people of the United States) cherish and desire to see enforced." *Cong. Globe,* 35th Cong., 1st Sess., p. 1682, April 20, 1858.

anarchy and disregard for the rights of foreigners in Mexico produced a situation which tempted to a more vigorous policy. The administration's hopes of territorial gain led in the same direction. Overtures looking to a cession were first made of the Zuloaga régime, but these overtures completely failed. By May Forsyth, acting on his own initiative, had broken off relations, using as his reason for doing so, the levy of what he considered as a forced loan on the property of foreigners. His action was sustained at Washington, and the administration embarked upon a policy which developed more and more into one of support of the Liberal faction in Mexico.

Into this new policy an element of distrust of European purposes entered. The prepossession of the reactionaries for Europe was obvious. From Mexico City Forsyth wrote disquietingly of the reactionary tendencies of the French minister, De Gabriac, of his intense anti-Americanism, of his dreams " of a European protectorate to be followed by a Mexican kingdom or empire." [29] Even more portentous was the state of tension which existed between the Zuloaga régime, and the government of Spain. For some years the two governments had been at odds with regard to the inevitable question of claims; negotiations had been undertaken in 1856, but had broken down; at the beginning of 1858 relations were completely severed; and in the course of the summer and early fall disquieting rumors

[29] Washington, Dept. of State, Despatches, Mexico, June 25, 1858.

of the preparation of a Spanish squadron which should sail for Mexico reached the ears of the authorities in Washington. From London Dallas wrote disquietingly of Spanish designs.[30]

In his message of 1858 Buchanan took an aggressive stand. Describing the situation to Congress, he declared that only the possibility of the triumph of the Juarist forces restrained him from recommending to the national legislature the partial occupation of Mexican territory, to be held in pledge for the redress of grievances. He also proposed the occupation of northern Sonora and Chihuahua, for the better protection of the border. Finally, his message contained a distinct warning to Europe. " It is a duty which we owe to ourselves," wrote Buchanan, " to protect the integrity of Mexico's (its) territory against the hostile interference of any other power. Our geographical position, our direct interest in all that concerns Mexico, and our well-settled policy in regard to the North American continent render this an indispensable duty."

The message of 1858 received no very favorable reception in Congress; indeed a motion to authorize the President to use the armed forces of the United States for the protection of American citizens in Mexico failed to reach the floor of the Senate; but the administration during 1859 pressed forward in a policy which represented a more and more definite alignment with the Liberal faction in Mexico. In December a special agent

30 G. M. Dallas, *Letters from London* (2 vols., London, 1870), II, 127.

23

was sent out to investigate conditions,[31] and on favorable reports with regard to the Juarez régime, and its willingness to cede territory to the United States a regular minister was accredited in March, 1859, in the person of Robert M. McLane of Maryland. Torn between loyalty to the policy of nonintervention in Latin American factional disputes, and an eager desire to buttress the Mexican elements most friendly to the United States, Cass instructed McLane to recognize the Juarez régime " at the earliest period when its condition and prospects would justify us in doing so," and even added that " possession of the capital need not be regarded as a *sine qua non* of recognition." [32] Within a month after the date of these instructions official relations had been established with the Liberal government, though the civil war continued unabated. Though efforts at a treaty for the cession of territory failed to make much headway, President Buchanan took a still more decisive stand in favor of the Juaristas in his message of 1859. Alluding in detail to the outrages committed upon American citizens in Mexico, especially by the reactionary government at Mexico City, he went on to declare that for the vindication of these outrages it would be necessary to penetrate into the interior of Mexico. " This can only be done," he declared, " by passing through the territory in the occupation of the constitutional Government. The most acceptable and least difficult mode of accomplishing the object will be

[31] Washington, Dept. of State, Instructions, December 27, 1858.

[32] *Ibid.*, March 7, 1859.

to act in concert with that Government." Recommending the raising of a military force for this purpose he declared, " Such an accession to the forces of the constitutional Government would enable it soon to reach the City of Mexico and extend its power over the whole Republic. In that event there is no reason to doubt that the just claims of our citizens would be satisfied and adequate redress obtained for the injuries inflicted upon them." [33]

Conscious that so frank an advocacy of intervention in the affairs of a neighboring republic was bound to arouse opposition, Buchanan called the Monroe Doctrine to his aid. Declaring that Mexico was now " a wreck upon the ocean, drifting about as she is impelled by different factions," he went on to say, " as a good neighbor, shall we not extend to her a helping hand to save her? If we do not, it would not be surprising should some other nation undertake the task, and thus force us to intervene at last, under circumstances of increased difficulty, for the maintenance of our established policy." Thus once again the language of 1823 became the basis for a policy, not of nonintervention, but of intermeddling in the affairs of an American state.

The Congress of 1859-60, preoccupied with the slavery question and with the approaching presidential election, paid no attention whatsoever to the recommendations of Mr. Buchanan. They do not appear even to have been debated in either House. But the administration went ahead along the path which it had chosen;

[33] Richardson, *Messages,* V, 567-8.

and in December of 1859, at the very time that these
recommendations were put forward, McLane succeeded
in negotiating with the Juarez government, more and
more desperate for want of funds, the extraordinary
treaty known as the McLane-Ocampo treaty. By this
treaty in exchange for a loan of $4,000,000 the United
States secured perpetual rights of way across the Isthmus of Tehuantepec, and also from Matamoras, or some
other convenient point on the Rio Grande to Mazatlan,
and from Guaymas to Rancho de Nogales. It was given
free ports of entry at the end of these routes, the right
to transport supplies and troops, and more striking still,
the right to employ military force for the protection of
transit, and to intervene, in cases of extreme danger,
even without the consent of Mexico. And in addition
to all these privileges, the treaty was accompanied by a
convention, the first article of which virtually gave to
the United States a general power of police over Mexico. Not till the turn of the twentieth century was a
document of such far-reaching character to be negotiated with any Latin American nation.

Once again, however, the views of the administration
were not the views of the national legislature. The
McLane-Ocampo compacts were defeated by the decisive vote of 27 to 18 in the Senate, in May of 1860, and
with their rejection ended all hope of a solution of the
Mexican difficulty by the Buchanan administration. The
presidential campaign and the crisis which followed
Lincoln's victory thrust the Mexican question into the
background.

The aggressive policy which we have just outlined is of the highest interest. It illustrates in the most forcible fashion, more forcibly indeed than any other episode, the way in which the Monroe Doctrine could be brought to the service of a policy of expansion; and it furnishes the only proper background in which to study the designs of European powers. The European intervention whose course we shall have to trace in succeeding chapters has naturally been regarded by many Americans as a singularly reprehensible challenge to the United States; so, indeed, from one point of view, it was; but from another angle it must have appeared to many trans-Atlantic observers as a kind of counter-agent to the rapacity and insatiable ambition of the Colossus of the North. The action and reaction of American and European policy deserve to be carefully examined.

I shall have something further to say on this matter in the course of this chapter, but before turning to the European view of things it may be well to examine one other aspect of Buchanan's policy. If the United States were prepared to pursue a policy of expansion, the principles of 1823 might be used not only to justify such a policy, but to warn off all intruders. The territorial ambitions of the United States might be justified by the invocation of Monroe's dogma; and still more reasonably that dogma might be used as a basis for fine moral indignation with regard to any ambitious views on the part of European powers. There are several important pronouncements of this kind. The first is to be found in the instructions to Dodge, the American minister in Madrid. At a time when Spanish action against Mexico seemed imminent, in the fall of 1858, Cass instructed this minister to make enquiries at Madrid, and if the occasion should arise to assert the principle that the United States would not " consent to the subjugation of any of the independent states of this continent by European powers, nor to the exercise of a protectorate over them, nor to any other direct political influence to control their policy or institutions." [34] This instruction Dodge furnished, with a translation, to the Spanish foreign minister, Calderon Collantes. It brought forth a complete disclaimer as to " interfering with the well-known policy of the United States as expounded by Mr. Monroe [sic!], and reiterated by yourself." [35] For sometime after this exchange of view the despatches with regard to Mexico, whether from European capitals or Mexico City itself, contained nothing that was threatening ; but the course of the year 1860 found the administration once more ready to assert its principles.   In August, replying to a proposal for common action on the part of France, Great Britain, Spain, and the United States to mediate between the contending factions in Mexico, the American Secretary of State took occasion once more to state rather fully the position of his government. [36] In September, new rumors

[34] Quoted in Moore, *Digest of International Law,* VI, 477.

[35] Washington, Dept. of State, Spain, Despatches, vol. 41, November 15, 1858.

[36] Washington, Dept. of State, Instructions, Mexico, vol. 17, No. 38, August 8, 1860.

of Spanish action being in the air, he expressed the American opposition to intervention in an interview with the Spanish minister, Tassara.[37] At the same time he instructed Mr. McLane, then about to return to Mexico, along similar lines.[38] Finally, the American point of view was most strikingly and definitely asserted in a circular which Mr. LaReintrie, an American agent sent to Mexico City by McLane, transmitted to the members of the diplomatic corps there in December, 1860. " The United States," read this circular, " has determined to resist any forcible attempt to impose a particular adjustment of the existing conflict against the will and sanction of the people of Mexico, and, also, any forcible intervention by any power which looks to the control of the political destiny thereof. . . . .

" The government of the United States does not deny to the European powers the right to wage honorable warfare for a sufficient cause, anywhere, or against any nation; nor does it deny their right to demand redress for injuries inflicted on their respective subjects . . . . but it does deny them the right to interfere, *directly* or *indirectly,* with the political independence of the republic of Mexico, and it will, to the extent of its power, defend the nationality and independence of said republic." [39]

The opposition of the United States to a genuine intervention in Mexico was thus well known by the

[37] Moore, *Digest,* VI, 481.

[38] Washington, Dept. of State, Instructions, Mexico, vol. 17, No. 39, September 20, 1860.

[39] 37th Cong., 2nd Sess., H. Exec. Doc. No. 100, pp. 17-18.

end of the Buchanan administration. But the door had been left open, none the less, for just such action, for, though denying the right to interfere with the political institutions of Mexico, the American government had more than once admitted the right of European states to take punitive action for the redress of grievances. As will have been noticed, the La Reintrie circular stated explicitly that there was no denial of the " right to wage honorable warfare, for a sufficient cause, anywhere, or against any nation," and this point of view appears in most of the other despatches to which reference has just been made. The distinction is an important, and, in some respects, a sound one. It was, in the main, in accordance with the historic interpretation of the Monroe Doctrine. The French war against Mexico in 1838 had awakened no resistance at Washington. Neither had the contemporary action in the Argentine. Though Buchanan had looked askance at the Franco-British meddling in La Plata in 1846, he had never protested against it directly. No blockade or threat of blockade by a European power had ever met with a veto on the part of the government in Washington. But, soundly based as the distinction between political intervention and international war might be, it was clear that one might be merged into the other. The actual course of events was to demonstrate that what might begin as a movement for the redress of grievances might easily be transformed into something far more dangerous.

Let us turn, then, from the policy of the United States to the policy of the European powers. The most important of these is doubtless France. And what will appear at the outset, picking up the story at the year 1856, where it was abandoned, is the steady development of French interest in Mexico in the years from 1856-61. In February of the first-named year, appears another of those numerous Mexican memoirs which are to be found in the French Ministère des Affaires Etrangères. The author is Tomás Murphy, identified with Mexican diplomacy over a period of more than a quarter of a century. The familiar note of antagonism to the United States is sounded once again; the notion of an American balance of power is again reiterated; the reader is assured that the Monroe Doctrine can be made an end of through the combined efforts of France and England.[40] The appeals of Murphy are supplemented by the language of the French minister in Mexico City, the Comte de Gabriac. Throughout the year this diplomat writes insistently of the desirability of intervention, of founding a monarchy in the Constantinople of the West,[41] of the strength of monarchical sentiment in Mexico, and of its steady increase, and the tone of the observer is exchanged for that of the advocate and the partisan.[42]

[40] Paris, Min. des Aff. Etr., Corr. Pol., vol. 45, Mexique, February 17, 1856.

[41] *Ibid.*

[42] *Ibid.,* September 1, 1856, September 5, September 9, October 2, October 27.

On September 1 De Gabriac directly recommended the establishment of a monarchy. "It would cost less," he wrote, "than making war on Mexico every fifteen years," and would be a mortal blow to universal demagogy, and above all to that of America. France has checked Russian ambitions in Asia, he

In 1857 the famous despatch of Forsyth, of April 4, 1857, is somehow gotten hold of and transmitted to Paris, with a view to whipping up hostility to the United States; [43] and later in the year another despatch bears witness to the close association of De Gabriac with the royalist faction in Mexico City.[44]

With the beginning of 1858, it will be remembered, the reactionaries regained control of the government at the capital. They lost little time in making overtures, no longer unofficial, but distinctly official, for assistance from Europe, with the usual plea for an American balance of power. In May the Mexican President definitely sounded De Gabriac with regard to the possibility of aid from France, or France and Great Britain combined,[45] and in August the appeal was reiterated.[46] The French minister's urging in behalf of an active policy became more and more striking. Buchanan's message of 1858 caused him the most acute anguish. It was received at Mexico City, he declared, with " general stupor." " More than ever, all eyes are turned toward Europe and especially toward France." [47] The recog-

---

added, why should it not put a check to demagogic passion in America? On October 2, he asks the question whether it is not better to chastise the Americans now rather than later. " Do not let the United States become as strong as the Russians, and force us to spend 1500 millions and sacrifice 200,000 men."

[43] *Ibid.*, April 22, 1857. De Gabriac speaks of monarchy, as being, from Forsyth's point of view, an " infraction of the laws of Monroe."

[44] *Ibid.*, September 17, 1857.

[45] *Ibid.*, May 31, 1858.

[46] *Ibid.*, August 8, 1858.

[47] *Ibid.*, December 26, 1858.

nition of Juarez in April, 1859, was " the application of the Monroe Doctrine in the form of a defiance of Europe," [48] and the McLane-Ocampo treaty little less than a catastrophe of the first order.[49] In despatch after despatch De Gabriac pled for an active policy on the part of his government in Mexico. And always the theme was the same, that Mexico could only be saved from absorption by the United States through the intervention of European governments. Again and again is the clash of systems illustrated in the correspondence in the French archives.

In the meantime what was the attitude of Louis Napoleon himself, and of his ministers? In early October of 1856, a Frenchman by the name of Radepont appeared in Paris as the emissary of the Mexican monarchists. He was sent by a rich Mexican, and his mission was to secure from France a small amount of military

[48] *Ibid.,* April 18, 1859.

[49] *Ibid.,* December 19, 1859.

De Gabriac had this to say of the McLane-Ocampo treaty : " It is evident that, in securing from a shadow government, composed of Indians and mulattoes, like Messers. Juarez, Ocampo, and their associates, the keys of Northern and Southern Mexico, the moment may arrive when Europe, taking thought and understanding all the importance of such concessions, and ready to unite to rule the destinies of the Old Continent, will find the means of taking charge of the affairs of the New World, in order to establish there the equilibrium become so necessary to its interests, and of making America enter into European public law, since the relations between the two hemispheres have become so rapid, so numerous, and so vital that their rupture would produce a profound check or a general catastrophe."

aid.[50] It is clear from the records at the Quai d'Orsay
that sometime late in 1856 or early in 1857 he had two
interviews with the Emperor himself and that the project
of founding a monarchy in Mexico was discussed in
some detail, apparently with a Spanish prince as the
most likely candidate.[51] More important still, by the
middle of 1857, Gutierrez de Estrada had established
relations with the French court. Sometime in June he
saw Louis Napoleon himself, and not only talked with
him about the monarchical idea, but also left with the
Emperor a long memoir which reiterates the now
familiar arguments for European intervention in the
distracted republic across the seas.[52] In the fall of the

[50] Radepont had once been French military attaché at Washington. He had gone to Mexico City in 1846 and had remained
there as a resident, without any official status. *Ibid.*, October
4, 1856.

[51] *Ibid.*, February 25, 1858.

[52] *Ibid.*, June—1857, and June 17, 1857.

We may note parenthetically here the appearance in 1857 of
an interesting work on Mexico, by Mathieu de Fossey, a Frenchman who had lived for a considerable number of years in that
country. (Matthieu de Fossey. *Le Mexique* (Paris, 1857.))
De Fossey is a strong advocate of monarchy. He pleads for a
European guarantee of Mexico (p. 450) against the " ambitious
republicans " of the North, for joint action by England, France,
and Spain against a people in whom " the good sentiments of
a candid adolescence " have been " succeeded, almost without
transition, by the shameful vices of a disordered youth." In his
judgment 6,000 men would suffice to protect the country from
the Americans (p. 451), and ninety-nine hundredths of the population would welcome such an intervention (p. 574). He pleads,
too, for the colonization of Mexico by Europeans, the sending
out of small farmers to the country (pp. 469-485). I have been

same year José Hidalgo, who had been occupied as we have seen in the Spanish negotiations of 1854, but who was now no longer in any official position, established personal relations with the Empress, who was to be the pronounced partisan of the Mexican adventure, and in the course of 1858 this man was entertained at the imperial chateau of Compiègne, and there held long conversations with the Imperial pair on the grand design of the restoration of monarchy in Mexico. Moreover, in the summer of 1858, evidently under the influence of the overtures of President Zuloaga to De Gabriac, an attempt was made to enlist British support in behalf of a possible intervention.[53] It is not impossible that action might have been undertaken thus early if the attitude of the British government had been favorable. But Lord Malmesbury, the Foreign Secretary in the Derby ministry, far from welcoming such a proposal, declared that the easiest way out of the Mexican imbroglio was annexation by the United States, and this chilling reply put an end to all further discussion of an aggressive policy at that time.[54] The course of events in Europe, indeed, soon thrust the whole question of monarchy in the New World into the background. At the very time of the overtures of '58, just mentioned, Napoleon III had already held the famous interview of Plombières

---

unable, however, to discover any connection between De Fossey and the Mexican monarchists, or, on the other hand, any contact on his part with governmental authorities.

[53] Paris, Min. des. Aff. Etr., Corr. Pol., vol. 45, Mexique, September 9, 1858.

[54] *Ibid.*, September 27, 1858.

with Cavour, and the stage was being set for the quarrel with Austria, and the active support of Sardinia in its strivings for the unification of Italy. In April war broke out. For the next year, until the treaty of Turin, ceding Nice and Savoy to France, the Italian question preoccupied the mind of the Emperor of the French. The most cautious policy was pursued with regard to Mexico. Though De Gabriac remained as interventionist in temper as ever, the French government, it would appear, gave no thought whatever to any policy of force between the date of the overture to Malmesbury and the negotiations of the fall of 1861.

In these three years, indeed, the chief apprehensions that were felt with regard to European armed action against Mexico had to do, not with the Court of the Tuileries, but with the Court of Madrid. We have already seen that relations were badly strained in 1858, and that they awakened the apprehensions of the United States. The danger may have seemed greater than it actually was, for as early as the spring of that year the reactionary régime at Mexico City had instructed its minister at Paris, Almonte, to open negotiations with Madrid; the friendly offices of France and Great Britain were exerted to make these negotiations a success; and though the situation remained somewhat threatening at the end of the year, concessions made by the Mexican government to Spain, largely as a result of French and British urging, paved the way for the Mon-Almonte convention of 1859.[55] But there were certainly elements

[55] For these negotiations see *Archivo Histórico Diplomático Mexicano*, vol. 13, El Tratado Mon-Almonte, Mexico City,

in Spanish politics, who dreamt, as had been dreamt before, of the restoration of monarchy in Mexico. A despatch of Señor Mon, the Spanish ambassador at Paris, in November, alluded to the strong interest which Europe had in the establishment of a strong and durable government in Mexico ("strong and durable government" being a favorite euphemism for monarchy), and expressed the fear that the Anglo-Americans would take advantage of the prevailing anarchy to take possession of their unhappy neighbor.[56] That the Spanish government itself had Mexico very much on its mind is shown by what followed on the heels of the Mon-Almonte convention, that is, a proposal, made in January, 1860, for a triple guarantee, by Great Britain, France, and Spain, of the territorial integrity of the Mexican republic.[57] In the fall of 1860, moreover, the natural hostility with which Madrid viewed the régime of Juarez, the protégé of the Washington administration, came near to culminating in action. Orders went forth for a blockade of Vera Cruz, and had it not been for the reluctance, indeed the refusal, of Serrano, the Captain-General of Cuba, to embark upon any such measure, a genuinely serious situation might have resulted. Nor was the Spanish attitude made more yield-

---

1925. It is even doubtful whether the Spanish government would, in any case, have resorted to hostilities. Count Waleski, the French foreign minister, told Almonte that he believed the warlike talk of the ministry was intended to influence the next elections, and was not seriously meant. (*Ibid.*, p. 29)

[56] *Archives Diplomatiques*, Paris, 1862, III, 205.

[57] Becker, *op. cit.*, II, 488.

ing by the events of early 1861. In January Benito
Juarez made his triumphant entry into Mexico City,
and one of his first acts was to dismiss the Spanish
minister, Pacheco, who had been guilty of the indis-
cretion of delivering his credentials to the reactionary
government in the last days of its rule. The obligations
assumed by the Mon-Almonte convention remained
undischarged; and Spanish honor and Spanish interest
alike might be readily conceived as demanding action
against inglorious Mexico.

The year 1861, as a matter of fact, saw the long policy
of patience pursued by the European powers in dealing
with Mexico give way to a policy of action. The British
government, long the partisan of a policy of moderation
and of mediation between the opposing factions, finally
found its patience nearing exhaustion. British private
claims against the Mexican government, in the conditions of anarchy which existed, had been steadily
mounting; the British embassy had been robbed of
$660,000 by persons connected with the Miramon gov-
ernment; a convoy of specie on the way to Vera Cruz
had been plundered by a Juarez partisan; and when
a new minister, in the person of Sir Charles Wyke, was
sent out in March of 1861, he was instructed to demand
satisfaction for the injuries sustained, and, if necessary,
call upon the naval forces of Great Britain in Mexican
waters to enforce his demands.[58] Faced with continued
obstruction and delay by the Juarez government and

[58] Wyke's instructions are in *British and Foreign State
Papers,* 1861-2, LII, 237.

with Mexico still in turmoil and disorder, Wyke's despatches from the beginning disclosed a distinctly interventionist bias.[59] By August 21 Lord John Russell, the British Foreign Secretary, was writing to him, instructing him to demand that the British be put in control of the customs at Vera Cruz and at Tampico, and if this demand was refused, the British minister was instructed to leave Mexico City.[60] And not long after the sending of this instruction came news of the suspension by the Mexican government, by a decree of July 17, of its international obligations, as defined in a series of conventions in force between it and foreign powers, and of the murder of a British vice-consul at Tasco. That such a series of events should have led the British government to consider a policy of coercion rather than of persuasion is not entirely remarkable.

As for France, her claims against Mexico, as compared with those of Great Britain and Spain, were really quite inconsiderable. But the hands of the Emperor were now freer than they had been for some time, so far as Europe was concerned; intervention in Mexican affairs would no longer violate the principle of co-operation with Great Britain, to which Louis Napoleon attached considerable importance; and the position of the United States was no longer such as to make action very difficult. Dubois de Saligny, the new minister sent out to Mexico in December, 1860, had made himself the earnest partisan of a forward policy, and on the

---

[59] See *ibid.*, p. 269 *et passim.*
[60] *Ibid.*, p. 285 *et seq.*

24

publication of the Mexican decree of July 17 he had, on his own initiative, broken off relations with the authorities in Mexico City. On August 18 he addressed to his government a despatch in which he pleaded for intervention in the affairs of Mexico, taking advantage of the troubled conditions which prevailed in the great republic to the North.[61] Early in September the Quai d'Orsay began to set the wheels in motion for common action against the unhappy régime of Juarez.

The Spanish government, as has been seen, had long had its grievances against Mexico; it had addressed a virtual ultimatum to the Mexican government in April; and by September the unwieldy Spanish machine was moving toward the despatch of a naval expedition to Vera Cruz. The way was clear, then, for an understanding of the three powers, and the diplomatic conversations of September and October culminated in the London Convention of October 30, 1861. The document thus signed was to open a new chapter in the history of the relations of Mexico and Europe.

[61] Paris, Min. des Aff. Etr., Corr. Pol., Mexique, vol. 55, August 18, 1861.

CHAPTER VII

INTERVENTION IN MEXICO

Before the convention of London had been signed, there had already been set in motion from Paris the train of events which was to lead to the rebirth of monarchy in Mexico, and to the acceptance of a throne in the New World by the unhappy Austrian Archduke Maximilian. No episode in the history of the nineteenth century involves more dramatically the clash of the systems of the New World and the Old, and none bears more directly upon the evolution of the Monroe Doctrine. It will not be necessary, of course, to examine it in all its details. That task, indeed, has already been done, never better than in the richly documented study of Count Egon Cesar Corti. The object of this and the succeeding chapter is not to add one more account of the enterprise of Mexican monarchy to those already extant, but to underline, and develop in detail, those aspects of that enterprise which relate themselves to the general principles under examination in this volume.

It is obvious that such a task must begin with an examination of the motives and point of view of the government of Louis Napoleon at the time when the project of Mexican monarchy emerged from the sphere of vague if pleasing speculation and romantic dreaming, and became a positive element in the foreign policy of the Second Empire. This emergence had begun, it ought to be observed, as early as September, 1861. At that time José Hidalgo had a long discussion on Mexican affairs with the Emperor and the Empress at Biarritz. The Emperor still remained extremely cautious; while conceding that intervention might be desirable he spoke only of sending ships, and no landing troops; but at the same time he discussed in tentative fashion the possibility that the action of the European powers might lead the country " to organize itself " and offered no opposition to the sounding of the Austrian government as to its views on the eventual candidacy of the Archduke Maximilian.[1] On October 9, having ascertained that the Austrian government was not entirely unfavorable, Louis Napoleon went a step further, and penned an important confidential letter to the Comte de Flahault, the French minister in London, in which he developed the project in more detail. Alluding to the tripartite intervention now clearly in prospect he went on to say, " According to the information I have received," he wrote, " as soon as the squadrons arrive off Vera Cruz a considerable party in Mexico is prepared to seize the supreme power, summon a national assembly, and proclaim the monarchy. I was asked confidentially who would be my candidate in the event of this happening. I declared that I had none, but should the occasion arise, it would be necessary to choose a prince informed with the spirit of the age, endowed with sufficient intelligence and firmness to found a durable order

[1] Notes Secrètes de M. Hidalgo, Vienna, Staatsarchiv, quoted in Corti, *op. cit.,* I, 100 *et seq.*

of things in a country disturbed by so many revolutions; and lastly that this choice should not wound the susceptibilities of the great naval powers; and I put forward the name of the Archduke Maximilian." [2] Two days later the French foreign minister, M. Thouvenel, made a somewhat similar declaration to Señor Mon, the Spanish ambassador at Paris.[3]

It is evident, then, that the setting in motion of the Archduke's candidacy for the Mexican throne preceded by some three weeks the signing of the convention of London, on which the intervention in Mexico was at first to be based. Yet the second article of that convention contained a specific engagement by which the contracting parties bound themselves not to " exercise in the internal affairs of Mexico any influence of a nature to prejudice the right of the Mexican government to choose and to constitute freely its own form of government." There seems here to be an inconsistency amounting to absolute duplicity, stamping the policy of Louis Napoleon from the outset as lacking in the most essential elements of good faith.

Yet it is doubtful whether such would be an absolutely fair view of the matter. At the outset it seems fair to say that the Emperor of the French did not regard the intervention in Mexico as one having for its object the imposition of a form of government upon the Mexican people against their will. The theory of his action was quite a different one. It is to be found devel-

2 Quoted in Corti, *op. cit.,* I, 362.
3 *Archives Diplomatiques,* 1862, III, 313.

oped in some detail in the instructions given to Admiral Jurien de la Gravière, who was placed in command of the forces sent out to Mexico in the fall of 1861. " The Allied powers," wrote Thouvenel, " do not propose, as I have said to you, any other object than that indicated in the convention ; they obligate themselves not to inter- fere in the internal affairs of the country, and especially not to exercise any pressure upon the will of the popu- lations as to the choice of their government. There are, however, certain hypotheses which foresight must take into account, and which we ought to examine. It may be that the presence of the allied forces upon the terri- tory of Mexico will encourage the healthy part of the population, tired of anarchy, eager for order and quiet, to make an effort to constitute a government presenting those guarantees of strength and stability which have heretofore been lacking in all those régimes set up since emancipation. The Allied powers have a common inter- est of the clearest kind in seeing Mexico emerge from the state of social dissolution into which it is plunged, and which paralyses the development of its prosperity, renders worthless for itself and all the world all the riches with which Providence has endowed its favored soil, and obliges other governments to have recourse periodically to expensive expeditions to remind ephem- eral and senseless régimes of the duties of government. This interest ought to lead them not to discourage at- tempts of the nature which I have just indicated, and you ought not to refuse your encouragement and your moral support, if as a result of the initiative of individ- uals and the sympathy that such individuals meet with

in the mass of the population there are chances of success for the establishment of an order of affairs assuring
to foreign interests the protections and the guarantees
which have hitherto been lacking." [4]

This important despatch, though written by the Foreign Minister, Thouvenel, gives an accurate impression
of the Emperor's mind in the fall of 1861. There was
no fixed intention to impose a government upon the
Mexican people by force, and there was not, indeed, any
absolute commitment to the monarchical idea itself.
But what was hoped, and no doubt expected in Paris,
was that the intervention would be the signal for a national rising, and that a monarchical government would
follow as a matter of course. The odious régime of Juarez
would be overthrown, and a stable and ordered government take its place.

It is today entirely clear, of course, that Louis Napoleon grotesquely misjudged the actual situation in
Mexico. He was misled by the interventionist ardor of
Dubois de Saligny, whose despatches reflected an incon-
sequent optimism; he was surrounded by the fuglemen
of Mexican monarchy, and hearing from their lips what
he ardently desired to believe, took their rosy predictions for gospel truth; he was urged on by his impetuous consort, who never denied her immense interest in
the Mexican intervention. [5] He assumed, as is clear from

[4] *Documents Diplomatiques,* Paris, 1862. Also quoted in
Ernst Schmit Ritter von Tavera, *Geschichte der Regierung
des Kaisers Maximilian I und die Französische Intervention in
Mexico* (2 vols., Vienna, and Leipzig, 1903), I, 77 *et seq.*

[5] For evidence of Eugénie's ardor, see Library of Congress
Transcripts, Haus-Archiv Kaiser Maximilian von Mexico

the letter to the Comte de Flahault already quoted, that
the monarchical cause would triumph as soon as the
intervention had begun, and in one of the first of his
letters to the Archduke Maximilian written in January,
1862, he again declared that he did not believe there
would be any important resistance.[6]

To this general conception that the Mexican people
were to be liberated rather than to be enslaved, were,
under the aegis of France, to have an opportunity to
constitute a government of their own choice, Napoleon
remained during all the earlier period of the intervention
consistently attached. To Lorencez, for example, who
was sent out to take command of the French land
forces in January, 1862, the Emperor wrote in June,
" It is against my interests, my origins, and my principles, to impose any government whatsoever upon the
Mexican people. Let it choose in all freedom the form
which is best suited to it." [7] To Forey, who succeeded
Lorencez, he expressed himself as follows : " The end
to be attained is not to impose upon the Mexicans a
government which will be antipathetic to them, but to
support them in the effort to establish according to their
own desire a government which has chances of stability
and can guarantee to France the redress of the grievances of which she complains. It goes without saying
that if the Mexicans prefer a monarchy it is France's

Karton 1, Docs. 3 and 9, Waleski-Metternich, July 16, 1861,
Metternich-Rechberg, October 6, 1861.

[6] Quoted in Corti, *op. cit.,* I. 365.

[7] Quoted in G. Niox, *Expédition du Mexique* (Paris, 1874),
p. 199.

interest to support them in this preference, and in this case the general may indicate the Archduke Maximilian as the candidate of France." [8] The same point of view he continued to express throughout 1862. Thus in November of that year he wrote, " Once order is established, before convoking a legislative body, I think it would be necessary to have all the Mexican people vote, Yes or No, by means of universal suffrage, as to whether they desire a republic or a monarchy.[9] And again on December 17, he wrote, " The only policy to pursue is to march on Mexico to install a government of the honorable men that you can yourself choose, and then have the Mexican people vote by universal suffrage as to the form of government they wish to establish." [10] It may seem fantastic to assume that a foreign intervention could be the means of constituting a government freely constituted by the Mexican people, and matters certainly did not work out this way in practise, as we shall see ; but, after all, making allowance for the sources of the Emperor's information, and the natural inclination of human beings in general to believe what they desire to believe, it is not difficult to see that Louis Napoleon thought of himself as liberating rather than enslaving the Mexican people, and that he was not completely insincere when he declared in the letter to the Comte de

[8] Genaro García, and Carlos Pereyra. *Documentos inéditos ó muy raros para la historia de Mexico. Correspondencia secreta de los principales Intervencionistas Mexicanos* (36 vols., Mexico, 1903), XIV, 12.

[9] *Ibid.,* I, 41.

[10] *Ibid.,* p. 51.

Flahault, already mentioned, " I seek nothing but good, convinced that to try to make a people prosperous is to work effectively for the prosperity of all." It is a difficult matter to analyze intentions, even our own; but it seems fairly clear that when the Emperor of the French gave his consent to the convention of London, he did not conceive of his own purposes as running absolutely counter to its provisions. If one chooses to call this self-deception, well and good. But there is a case for the argument that downright hypocrisy would be too strong a term.

This does not mean, of course, that the purposes of the French government were wholly or preponderantly altruistic ones. A variety of motives prompted the Mexican expedition, from the point of view of French interests. From a purely political angle, it was no doubt hoped by the imperial politician to win the support of the Catholic party at home, whose susceptibilities had been badly rasped by the Italian intervention of 1859; there was also a vague hope, expressed by Thouvenel,[11] that the setting-up of an Archduke upon a Mexican throne might facilitate the solution of the question of Venetia, and perhaps lead to the cession of that province to Italy by Austria. There was the desire to build up a market for French manufactures in the New World, and perhaps also a source of supplies, especially for cotton, that would free France from its dependence upon the United States, dependence emphasized by the Civil War

[11] L. Thouvenel, *Le Secret de l'Empereur* (Paris, 1889, 2 vols.), II, 176.

and the Northern blockade of the South, and there was also, beyond a shadow of a doubt, a conviction that the creation of a Latin and Catholic monarchy would furnish a useful counterpoise to the Protestant republic to the north.

It is, of course, the last of these motives that particularly interests the student of the Monroe Doctrine. There can be no exact balancing of the various elements which determined the Emperor of the French to embark upon the Mexican adventure; but it can be stated beyond a doubt that hostility to the United States was one of them, and that the existence of the Civil War in 1861 had a great deal to do with his decision. In the letter of October 9 to the Comte de Flahault, Louis Napoleon expressed himself as follows: " There is no need for me to enlarge upon the common interest which we in Europe have in seeing Mexico pacified and endowed with a stable government. Not only has that country, which enjoys every advantage, attracted much of our capital, and many of our fellow-countrymen, but, if it were regenerated, it would form an impassible barrier to the encroachments of North America, it would afford an important opening for English, Spanish, and French trade, while exploiting its own wealth, and lastly it would render great services to our manufactories by extending its cultivation of cotton. . . . . Today unexpected events have arisen and changed the face of affairs. The American war has made it impossible for the United States to interfere, and what is more, the outrages committed by the Mexican government have provided England, Spain, and France with a legitimate motive for interference in Mexico."

Such a statement of the case for intervention does not stand alone. It would be tedious to cite instance after instance of similar language, but there is perhaps room for the classical expression of the Emperor's views on North America, contained in the famous letter to Forey, of July 3, 1862. " There will not be lacking," wrote Napoleon at this time to the commander of his military forces in Mexico, " people who will ask why we are going to spend men and money to place an Austrian prince upon a throne.

" In the actual state of the civilization of the world, the prosperity of America is not indifferent to Europe, for it nourishes our industry and gives life to our commerce. We are interested in seeing the United States powerful and prosperous, but we have no interest in seeing that republic acquire the whole of the Gulf of Mexico, dominate from this vantage-point the Antilles and South America, and become the sole dispenser of the products of the New World. Mistress of Mexico, and consequently, of Central America and of the passage between the two seas, there would be henceforth no other power in America than the United States.

" If, on the contrary, Mexico conquers its independence and maintains the integrity of its territory, if a stable government is constituted there by the arms of France, we shall have opposed an insuperable barrier to the encroachments of the United States, we shall have maintained the independence of our colonies in the Antilles, and of those of ungrateful Spain, and we shall have established our beneficent influence in the center of America, and this influence will radiate northward as well as southward, will create immense markets for our commerce, and will procure the materials indispensable to our industry." [12]

A franker expression of hostility than this could hardly be looked for. The irritation at American jingoism that characterized the later fifties, the suspicion of American purposes, based upon the recommendations of Buchanan's message, these may help to explain such a point of view as that expressed above, but they cannot alter its fundamental character, or shake in any manner the clearly established thesis that one of the principal objects of the Mexican intervention was to checkmate the United States. Though the phrase " balance of power " is not used by the Emperor, it is clearly the principle of such a balance that he has in mind. The clash of systems thus appears with crystal-like clarity in the evolution of his policy toward Mexico.

Before embarking upon the story of the intervention itself, it will be necessary to examine the attitude of the other parties to the candidacy of the Archduke Maximilian. What of the prospective candidate himself ? What of the members of his family, of the Emperor Francis Joseph ? And what still more of the attitude of the other parties to the convention of London, of Great Britain and of Spain ?

[12] *Documents Diplomatiques,* 1863. Frequently cited, as, for example, in Niox, *op. cit.,* p. 212 *et seq.* See also García, *op. cit.,* XIV, 9 *et seq.*

It was to be more than two years after the signing of the convention of London before the Archduke Maximilian was to accept the throne of Mexico. Yet there can be very little doubt that from the very outset this ambitious scion of the Hapsburgs was fascinated by the possibility of founding a throne in the New World. He received the project favorably when it was first broached; he sought contacts with the Mexican royalists in Paris,[13] and in his correspondence with Louis Napoleon himself his enthusiasm is barely concealed.[14] Not, of course, that there was an utter absence of reserve; dignity alone would have prevented an Austrian Archduke from rushing to accept a throne which had not yet been formally offered to him, and the path to which could only be opened by military force. In one of his earliest letters to the Emperor, Maximilian indicates that his acceptance of the task proposed for him must rest upon the will of the Mexican people. But that, like other candidates, he was prepared to strain his ears to catch the summons of the multitude is fairly obvious from the temper of his correspondence.

On the other hand, those to whom he opened himself upon the question, while not entirely unsympathetic, while indeed rather pleased with the idea in principle, were a little more impressed with the practical difficulties involved. Maximilian's father-in-law, the shrewd Leopold of Belgium, when asked for his advice, an-

[13] Corti, *op. cit.*, I, 119. See the report of his confidential agent Scherztenlechner in Library of Congress Transcripts, Haus-Archiv, Karton 1, Doc. 23, November 6, 1861.

[14] See the letters published in Corti, *op. cit.*, I, 363 and 367.

swered that Mexico was, of all the countries of Latin
America, that " best suited for a monarchy " and that
its acceptance of a monarchical form would " raise a
barrier against the United States, and provide a support
for the monarchical and aristocratical principles in the
Southern States." But, on the other hand, he warned
his son-in-law that the crux of the matter lay in " what
the country itself would do," and that until the facts
of the case were better known, " it might be necessary
to keep oneself free." [15] As late as May, 1862, he was
still urging the greatest circumspection.

In the case of Francis Joseph, the Archduke's brother,
a certain sympathy is to be deduced from the conversation which the two princes held together in Venice on
New Year's Eve of 1861. At this time, the Emperor
declared that he would make a small advance out
of the family funds, that he would permit the recruit-
ing of a volunteer force within the boundaries of his
dominion for service in Mexico, and would permit
certain officers from the General Staff to go out to the
New World, and further still that he would permit the
Archduke to make the voyage to his new kingdom on
an Austrian man-of-war.[16] But the temper of Francis
Joseph's ministers was decidedly more cautious, and
Count Rechberg, the Austrian Foreign Minister, had
laid it down at the time of the first discussions of the
Mexican projects that, not only should there be a clearly

[15] Leopold to Maximilian, October 25, 1861, Library of Congress Transcripts, Haus Archiv, Karton 1, Doc. 29.

[16] Maximilian-Rechberg in Library of Congress Transcripts,
Haus Archiv, Karton 1, Doc. 101, January 1, 1862.

formulated request from the Mexicans themselves, but
also that the success of the undertaking should be
guaranteed by the support of two great naval powers,
which meant, of course, both France and England.[17]
Prince Metternich, the Austrian minister in Paris, was
equally conservative, " What a lot of cannon-shots it
will take," he declared in a letter to his chief, " to set
up an emperor in Mexico, and what a lot to maintain him
there. Even granted the separation of the North and the
South as a result of the Civil War, why should it not
be the case that the South should continue to maintain
the Monroe Doctrine?"[18] In such observations one
finds evidence of a shrewd realism that characterized the
course of the Austrian government, in actual fact, with
regard to the whole Mexican enterprise.

The same practical good sense characterized the views
of the British government. In the period anterior to
the convention of London it is clear that Sir Charles
Wyke, the British minister in Mexico City, was favorable to a thoroughgoing intervention, with the aim of
bringing " the moderate party " into power ;[19] and at a
later date it may well be that Lord Palmerston, the
British Prime Minister, viewed with indulgence, if not
with approbation, the project of establishing a monarchy
in Mexico.[20] But the policy of the British government
in the Mexican business was fixed by the Foreign Sec-

[17] *Ibid.*, Doc. 7a, October 7, 1861.

[18] *Ibid.*, Doc. 75, December 2, 1861.

[19] *British and Foreign State Papers*, 1861-62, LII, 256, 293,
366.

[20] See below, p. 393.

retary, Lord John Russell, and Russell at every stage
not only sought to limit the intervention, but to avoid
arousing the antagonism of the United States. Thus,
at the very outset of the negotiations preceding the convention of London, he laid down two principles upon
which, in his opinion, they should proceed; in the first
place, that the combined powers should not interfere
by force in the internal government of Mexico, and in
the second, that the cooperation of the United States
should be invited.[21] " Without at all yielding to the
extravagant pretensions implied by what is called the
Monroe Doctrine," wrote he to Cowley on September
30, " it would as a matter of expediency be unwise to
provoke the ill feeling of North America, unless some
paramount object were in prospect and tolerably sure of
attainment." [22] It was due to British urging also that

[21] *British and Foreign State Papers,* 1861-62, Russell-Cramp-
ton, September 27, 1861, LII, 332. Also Russell-Cowley,
September 30, 1861 in *ibid.,* p. 367.

[22] Compare also Crampton's statement in Madrid that while
the British government " could never recognize what was commonly called the Monroe Doctrine, the repeated announcement
of this maxim by successive Presidents of the United States as
a fundamental principle of their policy, and its eager acceptance
as such by the American people, rendered it sufficiently evident
that European intervention in the affairs of Mexico would be
viewed by them as an infringement of an imagined right, and if
now undertaken without their being consulted, and at a time
when it would appear to them that advantage was taken of their
internal troubles to make light of their influence, and perhaps
to realize projects repugnant to their political sympathies, a
strong feeling of resentment would not fail to be created, in
which both sections of the now divided Union would concur."
Ibid., Crampton to Russell, September 21, 1861, p. 371.

25

the convention of London contained the much cited second article to which we have already alluded, and that it also provided for the adhesion of the United States. Both of these facts indicate with what good faith, from the American point of view, the British government approached the problem of Mexico. When it came to the intervention itself, moreover, only 700 marines were sent to Mexico, and Sir Charles Wyke was explicitly directed that this small force should not under any circumstances take part in any operations against the capital.[23] From the beginning Russell believed that extended operations were undesirable, and the establishment of monarchy impossible. As early as September 25, 1861, he had told Charles Francis Adams that little good came out of any intervention on a large scale.[24] With regard to the candidacy of the Archduke Maximilian, his position from the beginning was that Great Britain would not object to that candidacy, if it came about as a result of the spontaneous desires of the Mexican people.[25] But he doubted very decidedly the existence of these desires. The project, he wrote the British minister at Vienna, appeared to have originated with the Mexican refugees at Paris. " This class of people," he continued, " are notorious for unfounded calculation of the strength of their partisans in their native country, and for the extravagance of their expectations of support. Marshal O'Donnell, as your excel-

[23] *Ibid.*, p. 381.
[24] 37th Cong., 2nd Sess., H. Exec. Doc. No. 100, p. 195.
[25] *Ibid.*, p. 425.

lency will perceive by the printed papers laid before
Parliament, is of the opinion that the notion of establishing, by foreign intervention, a constitutional monarchy in Mexico is very chimerical. His Majesty's
government would lend no support to such a project,
although they would gladly see a government in Mexico
that would maintain order and tranquility. If our estimate of the disorganization of Mexico is correct, the
archduke, if he were to assume the crown, would have
to rely wholly upon the support of French troops. It
would take a long time so to consolidate the throne in
Mexico as to render the sovereign independent of foreign support, even if there can be created in Mexico elements out of which a stable support for a monarchy
could be built up; and in the meantime, if the foreign
support were withdrawn, the sovereign might possibly
be driven out by the republicans of Mexico." [26] To this
view of the matter Lord John Russell steadily adhered,
and not only did he adhere to it, but, on at least two
occasions, as the project developed, he expressed his
views to the Comte de Flahault.[27] The British government must be acquitted of any ulterior objects whatsoever in connection with the intervention of 1861.[28]

[26] 37th Cong., 3rd Sess., H. Exec. Doc. No. 54, p. 593.

[27] *Ibid.*, pp. 719-20, and 793.

[28] The intervention, it ought also be noted, was the subject of
sceptical criticism by Disraeli shortly after the opening of Parliament. Hansard, *Parliamentary Debates,* 3rd series, CLXV,
64. See also the speech of Lord Stanley at King's Lynn November 22, 1861. *London Times.* Romero reports that the Tory
party sent an agent to Mexico to report on the situation, and
gather ammunition against the ministry. M. Romero, *Corres-*

The prudence of the British government was not matched by that of Spain. No such limited intervention as that advocated by Great Britain was in the mind of the authorities at Madrid. As early as October 9 Carl Schurz, the American minister, reported that it was undoubtedly the object of the government to land troops in Mexico, and to operate in the interior of the republic.[29] And this view of the matter was confirmed by the language of Calderon Collantes. On October 21 Barrot wrote to Thouvenel from Madrid that Collantes had declared that he would rather abstain from intervention altogether than to go in on the terms proposed by the British, and two weeks later the Spanish minister, with extraordinary candor, told Schurz that it was hoped that the intervention " might give new strength and a new impulse to the conservative party in Mexico, and enable it to establish a strong government." [30]   When General

---

pondencia de la Legación Mexicana en Washington durante La Intervención Extranjera (10 vols., Mexico, 1870-92.) All this seems to indicate anything but enthusiasm for the whole venture in at least some sections of British public opinion.

On the other hand, such important and influential papers as the *Times* and the *Spectator,* while not strong for British action, were not averse to letting the French go ahead if they wanted to. (*Ibid.,* pp. 859 and 919.)

[29] 37th Cong., 2nd Sess., H. Exec. Doc. No. 100, p. 223.

[30] *Ibid.,* p. 226. The Spanish view was also well expressed in the note of Calderon Collantes to the Spanish ministers in London and Paris, written October 22, commenting on the first draft of the convention of London. " Article III of the projet," he wrote (this being the article which renounced any intervention in the domestic affairs of the Mexicans), is in entire conformity with the views which the government of the Queen has always manifested. It has always thought that the Mexicans should be

Prim, entrusted with the command of the force to
operate in Mexico, was given his instructions on November 17, emphasis was laid on the desire for a strong
government, and on the possible necessity of marching
on Mexico City.[31] Though the fear of offending England
and the United States gave to the acts of a ministry
naturally vacillating a character of more than ordinary
vacillation, the Spanish government was on the whole
ready to fall in with the views of Napoleon, and gave
its adhesion to the idea of a vigorous policy.[32] An actual
intervention, not a mere operation for the redress of
grievances, was what was contemplated at Madrid.

But more than this, too, was in the wind. There was
certainly a party at the Spanish Court which hoped that
as a result of the projected expedition, a Bourbon prince
might mount the throne of Mexico. As early as August,
1861, the Mexican royalist Tomás Murphy visited London to ascertain the views of the British cabinet with

---

left entire freedom to constitute their government in the manner
most conformable to their interests, their habits, and their be-
liefs. . . . . But if it has believed and still believes that the
Mexicans ought to be the arbiters of their destinies, it also believes that it is necessary to put them in a position to examine
without passion or self-deception the situation in which their
errors have placed them, in order that they may adopt the most
suitable means for improving it." Cited in E. Lefèvre, *Documents Officiels Recueillis dans la Secretairerie Privée de Maximilien* (2 vols., Paris, 1870), I, 91.

[31] *Archives Diplomatiques,* 1862, III, 320 *et seq.*

[32] Paris, Min. des Aff. Etr., Corr. Pol., Espagne, vol. 859.
Instructions of November 5, 1861 and Barrot's reply of November 11.

regard to this possibility.[33] On September 6, 1861, Señor Mon, the Spanish minister at Paris, had reported that in view of the enfeebled condition of the United States, the time was ripe for the establishment of a monarchy in Mexico.[34] Not much later Schurz reported that it was the obvious ambition of Queen Isabel to gain new glory in the New World, and that Calderon Collantes appeared to fall in with the ideas of his sovereign. According to Schurz's account, the intended Spanish candidate was Don Sebastian, the uncle of the Queen, in whose behalf agents had already been sent to Mexico.[35] Schurz also indicated that the idea of a monarchy was being extensively discussed in the Spanish press.[36]

In the months that followed the course of the Spanish government was marked by extraordinary contradictions. The existence of monarchical ambitions was now admitted, at any rate by implication, and now denied. The French government, as has been seen, had notified the Spaniards of the projected candidacy of Maximilian early in October.[37] Its views were not hailed with enthusiasm in Madrid. The instructions of Calderon Collantes to Mon, dated October 22, exhibit a considerable coolness toward the plans of Louis Na-

[33] Lefèvre, *op. cit.*, I, 101, citing a despatch, from London, September 17, 1861, of M. Andres Osegura, secretary of the legation at Paris to M. de la Fuente, the Mexican minister there. It is needless to say Murphy got no satisfaction.

[34] Cited in E. Domenech, *Histoire du Mexique* (3 vols., Paris, 1868), II, 379.

[35] Washington, Dept. of State, Despatches, Spain, September 27, 1861.

[36] 37th Cong., 2nd Sess., H. Exec. Doc. No. 100, p. 225.

[37] See above, p. 359.

poleon. Granting that Mexico desires a sovereign, wrote the Spanish Foreign Minister, " it would be in conformity with historical tradition and with the bonds which unite the two peoples if a prince of the House of Bourbon, or closely associated with it, should be preferred," [38] and this view was reiterated in February. As late as April, 1862, talking with the Mexican reactionary, Arrangoiz, the Spanish minister clung to the idea that Spain might select the prince to rule over Mexico. At this time the choice seemed to fall on the Infanta Isabella, the niece of the Queen.[39] But at the same time that they harbored these ulterior views, he and his chief O'Donnell talked the language of moderation and restraint to Sir John Crampton, the British minister. O'Donnell, indeed, seems from the first to have disbelieved in the possibility of monarchy in Mexico. He declared to Crampton, the British minister, that any such project must be regarded as entirely chimerical, and that a monarchical government, if founded in Mexico, would be driven out by the United States.[40] In the meantime, both he and Collantes emphatically denied any intention of imposing any government upon the

[38] *Archives Diplomatiques,* 1862, III, 315.

[39] Francisco de Paula de Arrangoiz, *Apuntes para la Historia del Segundo Imperio Mexicano* (Madrid, 1869), pp. 116-17.

[40] London, P. R. O., F. O., Spain, vol. 1009, October 13, 1861. " A monarchy under a European prince," he declared, " if not guaranteed by Europe, would not last a year; if guaranteed and supported by Europe, it would be a fruitful source of struggle between European powers and those of America, who had adopted Republican Institutions, and repelled European interference in the New World." *Ibid.,* vol. 1030, January 30, 1862.

people of Mexico.[41]   When one analyzes and seeks to
reconcile these various declarations, one comes to the
conclusion that the Spanish government, like the French,
did not anticipate a strenuous resistance in Mexico, and
that there were hopes, certainly on the part of Collantes,
that out of the intervention a monarchy might emerge.

So much for the attitude of the government itself.
But before taking leave of Spanish policy in 1861, it
will be worth while to take a fleeting glimpse at the attitude of the Spanish press.   There was a very considerable press campaign afoot in behalf of the monarchical
idea, as Schurz had observed.   Papers in all parts of the
country, such as *La Cronica* in Madrid, *La Andalucia*
in Seville, and *El Porvenir* in Granada, took a hand.[42]
There also appeared two interesting pamphlets, advocating the candidacy of the Infanta Maria Luisa, the
sister of the Queen.   In one of these the Monroe Doctrine was handled without mercy, being described as
" most unimportant and common-place on its face, but
subversive and anarchical in its results." [43]   In the other,
on the contrary, it was admitted that the Mexicans must
do their own choosing, " thus practising in part the
doctrine of the renowned Monroe." [44]   Both afford interesting evidence that in Spain, as elsewhere in Europe,
the principles of 1823 were beginning to be known by
1861.

[41] *Ibid.*

[42] Fr. M. Tubino, *Un Trono en Méjico* (Madrid, 1862), p. 51.

[43] *La Cuestión de Méjico.* Si la monarquía constitucional es
conveniente y posible en Aquel País bajo el punto de vista de
los Intereses Mexicanos y de la Política Española. p. 25.

[44] *Un Trono en Méjico, op. cit.,* p. 21.

What stands out with crystal clearness, indeed, in a review of the point of view of the various parties in interest to the Mexican intervention, is the clear appreciation of the attitude of the United States. There might be a willingness to concede to that viewpoint or there might not; there might be a favorable or an unfavorable estimate of the future power of the United States to enforce its principles. But the existence of those principles was by the outbreak of the Civil War widely recognized among intelligent men; the Monroe Doctrine was already a force either to be reckoned with, or to be challenged. When the Allied powers went into Mexico they knew that it was very decidedly an element in the situation. The clash of systems was from the beginning implicit in the sailing of the squadrons for Vera Cruz.

It is from the standpoint of this deep-seated political antagonism, one with the very largest political implications, that we must analyze the events which culminated in the acceptance of the throne of Mexico by the Archduke Maximilian, and in his departure from Trieste to challenge destiny in the New World. It will be interesting to observe how much distrust and how much scepticism was felt with regard to the whole project of Mexican monarchy, and how, throughout the whole period, in the expressions of European public men and in the fluctuations of European public opinion, the recognition of the importance of the American viewpoint continues to make itself clearly felt.

We have seen that, when the Allied governments began their intervention in the fall of 1861, the French

and the Spanish Courts, if not the British, were inclined
to a vigorous policy. Nothing less than the regeneration
of Mexico was the object proposed. But the injection of
the candidacy of Maximilian had already introduced a
principle of division into the relations of the two Latin
powers. Nor did it help particularly that the officer to
whom was confided the command of the troops in
Mexico was anything but conservative in his political
viewpoint, and sceptical from the beginning as to the
possibility of founding a monarchy in Mexico.

General Prim y Prats, in some respects, seemed an
ideal choice for the projected expedition. He was a
friend of the Emperor Napoleon, and was thought by
Schurz to have been given the command at his request.[45]
Moreover, a government presided over by an O'Donnell,
with a Calderon Collantes as foreign minister, would see
some advantage in giving a liberal politician-soldier a
job to do a long way from home.[46] But these considerations, from the viewpoint of the Spanish ministers,
should have weighed as nothing against the fact that
Prim, from the very beginning, approached the whole
Mexican problem from a wholly different point of view
from that of the government whose orders he carried to
the New World. Before his departure he had an interview with Schurz, in which he expressed himself with
extraordinary candor and absence of reserve. Monarchy

[45] Washington, Dept. of State, Despatches, Spain, November
16, 1861.
[46] See the excellent article "L'Espagne et la Question du
Mexique," by H. Léonardon, in *Annales des Sciences Politiques,*
XVI, 59-95, especially 69-70.

in Mexico, he told the American minister, was an absurdity. He did not care what the government might think; he would work, not for the clerical party, but for a fair and free election, and if Juarez should win, as he probably would, so be it. The Mexicans would find him no foe of Mexican independence, but a helpful friend.[47] Holding such views, it is not strange that upon his arrival in Mexico he sought to negotiate with, and not to overthrow, the government in Mexico City, and that he assumed from the beginning an attitude highly unfavorable to the ambitious hopes of Dubois de Saligny, the strongly monarchist representative of the Emperor, and to the views of Louis Napoleon himself.

It is not necessary to detail the events which led to the actual breach of relations between the cooperating powers in April, 1862. At the beginning common action was somehow maintained: the forces that had been sent out were obviously inadequate for a march into the interior, in view of the fact that there was no sign of the hoped-for monarchist rising, and the French plenipotentiaries, Admiral Jurien and Dubois de Saligny, thus gave their assent to negotiations with Juarez and to the signing of the preliminary convention of La Soledad. By this convention the Allied troops were allowed to advance into the interior outside the yellow fever zone; but what was more important, it was definitely stipulated that the powers had no intention of infringing upon the independence or sovereignty of Mexico.

[47] Washington, Dept. of State, Despatches, Spain, November 16, 1861.

Soon, however, dissensions broke out in earnest. Dubois de Saligny, a furious partisan of intervention, had never approved of the course of action outlined above, and he now proceeded to put forward the most extravagant demands in behalf of his government, for financial redress to French citizens.[48]

To these claims the British and the Spanish commissioners refused to subscribe. A new and even more irritating source of friction arose with the arrival of the Mexican reactionary, General Almonte, in Vera Cruz. Almonte had come over in the same vessel which brought General Lorencez, with French reinforcements, and from the moment of his setting foot upon Mexican soil he made no secret of his intimate relations with Louis Napoleon, and of the intention of setting up a monarchy

[48] Amongst these claims was the famous Jecker claim. Jecker was a Swiss, who, in February, 1859, had made a loan to the Miramón government of the nominal value of 75,000,000 francs, but from which the Mexican government actually received only three and three-quarters million francs. In 1860 Jecker failed, many of his creditors being French. The French government therefore had an indirect interest in seeing his claims sustained from the beginning. But this interest was immensely increased when the Duc de Morny, the half brother of Louis Napoleon, and the President of the Corps Legislatif, entered into a deal with the Swiss banker, by which he was to receive 30 per cent of the profits, if the bonds were made to be respected and paid. (*Les Papiers Secrets du Second Empire* (*Bruxelles,* 1870), p. 34.) This sordid financial intrigue, which took place in January, 1861, is sometimes thought actually to have produced the intervention in Mexico. It is clear, however, from what has been said, that there were numerous other and much more powerful motives. And, as a matter of fact, Thouvenel, who favored the intervention, showed a decided reluctance to press the Jecker claim at all. (Niox, *op. cit.,* p. 119.)

under the Archduke Maximilian. In disregard of the desire of Prim that he be detained in Vera Cruz, the Mexican monarchist was permitted to advance into the interior under French escort, and mutual recriminations naturally followed. Already by March 29, the Spanish commander had written to his government that it would be necessary to withdraw.[49] Twelve days later, a crisis in the relations of the commissioners took place in the stormy conference of Orizaba. The British and the Spanish commissioners reproached the French with the protection of Almonte, and with the intention of disregarding the terms of the convention of London. Dubois de Saligny replied with a sneer that General Prim's opposition to the candidacy of the Archduke was only because he desired to proclaim himself Emperor. The Spanish commander answered back in profound irritation. The tempers of all the commissioners rapidly mounted. By evening the withdrawal of the Spanish and British contingents had been decided upon. The cooperation of the Allied powers in Mexico was at an end.

The charge of personal ambition which was brought against General Prim by Saligny, and to which we have just alluded, appears to be little less than an absurdity. It was based upon a statement of the Spaniard's that only " a fortunate soldier " could make himself the ruler of Mexico, and upon the activities of a Spanish newspaper, *El Eco de Europa,* published in Vera Cruz, which

[49] Pirala, *Historia contemporánea, op. cit.,* II, 415, text and note 3.

descanted in dithyrambic terms on the merits of the
Spanish commander. With these things to go on, the
malicious and jealous imagination of Saligny managed
to fabricate the charge that was hurled at Prim in the
conference of Orizaba. But as a matter of fact, Prim's
whole policy had from the first been conciliatory. He
had indicated this point of view to Schurz before his
departure; he had taken the lead in negotiating with
the government of Juarez, and had been chiefly responsible for the convention of La Soledad; and he had
written to his government, shortly after his arrival at
Vera Cruz, that " at the opportune time the moral influence which we are now acquiring in Mexico will be
utilized to establish an order of affairs which results
from the will of the majority, while offering guarantees
of solidity and stability as to internal affairs, and respect
for the rights of foreigners and for international treaties abroad." [50] In a letter of March 17 to Louis Napoleon he had expressed his complete scepticism with regard to the possibility of founding any monarchy whatever in Mexico. In his judgment, the number of men
of monarchical sentiment was extremely few; the rule
of Spain had left neither the interests of a landed no-
bility, nor moral interests; the neighborhood of the
United States and the " always severe language of these
republicans against monarchical institutions " had contributed to a very high degree to create a positive hostility to such forms. The reception accorded to the troops

[50] Cited in *La Gaceta de Madrid,* June 13, 1862, quoted in
Léonardon, *op. cit.,* p. 77.

of the Allied powers, he added, afforded additional evidence of the weakness of royalist sentiment, for there
had been not the slightest demonstration of any kind
from which to draw encouragement.[51] That these views
represented his mature judgment on the Mexican question it is impossible to doubt. There is, indeed, not a
scintilla of evidence to lead one seriously to believe the
accusations of Saligny. From beginning to end, Prim
approached the Mexican question as his speech, his despatches, and his line of conduct show, from a point of
view extremely different from that of France.

The action of the Spanish commander in bringing the
intervention to an end took place, it will be understood,
entirely upon his own initiative. The Spanish government, faced with the indignant protests of the French,
had disapproved the convention of La Soledad, and had,
so Calderon Collantes informed Barrot, despatched instructions to Prim to undertake a more aggressive policy.
The news of the rupture of Orizaba was therefore
received with a good deal of consternation in Madrid.
It is said that O'Donnell's first impulse was to disavow
the acts of General Prim, and use the whole incident to
humiliate one who might be regarded as a dangerous
political rival.[52] But other counsels prevailed. The

[51] This famous letter is to be found quoted in full in Léonardon, *op. cit.*, pp. 81-83.

[52] He is even said to have carried to the Queen a decree dis-
avowing the Spanish commander, but to have been met with
such enthusiastic approbation of Prim's action on her part that
he kept the decree in his pocket. D. M. La Fuente y Zalmalloa,
*Historia general de España desde los tiempos más remotas hasta
nuestros días* (Madrid, 25 vols., 1877-90), XXIII, 277.

damage had been done and could not be repaired. The
Queen was enthusiastically in favor of Prim's course.
It was decided to approve the acts of the Spanish plenipotentiary, and O'Donnell and Calderon Collantes
found themselves obliged to defend what had been done
when the Mexican question came up for debate in the
Cortes. In their heart of hearts, however, both the
prime minister and the foreign minister would have
preferred to pursue a policy of cooperation with France.
At the end of July, General Concha, a severe critic of
Prim, was sent to Paris to replace Mon, who had resigned. He was instructed to inform the French government that it was the view of the Spanish government
that the treaty of London had never been terminated,
but merely suspended, and that it was the desire at Madrid to enter into negotiations for its revival, based upon
respect for the will of the Mexican people, but also upon
the vigorous prosecution of the intervention until Mexico City had been taken, and upon the determination of
guarantees to be determined upon by common agreement, and exacted from the new government which
should be set up in Mexico. Despite an initial rebuff
from the Emperor, the Spanish ambassador, by instructions of August 25, was ordered to press the matter
upon the attention of Louis Napoleon, and discussions
took place at this time, and again in October. But in June
of 1862 the French troops, marching on Mexico City,
had suffered the defeat of Puebla ; and General Concha
was coolly informed that the French government could
not enter into negotiations of the sort suggested until
the affront to French arms had been avenged, and until

the victorious legions of Marshal Forey had made their triumphal entry into the City of Mexico. With the door thus closed to further discussions, the Spanish ministry found itself compelled to content itself with observing the Mexican adventure from afar. As time went on, its own activities in the New World were more and more occupied with the thorny question of Santo Domingo. Though it was to recognize the régime of Maximilian, when that régime was established in 1864, it took from this time on no important part in the solution of the problem which we are examining.[53]

The withdrawal of Spain from Mexico was, of course, variously judged in the Cortes, and by the newspaper press of Spain. The anti-ministerial group in Parliament and in the press naturally found in Prim's action the basis of a slashing assault upon the government. The first debates took place in June of 1862. The liberal deputy Olózaga, in a scathing speech, declared that the policy pursued had been most maladroit. "The United States," he declared, " against whom it was intended to erect a barrier to check the invasion of the Anglo-Saxon race, have the same motives of hatred and complaint against us, as if we had actually erected such a barrier. For it is clear that our lack of success is due, not to the absence of desire, but to the exercise of so little intelligence and foresight." [54] " President Lincoln, or Monroe

[53] For this whole episode, see the *Annuaire des Deux Mondes,* 1862-63, pp. 320-26. See also *Diario de las Sesiones . . . .* Senado, appendix to no. 5, December, 1862, and *ibid.,* Congreso, 3rd appendix to no. 12, January, 1863.

[54] Anon., *Le Général Prim, le Sénat, les Cortes, et la Presse Española dans la Question du Mexique* (Paris, 1863), p. 120.

26

with his celebrated doctrine," declared another deputy, "must have smiled" at the policy of submissiveness to Great Britain pursued by General Prim.[55] In the main, however, the debates of June did not turn upon the attitude of the United States, and the long defense of Calderon Collantes of the course of action pursued by the government had not a word to say of the attitude of Washington. Though Collantes was not unwilling to use the turn of affairs in Mexico to gain the good graces of the able American chargé, Horatio J. Perry,[56] he rested his case in the Cortes upon an appeal to Spanish pride. Although obviously laboring under some embarrassment, he proceeded to the complete vindication of General Prim.

At this time the Spanish commander was in the United States, where he was hailed with enthusiasm by Spanish-American groups, and where, too, he had an opportunity of talking with Seward, and of visiting the army of the Potomac. By the end of the year, however, Prim had returned to Spain, and brought his case before the Cortes itself, where a new debate ensued. Whoever reads the speeches which Prim made in his own defense in the sessions of December 10, 11, 12, 1862, will find in them, along with much egotism and self-praise, the elements of statesmanship.[57] Prim's conception of the

[55] *Ibid.,* p. 21.

[56] Washington, Dept. of State, Despatches, Spain, May 30. 1862.

[57] For the speech itself, see *Archivo Histórico Diplomático Mexicano,* " Don Juan Prim y Su Labor Diplomática en México," Num. 25, Con una Introducción por Genaro Estrada (Mexico, 1928), p. 149 *et seq.*

Mexican question had from the beginning been very different from that of the government; it was based, indeed, upon a much clearer perception of realities. For Prim realized, as he declared in his discourse to the Senate, that the material power of the United States was very great; he had, indeed, been much impressed with the military strength of the North; and he knew, too, that even were the Civil War to end in the break-up of the Union, the South would be no less jealous of the Monroe Doctrine than the Union itself had been. A policy which alienated the sentiment of North and South America, to trail at the chariot wheels of Louis Napoleon, was no policy for proud Spain to pursue. Such was the line of argument which Prim put forward, and it was very far from a contemptible one. It was more realistic and more forward looking than that of the government itself. Though the amendment which Prim presented was voted down by great majorities, though, indeed, it must have been voted down, the principles which he set forth in his own defense show that strong as was the antagonism to the democratic system of the New World in many quarters there were men who saw the facts clearly, and stated them no less so.

Very naturally Prim's speech only aroused the opposition to new attacks upon the ministry. There had been plenty of shuffling on the part of O'Donnell and Calderon Collantes, and the orators made the most of this fact. They roundly accused the cabinet of having sacrificed Spanish interests to no avail, of having alienated the United States without arriving at any desirable end,[58] of having abandoned a policy of monarchical regeneration for Mexico which would have opposed a barrier to the absorption of that country by the United States, and broken down the isolation of the New World. The time was ripe for such action. The American Civil War had made monarchy in Mexico a practicable thing. " Those men," exclaimed Señor Rio y Roas, " who said, America for the Americans, that is, America for the Anglo-Americans, for the Yankees, for the United States, America surrounded by an ideal wall, like the great wall of China, America cut off from the world, divorced from human civilization, those men who professed that insolent, absurd, and inhuman doctrine, have begun to see what they called the manifest destiny of America was not a decree of God, and that the order of his Providence was a very different one." [59] Señor Rio y Roas's denunciation of the Monroe Doctrine was echoed by other speakers. Bermudez de Castro and the Marquis de Habana declared that Spain neither had recognized nor could recognize any such principle.[60] General Prim was roundly denounced for having appeared to do so. The principles of 1823, indeed, figured more definitely in the Spanish debate of December, 1862, than they had ever done at any previous time in any foreign parliamentary body. General Prim's friendly references to those principles are also virtually the first of their

[58] *Question du Mexique devant les Cortes d'Espagne* (Paris, 1863), p. 119.

[59] *Ibid.*, pp. 197-8.

[60] *General Prim,* etc., *op. cit.,* pp. 108-9.

kind. The whole episode has thus a high interest for the student of American foreign policy.

The decisions that General Prim had taken in April, 1862, were shared in, it has already been observed, by his British colleague. British policy from the beginning had been far removed from that of France; and the personal relations between the British commissioner, Sir Charles Wyke, and the Frenchman Dubois de Saligny, were, from the beginning, distinctly bad. To Wyke Saligny was an ultra, a supporter of clericalism and reaction; to Saligny Wyke, with his sympathies for the moderate party, was nothing more or less than a supporter of the abominable Juarez. That these two men should have quarrelled was natural, and that Wyke should have followed the lead of Prim was hardly less so. The government at London was prompt to approve the decision of its plenipotentiary to withdraw troops, and from April, 1862, Great Britain plays only a subordinate part in the whole Mexican adventure.

It will be well, however, to examine very briefly the views of British statesmen and the reactions of British public opinion to the events in Mexico from the rupture of Orizaba to the acceptance of the throne by the Archduke Maximilian. Lord John Russell, as we have seen, was, from the beginning, definitely opposed to any real intervention in Mexican politics, and the official policy of Great Britain had been definitely directed at limiting the scope of allied action in Mexico. British scepticism with regard to the possibility of monarchy had been expressed quite candidly both at Paris and Vienna. For a considerable period after the rupture of Orizaba, the Foreign Office appears to have held its peace. There is nothing strange in this, for the French troops in Mexico, when they began their advance toward Mexico City, were subjected to a genuine reverse at Puebla, and it was not until large reinforcements had been sent out, and a new commander put in charge that they finally entered Mexico City in the early summer of 1863. Then only did the monarchical project begin to take more definite form. A Council of Notables, summoned by the French commander, established a regency, and elected the Archduke Emperor of Mexico. During the fall of 1863 and the winter of 1864 occurred the important negotiations which were to culminate in his acceptance of the throne.

In this critical period, it would appear, the British Foreign Office was not idle. It can hardly be possible that it did not have a hand in the activities of Sir Charles Wyke at this time. In September of 1863, Wyke had an interview with a member of the Archduke's entourage at Karlsbad. He told Maximilian's emissary that he much mistrusted the whole Mexican adventure, not so much on the ground that monarchy in Mexico was impossible (Wyke had never held this view), but on the ground that the identification of the intervention with the clericals and the reactionaries had made it odious from the beginning.[61] He took the same tone in further conferences with Rechberg, the Austrian foreign minister, in Vienna.[62] He reiterated these warnings a month

[61] Vienna, Herzfeld-De Pont, September 7, 1863.

[62] Library of Congress Transcripts, Haus-Archiv, Karton 5, Doc. 838, September 25, 1863.

later,[63] and in conversations with the Emperor Louis Napoleon in Paris.[64] Finally, in March of 1864, he had an interview with the Archduke himself in which he again expressed himself unreservedly as opposed to the enterprise in which Maximilian was about to embark. Most emphatically, if his counsels had been listened to, the Mexican adventure would have turned out very differently from what it actually did.[65]

It is not to be imagined, however, that the policy of establishing a monarchy in Mexico was entirely without its sympathizers. There is no doubt whatsoever that Lord Palmerston was not unfriendly to the projected enterprise. Wyke indicates this quite clearly in one of his letters to Herzfeld, and another purveyor of information on Mexico, one Bourdillon, testifies to the same effect.[66] Even more important, Palmerston expressed to the Mexican Arrangoiz, in September, 1863, his genuine desire for a fortunate outcome of the Mexican business, as useful to Europe as a whole.[67] It may have been due to his influence that at a later date (October, 1864), when the Archduke seemed to be in possession of most of the territory of Mexico, the British government recognized the monarchy.

The withdrawal of Britain and Spain from the Mexican intervention was not without influence upon the attitude of Austria. The point of departure of Austrian

[63] *Ibid.*, Doc. 928, October 19, 1863.

[64] *Ibid.*, Doc. 1036, Wyke-Herzfeld, November 27, 1863.

[65] Schmit von Tavera, *op. cit.*, I, 213. A personal interview of Wyke with the author is the basis for this statement.

[66] Library of Congress Transcripts, Haus-Archiv, Karton 3, Doc. 451, March 4, 1863.

[67] Arrangoiz, *op. cit.*, p. 146.

policy from the beginning had been the support of two
naval powers; and after the rupture of Orizaba it was
certain that such support would not be given. Moreover,
in February of 1862 Count Rechberg, the Austrian
foreign minister, had had the prudence to converse upon
the Mexican question with Motley, the American representative at Vienna. He began by stating his conviction that the North would surely win the struggle for
the preservation of the Union. He went on to ask if it
would be likely to oppose the establishment of a monarchy in Mexico. Motley's answer was that the opposition would be " universal and intense." [68] Language
such as this must have had its effect upon cooling still
more the very well-controlled sympathy of Rechberg
for the Mexican adventure. As early as March the
Austrian foreign minister had written Maximilian that
the indispensable condition for the Mexican enterprise,
i. e., the support of two maritime powers, had only
been half fulfilled.[69] By May of 1862, when the news
of the rupture of Orizaba had reached Vienna, he was
ready to counsel the Archduke to withdraw from the
whole enterprise; and the sagacious Metternich, from
his vantage point in Paris, took the same view some
months later.[70] The same attitude was maintained in

[68] Washington, Dept. of State, Despatches, Austria, February 12, 1862.

[69] Library of Congress Transcripts, Haus-Archiv, Karton 2,
Doc. 232, March 22, 1862. Also *ibid.,* 233a, March 20. Rechberg-Metternich.

[70] Corti, *op. cit.,* I, 171, Rechberg-Metternich, May 30, 1862.
Rechberg in this despatch mentions the attitude of the United
States as a reason for circumspection.

1863. When a Mexican delegation, composed of the secure royalists who promoted monarchy from the Faubourg Saint-Germain, proposed to come to Miramar to offer Maximilian the crown, Rechberg's influence was exerted to persuade the Archduke to give only a contingent answer, while at the same time it was made clear that the attitude of the Austrian government would be one of entire reserve.[71] The conversations of Sir Charles Wyke with the Austrian minister were duly reported at Miramar. As late as October, 1863, it was still the view of the Austrian government that the enterprise was highly undesirable without the support of England, and the Emperor telegraphed his brother to that effect after the reception of the Mexican deputation at Miramar.[72] It was, as we have seen, clearly recognized that the monarchical project would arouse the opposition of the United States.

Nor does it seem at all probable that the enterprise was popular with Austrian public opinion. Motley wrote that it was regarded with hostility by all classes of society, and that the language of the press was almost universally unfavorable.[73] The same view was taken by the British minister at Vienna. And it can be readily understood how many Austrians would judge the de-

[71] Library of Congress Transcripts, Haus Archiv, Karton 3, Doc. 624, Maximilian-Francis Joseph, September 10, 1863.

[72] *Ibid.*, Karton 4, Doc. 871, Francis Joseph-Maximilian, October 4, 1863.

[73] Washington, Dept. of State, Despatches, Austria, August 17, 1863. For some interesting press comment, see Lefèvre, *op. cit.*, I, 357.

parture of a scion of the proud house of Hapsburg to attempt to govern a nation which had been uniformly turbulent and ungovernable for a period of some forty years, and this under the tutelage of a power which had only a short while ago bereft this same house of Hapsburg of the fairest portion of its heritage.

And yet despite Spanish and British withdrawal and the cold reserve of Austria, the project of Mexican monarchy marched forward in 1862 and 1863 to its climax with the Archduke's acceptance of the throne in April of 1864. For the Emperor Louis Napoleon still cherished, in a measure, his illusions; and the royal dreamer of Miramar put aside all unfavorable reports to listen to the voices of the tempters who were beckoning him on to the tragic morning of Querétaro.

In turning back, however, to the policy of France, one must not expect to find therein an instance of unswerving and tenacious purpose, a resolute will to press on toward a given goal. For the truth of the matter is that no such purpose governed French policy. The Emperor Louis Napoleon was an opportunist-politician, and as an opportunist-politician he handled the question of Mexico. He wished, wished beyond all question, to see a monarchy in Mexico, but, as we have already seen, he did not begin his enterprise with the purpose of coercing the Mexican people into the acceptance of the monarchical form, and the policy of setting up a monarchy was not definitely adopted, without qualification, until events in Mexico itself, combined with the turn of French policy, made any other course impossible.

When the rupture of Orizaba occurred, in April of 1862, it was certainly the intention of Louis Napoleon that his troops should march upon the City of Mexico, and displace the government of Juarez. But as we have already seen, the Emperor immensely overestimated the aid that he might expect from the Mexicans themselves. He was still nursing the delusion that the project on which he had embarked would be easy of execution. And the language of General Lorencez, and, of course, of Dubois de Saligny, furnished ample support for this point of view.[74] In May came the defeat of the French at Puebla, a solemn warning of the difficulties ahead. But the Emperor took no heed of this; though admitting his discouragement and revealing his doubts as to the future, he decided that it was necessary to redeem the tarnished prestige of the French arms, and sent a new and very large force out to Mexico under General Forey. At the same time the extremely cautious language of his spokesman in the Corps Législatif, the character of the allusions to the candidacy of the Archduke in the debates of June, 1862, the virtual suspension of the correspondence with the Archduke himself, and the tone of the instructions to General Forey, with their obviously mixed motives and impressions show pretty clearly that in his own mind the Emperor was by no means as certain of the success of the enterprise to which he had put his hand as he had been some months before. Nor can there be much question that the doubts which he had indulged at this time were shared by mem-

[74] Niox, *op. cit.*, p. 106-7.

bers of his administration. Marshal Randon, the Minister of War, was certainly no violent partisan of the Mexican expedition. After Puebla he believed, with his sovereign, that the honor of French arms must be redeemed by a victory, but he also was of the opinion that there should be no hasty advance on Mexico City. As time went on his aversion to the Mexican expedition obviously increased. In the fall of 1863 he was opposed to the sending of further troops to Mexico, though they had been demanded by General Forey,[75] and spoke mournfully of the drain of the intervention on French military resources. Randon was not alone in his viewpoint. It is, indeed, one of the most interesting things about the whole Mexican adventure that there seemed to be an excellent chance that it might be brought to an end in the early summer of 1863. By this time Marshal Forey had begun his advance on Mexico City, but had again been checked by the resistance of Puebla. The European situation was very far from a settled one. The Polish insurrection was producing a tense international situation, and there had been a progressive worsening of the relations of France with Great Britain. Public opinion in France itself was reacting against the policy of the government in Mexico. On June 5, 1863, Drouyn de l'Huys, who succeeded Thouvenel as foreign minister, penned instructions to Marshal Forey which, if they had been carried out, might have altered the whole course of events in the years im-

[75] J. L. Randon, *Mémoires du Maréchal* (2 vols., Paris, 1875-7), II, 74.

mediately ahead. These instructions have not a word
to say of the Archduke Maximilian. They declared
that the engagements of France do not go " beyond the
prosecution of our just claims and the support that we
have promised to give sooner or later to attempts to displace the existing government." " We would have no
objection," Drouyn de l'Huys continued, " to entering
into relations with a new régime having the support of
the country, and ready to treat upon the basis of indemnities and guarantees of the general interest such as we
have a right to claim." Nor was this all. " In a country
in which the power has so often changed hands," wrote
the French minister, " the difficulty is not to find men
who have already possessed it, and who desire to regain
it, or a considerable number of individuals sufficiently
well known to aspire to it. But a society, whose ills
arise principally from its divisions, needs at its head a
name capable of uniting the rival parties whose alter-
nating successes have again and again troubled the country. Our desire would be that the man with whom you
try to put yourself in relations be as competent as
possible to undertake this work of reconciliation, and
previously receive from the nation itself, under some
form, if only provisional, the power to treat with you.
It may be," and here there is adumbrated a policy very
different from that centering on the candidacy of Maximilian, " it may be that it will be necessary to look for
him among those very leaders, who, deceived by their
patriotism, believe they are serving the national cause
by resisting us. Our policy has been, from the beginning

to appeal to all those whose aid could be useful to us, and it is the same thought which ought to guide you in the overtures which it appears opportune for you to initiate." [76]

This important despatch reveals with the utmost clarity the doubts and hesitations which existed at the Tuileries in the early summer of 1863 with regard to the whole question of Mexico. But unfortunately, it was to arrive on the other side of the Atlantic only after Forey, with the active support, indeed, one might almost say, at the instigation of Saligny, had summoned a Council of Notables in Mexico City, which, picked almost exclusively from the clericals and the reactionaries, made haste to offer the throne of Mexico to the Archduke Maximilian. When this body came to a decision, the Emperor of the French was faced with something in the nature of a *fait accompli.* It did little good now to recall Forey, and the chief of the mischief-makers, Saligny; nor was the situation appreciably changed by the instructions to Bazaine, Forey's successor, that the views of the capital could not be taken as a sufficient indication of the views of the Mexican people, and that the opinions of the provinces must also be collected upon the question of monarchy. In the very nature of the case, a vote taken under the protection of French arms was bound to have very little weight with the sceptical, and to have an entirely different look about it than that spontaneous rising which had been hoped for in 1861 and 1862. Face-saving such

[76] Quoted in Niox, *op. cit.,* pp. 315 *et seq.*

an expedient might be; but it could not be expected to carry conviction. From July, 1863, whatever the phrases in which it was veiled, French policy was in fact directed at imposing the monarchy upon Mexico.

But, once again, let it be observed that it was with reluctance that the Emperor of the French embarked upon this course. In an interview with Sir Charles Wyke in November, 1863, Louis Napoleon unbosomed himself quite frankly with regard to the whole problem of Mexico. He acknowledged that he had been mistaken about the state of the country, but still held to the opinion that a strong monarchical party existed there, which had been frightened off by the pronouncedly reactionary character of Almonte and the leading Mexicans who had cooperated with the French. " I realize that I have got myself into a tight place," he declared to Wyke, " but the affair has got to be liquidated." His hope was that the arrival of the Archduke would do much to solve the situation; that the parties would rally around him; that it would be possible to withdraw many of the French troops, leaving a small nucleus to form the basis of a native force, and thus to extricate France from what he recognized as a highly unpleasant situation. But retreat in the fullest sense he would not consider. Wyke urged that the Council of the Regency be dissolved, and that in order to ascertain the will of the Mexican people, a Congress be summoned in accordance with the fundamental laws of the country. " That," replied the Emperor, " would amount to admitting a mistake, and in France it is no longer permissible to make mistakes." Not strong enough or brave enough frankly to admit that his hand had been forced, and to shape his policy on a new basis, the imperial politician was now determined to see the monarchical project through. He even told Wyke that in the case of the refusal of the Archduke Maximilian, he would turn to Spain, and seek in Madrid a candidate for the throne of Mexico.[77]

It is not necessary for us here to follow the negotiations of the fall of 1863 and the winter of 1864 which finally pledged France to the support of the Hapsburg, in the enterprise of monarchy across the seas. It is sufficient that we should understand the angle from which these negotiations should be approached. As Leopold of Belgium wrote to his son-in-law, the French government needed Maximilian fully as much as Maximilian need the French;[78] and the result of all this was that on the military side generous promises had to be made by Napoleon. On the other hand, the aspiring candidate to the Mexican throne, being entirely unfamiliar with the real financial situation in Mexico, could light-heartedly agree to very considerable financial concessions, which could be exhibited to French public opinion as an indication that the sums which had been spent in Mexico would be repaid.

The convention of Miramar signed April 10, 1864, was, from the beginning, based upon illusions, and not

[77] Library of Congress Transcripts, Haus-Archiv, Karton 5, Doc. 1036, Wyke-Herzfeld, November 27, 1863.
[78] *Ibid.*, Doc. 1092.

only upon illusions but upon deceptions. Thus, the published articles of the treaty provided that as soon as
possible the French troops should be reduced to 25,000
men, including the Foreign Legion; but a secret article
stipulated that the French army should for the present
consist of 38,000 men, to be reduced to 28,000 in 1865,
25,000 in 1866, and 20,000 in 1867. On the financial
side, the French finance minister, Fould, extorted terms
not a little severe, and worthy of the worst traditions
of French bourgeois haggling. The Mexican government was to pay back 270,000,000 francs for the expenses sustained in Mexico up to July 1, 1864, and it
was thenceforward to pay 100 francs per annum for
each French soldier retained in service over seas. A
loan was to be floated, and of this the French treasury
was immediately to receive 66,000,000 at the price of
issue. In such provisions as these clearly appear the
evidences of the increasingly strong desire of the French
government to liquidate the financial side of the Mexican question, becoming more and more the object of
criticism in the Corps Législatif.

There was one concession demanded by Napoleon in
the treaty of Miramar, again a concession on the financial side, with which the Archduke Maximilian would
have nothing to do. In December of 1863, Louis Napoleon had written to Bazaine, commenting upon the
report of a French engineer with regard to the mines
of Sonora. He had mentioned the fact that a French
company had been formed to exploit those mines, and
had directed the commander-in-chief to secure a con-

27

cession from the Mexican provisional government.[79]
The Comte de Montholon, who was sent out to Mexico
at about the same time, bore similar instructions. Accordingly, there was negotiated early in 1864 a convention by which the French government was granted the
right of exploitation of all the mines of Sonora, not
actually being exploited or to which rights of exploitation had not been established. It was further stipulated
that troops might be maintained in Sonora to protect the
properties thus conceded.[80] This extraordinary agreement has sometimes been represented as a cession of
territory. A cession of territory, in the strict sense of
the word, it was not. But it gave to France far-reaching
privileges on the soil of another state, and could hardly
be regarded otherwise than as highly objectionable.
Maximilian very properly refused to give his assent to it.
For the time being, Louis Napoleon was obliged to
forego his ambitious plans for capitalizing his intervention in Mexico, and to put his name to an agreement
from which this piece of sharp business practise was
excluded.

The convention of Miramar is the definite and final
commitment which determines that the great experiment
of monarchy in Mexico shall be carried through. This
commitment was not taken by Louis Napoleon with
enthusiasm, it has already been made clear ; it was taken
because the course of events seemed to the Emperor to
render it imperative. It was taken because it was

[79] García, *op. cit.*, XVII, 76.
[80] *Ibid.*, p. 270.

thought that the candidacy of the Archduke was the only way out of a bad situation.

From the very beginning the tone of the Emperor himself in addressing the legislative bodies seems apologetic, the tone of one who does not anticipate ardent support. In his speech of January 28, 1862, he alluded only briefly to the Mexican expedition, and declared that " nothing could issue from this conflict of a nature to alter our confidence in the future." [81] There was not even a contingent reference to the ulterior purposes of the expedition. The action of France was placed squarely and unequivocally upon the ground of redress of grievances. It was not long, however, before the other aspect of the question began to be known and discussed. As early as March 13 a speaker in the Corps Législatif, addressing himself to the Mexican question, declared that while he willingly supported action for the redress of grievances, he could not approve of any intervention in the internal affairs of Mexico, or believe in the possibility of setting up a monarchy in that distracted country. The rupture of Orizaba and the appearance in the press of the protocol of the final conference and the news of the check at Puebla offered an occasion for further and more intensive discussion of the Mexican question. On June 26, in a speech of genuine power, Jules Favre assailed the policy of the government. He dwelt at length upon the folly of intervention in Mexico; he alluded directly and with scorn to the candidacy of the Archduke Maximilian; and he made incidental

[81] *Moniteur,* January 28, 1862.

reference to the danger of affronting the public opinion of the United States. He was answered in a speech hardly less able, and perhaps even more adroit, by Billault, minister without portfolio. As always from beginning to end of the Mexican adventure, the spokesman for the government denied any intention of imposing a government upon the Mexican people. The displacement of Juarez, the liberation of Mexico, the choice by the Mexican people of some other government, these were the themes of his discourse. With unscrupulous skill he sought to buttress French policy in Mexico by reviving the memories of Buchanan's messages of 1858 and 1859. Implicit in the speech which he made was the assumption that the Mexican expedition was a necessity to save that disorganized country from the rapacity of the United States. Arguments such as these were received with attention and even with applause, but the members of the Chamber had none the less listened with an unwonted attention and respect to the powerful assaults of the opposition. On the morrow of the defeat of Puebla, French pride made it imperative that the credits necessary to the prosecution of the Mexican expedition should be voted with unanimity; but this unanimity was certainly not the expression of general approval.

In the meantime, the tone of the French press was very far from enthusiastic. At the beginning there was little newspaper opposition. In the *Journal des Débats,* an Orleanist paper, Prevost-Paradol advocated the temporary occupation of Mexico, though he realized clearly that such action might be a challenge to the Monroe Doctrine.[82] Eugène Forçade, later anything but friendly, writing in the *Revue des Deux Mondes,* supported the expedition in principle, and even expressed the wish that the United States had departed from its vain-glorious isolation to take part in it.[83] But as time went on, and the ulterior objects of the venture began to become clear, there was general attack upon those objects in all of the press not devoted to the government. In the Republican *Siècle* the well known journalist Taxile Delord predicted future complications in the New World from the policy of the Emperor,[84] and his views were echoed by the equally republican *Presse.* By June, Romero reported the liberal papers were attacking the Mexican intervention with an energy of which there had been no example since the inauguration of Louis Napoleon.[85] The *Journal des Débats* expressed the opinion that the expedition might well end with the fall of Puebla,[86] and this view of matters, to judge from the reports of Dayton, the American minister in Paris, seems to have been general. In the summer of 1862 the American minister wrote to his government that there was not the slightest support for the project of Maximilian, and that it might, indeed, be considered to have been abandoned.

In this, Dayton, though doubtless reflecting a view widely held, was obviously guilty of exaggeration. The

[82] *Journal des Débats,* October 9, 1861.

[83] *Revue des Deux Mondes,* XXXV, 755-7.

[84] *Siècle,* February 1, 1862.

[85] Romero, *Correspondencia, op. cit.,* II, 232.

[86] *Journal des Débats,* June 13, 1862.

Mexican project, of course, had its defenders in the
Imperialist press, and to it Michel Chevalier, one of the
best-known economists in France, lent the authority of
his great name in the article which he wrote for the
Revue des Deux Mondes in April, 1862. This article
has a certain ingenuity, it must be confessed. It was obviously written in part with a view to allaying the dis-
quietude felt by many persons as to the possibility of a
clash with the United States; to Chevalier the Monroe
Doctrine seemed inapplicable to this particular case; the
United States, he pointed out, had recognized Iturbide
in Mexico, and Dom Pedro in Brazil; why should it not
recognize a possible Maximilian? The Northern states
themselves would have an interest in limiting the further
extension of slavery; a strong government in Mexico
would limit the expansion of the South, and should be
welcomed rather than feared. The extension of Latin
and Catholic civilization was also stressed by the great
economist. Indeed, this note, by no means unfamiliar,
was sounded by him with particular effectiveness. And
yet there are indications in his article that he was not
without some perception of the huge difficulties involved
in the Mexican adventure; one has the feeling in reading it that, summoned to make a defense of Imperial
policy, Chevalier nevertheless incorporated therein just
those insidious doubts which he must himself have felt.
The tone of the article is not ardent, by any means; and
the very absence of enthusiasm carries with it its own
powerful implications as to the views even of those who
defended the policy of the government.

Nor did any such enthusiasm develop with time. In the legislative session of 1863, in answer to the speech of the Emperor, the Corps Législatif expressed the hope that it would see " the happy and early end " of the whole expedition,[87] and the opposition again attacked the project with some vigor. Picard, one of the small group of republicans in the Chamber, declared that, far from preventing American encroachment, the use of armed forced in Mexico encouraged the development of American antagonism to Europe, and Favre again condemned a policy which brought France into antagonism with the United States.[88] Even such a defender of the policy of the government as David admitted that the policy of the Emperor had " caused profound emotion in the country," and declared that he was in favor of the briefest possible stay in Mexico.[89] It was difficult, however, for the opposition to make much headway against the studied silence of the government; and, for that matter, as has already been seen, the Emperor himself was disposed to the abandonment of the Archduke's candidacy in the early summer of 1863.

In the press, the year 1863 saw two rather remarkable attacks upon the Mexican policy of the Emperor. One of these is the volume of Mercier de La Combe, entitled *Le Mexique et les Etats-Unis*.[90] This work is extremely temperate in tone; it indulges in no invective; it does

[87] *Moniteur,* January 31, 1863.

[88] *Ibid.,* February 7, 1863.

[89] *Ibid.*

[90] Mercier de La Combe, *Le Mexique et les Etats-Unis* (Paris, 1863).

not even urge the abandonment of the Mexican enterprise, but it does develop at some length its dangers and
difficulties. Should the North win the Civil War, it
" will emerge a military democracy, led by a more centralized and compact government. Imagine peace concluded, will these arms and hearts disarm as if by en-
chantment? What is to be done with them? What
employment shall be offered to their ambition? What
diversion to these hatreds? What food for these passions? . . . . The field of battle," predicts Mercier de La
Combe, " the common ground on which reconciliation
will take place, is already indicated; it will be Mexico.
On the other hand, the South has always been expansionist in character; an independent Confederacy will
soon absorb the regions which lie nearest at hand to
satisfy its rapacity and its ambition." [91] Somewhat later
in the year appeared a slashing attack in the *Revue des
Deux Mondes* from Eugène Forçade. Forçade, like La
Combe, indulges in melancholy predictions of the future.
" Once the Civil War is over," he writes, " the perils of
our enterprise are obvious. American popular feeling
will turn from Canada toward Mexico. In a country
where power belongs to those who flatter the passions of
the multitude, the Presidency will go to the party most
hostile to the new Mexican Constitution. Military elements will survive the Civil War; there will be a host
of generals and officers without employment; a thousand
influences will press the government to vindicate the
Monroe Doctrine by force of arms. . . . . And if the

[91] *Ibid.,* p. 121.

government is moderate enough to resist impulses so natural, the figure of the American filibuster will make his appearance, as he has made it before, to undertake a similar enterprise." [92] Views like these make it clear that the difficulties and dangers of the Emperor's course in Mexico were fully appreciated, not only by the republican opposition, but by men of views far more moderate and far less colored by partisan antagonism to the Imperial régime.

In November, 1863, at the opening of the Chambers, despite growing evidences of criticism, Louis Napoleon announced his policy in Mexico with frankness for the first time. " In Mexico," he declared, " after an unexpected resistance, surmounted by the courage of our soldiers and sailors, we have been received as liberators. Our efforts will not have been in vain, and we shall be generously compensated for our sacrifices when the destinies of that country have been confided to a Prince whose talents and virtues make him worthy of so noble a mission." And then in a tone of high argumentation, he went on, " Our foreign expeditions, the object of so many criticisms, have not been the execution of any premeditated purpose. The course of events made them necessary, and they are by no means to be regretted. How, indeed, develop our foreign trade, if we abdicate all influence in America and in Asia? " [93]

These declarations did not go unanswered. On the contrary, they produced the most formidable attack on

[92] Revue des Deux Mondes, XLVII, 489.
[93] Moniteur, November 6, 1863.

the Mexican policy of the government yet launched, and
the views of the opposition were echoed in milder form
by the supporters of the imperial régime. Thus, the report of the Minister of Finance for 1863 declared that
France desired the end of the war; [94] the Senate, in
answering the speech from the throne, declared that it
desired that "the enterprise gloriously commenced
should receive as soon as possible a·solution worthy of
the Emperor and of French interests," [95] and the Corps
Législatif, on its part, spoke of the course of events
across the seas as "having beyond question disquieted
many minds." [96] If the subservient majority of the
Chambers could use such language, what of those who
bore no good will to the occupants of the Tuileries?
Their assaults were to be expected, and, most assuredly,
they came.

What is particularly interesting about the debates
of 1864 is the increasing emphasis laid on the position
of the United States. There had been allusion to the
attitude of the American government by members of the
opposition at an earlier date, as has already been pointed
out; but the spokesmen of the government had held
their peace. But in the discussions of 1864 the rôle of
Washington is given a much larger significance than
ever before; and well it might be, for though in the
eastern theater of the Civil War many months of bitter
struggle were ahead, by the end of 1863 the tide of battle
as a whole was certainly swinging toward the North.

[94] *Ibid.*, December 5, 1863.
[95] *Ibid.*, December 18, 1863.
[96] *Ibid.*, January 26, 1864.

Gettysburg and Vicksburg must have led men's minds to think seriously of the dangers of the Napoleonic policy in the New World. In speech after speech, therefore, the orators of the opposition raised the specter of American opposition. Guéroult declared that the enterprise was extremely unpopular and would never have been attempted had it not been for the Civil War, and predicted the growing hostility of the United States; [97] Thiers predicted the onrush of a horde of American adventurers upon Mexico when the Civil War was over, and in one of the most powerful and effective speeches of his career pleaded with the government not to let Maximilian go out to Mexico, but to treat with Juarez instead; [98] the veteran Berryer declared that the French policy was contrary to the Monroe Doctrine, mentioning that Doctrine by name,[99] and Jules Favre read with telling effect some of the despatches from Washington, and some of the debates in the American Congress.[100] It would be too much to say that the position of the United States occupied a central place in the debates; but that it now furnished a major argument to the speakers can now be fairly asserted.

The criticisms of the opposition in Parliament and the emphasis on the attitude of the United States were echoed in the press. Even before the monarchical project had been publicly avowed by Louis Napoleon, Prévost-Paradol had declared that neither the United States,

[97] *Ibid.,* January 26, 1864.
[98] *Ibid.,* January 27, 1864.
[99] *Ibid.,* January 28, 1864.
[100] *Ibid.,* May 13, 1864.

if its unity were restored, nor the South if it became independent, would ever consent to the establishment of monarchy in Mexico.[101] The able and influential Eugène Forçade wrote with remarkable frankness, "Certain frivolous and reckless spirits would like to change an eccentric expedition into a system of permanent hostility to the United States. . . . . In attempting to found an empire in Mexico, it is unfortunately true that we are creating gratuitously an antagonism between American patriotism and France." [102]

In answer to these attacks the government for the first time was compelled to unmask itself. Some of its supporters either ignored the United States, or contented themselves with references to the " selfish and tyrannical doctrine " of the American government,[103] or with gloomy predictions of the gobbling up of Mexico if a monarchy were not established.[104] But the able Rouher, minister without portfolio, attempted to answer the arguments of the opposition in some detail. He was expressing himself as the official spokesman of the Emperor, and his speech is obviously an attempt to justify all that had been done; but its views must have represented the hopes, if not the actual convictions of the Emperor himself. They offer interesting evidence of what was the official theory of the position of the United States in 1864.

[101] *Courrier du Dimanche,* August 23, 1863.
[102] *Ibid.,* September 15, 1863.
[103] *Moniteur,* Dalloz, March 10, 1864.
[104] *Ibid.,* January 28, 1864.

Rouher's line of reasoning ran as follows: The United States had left Mexico in 1848; it had carried through no policy of absorption at that time, and hence it would not view with apprehension the French policy which aimed after all at nothing more than establishing a stable government in Mexico. The Civil War would in any case make it impossible for some time to come for the American government to interfere, and in the meantime the régime of Maximilian would consolidate itself. The commercial interests of the United States would re-assume their dominance when the war was over, and would insist upon a policy of peace. As for the Monroe Doctrine, it was not at all involved. The Monroe Doctrine was not hostile to monarchy in principle, as witness the American recognition of the Empire of Brazil. The establishment of a monarchical government in Mexico by the act of the Mexican people themselves could not be regarded as a breach of the principles of 1823. The United States ought to welcome the setting-up of a régime which would give peace and prosperity to a hitherto distracted country.[105]

The arguments of Rouher to the Chambers were echoed and supplemented by an article in the ministerial organ, the *Constitutionel*, a few days later. The Mexican people, so ran the reasoning of this article, had freely accepted the monarchical form. It was impossible to deny their preference for this type of government. The United States could have no real objection there-fore to the new régime of Maximilian. Whatever the

[105] *Ibid.,* May 13, 1864.

results of the war, there was no real danger of hostility, for the victory of the North would lead to long military occupation of the defeated section, and would make undesirable any policy of expansion which would increase the strength of the vanquished. Mexico, better organized than ever before, would become a market for the United States. " The American people, ... when it has comprehended all that is to be gained from the new state of things without any injury to its legitimate pride, ... is intelligent enough to renounce puerile susceptibilities that its government was from the beginning wise enough not to excite." [106]

There were many vulnerable points in this line of reasoning, and perhaps some disingenuousness as well. By May of 1864, as we shall see in the next chapter, it might have been reasonably foreseen that the United States would oppose a formidable obstacle to monarchy in Mexico; but so prone is the mind of man to believe that which it desires to believe it is possible to assume that the Emperor's apologists deceived even themselves. If their view of matters suggests an ostrich-like indifference to facts, it can only be said that there was a good deal of such indifference in the whole policy of Napoleon III in Mexico.

As for the Archduke Maximilian, the same indifference must most certainly be ascribed to him. In the bottom of his heart he understood only too well how important would be the attitude of the United States, and as late as August, 1863, he wrote to the Emperor

[106] *Ibid.*, May 16 and 17, 1864.

declaring that " the most serious obstacle " to the carrying out of this work " would come from North America, the recent news from which appears to foreshadow the reconstitution of the Union, which is as greedy of aggrandizement as it is hostile to the monarchical principle in the other hemisphere." [107] Yet even so he persisted in moving forward, and at a time when he ought to have been analyzing with the greatest care the difficulties immediately in the way, he was dreaming romantic dreams of the marriage of his brother, Ludwig Viktor, to one of the daughters of the Emperor of Brazil, and even of the gradual absorption of Central America by the government which he was to found in Mexico.[108] The tragic doom of this amiable Hapsburg prince has always induced a charitable judgment of the enterprise to which he committed himself. But it must be freely conceded by all who examine the facts that there were ample warnings given him, from Sir Charles Wyke, from Rechberg, from his own brother; and the fateful decision which he took in April of 1864 was one that might and should have been avoided if prudence and critical judgment had played their due part in the forming of his resolution. The time had long gone by to dream of monarchy in the New World; Maximilian was to pay the penalty for being so thoroughly out of date. Chivalrous and generous his attitude may well have been; founded upon a clear realization of the facts it certainly was not.

[107] Quoted in Corti, *op. cit.*, I, 378.
[108] *Ibid.*, p. 280.

Yet it is interesting, after all, to see how far down into the nineteenth century reaches the idea of rescuing America from democracy. By this time the reader has had ample evidence of the strength of this motive in connection with the whole Mexican expedition. The checking of American expansion has been again and again referred to as one of the major justifications of the whole enterprise. The hoisting of the monarchist flag, " in the face of dangerous Utopias and bloody disorders," as Napoleon put it, was one of the principal objects which the Emperor of the French had in view.

And along with all this went, as is clear, the conception of a new balance of power in the Americas. The policy of Guizot and of Canning found fresh expression in the policy of Louis Napoleon. If the British Foreign Secretary who had so much to do with the origins of the Monroe Doctrine could boast of " calling the New World into existence to redress the balance of the Old," the Emperor of the French and his Hapsburg protégé might hope with equal ardor to call Old World monarchy into existence to redress the balance of the New.

The ambitions of these two men, however, were to be shattered upon the resistance of the Mexican people, the indifference or hostility of French opinion, and the antagonism of the United States. Of the existence of the first two, the reader has already had evidence. The last, in such a work as this, may properly claim a chapter to itself.

CHAPTER VIII

AMERICAN OPINION AND MEXICO

The events which have been described in the last chapter, beyond all question constitute the most serious threat that has ever been offered to the integrity of the Monroe Doctrine, and the clearest challenge to the principle of the two spheres upon which that Doctrine is founded. It is true, as has been pointed out, that there were hesitations and dubieties in the foreign policy of Louis Napoleon; it is even true that there was a time in 1863 when the project of monarchy in Mexico was near abandonment; but it is also true that from first to last the enterprise was conceived, in one aspect, at least, as a means of checking the development of the United States, and of creating a counterpoise to the forces of republicanism in the New World. The notion of the balance of power, touched upon in the speeches of Huskisson and Palmerston, developed in the parliamentary discourses of Guizot, applied by France and Great Britain in Texas, and reapplied in Santo Domingo, was now to be given new expression. The integrity of the principles of 1823 depended upon the outcome of events in Mexico.

It is necessary, therefore, to turn to the American side of the problem, and to see how public opinion in the United States and the policy of its statesmen reacted to the threat to the principle of nonintervention. At the risk of anticipating the story itself, it is worth while to say at the outset that the Monroe Doctrine played an enormous rôle in public discussion and diplomatic action in connection with the Mexican question. It has more than once been pointed out that Seward never mentioned the Doctrine in his copious diplomatic correspondence on Mexico; and this statement is correct. But it would be more to the point to indicate that the upholding of the principles of 1823 is implicit in all the more important of his despatches; that those principles were again and again invoked by the Mexican minister in Washington; that they were on the lips of most American public men, and in the columns of many of the newspapers; and that they exercised a powerful influence upon the course of events at home and abroad. It is my purpose in the following pages to retraverse the already well traveled ground of Seward's Mexican policy from this point of view,[1] not so much with the object of developing it in its every detail, as with the purpose of showing its relationship to the evolving message of President Monroe. The outcome of this examination will no doubt demonstrate that whereas in 1860 the Monroe Doctrine had not yet attained the importance of a truly national principle, whereas some atmosphere of partisanship still clung to it in the fifties, it emerged from the events which we are about to exam-

[1] The best treatments are J. M. Callahan, *The Evolution of Seward's Mexican Policy* (West Virginia University Studies in American History. Morgantown, 1908), and J. F. Rippy, *The United States and Mexico, op. cit.,* chs. 14 and 15, pp. 252-282.

ine immensely strengthened, and firmly anchored in the thought of the American people and in the policy of their government.

We have already seen in our discussion of the question of Santo Domingo that Seward's first thought was " to arouse a vigorous continental spirit of independence on this continent against European intervention." The document in which this principle was embodied had brought a mild and yet firm rebuke from Mr. Lincoln; and the attempt to adopt a truculent tone toward the government of Spain had produced no very flattering results. The Secretary of State learned much from experience, and he received with coolness the suggestion of Cassius M. Clay, writing from St. Petersburg in August, 1861, that the United States ally itself with Mexico, assume the lead in the liberal governments of the West, and cooperate with Russia in restricting the dominating policy of England in both hemispheres.[2] But his purposes and his outlook were not changed; and though prudent restraint governed the evolution of his Mexican policy, its essential objects were those which are expressed in the Monroe Doctrine. After the disillusion of Bull Run, it was clear that the time for braggadocio was over; the temper of the Seward policy is altered; but the purposes remain the same.

The possibility of European action in Mexico began to come under the consideration of the Secretary in the early summer of 1861. From Mexico City Corwin

[2] Washington, Dept. of State, Despatches, Russia, August 3, 1861.

wrote of the danger of European intervention, and suggested the desirability of a loan to Mexico.[3] " The United States," he wrote, in support of his viewpoint, " are the only safe guardians of the independence and true civilization on this continent." Accepting the principle, if not the details of Corwin's suggestion, Seward instructed the American minister to negotiate a treaty by which, provided that the European powers would consent to abstain from hostilities against the Mexican government, the United States would agree to pay 3% interest on the Mexican funded debt for a period of five years, from the date of the July decree suspending those payments. In exchange, Mexico was to give the United States a lien on the public lands and mineral rights in Lower California, Chihuahua, Sonora, and Sinaloa, which would become the property of the United States at the end of six years in default of reimbursement.

It is amusing to reflect for a moment upon this proposal. Thomas Corwin, who had so much to do with it, was that same Thomas Corwin who, not fifteen years before, had ardently opposed the Mexican war, and expressed the not particularly patriotic hope that the Mexicans would welcome their American foes with bloody hands to hospitable graves. We find him in 1861 advocating a proposition which, by his own view, would " probably end in the cession of the sovereignty " to the United States.[4] It is almost equally delightful to wit-

[3] 37th Cong., 2nd Sess., H. Exec. Doc. No. 100, pp. 13-4, Despatches of June 29 and of July 29.

[4] *Ibid.*, p. 15.

ness the Secretary of State of the United States attempting to retard or prevent the action of European powers by means of a proposal which had been so frequently condemned and feared by the statesmen of the Old World. As a matter of fact, the Corwin-Seward proposition was entirely impracticable. Not only did it fail to cover the grievances of Great Britain, France, and Spain, which were based on many other claims than those involved in the suspension of payment on the debt, but it inevitably aroused suspicion of American intentions. From London Adams wrote that it was not only inacceptable to the British government, but also that it naturally became the ground of an outcry that it was " but the preliminary to an entry for inevitable foreclosure. And then follows the argument," wrote Adams, " that if this process be legitimate in one case, why not equally in all? As against Great Britain and France it would be difficult to oppose to this the abstract principle contained in what has been known as the Monroe Doctrine, however just in substance." [5] The point of view of the British government was obviously shared by France and Spain. M. Thouvenel, like Lord John Russell, declared that the American proposition did not cover the case, and pointedly hinted to Dayton that the danger of Mexican extinction had hitherto come from the United States.[6] At a somewhat later date, Perry reported from Madrid that the intervention of the United States in the Mexican business was the subject

[5] *Ibid.*, p. 201, Despatch of November 1. See also pp. 193-4, Despatch of September 28.

[6] *Ibid.*, p. 212, despatch of September 27.

of considerable apprehension, and that the journals of the capital were hinting that the allied intervention was the only alternative to an American protectorate.[7]

Moreover, the loan project met with no favorable reception in the United States itself. In advance of the actual negotiation of a treaty by Corwin, the administration decided to try to get a resolution of approval from the Senate of the United States, and Seward apparently worked energetically to this end. He was aided by the indefatigable Mexican minister at Washington, Matias Romero. This remarkable man, of prodigious industry and energy, and a mere youth of twenty-nine in 1861, seems to have been a master of the art of personal politics. He formed contacts with all the most influential people in Washington; through Montgomery Blair, the Postmaster-General, he gained a knowledge of what went on even in the secrecy of the cabinet; he enjoyed cordial relationships with Charles Sumner, the chairman of the Committee on Foreign Relations in the Senate; and, with an understanding of democratic institutions remarkable in a Mexican of the sixties, he resorted to an active propaganda in newspapers and periodicals. Romero had not really hit his stride at the end of 1861 and the beginning of 1862, but he managed to win the members of the Committee on Foreign Relations to his point of view of the Mexican business. When the resolution endorsing the project of a loan was brought to the floor of the Senate, however, it was decisively rejected, and

[7] 37th Cong. 3rd Sess., H. Exec. Doc. No. 54, p. 552, despatch of March 26, 1862.

a resolution of wholly contrary tenor adopted declaring
that it was not advisable to negotiate a treaty that would
require the United States to assume any portion of the
principal or interest of the debt of Mexico, or that would
require the concurrence of foreign powers.[8] As Romero
wrote to his government, a " supine egoism " led the
members of the Senate to believe that the whole energies
of the United States should be devoted to the prosecution of the war at home, and no cause of affront given
to foreign powers.[9] Though the loan project lingered
on, though a treaty was actually negotiated by Corwin,
and submitted by the administration to the Senate, there
was never any real prospect that this mode of solving
the Mexican difficulty would be adopted. The European
powers brushed aside the suggestion that was made to
them, and, as has already been seen, had decided upon a
vigorous course by the end of October, 1861.

None the less, the expedient of a loan to Mexico has
its very real interest. It represents a new development
in American diplomacy, a policy of direct aid to distracted American republics with a view to warding off
European intervention. The times were not propitious
for its acceptance; it could hardly be expected that the
public opinion of the United States would sanction any
such scheme in the midst of the Civil War, or that it
would be otherwise regarded than as a veiled form of
expansion by the jealous diplomats of Europe; but it

[8] See 37th Cong., 2nd Sess., H. Exec. Doc. No. 100, p. 49.
[9] *Correspondencia de la Legación Mexicana durante la Intervención Extranjera* (10 vols. Mexico City. 1870-92), edited by
Matías Romero, II, 67.

must be admitted that, in putting it forward, Seward was only proposing a course of action not far removed from that actually followed by American administrations of a later era. In this, as in some other aspects of his foreign policy, for example, his views with regard to the Caribbean, he was the exponent of ideas, after a lapse of many years, to be accepted by his successors. On the other hand, one must admit a certain naïveté to be apparent in a proposal which smacked so much of expansion, and was none the less submitted for approval to those very European states which might be expected to be most critical of the territorial aggrandizement of the United States. It is possible that a more experienced Secretary would have doubted the value of any such expedient from the beginning.

But if the European powers could not thus be diverted from their purpose, what were to be the main lines of the foreign policy of the United States with regard to the Mexican question? Seward answered these questions in two notable despatches, the circular of December 4, 1861, and the equally important circular of March 3, 1862.

The first of these two documents was in response to the invitation of the signatories of the convention of London that the United States adhere to that convention. After summarizing the convention itself, the American Secretary of State proceeded to state the principles by which the action of his government would be guided. The first of these was to the effect that the right of the European powers to wage war against an American state, either singly or collectively, was not to be challenged. Such a position was, of course, consistent both with past precedents, and with the realities of the existing diplomatic and domestic situation. There had been no case, down to 1860, of a direct prohibition of armed action for the redress of grievances by the states of the Old World against the states of the New. The French interventions in Mexico and Argentina in 1838 has passed unchallenged by the executive. The Anglo-French intervention of 1845, however distasteful, had been the subject of no protest from Washington. The Buchanan administration itself, most sensitive on the subject of the Monroe Doctrine, had never assumed to veto the use of force for the vindication of national claims, and had indeed specifically asserted a contrary view at the time of the impending action of Spain against Mexico in 1858. It was not until the beginning of the twentieth century that American public opinion became so sensitive as to all armed action by European states in the New World as to force a revision of this viewpoint. In taking the stand that he did take in 1861, Seward was guided by the traditional attitude of the United States.

Nor can he be said to have deviated from this attitude in his refusal to accept the invitation that was tendered him. The matter was the subject of very careful consideration; it was discussed by the cabinet; and at least one member of that body, Francis Blair, was favorable to acceptance, on the ground that American participation would serve as a check on the other intervening states.[10] Romero himself urged Seward to give an

[10] *Ibid.*, I, 620.

affirmative reply to the overture of the signatories of
the London convention. But the weight of opinion was
against it, and the refusal to accede to the convention
was placed upon the sound traditional ground that it
was contrary to the policy of the United States, for them
to make alliances with foreign countries, and upon the
fact that Mexico " being a neighbor of the United States
on this continent, and possessing a form of government
similar to our own in many of its important features "
was entitled to some measure of patience and indulgence,
despite the existence of valid claims against it.

In the phrase that has just been quoted above, appears a hint of that doctrine of the two spheres that, on
the one side and on the other, was to play so large a
part in the Mexican question. But the circular of December 4 contains a more striking statement, which may
be regarded as the first of the warnings which the American Secretary communicated to the powers of the
Old World with regard to Mexico. " The United
States," he declared, " have a deep interest which, however, they are happy to believe is an interest held by
them in common with the high contracting powers and
with all other civilized states, that neither the sovereigns
by whom the convention has been concluded shall seek or
obtain any acquisition of territory or any advantage
peculiar to itself, and not equally left open to the United
States and every other civilized state within the territories of Mexico, and especially that neither one nor
all of the contracting parties shall, as a result or consequence of hostilities to be inaugurated under the convention, exercise in the subsequent affairs of Mexico

any influence of a character to impair the right of the Mexican people to choose and freely to constitute the form of its own government.

" The undersigned renews on this occasion," Seward went on, " the acknowledgment heretofore given, that each of the high contracting parties had informed the United States substantially that they recognized this interest, and he is authorized to express the satisfaction of the President with the terms in which that recognition is clearly embodied in the treaty itself."

In thus treating of the threat of the subversion of the régime of President Juarez, the American Secretary of State might be thought to be practicing the familiar diplomatic manœuver of assuming complete good faith on the part of an adversary really the subject of distrust. As early as September 27 Carl Schurz had written him of the monarchical leanings of Spain; [11] at an even earlier date the vigilant Charles Francis Adams had declared that the projected intervention might result in the establishment of monarchy and the creation of new combinations based upon the balance of power, introducing " a new principle of action into American affairs," [12] and though Dayton, up to this time, seems to have allowed himself to be lulled into indifference by Thouvenel,[13] Romero had not failed to insinuate into Seward's mind the idea that the purposes of France

[11] Washington, Dept. of State, Spain, Despatches, September 27, 1861.

[12] 37th Cong., 2nd Sess., H. Exec. Doc. No. 100, despatches of September 19 and September 28, pp. 191 and 193.

[13] See especially the despatch of September 27, published in ibid., pp. 211-12.

were not so innocent as they seemed.[14] The best way to deal with all these disquieting suggestions would be to assume and to declare with every appearance of conviction that there was nothing in them. Yet it would seem as if, despite all these warnings, Seward was rather inclined at first to take the danger lightly. His general tone in talking to Romero was one of incredulity with regard to the intentions of the intervening states, and on more than one occasion he declared his opinion that the divergence of purpose amongst the three powers themselves would remove the sting from any far-reaching plans, or the subversion of the republican régime of President Juarez.[15] It was not until the idea of the candidacy of the Archduke Maximilian began to be freely discussed in the American newspapers, and was for the first time mentioned in the despatches of the not extraordinarily alert Dayton, that the Secretary took his pen in hand, and gave solemn warning of the policy of the future in the circular of March.[16] This circular is so important that it deserves quotation in full. It may be considered as the platform on which Seward took his stand as soon as the issue was definitely presented to him, and on which he stood from that day forward.

[14] Romero, I, 604.

[15] *Ibid.*, pp. 604 and 618.

[16] Some importance may also be attached to the speech which Gerrit Smith delivered at the Smithsonian Institution on the night of March 1, in which his declaration that the people of the United States would not permit the establishment of a monarchy in Mexico was received with great applause. *Ibid.*, II, 72.

DEPARTMENT OF STATE,
WASHINGTON, MARCH 3, 1862.

SIR: We observe indications of a growing opinion in Europe that the demonstrations which are being made by Spanish, French, and British forces against Mexico are likely to be attended with a revolution in that country which will bring in a monarchical government there, in which the crown will be assumed by some foreign prince.

This country is deeply concerned in the peace of nations, and aims to be loyal at the same time in all its relations, as well to the allies as to Mexico. The President has therefore instructed me to submit his views on the new aspect of affairs to the parties concerned. He has relied upon the assurances given to this government by the allies that they were seeking no political objects and only a redress of grievances. He does not doubt the sincerity of the allies, and his confidence in their good faith, if it could be shaken, would be reinspired by explanations apparently made in their behalf that the governments of Spain, France, and Great Britain are not intending to intervene and will not intervene to effect a change of the constitutional form of government now existing in Mexico, or to produce any political change there in opposition to the will of the Mexican people. Indeed, he understands the allies to be unanimous in declaring that the proposed revolution in Mexico is moved only by Mexican citizens now in Europe.

The President, however, deems it his duty to express to the allies, in all candor and frankness, the opinion that no monarchical government which could be founded in Mexico, in the presence of foreign navies and armies in the waters and upon the soil of Mexico, would have any prospect of security or permanency. Secondly, that the instability of such a monarchy there would be enhanced if the throne should be assigned to any person not of Mexican nativity. That under such circumstances the new government must speedily fall unless it could draw into its support European alliances, which, relating back to the present invasion, would, in fact, make it the beginning of a permanent policy of armed European monarchical intervention injurious and practically hostile to the most general system of government on the continent of America, and this would be the beginning rather than the ending of revolution in Mexico.

These views are grounded upon some knowledge of the political sentiments and habits of society in America.

In such a case it is not to be doubted that the permanent interests and sympathies of this country would be with the other American republics. It is not intended on this occasion to predict the course of events which might happen as a consequence of the proceeding contemplated, either on this continent or in Europe. It is sufficient to say that, in the President's opinion, the emancipation of this continent from European control has been the principal feature in its history during the last century. It is not probable that a revolution in a contrary direction would be successful in an immediately succeeding century, while population in America is so rapidly increasing, resources so rapidly developing, and society so steadily forming itself upon principles of democratic American government. Nor is it necessary to suggest to the allies the improbability that European nations could steadily agree upon a policy favorable to such a counter-revolution as one conducive to their own interests, or to suggest that, however studiously the allies may act to avoid lending the aid of their land and naval forces to domestic revolutions in Mexico, the result would nevertheless be traceable to the presence of those forces there, although for a different purpose, since it may be deemed certain that but for their presence there no such revolution could probably have been attempted or even conceived.

The Senate of the United States has not, indeed, given its official sanction to the precise measures which the President has proposed for lending our aid to the existing government in Mexico, with the approval of the allies, to relieve it from its present embarrassments. This, however, is only a question of domestic administration. It would be very erroneous to regard such a disagreement as indicating any serious difference of opinion in this government or among the American people in their cordial good wishes for the safety, welfare, and stability of the republican system of government in that country.

I am, sir, your obedient servant,

William H. Seward.

Charles Francis Adams, Esq., &c., &c., &c.

The suavity of this despatch should not be permitted to becloud its real definiteness of outline. The circumstances were not propitious for the language of bluster, and Seward had grown immensely since the *Thoughts for the Consideration of the President* in April, 1861. He no longer took the great struggle in which the North was now engaged with a frivolous optimism; and he was well aware of the danger involved in antagonizing Europe before that struggle was concluded. He must, therefore, use moderate language in making his essential purpose clear; he must avoid creating a sharp issue of any kind. This he undoubtedly did with great skill. Once more the pious professions of the signatories of the London convention were taken as the measure of their purposes; the assumption was made that the project of monarchy was one of Mexican refugees alone; but the occasion was seized for a disquisition on the political conditions of the New World, which left no room for doubt as to the views of the United States. And as if to make assurance doubly sure, Seward followed up the circular of March 3 with a despatch of March 31 to Dayton, in which, in the most tactful language, the American minister was authorized, not to ask for explanations, but to intimate that any information which might be "calculated to relieve anxiety" would be gratefully received. The concluding sentence of this despatch was unequivocal. "We have more than once . . . . informed all the parties to the alliance that we cannot look with indifference upon any armed European intervention for political ends in a country situated so near and connected with us so closely as Mexico." [17]

In penning these diplomatic documents the American Secretary of State was, to all practical purposes, acting upon the basis of the Monroe Doctrine. If he did not mention the Doctrine itself by name, there was ample justification of his action, both in his own past, and in the existing diplomatic situation. He had contended a decade before for a point of view which judged practical questions upon a practical basis, and not upon the basis of dogma; there was something solid and important behind the principles of 1823; but what *was* solid and important gained neither in solidity nor importance by constantly invoking them. It was clear that the Monroe Doctrine was profoundly unpopular abroad; and it was only a few months before, after all, that Calderon Collantes had returned a crushing reply to Perry when the latter tried to lecture him on the great American dogma. Why, then, flaunt it in the face of a jealous and unfriendly Europe? And yet the essential truth must be stated, the truth that intervention in Mexico might easily be the beginning "of a permanent policy of armed European monarchical intervention, injurious and prac-

[17] 37th Cong., 2nd Sess., H. Exec. Doc. No. 100, p. 218.

tically hostile to the most general system of government prevailing on the continent of America," in opposition to which the " permanent interests and sympathies of this country would be with the other American republics."

There can be very little question that in taking the position which he did in fact assume, Seward was interpreting the developing public opinion of the United States. At the outset of the Mexican episode, the policy of the European governments came in for virtually no comment from American public men, and there are various indications that this public opinion was little aroused. Papers which were as divergent in their views as the New York *Tribune* and the *Herald* united in declaring that a little chastening might be good for the Mexicans. Horace Greeley, with that delightful inconsequence which sometimes inspired his views, declared that Mexico really needed a monarchy, but that since it would be difficult to find a monarch, it might be desirable to move the Pope to Mexico, and set up his rule there, thus solving the Roman question.[18] At a later date, Greeley devoted two elaborate editorials to proving that the Monroe Doctrine was not in any way involved.[19] In Congress not a word was spoken on the subject, and Romero felt obliged to labor unremittingly in an effort to stimulate a movement of indignation ; the vote of the Senate on February 25 rejecting the Corwin treaty proposal may very possibly reflect indifference as well as

[18] Romero, I, 522.
[19] *Ibid.*, p. 622.

29

caution. But there are signs of increasing interest in Mexico in the winter and spring of 1862. Representative men began to express themselves upon the matter. George Bancroft, speaking in Cooper Union on Washington's birthday, found occasion to declare that any effort to establish a monarchy upon the flank of the United States would " have an importance not to be denied." And his remarks were received with applause. Gerrit Smith, speaking at the Smithsonian Institution a week later, declared that the American people would never permit the setting-up of a monarchical régime in Mexico, and he, too, was loudly cheered.[20] Francis Blair told Romero that the United States, once its own unhappy conflict was ended, would drive the forces of European powers from Mexico.[21] General McClellan took the same view in a letter to the Mexican refugee, Ghilardi.[22] John J. Crittenden, the chairman of the House Committee on Foreign Relations, gave every encouragement to the Mexican minister.[23] The papers began to take the same tone.[24] As popular hopes of the early ending of the war rose with the advance of the Army of the Potomac toward Richmond, it seemed as if already the thoughts of public men were turning to the southward, and to the vindication of the republican system in the New World.

Even Seward and the cautious Lincoln gave some indication of sharing in this popular indignation. The

[20] *Ibid.*, II, 72.
[21] *Ibid.*, p. 170, May 9, 1862.
[22] *Ibid.*, p. 257.
[23] *Ibid.*, p. 177.
[24] *Ibid.*, p. 171.

Mexican minister had had great difficulty in seeing the latter. He finally managed to get an interview with him on May 16. Lincoln told him that the settlement of the Mexican question would depend on the course of events in the United States, a clear indication of sympathy.[25] In general Seward, when Romero talked to him, remained impassive. But on one notable occasion he unguarded himself. Romero had brought to him the news of the fiasco of Puebla. A sarcastic smile curled about the lips of the Secretary. " I hope you can hold out three or six months more," he remarked. And then, as if he realized that he had gone too far, he tried to pretend that all he had meant to say was that it would not take much longer than that for the Mexicans to settle their own problems.

Romero, on his part, was doing all he could do indoctrinate Seward and indeed all others with whom he came in contact with a deadly suspicion and hatred of the French, and a clear understandnig of the great issue which he held to be involved. His despatches to the Secretary of State are marvels of industry; they rest, not upon theory alone, but upon the most careful study of the public documents which the various European governments had published; and their only weakness is in their very thoroughness. There is a question of diplomatic method involved in submitting a diplomatic note that takes up more than 100 printed pages! With relentless logic the Mexican revealed the bad faith of the French, and shattered the optimism which still permitted

[25] *Ibid.*, p. 184.

Seward from time to time to accept the disclaimers of
Thouvenel, and the obtuse despatches of Dayton; with
a pertinacity no less relentless he went to the State Department again and again to keep the Mexican question
in the forefront of discussion; between October 1, 1861
and June 30, 1862 he had 53 personal interviews with
Seward. The conversation turned upon many aspects
of the Mexican question, of course; but the object and
purpose was always the same.

In the course of this besieging of the Secretary
Romero of course found room for a direct appeal to
the Monroe Doctrine. His despatch of June 2, 1862
declares, "I cannot believe for even a moment," that
"the government of the United States can remain indifferent to the dangers which threaten in America the
system of republican government, and that she can be
an impassible spectator of the contest in which is involved (I say this without fear of being held to exaggerate) the future fortune of the continent, and whatever can be of most value to man on earth—its independence, its freedom, its autonomy. It is not possible that
the people and government of the United States can
forget the principles bequeathed to them by one of the
most distinguished of their Presidents, James Monroe,
who, in his message of the 2nd of December, 1823 . . . .
traced the following lines, which seem to be written for
the present occasion." Not content with quoting the
message itself, the Mexican also quoted the instructions of Clay to Poinsett of May 25, 1825. He brought
together both the non-colonization principle and the

other portion of the Doctrine. The former, he declared, was more important than ever when the question was not " of establishing a colony on an uninhabited and unknown part of this continent," but when it was intended " to reduce to the colonial condition a state . . . . which occupies a prominent position among those which compose the American continents."

To the note of June 2, and to many others, for the matter of that, the Secretary of State returned noncommittal replies, often promising no more than to include them in the documents to be transmitted to Congress. In the meantime the fortunes of the Civil War seemed to turn for a time against the North; McClellan was compelled to withdraw from before Richmond, and as the summer wore on there followed the second defeat at Bull Run, Lee's invasion of Maryland, and the battle of Antietam. The year closed in gloom with the wintry holocaust of Fredericksburg. The turn of events in the United States might of itself have forced the Mexican question into the background, for a time. But in Mexico itself there is little to record in the second half of 1862. Marshal Forey was preparing slowly and cautiously for the advance which was to culminate in the taking of Mexico City; he did not begin his forward movement till the spring of '63. Meanwhile it was still possible to assume, as Seward did assume, and as Dayton encouraged him to do, that the project of monarchy was in abeyance; and though the American Secretary of State found occasion to reiterate the views of the United States from time to time his instructions of this period add nothing essential to the understanding of his policy.[26]

It is not thus with the year 1863-64. Both in the sphere of public opinion and of diplomatic policy there are important developments to record. In the first place, Mexico found its first real champion in the Congress of the United States. Senator MacDougal of California was a Democrat, critical of the administration, and devoted to the Monroe Doctrine as a Democratic dogma; and he looked with distrust upon the French intervention in Mexico not merely on theoretical grounds but also because it interrupted and dislocated the commerce of the Pacific Coast. He had also undoubtedly undergone a little education from Romero when he introduced into Congress on January 19, his resolution condemning the policy of Louis Napoleon as contrary to good faith and to international law, and requested the administration to require the withdrawal of the French armies and to afford such aid to Mexico as might be required " to prevent the forcible interposition of any of the states of Europe in the political affairs of that republic." [27] On February 3 he secured consideration for his reso-

[26] Dayton had a long conversation with Thouvenel on Mexico in the middle of April. (Washington, Dept. of State, France, Despatches, April 22, 1862.) The French minister on this occasion, and again in an interview in early June, declared that France did not mean to establish a monarchy. (37th Cong., 3rd Sess., H. Exec. Doc. No. 54, p. 529.) Dayton reported in a despatch of June 13 that the project had been abandoned. (*Ibid.*) Seward wrote to Corwin in this sense, July 14. (*Ibid.*, p. 21.)

[27] *Cong. Globe,* 37th Cong., 3rd Sess., p. 371.

lution by a vote of 29 to 16. Speaking at length on the subject with which he dealt, he declared the policy of the government to be weak beyond description, and the Monroe Doctrine to be the "established law" which ought to be invoked on such an occasion. He was followed by Sumner, who strongly deprecated any action which might be offensive to France, and his resolution was temporarily smothered by a vote to go into executive session. Obviously MacDougal's move was contrary to the desires of the administration. It was pigeonholed in the Foreign Relations Committee, and MacDougal's effort in July to get it on to the floor of the Senate was defeated by the decisive vote of 23 to 5.[28]

It would be easy to deprecate MacDougal's manœuver as nothing more nor less than partisanship. But the cry of partisanship is more often than not a very shallow explanation of political warfare. What lies behind so-called partisanship is the attempt of an opposition to capitalize public discontent with the conduct of the administration, and for this purpose it must inevitably choose issues on which such discontent exists, and exists widely. It is to be assumed, therefore, that the Democratic Senators who voted for the MacDougal resolution did so because such action was not altogether unpleasing to their constituents. If they had been charged with responsibility they would have been forced to recognize the prudential reasons for avoiding a clash with France when the fortunes of war were by no means brilliant;

[28] Senate *Journal*, 38th Cong., 1st Sess., p. 486.

as it was, however, they could afford to express a feeling which the supporters of Lincoln and Seward may have shared, and which was certainly felt in a growing measure by many Americans.

In his speech of February 3, MacDougal quoted from the famous letter of Louis Napoleon to Marshal Forey. That letter had, most imprudently, it would appear, been published in the *Documents Diplomatiques* for 1862, and from France it had found its way to England and America. It was, the French minister wrote to his government, widely noticed in the press, and vigorously criticized. It supplied the proof, hitherto lacking, of ulterior purpose in the Mexican intervention. It could not fail to be highly irritating to American public opinion.[29] It was again and again republished in the course of the year,[30] and must have had an influence worth taking into account.

The rising interest in Mexico in the year 1863 is revealed, moreover, in a very considerable number of pamphlets and books which deal with the subject. The first of these books in point of time, Vine W. Kingsley's review of Mercier de la Combe's book, erroneously ascribed to Chevalier, is in no way remarkable. It is a clear analysis of French purpose, and it contains the Forey letter in full, but it deals little with general principles, and hardly mentions the Monroe

[29] Paris, Min. des Aff. Etr., Corr. Pol., Etats-Unis, February 6, 1863.

[30] For example, in Vine W. Kingsley, *French Intervention in America* (New York, 1863), and Joshua Leavitt, *The Monroe Doctrine,* and John Jay, *Letter on the Relinquishment of the Monroe Doctrine.*

Doctrine. A second pamphlet, which bears the imposing name of Edward Everett, which was published in September, and which bears as its title, *The Monroe Doctrine,* is mostly devoted to proving that the Doctrine did not draw its inspiration from England. Still a third, devoted to a bitter excoriation of the administration is the brief brochure of John Jay, son of the great John Jay, *Letter on the Relinquishment of the Monroe Doctrine.* But there is far more merit and importance in the work of Joshua Leavitt, published toward the end of 1863, and entitled *The Monroe Doctrine.*[31]

Leavitt's work, coming as it does from a man well known in the circles of abolitionism and of radical republicanism, deals with great clearness with that clash of systems on which we have so often insisted in this volume. It contrasts sharply the dominating motives of European and American diplomacy; it develops in some detail the general thesis of the conflict between the balance of power on the one hand, and the principle of nonintervention on the other, and illustrates that thesis by the march of existing events; it contains an excel-

[31] Passing notice should also be taken of the interesting work of C. B. Boynton, *English and French Neutrality and the Anglo-French Alliance in their Relations to the United States and Russia, including an Account of the Leading Policy of France and of England for the last two hundred Years—The Origins and Aims of the Alliance, The Meaning of the Crimean War—and the Reason for the Hostile Attitude of these two Powers toward the United States, and of the Movement on Mexico, with a statement of the General Resources—The Army and Navy of England and France—Russia and America—showing the Present Strength and Probable Future of these Four Powers* (New York, 1864).

lent historical account of the Doctrine, singularly sober and free from exaggeration, and it declares the principles of 1823 to contain an " axiomatic truth " that never dies. " We shall not shrink from our proper responsibility, as a free people and the friend of free institutions. . . . . And the Powers may be sure that we shall not stand wholly on the defensive. . . . . If, by their machinations or aggressions, we are once involved in their conflicts against our will, there will be no more peace for us and them, until the American ideas of national independence and responsibility have been spread over the countries of the Old World, and the doctrines of national interference and the Balance of Power have been cast among the rubbish with the systems of absolutism and popular ignorance which they were devised to support. And let God give victory to the right." [32]

Leavitt's article is also interesting for its invocation of a motive not commonly discovered in the literature on the intervention in Mexico. The appeal is made to religious prejudice ; the intervention of the French is assailed as being only one of many of the evidences of the connection between " Popery " and reaction. In every part of the world, declares Leavitt, France has been the subservient tool of the Church ; and in every part of Latin America, he goes on, the struggle is between the outworn traditions of the " Priests' Party " and the interests of the body of the people. The invasion of Mexico, Leavitt declares, is only one aspect of a

[32] J. Leavitt, *The Monroe Doctrine* (New York, 1863), p. 49.

mightier struggle, and " is aimed by the Papacy against our Protestant faith." " No true American," he goes on, " will object to a Church of the Catholic form in this country. . . . . But it is quite another thing to stretch over this continent, and over this Republic, the power of that politico-ecclesiastical despotism called the Papacy, of which Louis Napoleon is one head and the Pope the other; of which the Jesuits are the inspiring soul, and French and Latin armies and navies to be the executive powers. Could Europe and America, as France and the Jesuits design, be brought under the control of the Papacy again, it would bring upon the world a more fearful despotism, a bitterer curse than it felt under Hildebrand and the Innocents."

Waiving the question of the soundness of views such as these, it is extremely interesting to find that they existed. The language of Leavitt was quoted by approval in a work published in the course of the next year, Charles B. Boynton's *English and French Neutrality*. One would like to know to what degree it expressed a widely-held opinion. There can be no doubt of the religious color of the Mexican expedition; it was, as has been said, in part undertaken to conciliate the Catholics in France, and it was supported, beyond question, by the most extreme reactionaries in the ranks of Mexican politicians; but it is to be regretted that it is not possible to measure more accurately the effect of these facts upon American public opinion. No doubt monarchy under any circumstances would have been profoundly unpopular; but having in mind the strong anti-Catholic bias always latent in certain elements in the population of the United States, is it not possible that Leavitt's argument in this regard was to some degree an effective one? At any rate, it is highly amusing and not uncharacteristic of the thought of some Americans to find the aura of Protestant Christianity brought to illumine the foreign policy of the United States.

Before leaving this New England radical to his devices, it is worth while, perhaps, to call passing attention to the article which he published in the *New Englander* in July of 1864, if only for its title, " The Key to a Continent." In this, as in the preceding work, there is many an appeal to religious prejudice ; but the guiding conception is of the danger to the United States from French control of the trade routes between the Atlantic and the Pacific. With this idea the article opens, and with this idea it ends ; and the imagination of its author finds the Emperor of the French master not only of all Mexico, but of Central America and New Granada, and in full possession of the key to the riches, not only of the New World, but of Asia as well. Curiously enough this aspect of the matter is little touched upon in most of the literature on the subject, and for that reason this word of comment on the Leavitt article seems justified.

In the protests against French policy which signalized the year 1864, a rôle of some importance must be given to Matias Romero. As a propagandist for his own cause, there has, perhaps, never been a more skilful diplomatic agent in Washington. By the end of 1863 he despatched to his government a long list of newspapers in every part of the country to which it was desirable to send such news materials as would aid in the formation of a healthy public opinion,[33] and at the same time he got together a dinner group in New York to discuss the Mexican question. It is remarkable to note the type of person whom he succeeded in interesting in the woes of his country. The dinner was attended by William Cullen Bryant, by William E. Dodge, a banker of great influence, by James W. Beekman, one of the wealthiest real estate owners in New York, by John Van Buren, son of President Van Buren, by Hiram Barney, the Collector of the Port, and by John W. Hammersley, a leading New York lawyer. Others who showed themselves favorable to its purposes were General McClellan, John A. Dix, George Bancroft, and the distinguished lawyer, William M. Evarts.[34] A mouth-watering repast was provided by the enterprising minister, and then followed speech after speech on the unhappy condition of Mexico. Romero himself naturally had an opportunity to express his views in full, and to see to it that the meeting was reported in the press. It was decided, after a truly amazing flow of oratory, to take no action for the present, but the way was cleared in this preliminary banquet for a new dinner on March 29. Beekman, Dodge, and Hammersley, acting on the instigation of Romero, proceeded to organize the affair. They at first intended to get General Winfield Scott to preside, but this indelicate reminder of the events of 1846 and '47 was, perhaps not unnaturally, frowned

[33] Romero, III, 491.
[34] *Ibid.*, p. 606-7.

upon by Romero. But the turnout to this new feast was truly a noble one. There were 22 guests, and they included George Bancroft, Hamilton Fish, J. J. Astor, Jr., Henry Clews, David Dudley Field, Charles King, the President of Columbia, Washington Hunt, an ex-Governor of New York, and George Opdyke, an ex-Mayor of New York City.

Of less importance than the Romero dinners, and yet not wholly without interest, is the club which was formed in New Orleans in the winter of 1864, and which took the name of the D. M. D., or the Defenders of the Monroe Doctrine. This organization seems to have been due to Mexican initiative, and specifically to one Colonel Bordon, who was sent by General Comonfort, perhaps with authority of the Mexican government, to the United States for propaganda purposes.[35] It seems to have included a good many American officers, as well as some Mexican refugees, and one of the most conspicuous of them, General Hahn, expressed in public the view that the North and South should combine to expel the French from Mexico.[36] In the course of the year 1864, the D. M. D. offered a prize for the best essay on the Monroe Doctrine, and several such essays were submitted and published. The quality of the paper on which they were printed, however, suggests that this worshipful company had no very large funds on which to operate, and the quality of the essays suggests that its competition was principally participated in by the

[35] *Ibid.*, IV, 80.
[36] Paris, Min. des Aff. Etr., Corr. Pol., vol. 131, May 5, 1864.

adolescents of New Orleans.[37] None the less, it is worth
noting. Geoffroy, the French chargé, acting on instructions, protested against this organization on the ground
that it was formed to smuggle arms into Mexico, and
received a suave, but not particularly satisfactory, reply
from Seward.[38]

While Mexican propaganda and American natural
indignation were thus developing in the United States,
once again notice was taken in Congress of the course of
events in Mexico. In the Senate MacDougal reintro-
duced a resolution condemnatory of French action; but
it was sent to the Committee on Foreign Relations without debate, and was long to slumber there. The administration was anxious to prevent any action that might
be offensive to France, and it controlled the situation.
It was not so in the House of Representatives. Early
in January the ever active Romero had an interview with
John A. Kasson, a prominent member of the House.
Kasson told him that he intended to introduce a resolution condemnatory of the policy of the French government in Mexico, and that he was sure it would pass by
unanimity. Enchanted, Romero at once invited him to
dinner.[39] The dinner apparently did not come off, but
the resolution did, and was brought in by Kasson on

[37] *Arguments in favor of the enforcement of the Monroe Doctrine, contained in his annual message, in 1823, and its application to our sister republic of Mexico in 1864* (New Orleans,
1864).

[38] Paris, Min. des Aff. Etr., Corr. Pol., Etats-Unis, vol. 131,
May 5, 1864, and Seward's reply in Washington, Dept. of State,
Notes to Legations, France, May 22, 1864.

[39] Romero, IV, 9.

January 29. The next day Romero called on Henry Winter Davis, the chairman of the Committee on Foreign Affairs in the House, and found him extremely cordial.[40] Indeed, Davis indicated that he had intended to introduce some such measure himself. The Mexican's hopes, therefore, ran higher and higher. But the way was not yet wholly clear. Mr. Davis soon sought the views of the administration. Late in February he was for delaying action, on the ground that he had heard the French were getting tired of their intervention in Mexico, and that if their susceptibilities were not wounded they would probably withdraw. Horrified at such optimism, the Mexican minister proceeded to send him a copy of the speech of the French minister, Billault, delivered on February 17, in which the purpose of the French government was quite clearly stated.[41] At the same time he urged Kasson to ask for the correspondence with Mexico from the State Department, and Kasson acted on his request.[42] In the meantime the Archduke Maximilian visited Paris, and Romero returned to the charge. In an interview with Davis in the middle of March the Mexican argued earnestly for the resolution. It might prevent the Archduke from going to Mexico at all, he declared, and it would increase the unpopularity of the whole enterprise in France. At the same time it would not be dangerous, for it could never get by the Senate, which would satisfy the scruples of

---

[40] *Ibid.*, p. 21.
[41] *Ibid.*, p. 77.
[42] *Ibid.*

the most timid. Why not pass it then? Why not indeed?
So Davis appears to have thought. Just how far he was
influenced by Romero's arguments we cannot definitely
know, but at any rate, hesitating no longer, Davis reported out a resolution from his committee on the 6th
of April. It read as follows: "*Resolved*, That the Congress of the United States are unwilling by silence to
have the nations of the world under the impression that
they are indifferent spectators of the deplorable events
now transpiring in the Republic of Mexico, and that
they think fit to declare that it does not accord with the
policy of the United States to acknowledge any monarchical government erected on the ruins of any republican government in America under the auspices of any
European power."

The debate on this resolution was almost nil. It met
with not the slightest opposition. The Democratic
leader, Mr. Cox, lamented the fact that it was not
phrased in stronger terms, and had something to say of
the weakness of the attitude of the administration, and
of the good old Democratic Monroe Doctrine.[43] After
a short passage at arms with Davis, he announced his
purpose to vote for the resolution. It passed unanimously, 109 to 0.

It is probably true that there was a measure of partisan manoeuvering involved in the action of Davis. He
belonged to the radical faction of the Republicans, which
was more and more on the outs with the administration.
The political game of 1864, centering about the Repub-

[43] *Cong. Globe,* 38th Cong., 1st Sess., p. 1408.

30

lican nomination for the presidency, had now already
begun. The candidacy of John C. Fremont was already
in the offing, and Fremont himself was doubtless playing politics when he denounced the French intervention
in a speech of February 29. Secretary Chase, too, had
permitted his name to be put forward in the canvass, and
his partisans had inscribed the maxim of the Monroe
Doctrine on their standard. The foes of the patient
man in the White House were willing enough to capitalize the Mexican question for their own ends. They knew
well enough (for Seward had made his views clear [44])
that they were acting contrary to the desires of the Secretary of State and of the President. But grant all this,
and one has not explained away the importance of the
unanimous vote by which the House of Representatives
passed the Davis resolution. Congressmen do not yield
their unanimous adhesion to unpopular doctrine. The
student of democratic politics must inevitably discover
in such unqualified approval of the Monroe Doctrine
some indication of the strength of public opinion.

In the nominating conventions of 1864 popular feeling
reflected in the Davis resolution was once more, in some
degree, to be manifested. The radical Republicans met
first, at Cleveland. There they listened to a campaign
speech by the presiding officer, in which the Mexican
question played its part, nominated the man who made
it for the vice-presidency, and incorporated a declaration on Mexico in their platform.[45] But the Lincoln

[44] Romero, IV, 101.
[45] Ibid., IV, 224.

men were not to be outdone. When the regular Republicans met in Baltimore to renominate the President, they adopted amidst tremendous applause a plank no less definite than that of their rivals,[46] and Mr. Lincoln, in accepting the nomination, in language carefully guarded but none the less significant, approved the language of the convention. A ratification meeting in New York City at the end of June produced a new crop of speeches on the Mexican question.[47] Much to the disappointment of Romero, however, the Democratic convention, which met in Chicago at the end of August and nominated General McClellan, had nothing to say with regard to the Monroe Doctrine. There were certainly Democrats who would have liked to see some action taken, as, for example, McDougal, with whom the Mexican minister, as we have seen, was in close relations.[48] But the Democrats, in the campaign of 1864, adopted the extraordinary and injudicious course of seeking to capitalize the war weariness of the North. They were thus hardly in a position to challenge the foreign policy of

[46] It read as follows: "*Resolved,* That the people of the United States can never regard with indifference the attempt of any European power to overthrow by force or to supplant by fraud the institutions of any republican government on the Western Continent, and that they will view with extreme jealousy, as menacing to the peace and independence of their own country, the efforts of any such power to obtain new footholds for monarchical governments, sustained by foreign military force in near proximity to the United States." (J. G. Nicolay, and John Hay, *Abraham Lincoln. A History* (10 vols., New York, 1890), VII, 421.

[47] Cited in Romero, IV, 243.

[48] *Ibid.,* p. 283.

the administration in connection with the course of events in Mexico. Domestic problems held the stage, and the vigilant Romero, ever on the watch for important pronouncements on the Monroe Doctrine, could report only occasional comment. He had the satisfaction of noting a speech of Montgomery Blair toward the end of September, and one of Salmon P. Chase at about the same time,[49] but, in the main, if we are to trust this unusually accurate and full reporter, there was little attention paid to Mexican affairs, in the heat of the domestic controversies of 1864, and the struggle for the vindication of the administration.

In the events of 1864, however, speaking very broadly, there is certainly to be discerned a swelling tide of popular antagonism to the policy of the French in Mexico. Domestic questions undoubtedly crowded Mexico into the background in the second half of the year, but the resentment of the American people with regard to French policy had been expressed, and expressed without equivocation. It is not, of course, to be supposed that no voice was ever raised upon the other side of the question. The *New York World*, for example, was certainly not hostile to French policy in Mexico in 1863; neither was the *Journal of Commerce*,[50] and the *National Intelligencer* spoke of the Monroe Doctrine with contempt, as an outworn theory, and even went so far as to intimate that no less a person than the American minister to Mexico was not unfavorable to the establishment of monarchy. In the Senate, as has already been

[49] *Ibid.*, pp. 359-60.
[50] *Ibid.*, III, 282 and 455.

noticed, the influence of the administration was sufficient
to prevent a vote on the McDougal resolution, and no
other Senator raised his voice on the subject of Mexico.
The peace party which influenced the Democratic convention of 1864, and which was willing to see the Civil
War end in a peace without victory, could hardly have
been more anxious to involve the United States in a
war with France over Mexico. But preponderant opinion undoubtedly was strongly opposed to the Mexican
monarchy. The language of Seward with regard to the
Davis resolution, when he said that it expressed the
unanimous sentiment of the American people, may have
contained an element of exaggeration, but it was to a
large extent true. What is most interesting about it all
perhaps is that so many elements were represented in
the growing opposition to French policy. The supporters of the administration, and the Radical Republicans, native Americans and naturalized Americans, conservatives like the Blairs and radicals like Chase or
Chandler, the press without any great distinction of
party, the rank and file of democracy, and the representatives of the well-to-do, and of American scholar-
ship, all these elements are to be discovered in the ranks
of the supporters of the Monroe Doctrine.[51]

[51] For the naturalized Americans, see the convention of German radicals, at Cleveland, in December, 1863, and at Alton,
Illinois, in May, 1864. (*Ibid.,* p. 632 and IV, 191.) Chandler
told Romero in October, 1864, that the United States would
take on the French at the end of the Civil War. (*Ibid.,* p. 343.)
The government would have a great army, he said, which could
not be speedily disbanded, and which could have no better occupation than expelling the French from Mexico. Such a step

But what of Seward and his policy during 1863 and
1864? How far did the expression of public opinion
influence the foreign policy of the administration? How
far was the attitude of the Secretary of State determined by the Monroe Doctrine? The answer to this
question is precisely what it was in 1861 and 1862. The
essential principle Seward not only never surrendered,
but did not hesitate to state frankly to the government
of France. As he had written to Dayton in June of
1862, in view of the assurances of Thouvenel, the government of the United States " would in any case be
bound to wait for, and not anticipate, a violation " of
French good faith.[52] This attitude Seward maintained
until the latter part of 1863. As late as August of that
year Dayton had an interview with Drouyn de l'Huys,
who had succeeded Thouvenel, in which the French
minister assured him that " France had no purpose in
Mexico other than heretofore stated; that she did not
mean to appropriate permanently any part of that country, and that she should leave it as soon as her griefs
were satisfied, and she could do it with honor. When
Dayton suggested that she might leave a puppet behind,
Drouyn answered that " the strings would be too long
to work, and that they had had enough of colonial experience in Algeria." [53] To these assurances Seward re-

would be not only in conformity with American interests, but
would be an inescapable necessity which no Government could
ignore.

[52] *Papers Relating to Foreign Affairs, Accompanying the
Annual Message of the President,* more commonly known as
Diplomatic Correspondence, 1862, p. 355.

[53] *Ibid.,* 1863, Part II, p. 689.

plied suavely in a despatch of September 7, that "if
we were authorized to regard them as guaranteed by
the Emperor, it will go far to relieve a solicitude, which
I cannot but believe is becoming as inconvenient to
France as to the United States." [54] In October, however, the long dishonesty of the French government in
dealing with the American State Department underwent
modification. On October 8 Dayton was told by the
French foreign minister that there would be an election
in Mexico, and that the Archduke Maximilian might
be chosen Emperor. The dangers of the new government, continued Drouyn, would come from the United
States, and the sooner the American government showed
itself satisfied, the sooner the new government could
take care of itself, and France retire from Mexico; in
particular the early acknowledgment of the new government " would tend to shorten, or perhaps," he said,
" to end, all the troublesome complications of France
in that country; that they would thereupon quit Mexico." [55] Seward answered this despatch with promptness
on October 23. The United States, he declared, had
never concealed its conviction that the permanent establishment of monarchy in Mexico would be neither easy
nor desirable. " You will inform M. Drouyn de l'Huys
that this opinion remains unchanged. On the other
hand, the United States cannot anticipate the action of
the people of Mexico. . . . . It is proper, also, that M.
Drouyn de l'Huys should be informed that the United

[54] *Ibid.*, p. 697.
[55] *Ibid.*, p. 717.

States continues to regard Mexico as the theater of a war which has not yet ended in the subversion of government long existing there, with which the United States remain in the relation of peace and sincere friendship; and that, for this reason, the United States is not now at liberty to consider the question of recognizing a government which, in the further chances of war, may come into its place." [56]

This able instruction did not commit the United States too far or too definitely; it did not even close the door on the recognition of Maximilian. But it made the opposition of the American government to European monarchy in Mexico fairly clear, and it was followed up by instructions to Dayton that if the Archduke should come to Paris, the American minister should abstain from all relations with him. [57] There was no weakness in Seward's policy, and no denial of principle, only a wise restraint. In February of 1864 the Secretary told Romero that he had received word from a member of the French opposition (in all probability, Thiers), urging caution, lest French pride be enlisted behind the unpopular expedition in Mexico, [58] and this view of the case he doubtless accepted as his own. [59] In his conversations with the French chargé d'affaires, Seward took a remote and rather disinterested tone. When, for ex-

[56] *Ibid.*, p. 726.

[57] *Ibid.*, 1864, Part III, p. 45.

[58] Romero, IV, 24.

[59] A little later, Blair, who seems to have had a very mild sense of secrecy, told Romero that this was the view of the administration. (*Ibid.*, p. 52.)

ample, Geoffroy declared to him that sentiment for war with France at the end of the Civil War seemed to be almost unanimous, Seward answered that such would be the case, if guarantees were not given, but that all this was a long way off. " Neither you or I will be here, then," he said. In the same way, when Geoffroy inquired whether Maximilian might not give the United States what it wanted in Mexico, or at least the assurance of stability, the American Secretary answered, " Yes, he might last longer than others and couldn't be worse." [60] When the Frenchman protested against the Davis resolution, Seward, in a masterly reply, often quoted, pointed out that the House could not determine the policy of the government of the United States.[61]

With the approaching victory of the North at the end of the year, and the establishment of Maximilian upon his throne by the arms of France, we enter upon a new phase of the Mexican question, and one which I shall examine in a separate chapter. But before taking leave of these earlier years, we must turn back to observe certain other aspects of Seward's policy which are not unrelated to the Monroe Doctrine.

The American Secretary of State, in dealing with the problem of Mexico, was called upon, as some of his predecessors had been, to decide what should be his attitude toward projects of Pan-American cooperation. To put the matter in another way, in the period 1861-64, as in the period 1824-26, and to a less degree in 1847,

[60] Paris, Min. des Aff. Etr., Corr. Pol., Etats-Unis, vol. 131, May 29, 1864.

[61] *Diplomatic Correspondence*, 1865-6, Part III, p. 357.

efforts were made by some of the states of Latin America to give the principles of the Monroe Doctrine a continental backing. In the last of these instances, as in the two former, American diplomatic action was distinctly unfavorable to any such conception, if it involved any binding obligation to go to the defense of the liberties of the other states of the New World. The matter first came up in January, 1862, when Don Manuel Nicolas Corpancho, the minister of Peru to Mexico, had a conference with Seward in which he proposed the formation of a Pan-American alliance to drive the French from Mexico. Seward gave a polite but hardly encouraging reply, declaring that he would gladly explain his position fully, when Peru sent a regularly accredited minister to Washington.[62] In March the Chilean minister, Asta Buruaga, made a somewhat similar proposal for a continental demonstration against the intervention. Seward read him the instructions of March 3, but no demonstration was made.[63] In April came a third proposal, this time from Señor Barreda, the newly arrived minister from Lima. This was in the form of a rather elaborate continental treaty, of which the sixth article bound the contracting parties to protect each other against European intervention, protectorates, or conquest.[64] This time Seward declared that he could not commit himself to any such action, in view of the relations of the United States with European powers.[65]

[62] Romero, II, 8.
[63] *Ibid.*, p. 76.
[64] *Ibid.*, pp. 121-22.
[65] *Ibid.*, p. 153.

When the American minister to Costa Rica got wind a few months later of a projected Pan-American Congress, and learning that the Costa Rican government did not wish the United States to participate, wrote to Seward asking if he should protest against such an attitude, the Secretary of State not only told him to do nothing of the kind, but took care to tell Romero of the incident, and to remark that an alliance with the states of Latin America would have many more disadvantages than advantages for the United States.[66]

To Romero conduct such as this was proof positive of the craven timidity which guided American foreign relations. But if this aloofness was irritating, what was to be said of the shocking step which Seward took in the middle of '62, and of which, fortunately for his peace of mind, the Mexican only heard at the end of the year. Revolution had broken out in New Granada. The New Granadan government had called for American intervention to protect the right of way across the Isthmus in accordance with the treaty of 1846. Acting with the caution which, after his initial rashness, usually characterized his diplomacy, Seward sought the views of Great Britain and France as to the possibility of co-operative action. There is room for argument that this was a dangerous precedent to establish. The principle of joint intervention in the affairs of Latin American republics would not have been a wholly healthy one. It would not fall, perhaps, within the limits of the strict interpretation of the Monroe Doctrine, but it might

[66] *Ibid.*, p. 396.

easily lead into embarrassing situations. But no such modest view of its significance was held by the Mexican minister, or by his government. To him the whole American system was crashing into ruin. He saw to it that the offending correspondence was published in the *Continental,* a Spanish newspaper in New York, and with it an editorial declaring that the Lincoln administration had solemnly renounced the Monroe Doctrine, and " compromised all the principles upon which reposes the independence of the Republics of the New World." He must have been more than satisfied when, some two months later, he received instructions from his government, usually torpid in its correspondence with the Washington legation, to protest against an act " of such terrible importance to the peace and liberty of the continent, on which it would attract by such means the domination of the sovereigns of Europe." [67] A note was accordingly drawn up, in the best Monroe Doctrine style, but it received only a brief and rather tart answer from Seward. The truth is that by this time the possibility of intervention on the Isthmus had long since past. If ever there was a tempest in a teapot, this little incident was one.

From the middle of 1863, however, these incidental embarrassments of Seward's policy of caution were not particularly important. A Congress of Latin American states met at Lima in 1864; but there was no unanimity among the proponents of the Congress as to extending an invitation to the United States, and none was in fact

[67] *Ibid.,* p. 578.

extended. The Secretary was spared the necessity, therefore, of inditing a refusal. He could, of course, hardly have done otherwise if the matter had ever been referred to him. The interests of the United States could hardly have dictated any other course in 1864. On the other hand, the governments of Peru and of New Granada, the leaders in the movement for the Congress, took the only attitude that could have been expected of them in deprecating American participation. After Seward's original stand-offishness, in view of the domestic situation, and in view of the great circumspection of American policy and the normal American tradition, it was hardly to be hoped that the United States would put itself at the head of a great American coalition. Any change in American policy with regard to Mexico must wait upon the issue of the Civil War.

By the end of '64, however, that issue was not far away. The Old World and the New were soon to see the long withheld influence of the American government cast into the scale in behalf of American traditions. The vindication of the Monroe Doctrine was drawing near. The clash of systems, implicit in the whole policy of France in Mexico, was now to enter a more dramatic and a more decisive phase.

CHAPTER IX

THE MEXICAN ISSUE DECIDED

The years 1865 and 1866 represent a new phase in the development of the Mexican question. On the side of the United States, the cautious policy hitherto pursued is by degrees abandoned, and the tone of Seward gradually rises until it becomes positively shrill in the instruction of December 16, 1865. On the side of France, the discontent with the Mexican expedition, which we have already seen existed in 1864, mounts more and more rapidly, and is accompanied with an increasing anxiety as to the attitude of the United States. By January, 1866, the fatal decision to withdraw from Mexico has been taken, and before the end of the year the actual evacuation is to a large degree under way. Two aspects of the unfolding of these events particularly interest the student of the Monroe Doctrine. The first is the course of development of American public opinion, as reflected both within and without the administration; the second is the problem as to what degree the policy of Louis Napoleon was conditioned or determined by the attitude of the American government and the American people. Intelligent judgment with regard to either one or the other of these matters involves, very naturally, some knowledge of the diplomatic negotiations; but it is these two questions and not the negotiations themselves which form the core of this chapter.

The policy of Seward, at the end of 1864, and during the first half of 1865, still remained essentially cautious and conciliatory. It had never been his purpose to conceal the distaste of the American people for the monarchical experiment in Mexico from the French government, or to practise an emollient acquiescence in what was going on in the republic to the South. When he heard that Maximilian was negotiating with the French government with regard to a cession of territory, or a lien on the resources of northern Mexico, as a means of liquidating his debt to France, the Secretary of State instructed Bigelow, who had succeeded Dayton in Paris, that neither of these expedients would be " regarded with favor by the people of the United States." [1] He declined to hold any intercourse, official or unofficial, with any representative of the Mexican Emperor; [2] and in the interesting despatch of March 17, 1865, he reiterated with perhaps more emphasis than formerly the views of the American people in general with regard to Mexico. " The Emperor's persistence," he wrote to Bigelow, " implies that he yet believes it to be certain what we have constantly told him that the people of the United States, reasoning upon pre-conceived sentiments and national principles, cannot even apprehend to be possible, namely: that a new European monarchical system can or ought to be permanently established on the American continent and in territory bordering on this Republic." [3] But despite this language, nothing in the

[1] *Diplomatic Correspondence,* 1865, part 3, p. 363.

[2] *Ibid.,* pp. 378 and 484.

[3] Washington, Dept. of State, Instructions, France, March 17, 1865.

nature of a threat can be said to have come from the
Secretary of State until well along in 1865. He was
wholly aware of the attitude of the French government
itself ; in February Bigelow wrote that the Emperor had
said to him in private conversation, " What I really
want is to get out of Mexico altogether ; " [4] and it was
not Seward's purpose if he could help it to embroil the
situation by rasping the pride of an embarrassed government and of a sensitive people. His despatches, therefore, contain more than one assurance that no aggressive
action is intended, that the United States intended no
attack on Mexico, and that time and reason might be
expected to produce their natural effects with regard to
the delicate problem of Franco-American relationships. [5]

[4] Washington, Dept. of State, Despatches, France, February
9, 1865.

[5] See, for example, the despatch of March 6, in which Seward,
answering Bigelow with regard to French fears of a war with
the United States over Mexico, declared, " If we have war with
her (i. e., France), it must be a war of her own making either
against our ships or against our territory. We shall defend ourselves if assailed on our own ground. *We shall attack nobody
elsewhere.*" (Washington, Dept. of State, Instructions, France.)
Or see the despatch of March 17. " This government has not
interfered. It does not propose to interfere. . . . . It firmly
repels foreign intervention here and looks with disfavor upon
it anywhere; therefore, for us to intervene in Mexico would
be only to reverse our principles and adopt in that country the
very policy which in any case we disallow. I remain, however,
of the opinion that I have often expressed, that even this
vexatious Mexican question in the end will find its solution without producing any conflict between the United States and
France. The future of Mexico is neither an immediate, nor
even a vital question, for either the United States or France.
For both of them it is a foreign affair, and therefore time and

Always optimistic by temperament, the Secretary doubt-less believed, as he most certainly hoped, that the with-drawal of the French armies would come about without pressure on the part of the United States. His object, his highly laudable object, was to avoid an international crisis if it could be avoided.

Yet at the end of 1864 and during the first half of 1865, there was plenty of American opinion which did not judge the Mexican question from a point of view so elevated and so statesmanlike. Romero records with delight the story of a post-election dinner in New York City. William M. Evarts, responding to the toast, " The Foreign Relations of the United States," declared, " The nations of Europe will soon know and have to take account of the fact that the American continent has been irrevocably consecrated to the cause of republican liberty." He was answered by Senator John Sherman, who said that he believed in the Monroe Doctrine, but that he did not think the relations of the United States ought to be complicated by it at that time, and that the next generation could be left to vindicate it. These ob-servations apparently provoked a furor. Chauncey De-pew arose to eulogize the Doctrine, and to declare that to enunciate it at the present time, at the end of an un-equalled Civil War, was little short of sublime. Another speaker followed with warm defense of the principles of 1823, and still another. There could be no doubt of

reason may be allowed their due influence in its settlement."
(*Ibid.*, partially quoted in *Diplomatic Correspondence*, 1865, Part III, p. 387 and in John Bigelow, *Retrospections of an Active Life* (New York, 1909, 5 vols.), II, 412.

31

the sentiment of this particular gathering. Nor did the
New York meeting stand alone.[6] Men like John A. Dix
and Commodore Porter made no secret of their hostility
to French policy in Mexico;[7] there was tremendous
enthusiasm for a war with Mexico in army circles, as
we shall later see in more detail, and there was even
some discussion of a coalition of the North and South
reconciled and reunited, to oust the French from Mexico.

This interesting idea is particularly to be connected
with the name of Francis P. Blair, the father of Montgomery Blair, who had been Postmaster-General till
the fall of '64 in the cabinet of President Lincoln. At
the end of 1864 Blair secured permission from the
President to go to Richmond, and try to arrange peace
terms with the Confederates. In his own mind the idea
of peace was knit up with an expedition against the
French, and this possibility he discussed with Romero
before his departure for Richmond.[8] Blair got in touch
with Jefferson Davis, and proposed that an armistice
should be arranged, under cover of which the forces of
the South should be shifted to the banks of the Rio
Grande, there to be united with the liberal forces of
Juarez. The way might thus be cleared, he thought, not
only for the expulsion of the French, but for the possible absorption of the Mexican states into the American
Union. The Confederate President seems to have given
some favorable consideration to this rather wild conception. So, too, did Alexander H. Stephens. But Lin-

[6] Romero, IV, 443-4.
[7] Ibid.
[8] Ibid., V, 4.

coln had never authorized it, and he would, of course, have none of it. It was utterly inconsistent with the foreign policy of the administration, but it is interesting evidence of the hostility of a prominent American public man to the presence of monarchy in Mexico.[9]

A somewhat similar project was that of General Lew Wallace. It was Wallace's idea that the Confederates of the Trans-Mississippi Department might be persuaded to come to terms with the Northern commander, on the basis of a joint attack on the French in Mexico. Authorized by Grant to make a " tour of inspection " on the Rio Grande, Wallace got in touch with Brigadier-General James E. Slaughter and Colonel John S. Ford, commanding Confederate troops in Texas, and found they thought well of the idea. But the superior officer of these gentlemen refused to have anything to do with the project and by April it had completely collapsed.[10]

[9] The complete report of the Blair mission is given in the *Century Magazine,* vol. 16, pp. 839-46. In an abbreviated form it can be found in John G. Nicolay and John Hay, *Abraham Lincoln. A History. op. cit.,* X, 91-112. Blair told Romero about the mission, and there is interesting material in Romero, V, 4 and 42.

[10] An interesting account of this episode is in Lew Wallace, *An Autobiography* (2 vols., New York, 1906), II, 812 *et seq.* See also *Official Records of the Union and Confederate Armies,* I, vol. 46, p. 201, and vol. 48, part i, pp. 512, 937, 1166, 1276, and part ii, pp. 457 *et seq.* From a letter written by General Wallace in 1889, and, on account of its date to be taken with some scepticism, it would appear that Lincoln and Stanton knew of this project, and approved of it. Lincoln, Wallace says, told him not to mention it to Seward, and agreed that the time had come to help Juarez, at least privately. (*Autobiography, op.*

More important, perhaps, than these rather romantic dreams of policy, as illustrating a certain section of American sentiment, was the attitude of General Grant. The encouragement which Grant gave to Wallace, just described, is not untypical of his attitude in the Mexican question. In the spring of 1865, shortly after his return from Appomattox, he entered into close relations with Romero. Romero, whose ambitions had been stimulated by the Blair project, told him that he would like very much to enlist a sizeable force in the United States, under the leadership of some eminent commander. With a guileless guile, the Mexican declared that he would like to invite Sherman or Sheridan to lead it. " My wife would like to have me go to Mexico, myself," said the hero of the Civil War after a pause. " We would like nothing better," answered the agent of Juarez. " Perhaps, though," he added hopefully, " the United States will declare war on France, and then you can go as the commander of the forces of this Government." The conversation then passed on to other aspects of the Mexican question, but it is no wonder that Romero, in recounting it to his government, reported that he could count upon the ardent support of the victor of Appomattox.

In June, Grant attended a cabinet meeting to urge a vigorous policy against the French. President Johnson

---

cit., II, p. 843.) General J. O. Shelby indicates that Lincoln made a similar proposal to him. This, however, is a reminiscence of 1877, and like Wallace's, must be received with scepticism. (*Missouri Historical Review*, vol. 10, pp. 63-119, especially pp. 115-18, in an article by Walter B. Stevens, "Lincoln and Missouri.")

in his heart had probably sympathized with such a policy from the beginning. When nominated for the vice-presidency he had pronounced some violent words on the subject of the French in Mexico.[11] Though he was, on his assumption of the presidency, preoccupied with many other matters he was, Grant assured Romero, entirely sound upon the Mexican business. Indeed, at a later date, in one of his expansive moments, Seward told the Mexican minister that he had had a difficult time in holding the President down. However this may be, the President brought Grant before the cabinet in the meeting of June 16. The General urged immediate action in Mexico. Seward opposed him. The Empire was crumbling, he declared, and the whole miserable business would be over in six months, perhaps in sixty days. The consensus of opinion in the cabinet was that the question should be left to the Secretary, though it was generally agreed that the United States could not indefinitely suffer the French to remain. For the time being Grant's purposes were frustrated. The agitation which he felt on the Mexican question, however, was far

[11] See his Nashville speech of June 10, 1864. "The day of reckoning is approaching. It will not be long before the Rebellion is put down. The time is not far distant when the rebellion will be put down, and then we will attend to this Mexican affair, and say to Louis Napoleon, 'You cannot found a monarchy on this Continent.' (Great applause.) An expedition into Mexico would be a sort of recreation to the brave soldiers who are now fighting the battles of the Union, and the French concern would be quickly wiped out." *Biographical Sketch of Andrew Johnson of Tennessee, together with his Speech and his Letter Accepting the Nomination for the Vice-Presidency of the United States* (Washington, 1875).

from quieted. Indeed, he seems to have been just as much convinced as ever of the necessity of vigorous action, to judge from his conversations with Romero. It was with his consent, if not at his actual instigation, that Romero now began to sound General Schofield with regard to the possibility of going to Mexico.

This project, if only for the light it throws on the views of Grant,[12] and perhaps of the President, deserves to be recounted. It was worked out in its details by Grant and by Romero.

Ever after his interviews with the elder Blair in January of '65, Romero indulged the notion that an Ameri-

[12] For a further expression of Grant's views, see the letter which he wrote to the President on June 19, in which he declared the attempt to establish a monarchy in Mexico as "an act of hostility against the United States," and predicted that if it were "allowed to go on," he could "see nothing before us but a long, expensive and bloody war, one in which the enemies of this country will be joined by tens of thousands of disciplined soldiers, embittered against their Government by the experience of the last four years." Grant proposes "a solemn protest" and the recognition of equal belligerent rights to both parties, with an open market to both for the purchase of arms. (Official Records, I, vol. 48, part ii, pp. 923-4.) For the Schofield mission, see H. M. Wriston, Executive Agents in American Foreign Relations (Baltimore, 1929), pp. 780-89, Bigelow, op. cit., III, 265-7, 299-300, 572-3, J. Schofield, Forty-six Years in the Army (New York, 1897, pp. 379-80), J. Schofield, "Withdrawal of French from Mexico. A Chapter of Secret History." Century Magazine, vol. 32, pp. 129-30, Washington, Dept. of State, Instructions, France, vol. 17, p. 465, and Despatches, France, vols. 59 and 60, passim, F. Bancroft, Life of William H. Seward (2 vols., New York, 1900), II, 434-5, Moore, A Digest of International Law, VI, 498-99, C. A. Duniway, "Reasons for Withdrawal of French from Mexico," Ann. Rep., Am. Hist. Asso., 1902, I, 326, Diplomatic Correspondence, 1865, part 3, pp. 391, 394, 399, 421-22, 428-29.

can force could be raised to fight against the French, and
that such a force should be put under American command. In order to keep the letter of the law the elements of this force were to enter Mexico as emigrants;
there they were to be provided with arms; and there
they were to be put under American command. This
project was discussed by the minister with Grant early
in May. It was at first attempted to enlist the interest
of General Sherman,[13] but when he refused General
Schofield was next approached and appeared to be not
unfavorable. Romero, with a cavalier regard of diplomatic amenities, then went over the head of Seward
and carried his plan to the White House. The President was noncommittal; indeed he told the Mexican to
discuss the project with the Secretary of State;[14] but
only a little later he permitted himself to be talked into
a different attitude by General Grant. By the end of
June, a complete plan had been worked out. Schofield
was to go to the Rio Grande, bearing the title of In-
spector of the Army of the United States, and was to
receive a year's leave of absence. At the same time
Grant wrote a letter to Sheridan, a copy of which Romero actually saw, directing that war materials should
be concentrated on the border, and that whatever troops
in the Northern army in Texas desired should be mustered out, and permitted to cross over into Mexico.
Stanton was sounded, and found to be not unfavorable.
A contract was drawn up and discussed under which

[13] Romero, V, 332.
[14] *Ibid.*, pp. 475-6.

Schofield might operate. The consent of the President was now taken for granted.

And now came the hitch in the proceedings. Schofield went to Cape May to see Seward, and to consult him about the business. The result was to disrupt completely this ingenious plan for bringing American arms to the aid of republican Mexico.[15] The Secretary of State not only discouraged the plan, but obviously was disturbed by it. Irritated by Romero's jaunty appeals to the President, he dictated a circular, framed in general terms (and the delicacy of this is really delightful), requesting the diplomatic representatives in Washington to observe the usual amenities of diplomatic intercourse, and carry on their business through the medium of the Department of State.[16] At the same time, with a humor still more delightful, he offered the vainglorious Schofield a special mission to France.[17] That this was a mere ruse is of course perfectly clear. When Schofield arrived on the other side of the water, he was kept at arms' length from the really important people by Bigelow. Indeed, he confessed as much to Romero himself on his return.[18] But the plan of sending an American minister to Mexico was blown sky-high, as Seward intended it to be. And it is not an unrelated fact that from this time forward the Mexican minister had no more interviews with the President of the United States. The in-

---

15 *Ibid.,* pp. 513-18.
16 *Ibid.,* pp. 520-21.
17 *Ibid.,* p. 530.
18 *Ibid.,* VII, 263.

experienced and impetuous Johnson had obviously been taken in hand by his more judicious counselor.

The Schofield episode, involving as it does the opinions of the President, of Stanton, and of Grant, is an interesting illustration of the strength of the feeling against the French in high official quarters. It is the expression of a point of view which permeated American public opinion in 1865 as it had in 1864. The evidence of this is to be found in the numerous speeches on the subject of Mexico and the Monroe Doctrine delivered by representative politicians in the summer of the latter year. It would be tedious to analyze these speeches in detail. The theme and the attitude of them all are much the same. But note well some of the more important names. Henry Winter Davis at Chicago on July 4,[19] Montgomery Blair at Hagerstown on July 12,[20] Secretary James Harlan of the Department of the Interior at Washington on July 13,[21] former Secretary of War Cameron on July 23 at Harrisburg.[22] The speeches of such men not only expressed to a certain degree the prevailing mood, but also did something further to excite public opinion, and the newly arrived French minister in Washington, the Comte de Montholon, reported at this very time that a new press polemic had been started against the Mexican empire.[23]

[19] *Ibid.*, V, 466.
[20] *Ibid.*
[21] *Ibid.*, p. 477.
[22] *Ibid.*, p. 504.
[23] Paris, Min. des Aff. Etr., Corr. Pol., Etats-Unis, vol. 134, July 25, 1865.

There was, then, in the summer of 1865, it may fairly be assumed, a formidable body of sentiment which viewed with an open and demonstrative hostility the proceedings of the French in Mexico. But there were, of course, countercurrents as well. The country had passed through four years of a sanguinary Civil War, and it would have been curious, indeed, if no voices had been raised in favor of moderation and restraint in a situation which had so many dangerous possibilities.

Of these voices, one of the most significant is that of John Bigelow. More intellectual than emotional, less susceptible to shibboleths than the rank and file of human beings, Bigelow had never been precisely enthusiastic with regard to the Monroe Doctrine. As early as 1863 he had written to Seward his view that nothing was more unpopular in Europe, and (a personal judgment), " nothing was more absurd anywhere." [24] His views had not much changed in 1865. It would not be fair to say of him that he was willing to acquiesce in the presence of the French in Mexico; yet it could reasonably be stated that he had no hostility to the Empire of Maximilian as such, and that he was certainly not at all enthusiastic over any course of action which might provoke a clash with France. Indeed, he went further than he ought to have gone, perhaps, in the effort to conciliate the French government, until the receipt of despatches from Seward put him upon what, in the state of American public opinion, was the only feasible, if not the only intellectually justifiable, course of action.

[24] Bigelow, II, 46.

Thus, in February of 1865, Bigelow had a long conversation with Fould, the French Finance Minister. His language was that of reassurance. The Mexican question, he declared, had only a secondary importance in American public opinion. The United States had had enough of fighting. Democracies, anyway, were essentially selfish, and it would be fatal to any administration to plunge the country into a new war when the struggle with the South was liquidated. One might have thought, perhaps, that the moderation of this language was due to the fact that there were still irritating controversies over the Confederate navy troubling the relations of the United States with the government at Paris. But in reporting his conversation with Fould to his own government, Bigelow went on to argue for a policy far removed from that of Seward. " I do not know your views as to the policy to pursue toward Europe," he wrote. " Our only hostile act will be to withhold recognition of Maximilian, and perhaps we may later even recognize him. Mexico is to be conquered by immigration and not by the sword. No nation can afford to be so indifferent as ours to the efforts of Mexico to found an empire. We have nothing to do but set the example of a good government. All else shall be added to us." [25] In the same way, in a conversation with Berryer, a leading figure in the Corps Législatif, in the middle of March, the American minister declared that the United States had no " unreasonable

[25] Washington, Dept. of State, Despatches, France, Nos. 29 and 30, February 14, 1865.

tenacity " for the Monroe Doctrine, and that " if any
nation 3000 miles distant with an Imperial form of
Government can compete with a popular government
on its border for favor with the inhabitants of Mexico,
there is no reason why they should not." He then went
on, quite erroneously, to relate American reluctance to
recognize Maximilian to the resentment felt at the partiality of France for the Confederates, and for the aid
given to the Confederate cause, " especially in the dock-
yards of the Empire." [26]

This tone, Bigelow continued to hold during the
spring and summer of 1865. He was, of course, encouraged by the tenor of Seward's despatches to intimate that
the United States would not depart from its policy of
nonintervention, but it must be confessed that he was,
at any rate from the standpoint of an interpreter of
American public opinion, a little too complacent with
regard to the Mexican experiment. Thus, some time
in April, he told Drouyn that he did not think it was
the wish of any considerable portion of the American
people, and certainly not of the government, to offer it
more than a purely passive resistance, and that there
was no objection to seeing the " experiment of trans-
planting the prevailing system of European government
to Mexico, now that it has begun under such imposing
auspices, ... fairly tested. I went on to say," he
wrote to Seward, " that we had no particular reason to
be proud of the fruit borne by popular forms of government in Spanish America, and if European forms could

[26] Bigelow, II, 428-29, Bigelow-Seward, March 21, 1865.

yield more happy results, no nations were more interested in the application of them than their nearest neighbors." [27] This expansive utterance brought forth a mild, albeit a very mild, rebuke from Seward.[28] But the views of the American minister were not changed. Indeed, in an unofficial communication of August 21, Bigelow argued warmly in favor of a policy of restraint with regard to France. This communication is so important that it deserves to be quoted at considerable length. " I think you will find, when the question is raised in a practical shape, with all its attendant responsibilities before our people," he wrote, " that the opposition to the extension of European influence in the Western Hemisphere is a sentiment which they cherish, but not a policy for which they will fight. The moment the burdens of war waged upon such a pretext should begin to be felt, it would become unpopular, and the Administration would be driven to accept a peace perhaps upon humiliating terms. The abstract folly of making ourselves the armed champion of all or of any of the Spanish American States, whose people belong to a different race from ours, who speak a different language, who possess a different religion, and who have been trained under social and political institutions having very little in common with those of the United States, would be aggravated now by the state of our finances, which are likely for many years to tax all our resources to the utmost under the most favorable cir-

[27] *Ibid.*, p. 538.
[28] *Diplomatic Correspondence,* 1865, part 3, p. 394.

cumstances. As yet no action of the Latin race has succeeded in establishing a government worthy of being called republican, and nowhere have their attempts to do it proved more disastrous failures than in Spanish America. I think it safe to assume that the people of this race in our hemisphere will require for many years a much more highly centralized government than we can offer them under our present constitution, and it is hardly worth while, therefore, under the pretext of defending republican institutions, to get ourselves into a war with one and perhaps with several of the most powerful States of Europe, whose hostility in a twelvemonth would do us more damage than all our commerce with Mexico would repay in twenty years.

" I doubt if there is a power in Europe that would formally sustain our pretensions under what is called the ' Monroe Doctrine ' while England, France, Spain, Denmark, Austria, and Brazil would lend their moral support and some of them probably material support, to any sovereign that would resist them. The mere apprehension of such a state of things would impair our credit in Europe at a moment when a good credit there appears to offer us our only means of escape from bankruptcy, and it would indefinitely postpone our return to a Specie Standard of value and to a reduction of our tariff, the two measures upon which our national prosperity seems, humanly speaking, to be most immediately dependent ; it would check the current of emigration from the Old World, one of the most important items of our national wealth ; and finally, it would cost the finest opportunity ever offered any nation of indicating the superior sagacity and discretion of a real representative democracy. In a war involving our national existence, like the one just closed, we might resist the world in arms successfully; but in a war to redress the wrongs of Mexico or to propagate republicanism by the sword, we should, in my opinion, be likely to fail. Such a contest would accomplish for the Emperor of France what he had sought in vain to accomplish hitherto; it would rally all his subjects to his support; it would give him that Imperial position among the European powers which has always been his dream; it would speedily arm and equip in the Southern States more rebels than General Lee had under his command on the day of his capitulation, and would probably place our government so completely on the defensive before the close of the first campaign as to make it but too happy to retire from the contest without any other humiliation than the formal recognition of the Emperor of Mexico.

"I may seem to underrate the value of our troops and the military genius of our people when I speak of the expulsion of the Archduke Maximilian as a task involving difficulty and danger. I am sure no one can rate either higher than I do, but I can conceive of no more deplorable delusion for our people to fall into than for them to infer from their wonderful military achievements since 1861 that they are destined to be, under their present Constitution, a great military nation. No one knows better than you, My Dear Sir, how impossible it would have been for us to have over-

come the forces arrayed against us during the late rebellion if the struggle had concerned anything less dear,
less vital than our national existence. I am greatly
mistaken if there was any moment between the 1st of
January, 1862 and the 1st of January, 1865 when the
administration would have dared decline any terms of
peace the South might have offered that included a restoration of the Union and a respect for our plighted
faith. Our government is based upon the will of the
people who would not prosecute an expensive war for a
cause which is not of vital interest to a very great majority of them, and it is impossible to make them feel that
they have any such interest in the restoration of the
soi-disant Republican government of Mexico. Whoever
thinks the contrary, I fear, is deceived." [29]

It might be said, of course, in commenting on this
extremely interesting letter, that the American minister
to France was in no position to judge the public opinion
of the United States, or the feeling of the American
people with regard to Mexico. But the view which he
here maintained was one which was certainly not unknown or unexpressed by others. The *New York Times,*
which enjoyed, of course, through Henry J. Raymond,
a very close contact with Seward, expressed itself from
first to last on the Mexican question with very great
moderation. In the cabinet, the Secretary of the Treasury declared that the country could not sustain a new
war,[30] and Welles, the Secretary of the Navy, took the

[29] Bigelow, III, 152-4.
[30] G. Welles, *Diary of Gideon Welles* (New York, 3 vols.,
1909), II, 333.

same view. Two pamphlets published in 1865, one anonymously, and one by F. J. Parker, take the viewpoint that no real interest of the United States is involved in the overthrow of monarchy in Mexico. On the contrary, writes one of these authors, the American people have every interest in the establishment of orderly conditions there.[31] The Monroe Doctrine, declares the other pamphleteer, was no child of the mind of President Monroe. There was " nothing in his nature or genius to make him the author of a speculative doctrine, utterly without immediate or practical application. No American statesman at that time of any prominence ever imagined it to possess the transcendent importance now thought to be associated with it." [32] Maximilian was the free choice of the Mexican people. He was the best hope of a Mexico regenerated by firm administration.

The holding of views such as these is a matter that most certainly deserves to be noticed. But the drift of opinion can hardly be said to have been in this direction. The mounting tone of Seward in the latter half of 1865 is undoubtedly the reflection of the development of the public mind. The personal inclinations of the Secretary were certainly towards moderation. If, as the year wore on, his tone became increasingly acrid in his correspondence with Bigelow, it seems fair to trace this to the increasing pressure to which he was subjected.

[31] F. J. Parker, *The Mexican Empire and the American Union* (Boston, 1865), p. 10.

[32] *Mexico and the Monroe Doctrine* (New York, 1865), p. 3.

32

We shall have some illustrations of this fact to offer
in the course of this chapter. But before turning to the
second half of 1865, and examining it from the American angle, it will be convenient, at this point, to cast a
backward glance at the policy of France, and at the development of French public opinion in the period just
traversed.

It is first of all to be noticed in this connection that
for a very considerable period, certainly from April,
1864, the government of Louis Napoleon had begun to
look with some anxiety upon the development of public
opinion in the United States. When, shortly after the
passage of the Davis resolution, Dayton had gone to
read to Drouyn de l'Huys the note of explanation which
Seward penned on this subject, the French minister had
met him with the significant question, " Do you bring
us peace or war?" [33] Never was any question more
revealing of a state of mind. As by a lightning flash
Drouyn had given away the fact that he was seriously
concerned about American policy. His attitude is still
more clearly revealed in the protest which he instructed
Geoffroy to lodge against the club of the D. M. D. in
New Orleans.[34] A society of the smallest local significance, and of meager resources, was here given a very
considerable importance.

Drouyn's nervousness could hardly have been allayed
by the tone of Geoffroy's despatches in 1864 and early
1865. The French chargé at Washington was obviously

[33] *Diplomatic Correspondence,* 1865, part 3, p. 757.
[34] Paris, Min. des Aff. Etr., Corr. Pol., Etats-Unis, vol. 131,
May 4, 1864.

immensely impressed with the strength of the public
hostility to the Mexican adventure, and the language of
Seward, as we have seen, can hardly be said to have been
entirely reassuring. In the summer of the former year
Geoffroy wrote to his government that the occasion was
hardly propitious for raising the question of Mexico,
since both parties, in the midst of the electoral campaign, were hoisting the standard of the Monroe Doctrine.[35] In August he transmitted Seward's intimation
that Maximilian would not be recognized,[36] and at the
turn of the year the report of the Blair mission to
Richmond.[37] On February 13 he gave it as his sober
opinion that when the Civil War was over the people
of the United States would throw themselves upon
Mexico, and that no one would dare oppose such action.
On the 27th he declared that war with France was
thought to be in the offing. Puzzled and perturbed, the
Emperor wrote to Bazaine on March 1, 1865, a letter
which, while refusing to admit the danger of war with
the United States, directs the Marshal so far as possible
to concentrate his troops, rather than to diffuse them.[38]
A little later, Drouyn de l'Huys, who seems to have
been a jumpy sort of person, penned instructions to
Geoffroy which were apparently based upon the hypoth-
esis that the situation called for the tone of intimidation.
What was obviously feared was the direct invasion of

[35] *Ibid.,* July 21, 1864.
[36] *Ibid.,* vol. 132, August 1, 1864.
[37] *Ibid.,* vol. 133, January 24, 1865.
[38] Genaro García, and Carlos Pereyra. *op. cit.,* XXIV, 246.

Mexico, a step which would have been fatal alike to the existence of the monarchy of Maximilian and to the prestige of the French government. " We cannot believe," wrote Drouyn, " that they (the United States) are thinking of using them (their forces) in an expensive and unjust war against a country that has never given them cause of complaint—in a war, in fact (and we say it because we do not wish to repeat it) in which circumstances will force the United States to meet and oppose a power that was once their ancient ally." [39] The fear of American action indicated in this notable despatch was reflected in the press, and in the debates in the Corps Législatif. In the case of the former, it is not that predictions of hostile action on the part of the United States were particularly numerous. But the emphasis with which papers hitherto hostile to the Mexican expedition, and critical of its effects upon American relations, now began to assert that there was no real danger of a clash with the American government, is in itself significant.[40] And the studied effort of the *Memorial Diplomatique* to prove that the Monroe Doctrine was not involved in the case, since the Mexicans had chosen their own course of action, and had established monarchy of their own accord, is a typical instance of a line of thought not unlike that of the Queen who protests too much in the third act of Hamlet.[41] In reality, if Bigelow is to be believed, the ending of the American

[39] 39th Cong., 1st Sess., H. Exec. Doc. No. 73, part I, p. 266, March 23, 1865.

[40] See encl. in Bigelow's despatch of March 14, 1865. *Diplomatic Correspondence,* 1865, part 3, pp. 380-2.

[41] *Ibid.*

Civil War (combined with the sudden death of the Duc de Morny, one of the mainstays of the Imperial régime), "produced almost a panic in Paris." [42] In the Chambers, the opponents of the government did their best to capitalize this feeling. On March 10, amidst a chorus of protests, the Marquis de Boissy predicted that the termination of the contest between North and South would see the French army in Mexico taken prisoner.[43] A month later, in a speech signalized by brilliant eloquence and logic alike, Jules Favre attacked the Mexican venture, laying the principal emphasis upon the attitude of the United States.[44] In answer to these strictures the defenders of the government sought to minimize the peril. The United States had no real interest in Mexico, it was declared; the state of their relations with Great Britain would prevent a breach with France; the Northern soldiers were small farmers who would be anxious to return to their farms; the problems of reconstruction would occupy the full attention of American statesmen.[45] These were ingenious arguments, but there is ample indication in the diplomatic correspondence of the months that followed that the men who uttered them were merely attempting to whistle down a peril the existence of which they could not in their heart of hearts deny.

It must not be assumed, however, that in the spring of '65 the French government was yet ready to adopt

[42] *Ibid.*, p. 380.
[43] *Moniteur*, March 10, 1865.
[44] *Ibid.*, April 11, 1865.
[45] *Ibid.*, April 12, 1865, the speech of Corta.

the policy of scuttle to which it was later driven by the
logic of events. It is true that in his speech to the Chambers in February, Louis Napoleon assumed a tone of
jaunty optimism with regard to Mexico, and spoke of
the Mexican army as returning home; and, as we have
already seen, this was the language which he used in talking with Bigelow, and indeed with many others. But
it is clear that at this time, while ready to promise withdrawal, the Emperor was not ready to desert his protégé.
He wished to silence criticism at home and abroad by
talking as if the Mexican expedition were near its end;
in a sense he had long regretted the whole business, and
wished to be rid of it; but it was obviously desirable,
if it could be done, to permit Maximilian to consolidate himself in Mexico before the final departure of
the French troops. In January, 1865, the Prussian minister, who was obviously well informed of the Emperor's
purposes, told Bigelow that two years at least would be
required.[46] And the tone taken by Rouher, Louis Napoleon's fugleman, in the debates of April, 1865, was to
the effect that the French troops must remain long
enough to consolidate their work. This, it was of course
assumed, would not be long. But some time must be
given for it. The government was not prepared to withdraw under pressure; nor indeed at this time did it contemplate fixing a definite limit to the Mexican expedition. While obviously concerned as to the attitude of
the United States, the threatening language of Drouyn
de l'Huys seems to indicate that it was thought that,
despite the trend of public opinion across the Atlantic,

[46] Bigelow, II, 266.

it might be possible by a strong tone to intimidate the American government.

The attitude assumed by the French government, however, did nothing to liquidate the Mexican question; it altered not a jot, of course, the policy of Seward, which was to avoid putting pressure upon France, if possible; during the spring and early summer of 1865, on neither the one side nor the other, were any steps taken which tended to precipitate a vigorous discussion. The American Secretary of State continued to give assurances of the intention of the United States to observe neutrality; the French minister of Foreign Affairs, though sometimes a little tart and supercilious in his intercourse with Bigelow, did not undertake to utter menaces again.

The month of August, however, marks a considerable change in Franco-American diplomatic relations. Before entering upon an analysis of this change, it will be desirable to consider briefly the military situation which is intimately connected with it.

We have already seen that in February and March of 1865 it was the fear of the French government that the troops liberated from their task by the ending of the Civil War might be directed against Mexico. The actual ending of hostilities was followed by the gradual mustering out of the mighty armies that had vindicated the existence of the Union; but despite this mustering out a considerable force was maintained in Texas, and this force was actually increased in July of 1865, despite the ending of all Confederate resistance in this part of the

South.[47] All in all, it amounted to some 40,000 men,[48] a number which seems small in comparison with the hosts which had fought the Civil War, but which was large enough, so, no doubt, it was assumed in Washington, to make some impression upon the government of Louis Napoleon.[49] Its existence was a solemn warning of the fact that the Mexican question, in the opinion of the American government, was far from liquidated, and it must have strengthened Seward in the change of tone which he assumed in the midsummer of 1865.

The pressure to which the Secretary of State had been subjected in favor of a more vigorous policy was by June considerably increasing, as we have seen. He had had to defend his policy against criticism in the cabinet; he knew of the intrigues of Grant and Schofield; and in the press and the public hall the clamor for the vindication of the Monroe Doctrine grew louder. It

[47] *Official Correspondence,* I, vol. 48, part ii, p. 1024.

[48] *Ibid.,* pp. 865 and 1024.

[49] It is curious to see how relatively few are the references to this "army of observation" in the correspondence of Montholon, of Dano, the French minister in Mexico City, and of Bazaine. The tone of Montholon was at no time alarmist with regard to it; and although one finds signs of anxiety in a letter of Bazaine's written at the end of May, and of Dano at the end of July (García, *op. cit.,* vol. 30, p. 14, and Paris, Min. des Aff. Etr., Corr. Pol., Mexique vol. 63, July 28, 1865), neither the one nor the other of these personages can be said to have laid great emphasis upon the existence of this American force. Bazaine, indeed, seems more impressed with the unofficial encouragement given to the Juaristas than to the danger of hostile action from Washington. That the presence of the American army was taken seriously in Paris, however, will appear from what follows.

is not strange, then, that his tone began to change; in an instruction to Bigelow of July 6, a note of veiled hostility is struck for the first time. Directing a protest against the reception within the French lines in Mexico of property smuggled across the border by the Confederates, Seward went on to say, " You will inform Mr. Drouyn de l'Huys that renewed instructions have been given to the general commanding the United States military forces in Texas to permit no aggressive movements of troops under his command within Mexican territory, unless special instructions from the War Department should be rendered necessary by a condition of affairs not now anticipated." [50] This message was transmitted by Bigelow on July 26.

It was followed by another much more striking, having to do with the activities of William M. Gwin in Mexico. Gwin had been a Senator from California from 1849 to 1861, but was imprisoned as a Confederate sympathizer at the beginning of the war.[51] Released in 1863, he proceeded to Paris, and there got in touch with Louis Napoleon. He was encouraged by his interviews with the Emperor to go to Mexico, to undertake schemes of colonization, in conjunction with the exploitation of the mines of Sonora.[52] The administration had wind of this gentleman's ambitious projects in 1864. At that time, however, Seward held his peace. But in the sum-

[50] 39th Cong., 1st Sess., H. Exec. Doc. No. 73, part II, p. 463.
[51] The *Memoirs* of Gwin are in the Bancroft Library, University of California. See especially pp. 187-199.
[52] P. Gaulot, *La Verité sur l'Expédition du Mexique* 3 vols., Paris, 1889-90), I, 216, and II, 147, and Bigelow, *op. cit.*, II, 190 and 197.

mer of 1865, the ever active Romero transmitted to the Secretary of State certain intercepted documents, some of them Gwin's, all of them concerned with his plans, and one of them indicating that he had the support of the Emperor of the French. These documents Seward transmitted to Bigelow, and on August 1, the American minister, acting under instructions, transmitted a sharp diplomatic protest to Drouyn de l'Huys. " In submitting to his Excellency the Minister of Foreign Affairs copies of this correspondence," he wrote, " the undersigned is instructed frankly to state the sympathies of the American people for the Republicans of Mexico are very lively, and that they are disposed to regard with impatience the continued intervention of France in that country ; that any favor shown to the speculations of Dr. Gwin by the titular Emperor of Mexico or by the Imperial Government of France will tend greatly to increase the popular impatience, because it will be regarded, perhaps justly, as importing danger, or at least a menace to the United States.

" Could the Government of the undersigned be brought to believe that the statements of these speculators were worthy of entire confidence, the President of the United States would be forced to the conclusion that His Majesty the Emperor of France was pursuing toward Mexico a policy materially at variance with that of neutrality in regard to the political institutions of the country, which he avowed at the commencement of his war with that republic.

" The President, on the contrary, confidently and sincerely expects, in some form, an assurance that all the pretences of Dr. Gwin and of his associates are destitute of any sanction from the Emperor of France." [53]

The first instinct of the French minister was to resent such language. In a tart despatch of August 7, he declared that the Emperor was determined to " reject all interpellations which may come to us in a comminatory tone about vague allegations, and based upon documents of a dubious character." [54] But it seems not at all improbable that the note of August 1 in the long run produced something of a change in French policy, and opened the way for the diplomatic exchanges of the fall of 1865. On August 17 there went forward new instructions to Montholon. These instructions enclosed the exchange of correspondence with regard to Gwin, and emphasized by underlining the phrase which has just been quoted above. They seek to justify the Mexican adventure. They declare that France is " unwilling to leave anarchy behind in Mexico, and that the French government will recall all of its troops gradually, according to the reestablishment of order and the pacification of the country. They declare that France will not hasten its steps on account of " haughty injunctions or threatening insinuations." But they close with the suggestion of a frank exchange of views between the two governments.[55] While it cannot be said that there was much in the temper of this instruction to suggest that the French government might meet the views of the

[53] Despatch quoted in Bigelow, III, 123.
[54] Ibid., p. 146.
[55] Paris, Min. des Aff. Etr., Corr. Pol., Etats-Unis, vol. 135, August 17, 1865.

United States by a prompt withdrawal, there was, for the first time, the expression of a willingness to discuss the Mexican question.

It is not improbable, despite Seward's refusal to receive a minister from Maximilian in July, that the Quai d'Orsay had already formed the project, set forth in greater detail later, for some kind of bargain by which American recognition of Maximilian should be set off against French withdrawal. Marshal Randon mentions such an idea in a letter to Bazaine on August 31.[56] It seems reasonable to believe that it was already in the mind of Drouyn de l'Huys as well.

Beneath the proud external form of the despatch of August 7, there may well have been a considerable uneasiness. Whether Drouyn de l'Huys felt it or not (and the language of Bigelow must have been most reassuring), the Emperor himself and Marshal Randon certainly did. There is extant a letter of August 17 from Louis Napoleon to Bazaine, written on the very day of the instructions to Montholon. Relations with the United States, wrote His Majesty, while not bad, were assuming a character which might become grave. In case of an American invasion of Mexico, he added, it would be necessary to evacuate the points on the circumference, and concentrate French forces in a central place.[57] This advice was echoed by Marshal Randon, who, in a letter of the 21st, spoke also of permitting the intervention to last not a moment longer than would be necessary to accomplish the task that had been under-

[56] García, XXX, 224.
[57] Gaulot, II, 169.

taken.[58] These letters furnish an interesting commentary on the seriousness with which the Emperor and his Minister of War took the attitude of the United States, and on the practical importance they attached to it.

The instructions of Drouyn de l'Huys were communicated to Seward early in September. The Secretary of State, in his conversations with Montholon, was still quite conciliatory. " All we need is a little time," he declared, " in order to solve the Mexican question." [59] But the pressure upon him was undoubtedly becoming more and more severe. The President was extremely anxious to get the French out of Mexico; the sentiment of the army officers was distinctly bellicose; the Monroe Doctrine, as the judicious Montholon reported, was " the idol of patriotism " with the masses; [60] General Grant had just transmitted to the President a perfervid appeal for vigorous action, based, as he declared, on many contacts with " all parties and classes of the people " during a seven weeks' absence from Washington.[61] The

[58] *Ibid.*, p. 172.

[59] Paris, Min. des Aff. Etr., Corr. Pol., Etats-Unis, vol. 135, September 5, 1865.

[60] *Ibid.*

[61] *Official Records, op. cit.*, I, vol. 48, part ii, p. 1221. This statement deserves full quotation.

GALENA, Ill., Sept. 1, 1865

His Excellency A. Johnson,
    President:

Seven weeks' absence from Washington and free intercourse with all parties and classes of people has convinced me that there is but one opinion as to the duty of the United States toward Mexico, or rather the usurpers in that country. All agree that, besides a yielding of the long-proclaimed Monroe doctrine, non-intervention in Mexican affairs will lead to an

time was approaching when Congress would be in session. Confronted, as he frankly explained to Bigelow, with the reasonable anticipation that " the Congress of the United States, and the people in their primary assemblies, will give a very large share of attention to questions of extraneous character, and chief among

---

expensive and bloody war hereafter or a yielding of territory now possessed by us. To let the Empire of Maximilian be established on our frontier is to permit an enemy to establish himself who will require a large standing army to watch. Military stations will be at points remote from supplies, and therefore expensive to keep. The trade of an empire will be lost to our commerce, and Americans, instead of being the most favored people of the world throughout the length and breadth of this continent, will be scoffed and laughed at by their adjoining neighbors both north and south—the people of the British Provinces and Mexico. Previous communications have given my views on our duty in the matter here spoken of, so that it is not necessary that I should treat the subject at any length now. Conversations with you have convinced me that you think about it as I do, otherwise I should never have taken the liberty of writing in this manner. I have had the opportunity of mingling more intimately with all classes of the community than the Executive can possibly have, and my object is to give you the benefit of what I have heard expressed. I would have no hesitation in recommending that notice be given the French that foreign troops must be withdrawn from the continent, and the people left free to govern themselves in their own way. I would openly sell on credit to the Government of Mexico all the ammunition and clothing they want, and aid them with officers to command troops. In fine, I would take such measures as would secure the supremacy of the republican government in Mexico. I hope you will excuse me for the free manner in which I address you. I but speak my honest convictions, and then with the full belief that a terrible strife in this country is to be averted by prompt action in this matter with Mexico.

U. S. GRANT,
Lieutenant-General.

these . . . . our relations towards France with regard to Mexico," Seward wrote on the 6th of September the first of a series of despatches in which a rising tone with regard to France is distinctly apparent. The despatch contained no threat, but it alluded to the tension which the Mexican situation created, and to the preference of the United States for the republican form of government in the states of the American continent. It spoke also of the " necessity for expansion " of the American people, and of the fact that " the like necessity may reasonably be expected to occur hereafter." It declared that " peace and friendship between the United States and the other nations on this continent, and consequently the advance of civilization in this hemisphere, seem more likely to be secured when the other American states assimilate to our own." " I may remark," Seward added, " that France appears to us to be lending her great influence, with a considerable military force, to destroy the domestic Republican Government in Mexico, and to establish there an Imperial system, under the sovereignty of a European prince, who, until he assumed the crown, was a stranger to that country." [62] This despatch was submitted to Drouyn de l'Huys by Bigelow on October 5. The French minister received it with some displeasure; he made the statement, by no means novel by the autumn of 1865, that the French government wished to get out as soon as it could, but he refused to fix any precise time, and Bigelow received the im-

[62] Bigelow, III, 175 et seq., and Diplomatic Correspondence, 1865, part 3, p. 412 et seq.

pression that there was an intention to insure stability or financial compensation before withdrawal.[63] Seward's intimations had not much advanced the solution of the problem.

Indeed, the French government still nourished hopes of some kind of bargain with the United States. In the long discussion of October 5, Bigelow had inquired whether the recognition of Maximilian would enable him to dispense with a foreign army. Grasping at this hint of a compromise, Drouyn de l'Huys took up the question with him in a later interview, and argued warmly for some assurance from the American government that it would enter into relations with the Mexican Empire simultaneously with the withdrawal of the French army. On October 18 he drew up instructions to Montholon in this sense.[64] The next day Bigelow addressed a long and important despatch to Seward apprising him of the tenor of his conversations with the French minister.

In the meantime Seward, on his part, was being forced along the path of action. General Grant was as ardent as ever for intervention; and on October 6 a letter of his strongly urging a vigorous course was read by the President to the members of the cabinet.[65] The President himself felt almost as strongly; indeed, he told Schofield that he had always believed that action ought to have been taken the very moment the Civil War was ended.[66] In the cabinet Dennison and Harlan were the

[63] Bigelow, III, 194-6.
[64] Paris, Min. des Aff. Etr., Corr. Pol., Etats-Unis, vol. 135, October 18, 1865.
[65] Romero, V, 675.
[66] *Ibid.*, pp. 632 and 742.

partisans of a forward policy.[67] The fall conventions of the political parties produced a new crop of resolutions and speeches on Mexico. In the first days of November offices for the floating of a Mexican loan were opened in the principal American cities. If, in September, it had been possible for Seward to write that the political trend would compel more attention to Mexico, such a point of view was all the more cogent two months later.

The language of Bigelow's despatches may also have encouraged the American Secretary of State to take a sharper tone. The French government had not as yet made any clear-cut and definite announcement of its intention to withdraw; withdrawal, indeed, was still made contingent upon the satisfaction of France's interests and honor. But on the other hand, Drouyn had indicated that the reduction of the French forces in Mexico would go on as fast as possible,[68] and had declared very definitely that the Emperor was anxious to withdraw, and he had clearly indicated his willingness to conciliate the United States. The proposal of withdrawal on the basis of American recognition of Maximilian was accompanied by hints of the negotiation of a commercial treaty with the United States. For the menacing tone of March had been substituted the language of conciliation.

Early in November, therefore, the American Secretary took a series of important steps. In the first place,

[67] For Dennison, see *ibid.*, p. 662; for Harlan the speech already mentioned.

[68] Bigelow, III, 190.

33

he sent to Bigelow the famous despatch, No. 300, in which the French intervention in Mexico was stigmatized " as disallowable and impracticable," in which it was stated that recognition of the monarchical régime was absolutely impossible, and in which regret was expressed that " no communication, formal or informal, which has been received from the government of that country (*i. e.,* France) seems to justify us in expecting that France is likely soon to be ready to remove, as far as may depend upon her, the cause of our deep concern for the harmony of the two nations. I will leave you," Seward was cautious enough to add, " to present the opinions of the President to such extent and in such manner as your own views of propriety shall suggest." [69] Contemporaneously with No. 300 went two other important steps. Acting with the support, perhaps at the instigation of Johnson, Seward decided to announce the appointment of a minister to the wandering government of President Juarez. The individual selected for this post was General Logan, who had distinguished himself by his public denunciation of the French intervention, and by his strong support of the Monroe Doctrine.[70] Thirdly, General Schofield was directed to proceed to Paris. For some months, it will be remembered, he had been tempted with the promise of a mission across the seas. Yet Seward had long delayed; he had, it would appear, held the General back until he might hope for the maximum effect from sending him to Paris.

[69] *Diplomatic Correspondence,* 1865, part 3, p. 421, *et seq.*
[70] Romero, V, 373 and 789.

What instructions he gave him it is even today impossible to tell; and the biographer of the Secretary has treated the whole episode as if its whole object were to get a troublesome military man out of the way. Such an interpretation, however, seems hardly to do justice to the subtlety which Seward so often showed in things political and diplomatic; and if it were a true one it would be difficult to explain why it was that he waited so long before launching Schofield on his mission, and why he sent him at precisely the time when a vigorous course of action had been decided upon. It seems more likely that the object in view was to render just a little more nervous the already nervous government in Paris by the rather mysterious appearance of a prominent American soldier in that capital. On the other hand, Schofield's own assertion that Seward said to him that he wished him to get his legs under Napoleon's mahogany, and tell him to get out of Mexico, cannot be said to carry conviction. Schofield never really got in contact with the Emperor of the French, and if it had been the purpose of the Secretary of State to have him do so, the matter could certainly have been arranged. It looks, therefore, as if the Schofield mission was a sort of bluff, but a bluff with a very definite purpose. No doubt from the beginning the shrewd director of American foreign policy was not loath to distract the general from his schemes of Mexican adventure; but a more positive purpose may fairly be assumed to lie behind his course of action. That it was not wholly without effect will soon be seen.

The events of November which we have just described may fairly be said to mark, in the words of the Comte de Montholon, a new era in the story of the Mexican question.[71] They are indications that Seward was now clearly embarked upon a policy which involved exerting pressure upon the government in Paris. Before proceeding to examine that policy further, it may be worth while to pause for a moment to consider it in its relation to American public opinion.

No task of the historian is more difficult or more delicate than that which involves the interpretation of the state of mind of a whole nation. To speak, indeed, of such a thing in general terms is, of course, virtually impossible ; and the various citations which have already been made which illustrate the sentiment in favor of the

[71] Paris, Min. des Aff. Etr., Corr. Pol., Etats-Unis, vol. 135, November 20, 1865.

The month of November was also signalized by the interesting episode of James Watson Webb's interview with Napoleon. Mr. Webb, long a New York editor, was made minister to Brazil in 1861. On his way back from Brazil via Paris in 1865, he was received by the Emperor at Compiegne. On November 10, the two discussed the Mexican question, and Webb stated that in his judgment the American people would insist on the Monroe Doctrine. Napoleon indicated his desire to get out, but said that it would be dangerous to put pressure upon France. (Washington, Dept. of State, Despatches, Brazil, vol. 31, undated and unnumbered.) On the basis of this interview the most extravagant claims have been made for Webb. (See B. Jerrold. *The Life of Napoleon III.* (4 vols., New York, 1884), IV, 345-6.) The incident appears to me relatively unimportant. Webb claims to have decided nothing, and why should Louis Napoleon be more influenced as to the state of American opinion by an American returning from Brazil, even by an American minister, than by direct information from Washington?

upholding of the Monroe Doctrine may very possibly have produced an effect somewhat deceptive. It is to be remembered that there were newspapers which all this time urged caution, some from conviction, others, by this time, subsidized by Maximilian; it is to be remembered that all through the year 1865 the demobilization of the mighty armies which had fought to preserve American nationality went on without interruption; it is to be noted that in some sections of the country, notably in New England, there was very decided opposition on the part of the well-to-do classes to any breach with France.[72] It is possible, too, to discover some truth in the view of Richard Henry Dana that some of those who talked so loudly of the external issue wished to distract attention from the difficulties and dangers of reconstruction. Such a point of view may, for example, be attributed to the Blairs, and perhaps to some others. Finally, it is to be noted that the Congress which met at the beginning of December, 1865, was, as Romero confessed to his government with some disappointment, more concerned with the questions of reconstruction than with the question of the French in Mexico.[73]

Yet it is also true, as we have seen, that such conspicuous military leaders as Grant and Sheridan and Schofield were strong for a vigorous policy; that the President was drawn in the same direction; that the eulogies of the Monroe Doctrine came from the members of no single party, no single class, and even no single

[72] Romero, V, 862, and Bigelow, III, 209.
[73] Romero, V, 863.

section. If Seward exaggerated when he said to the Prussian minister, Gerolt, in November, 1865, that the whole nation wished the Monroe Doctrine upheld; if Romero may also have exaggerated when he said that all the members of Congress, even those who wished to take no action, were opposed to the French intervention, and that few of them would dare vote against a resolution to express that opposition, it is none the less true that there was much truth in both these statements. Whether the American people would have fought over the Mexican question we shall never know; but it seems safe to say that there were inflammable materials lying about in the fall of 1865. It is easy in this irrational but always interesting world to want a thing without wanting its consequences; so, at the time of which we are speaking, a considerable body of the American people wanted the Monroe Doctrine upheld without necessarily wanting war; but one wonders what their choice would have been if they could not have had one without the other. Would war weariness and the pressure of domestic questions have prevailed? Or would popular passion and prejudice, the aroused nationalism that followed on victory, have had its way?

There is, of course, no answer to this question; thanks to Seward the challenge to France was made only when it was prudent to make it, when it seemed certain that it would produce the desired result. By the end of November it was tolerably clear that France would yield. The President's message, December 4, 1865, spoke out clearly on Mexico, alluding to the system of " non-interference and mutual abstinence from propagandism " that had characterized the intercourse of Europe and America, and declaring, " We should regard it as a great calamity to ourselves, to the cause of good government, and to the peace of the world should any European power challenge the American people, as it were, to the defense to republicanism against foreign interference." [74] And on the heels of the message fol-

[74] The full text of the relevant portion of the message runs as follows: " From the moment of the establishment of our free Constitution the civilized world has been convulsed by revolutions in the interests of democracy or of monarchy, but through all these revolutions the United States have wisely and firmly refused to become propagandists of republicanism. It is the only government suited to our condition; but we have never sought to impose it on others ; and we have consistently followed the advice of Washington to recommend it only by the careful preservation and prudent use of the blessing. During all the intervening period the policy of European powers and of the United States has, on the whole, been harmonious. Twice, indeed, rumors of the invasion of some parts of America in the interest of monarchy have prevailed; twice my predecessors have had occasion to announce the views of this nation in respect to such interference. On both occasions the remonstrance of the United States was respected from a deep conviction on the part of European Governments that the system of non-interference and mutual abstinence from propagandism was the true rule for the two hemispheres. Since those times we have advanced in wealth and power, but we retain the same purpose to leave the nations of Europe to choose their own dynasties and form their own systems of government. This consistent moderation may justly demand a corresponding moderation. We should regard it as a great calamity to ourselves, to the cause of good government, and to the peace of the world should any European power challenge the American people, as it were, to the defense of republicanism against foreign interference. We can not foresee and are unwilling to consider what opportunities might present themselves, what combinations might offer to protect ourselves

lowed the prompt reply of Seward to Bigelow's despatch of November 30.[75] A few days before, the American minister had a long discussion with Drouyn at the
Quai d'Orsay, handing to the Frenchman the instruction
of November 6. The argument waxed warm at times;
there were the expected assertions to the effect that
France could not be bullied, a querulous question as to
why Seward did not say war, if he meant war, the not
novel defense of Maximilian's empire as based upon the
will of the people. But from the conversation as a whole
Bigelow drew the distinct impression that if the United
States "insisted upon it, of course there would be an
end of the Mexican experiment." [76] On receiving this
despatch, without a moment's delay, the Secretary of
State replied to it. He declared that friendship with
France "would be brought into imminent jeopardy,
unless France could deem it consistent with her interest
and honor to desist from the prosecution of armed intervention in Mexico;" he intimated that Congress
might soon have something to say about the subject;
and he declared with pointed candor that there was
nothing in the language of M. Drouyn de l'Huys which

---

against designs inimical to our form of government. The United
States desire to act in the future as they have ever acted heretofore; they never will be driven from that course but by the
aggression of European powers, and we rely on the wisdom
and justice of those powers to respect the system of non-interference which has so long been sanctioned by time, and which by
its good results has approved itself to both continents." Richardson, *Messages, op. cit.,* VI, 368.

[75] *Diplomatic Correspondence,* 1865, part 3, p. 429.

[76] Bigelow, III, 255.

authorizes " an expectation on our part that a satisfactory adjustment of the case can be effected on any basis that thus far has been discussed." In short, he went as far as he well could go without demanding in terms the ending of the Mexican expedition in a stipulated time. The day after writing this despatch he lunched with the members of the Foreign Affairs Committee of the House. " You can pass whatever resolutions you want now," he said. " I am ready for anything." [77] His confidence that France would yield was, it would appear, by this time unbounded. The French minister withdrew to New York in dudgeon at the language of the note of December 6, but Seward was sure that he, and not de Montholon, held the winning cards.

His optimism was soon to be rewarded. The despatches from Bigelow which came to him as the year closed were all that he could have desired. On the 21st of December the American minister wrote that he had had another talk with Drouyn de l'Huys, in which he had tactfully intimated that the fixing of a period when the French flag would be withdrawn from Mexico would have " a tranquilizing and salutary effect upon both sides of the Atlantic." The Frenchman had replied that the Emperor would speak upon the subject of Mexican affairs at the opening of the Chamber, if no earlier, and that " I might be sure that what he would say would be satisfactory." He added that this news might be communicated to Seward. The two men proceeded to discuss the possibility of an exchange of letters between

[77] Romero, V, 903.

President Johnson and the Emperor, initiated by the former, but which should result in formal assurances of French withdrawal.[78] This was gratifying enough, of course, but better news was to come. On Christmas Eve Bigelow had an opportunity of talking with Louis Napoleon. The Emperor had obviously been made nervous by General Logan's appointment and Schofield's appearance in Paris, as his inquiries with regard to both showed; and he told Bigelow that he expected all the French troops to be back by the following autumn.[79] Early in January Drouyn de l'Huys tried to enter into negotiations with Bigelow, looking to the protection of France's financial interests, but he made it clear that France would withdraw if assured that the United States would not interfere to overthrow Maximilian.[80] A similar position was assumed in the instructions which the French Foreign Minister now despatched to Montholon. With a view to French opinion, it was necessary, of course, in these instructions to enter into a justification of French policy in Mexico. With a somewhat labored logic, Drouyn de l'Huys fell back upon the theory that France had entered Mexico for the redress of grievances, and that the monarchy had simply happened. " The French army," he declared, " did not carry monarchical traditions to Mexico in the folds of its flag." Maximilian, he jauntily asserted, had been called by the will of the country. Why should not the United

[78] Bigelow, III, 288-92.

[79] *Ibid.,* pp. 298-300.

[80] Washington, Dept. of State, Despatches, France, January 5, 1866.

States hold as friendly relations with his government as with the government of Brazil? Why should it grudge to this régime a measure of support from outside? "What state is there that needs not allies, whether to form or defend it? . . . . When the United States fought for their emancipation, did the aid given by France to their efforts cause that great popular movement to cease to be truly national? And shall it be said that the contest with the south was not in like manner a national war, because the thousands of Irishmen and Germans were fighting under the flag of the United States?"

All this, no doubt, was excellent fooling. But there were realities which had to be faced. And Drouyn faced them. He informed Montholon that the Emperor had given orders to his minister in Mexico "to make with the Emperor Maximilian arrangements, which, by satisfying our interests and our honor, will permit us to consider as at an end the service of our army on Mexican soil." "We fall back from that moment," he continued, "upon the principle of non-intervention, and from that moment accept it as the rule of our conduct; our interest, no less than our honor, commands us to claim from all the uniform application of it. Trusting in the spirit of equity which animates the cabinet at Washington, we expect from it the assurance that the American people will themselves conform to the law which it invokes, by observing, in regard to Mexico, a strict neutrality. When you shall have informed me of the resolution of the federal government on this subject,

I shall be able to indicate to you the results of our negotiations with the Emperor Maximilian for the return
of our troops." [81]

The instructions of the 9th of January were transmitted to Seward on January 29. It was just a fortnight when he despatched his reply. He began by
summing up the French argument and the explanation
of French motives which Mr. Drouyn de l'Huys presents " as a true statement of the present case." He
then proceeded with delightful suavity to declare that
the American people, " without one dissenting voice "
rejected the thesis that the Empire of Maximilian was
the free choice of the Mexican people, and that all the
republican states in the American hemisphere had
adopted the same view. " Where a nation has established
institutions republican and domestic, similar to our
own, the United States assert in their behalf that no
foreign nation can rightfully intervene by force to subvert republican institutions and establish those of an
antagonistical character." The French minister had alluded to the right of Maximilian to seek alliances. To
this argument Seward replied, " Mr. Drouyn de l'Huys
seems to us to have overlooked two important facts,
namely: first, that the United States in this correspondence have assigned definite limits to the right of alliance
incompatible with our assent to his argument; and
secondly, the fact that the United States have not any
time accepted the supposed government of the Prince
Maximilian as a constitutional or legitimate form of

[81] *Diplomatic Correspondence*, 1865, part 3, pp. 805-8.

government in Mexico, capable or entitled to form alliances." After further refutations of the subordinate arguments in Drouyn's note, Seward came to the core of the communication, the request for assurances as to the future policy of the American government. A politician no less than a diplomat (or perhaps even more so), Seward concealed or veiled his virtual assurance of neutrality in sentences which had the air of conceding very little. He declared the United States could not assume that the Emperor " contemplates the establishment in Mexico, before withdrawing his forces, of the very institutions which constitute the material ground of the exceptions taken against his intervention by the United States." " On the contrary," he went on boldly, " we understand him as announcing to us his immediate purpose to bring to an end the service of his armies in Mexico, and in good faith to fall back, without stipulation or condition on our part, upon the principle of non-intervention upon which he is henceforth agreed with the United States. We cannot understand his appeal to us for an assurance that we ourselves will abide by our own principles of non-intervention in any other sense than as the expression, in a friendly way, of his expectation that when the people of Mexico shall have been left absolutely free from the operation, effects and consequences of his own political and military intervention, we will ourselves respect their self-established sovereignty and independence." The United States could not bind itself by treaty with regard to the matter, and even diplomatic assurances could be only " expressions of confident expectation " that the administration of the moment did not "misunderstand the settled principles and policy of the American people." "With these explanations," Seward added, "I proceed to say that, in the opinion of the President, France need not for a moment delay her promised withdrawal of military forces from Mexico, and her thought of putting the principle of non-intervention into full and complete practise in regard to Mexico, through any apprehension that the United States will prove unfaithful to the principles and policy which, on their behalf, it has been my duty to maintain in this now very lengthened correspondence. . . . . Looking simply toward the point to which our attention has been steadily confined, the relief of the Mexican embarrassments without disturbing our relations with France, we shall be gratified when the Emperor shall give to us, either through the channels of your esteemed correspondence or otherwise, definitive information of the time when French military operations may be expected to cease in Mexico." [82]

The note of February 12 arrived in Paris on February 27. Dignity alone would have dictated that the French government reply to it only after a decent interval. But, dignity apart, it was necessary to hear from the mission of Baron Saillard, the special representative of the Emperor sent out in January to Mexico, and still more from Marshal Bazaine. Word came early in April. The Marshal wrote that Baron Saillard had been fully informed by him of the situation, and that Maximilian had declined to consider any arrangement for the pro-

[82] *Ibid.*, pp. 813-22.

gressive repatriation of the French army. France must act, he declared, without the consent of Mexico. Withdrawal might take place in three contingents, the first in November, 1866, the second, in April, 1867, and the third and last in November, 1867.[83] Acting on the information just given, Drouyn de l'Huys addressed to Montholon on April 5 a note fixing the specific dates indicated above for the evacuation. At the same time an official notice to the same effect appeared in the columns of the *Moniteur*. The Imperial Government was now solemnly pledged to abandon its policy of building an Empire in the New World on the bayonets of its soldiers. The cause of the Monroe Doctrine had won a great victory.

It was, of course, reluctantly that the Imperial politician made up his mind to withdraw from Mexico. It was clear that the considerable period set for the evacuation, as Bigelow discerned, was intended to afford an opportunity for Maximilian to consolidate his power. Indeed, the Emperor had written just this to Bazaine in an interesting letter of January 31. " Circumstances stronger than my will oblige me to evacuate Mexico; but I wish to do so leaving behind me for the Emperor Maximilian every chance of maintaining himself with his own forces. You must put all your zeal and intelligence into the task of organizing something durable in the country, in order that our efforts may not be a dead loss. To accomplish this difficult task, you have a year or eighteen months." [84] Yet even Louis Napoleon

[83] Gaulot, III, 8.
[84] *Ibid.*, II, 237.

recognized that the tide was running strongly against the Empire. In this same letter to Bazaine, he alludes to the possibility of convoking a Junta, organizing a new government, and getting elected, through French influence, a President whose powers should last six to ten years. It does not seem unreasonable, particularly in the light of what was to come, to take the declaration of April 5 as the death knell of the Mexican monarchy. The diplomatic history of the matter is not to be terminated at this point; but the moment has now arrived to cast a backward glance over the period just traversed, and to seek to answer the central question which that period poses, the question as to the influence of the United States, upon the decision that was then reached, when considered in relation to all the factors involved.

In making a rapid survey of the diplomatic exchanges of 1865 and 1866, it is obvious that not all the factors in the Mexican question have been taken into account. The impression given, if the narrative stopped at this point, might be a very false one. No one would contend that the American attitude was the sole and simple explanation of French policy. Louis Napoleon, as we have seen, had tried to extricate himself from the Mexican adventure in 1863; he had welcomed the election of Maximilian in 1864 as opening the way to a solution of the problem; and he had expressed his desire to get out of Mexico to Bigelow as early as the winter of 1865. There were many elements which may have influenced him in 1866. In an interesting article which appeared nearly thirty years ago, Dr. C. A. Duniway put forward the view that the state of French public opinion, the condition of French finances, the friction that had been developed between the Emperor Maximilian and Louis Napoleon, and the general state of affairs in Europe all had their influence upon the final decision.[85]

The factors which Dr. Duniway thus mentioned are, in my opinion, of very varying importance. It may be worth while briefly to reexamine them. Let us look, first of all, at the theory that the general European situation influenced French policy. This theory, more concretely expressed, would assume that it was fully realized at Paris that the storm clouds were gathering over Central Europe. The Austrian and Prussian governments, having fought a common war together in 1864 against Denmark, had found it difficult to dispose of the spoils, the Duchies of Schleswig and Holstein. True, in the summer of 1865, they had arrived at a sort of makeshift solution of the problem in what is known as the Convention of Gastein. But this convention could hardly be regarded as a finality. Indeed the Prussian Chancellor in his conversations with the French ambassador at Berlin frankly stated with disarming candor that the convention was drawn up to contain calculated ambiguities, and that it was his purpose at a propitious moment to pick a quarrel with Vienna.[86] With the possibility of a European crisis ahead, in which France could hardly fail to take an interest, may it not be that Louis Napol-

[85] C. A. Duniway, " Reasons for Withdrawal of French from Mexico," *op. cit.*

[86] Paris, Min. des. Aff. Etr., Corr. Pol., Prusse, vol. 352, August 12, 1865.

34

eon felt keenly the necessity of bringing the Mexican adventure to an end in order to strengthen himself, both militarily and diplomatically, for a more active rôle in the affairs of Europe?

A close examination of the matter lends little support to any such thesis. From the diplomatic viewpoint the plain fact of the matter is that Louis Napoleon, by a fatality that appears curious enough in retrospect, watched with some complacency the unfolding of events in 1865 and 1866, until the victory of Prussian arms at Sadowa brought him face to face with some unpleasant realities. He was well informed as to the intentions of that rough and astute realist who had now become the Chancellor of Prussia, Prince Bismarck; and if, in the famous interview at Biarritz in October of 1865, he did not tie his own hands by promises, his silence, at least, emboldened the minister of Frederick William to press on with his policy of provoking the Austrians to war. In the Italo-Prussian negotiations of the late winter of 1866, negotiations which culminated in the treaty of alliance of April 8, the advice of the French Emperor was sought by Nigra, the Italian minister at Paris, and given in favor of the acceptance of Prussian overtures. With what now seems like a blind folly, the remaking of the map of Europe was actually encouraged, and when the prompt and decisive triumph of Sadowa finally came in July of 1866, France was diplomatically in a situation where a volte-face in favor of Austria was virtually impossible.[87] It would be extremely difficult

[87] For an excellent study of this period, see Pierre de la Gorce, *Histoire du Second Empire* (Paris, 1899, 7 vols.), IV,

to interpret the policy of Louis Napoleon in the first six months of 1866 in its relation to Central Europe as one which called for the strengthening of his military position. On the contrary, that policy was one of *laissez-faire, laissez aller,* to an extraordinary degree. Nor ought it, in seeking a relationship between the Mexican question and the German question, to be forgotten that the decision to withdraw from Mexico was already adumbrated as early as August, 1865, before the views of Bismarck were fully disclosed.[88] It may be, of course, that Drouyn de l'Huys, alike the foe of the Mexican adventure, and of Prussian ambitions, connected the two in his own mind; but if he did so, there is no hint of any such fact in the instructions to Montholon and Dano at Mexico City or in the instructions to Benedetti at Berlin.

Nor, even assuming that the military power of France was an important factor in her diplomatic policy in 1866, does it seem possible to prove that the withdrawal of the French troops from Mexico was necessary. There were but 28,000 of them, out of a total active force of 400,000, not counting reserves.[89] No doubt these forces

---

ch. xxix. The difficulties, from a diplomatic standpoint in taking a strong attitude in the summer of 1866, are well set forth in G. Rothan, *Origines de la Guerre de 1870. La Politique Française en 1866* (Paris, 1883). Rothan describes the proceedings of the famous Imperial Council of July 5, 1866, two days after Sadowa, and the arguments put forward for and against French mobilization. See especially chap. iv.

[88] See below, p. 493.

[89] Randon, *Memoires, op. cit.,* II, 153. For French army figures for this period see also Max von Szczepanski, *Napoleon III und sein Herr* (Heidelberg, 1913), pp. 136-40.

were among the best in the French army; but Marshal
Randon, who was the Minister of War, expressed the
opinion in 1866 that France was amply prepared for
eventualities.[90] In the famous Council of July 5, 1866,
held just after Sadowa to determine whether France
should mobilize in order to exert her full influence on
the future of Europe, both Randon and Drouyn de
l'Huys were of the opinion that on the military side the
situation was secure.[91] And there are more decisive
arguments than these which may be invoked to indicate
how little the Mexican question had to do with French
policy in Central Europe. In the fall of 1865, when the
decision to withdraw from Mexico was impending, an
actual reduction of the French military forces took
place.[92] What is more important still, the arrangements
under which the evacuation was to be carried on, it will
be remembered, called for the withdrawal of the first in-
stallment in *November, 1866*, and of subsequent installments in April and November, 1867. In the face of this
fact, it is difficult to contend that the Mexican adventure
was abandoned in order to utilize the troops engaged
therein as a support to the European diplomacy of the
Emperor. Any such explanation of the abandonment
of Maximilian must be, in my judgment, entirely ruled
out.

It is not the same with the contention that the financial
situation had something to do with Louis Napoleon's

[90] *Ibid.*, p. 146.
[91] *Ibid.*
[92] *Ibid.*, p. 136.

decision. There is no doubt that the Mexican expedition was extremely costly; it had never been popular with the Finance Minister of the Emperor, Achille Fould, as we have already seen; and by the end of 1865 it had already cost no less than 274,698,000 francs.[93] The drain was, of course, continuous, and it was counterbalanced by very meager payments from Mexico to the French Treasury. In addition, throughout 1865, the Mexican Finance Minister, Ramirez, was opposing an obstinate resistance to the payments of the French claims on the basis desired by France.[94] In the Chamber, the budget discussions of 1865 had revealed a very vigorous opposition to further expenditures. It would be foolish, indeed it would be impossible, to deny the significance of such facts.

Nor can the state of French public opinion with regard to the Mexican imbroglio be described as otherwise than increasingly hostile in 1865. The situation in the early part of the year has already been described; in June Bigelow wrote that he did not believe that there was a man in France who now thought that the Arch-duke could remain long in Mexico except " at an unprofitable waste of money and blood;" he expressed a similar view again in August, and early in December he wrote to his government of " the universal unpopularity of the Mexican expedition " as making it impos-

[93] The figures are in G. L. Niox, *Expédition du Mexique 1861-67* (Paris, 1874), p. 763. From this there might perhaps be substracted Mexican reimbursements to France amounting to 64,000,000 francs.

[94] Paris, Min. des Aff. Etr., Corr. Pol., Mexique, vol. 63, *passim*, but especially August 15, 1865.

sible for the Emperor to pursue any other course than withdrawal.[95] In the press attacks upon French policy continued. The *Revue des Deux Mondes,* of the highest standing and by no means anti-imperialist in its general views, expressed itself more and more frankly as the year wore on ; [96] and early in 1866 M. Saint Marc Girardin in a series of brilliant articles in the *Journal des Débats* vigorously attacked the policy of the Emperor.[97] In the Chambers the spokesmen of the government itself admitted that the whole trend of public opinion ran against the prolongation of the Mexican experiment. Tenacious though Louis Napoleon was, cling though he did, even after much had been yielded, to the hope that something lasting might yet come out of his grandiose dreams of monarchy in the New World, it cannot be denied that the unpopularity of his policy was a powerful factor in leading to its abandonment.

The same can be said, in some degree, of the state of affairs in Mexico itself. It is true that on the military side French arms, during 1865, vindicated themselves almost everywhere that they appeared ; and in the fall of 1865 the French invasion of Chihuahua drove the government of Benito Juarez, gallant and tenacious, to El Paso del Norte, on the Mexican frontier itself. The reports of Montholon, and of his successor, Dano, were, on the whole, not pessimistic. But there was plenty of news that was disquieting, none the less. Wherever the

[95] Bigelow, III, 49, 155, and 267.
[96] *Ibid.,* p. 497.
[97] *Ibid.*

French armies were not stationed, bands of guerillas sprang up, to contest with the Imperial authorities, and the letters of Bazaine, from a relatively early period in 1865, began to complain of the lack in energy and capacity of Maximilian himself.[98] In Mexico the French and Mexican authorities were frequently at logger-heads; and wrangling over financial questions increased the irritation which was felt in Paris at the protégé of France. The task of consolidating the new régime in Mexico was, undoubtedly, becoming more difficult and more irritating as time went on.

All these considerations taken together make it clear, as must frankly be admitted, that the Empire of Maximilian might have come to an inglorious end, and the French troops been withdrawn from across the seas without the intervention of the United States. Indeed, if I may make a purely hypothetical judgment for the little that any such judgment is worth, I believe that such would have been the case. But to say this is not to say that the influence which emanated from Washington was not of very genuine importance, and that it did not produce very concrete and recognizable effects. In candid willingness to recognize various other elements in the Mexican situation beside the position of the American government, Dr. Duniway, in my judgment, in the article to which I have already alluded, hardly did justice to the rôle played by American opinion. The despatches which crossed the Atlantic from Washington to Paris, whether those of Geoffroy and Montholon or

[98] See Gaulot, II, 223, 228, 261.

those of Seward, again and again, if the argument from synchronism holds, affected the point of view of the Emperor and of his ministers. Thus the alarmist despatches of Geoffroy in January and February of 1865 were followed by the Emperor's letter of March 1 to Bazaine, urging him to concentrate his troops, and by the nervous diplomatic note of Drouyn on March 23; and the initiation of a sharper tone in the diplomatic correspondence by Seward at the end of July and early in August, accompanied as it was by more alarmist despatches from Montholon, produced, or at any rate was followed by, a series of most interesting despatches which went forth from Paris. I have already mentioned in this connection the instructions to Montholon, dated August 17, which look toward an understanding with the United States, the letter of the same date from the Emperor to Bazaine, and the pessimistic tone of Marshal Randon in his letter of August 21. But to these there ought to be added the querulous despatch which Drouyn de l'Huys penned on the 15th of August to M. Dano, his representative in Mexico. On the whole, down to this time, the tone of Drouyn's instructions had not been unfriendly or such as to indicate any withdrawal of support from Maximilian. But in this communication the mood changes. Alluding to the amnesties which the Mexican sovereign too freely granted to those condemned by the tribunals for sniping at the French troops, alluding, also, to the complete failure of Mexico to keep her financial engagements, the minister declared that it was not wise for the government of Maximilian to compel France to think only of its own interests. "We would be obliged to do so," he continued, "if the task we have freely accepted were made more difficult, perhaps impossible, of accomplishment. In increasing the weight of the burden, we would not be forced to carry it indefinitely, but the moment would be hastened when imperious duties would force us to lay it down. We should, no doubt, regret to leave our work unfinished, and perhaps compromised, but we would have the conviction of having done our full duty to prepare its success, and there would remain to us the honor of having attempted it." [99] It seems impossible not to relate this interesting despatch to the communications of Seward. The transmission of the Gwin correspondence to M. Dano, the displeasure expressed by Drouyn de l'Huys at the "premature" mission of Degollado from Maximilian to Washington, seeking American recognition, both of these coming at the same time as the communication just quoted, strengthen the impression that the views of the American government had a very great influence indeed upon the policy of France.

Indeed, there can hardly be any other satisfactory explanation of the increased anxiety and discontent which Louis Napoleon and his ministers displayed in the month of August, 1865. The Chambers were not in session, and would not be for five months. It was not immediately necessary, therefore, to take account of the popular opposition to the Mexican expedition which

[99] Paris, Min. des. Aff. Etr., Corr. Pol., Mexique, vol. 64, August 15, 1865.

would focus there. The financial difficulties and divergences between France and Mexico were serious, but so they had been for months before. The situation in Mexico itself was described rather pessimistically by Dano in a despatch received on August 12,[100] but this was only one of a series which had started some time before. The European situation had not yet begun to be threatening ; and as we have seen, it relates itself very little to that in Mexico. While not regarding the policy of the United States as of exclusive importance, it seems reasonable, therefore, to assign to it a very important rôle in hastening, and indeed in forming, the decision of the Emperor of the French to cut the painter, and abandon his royal protégé.

The nervousness which both Louis Napoleon and Drouyn de l'Huys felt with regard to the attitude of the American government can be amply proven from this time forward. As early as September 14, 1865, Louis Napoleon proposed to Maximilian that he reorganize his army with Austrian troops. " When that has been done," he wrote, in a sentence which revealed the pith of the matter, " I can withdraw the greater part of our troops, which would deprive the Americans of all pretexts for their objections." [101] As for Drouyn, he frankly expressed to the Austrian ambassador, Prince Metternich, his fear that it would not be possible to preserve good relations with the United States, since the

[100] Ibid., July 10, 1865.

[101] Vienna, National Archives, Napoleon III to Maximilian, September 14, 1865, cited in Corti, II, 555.

new President was a radical demagogue, who might let himself be led by the mob and by the radicals, to whom monarchy in Mexico was obnoxious.[102] In his instructions to Dano, written September 21, he exposed his fears with equal clarity. The government at Washington had protested against the enrolment of Confederate soldiers in the Mexican Foreign Legion. We might, wrote Drouyn, have told Mr. Seward to go to Maximilian with these protests. But such action might incite him to a threatening attitude, and lead to a formal rupture, and in such a case it would be difficult for France to stand aside.[103] We have already seen the eagerness with which, early in October, the French minister seized upon the intimation of Bigelow that it might be possible to arrange a compromise on the basis of French withdrawal and American recognition of Maximilian; and it is worth noting, also, that the communication of Seward's despatch of September 6 is followed, at no very long interval, by a note from the French minister to Hidalgo, in which the view is expressed that the Federal government may have its hand forced, and that Maximilian had better be prepared to stand alone, and to take steps for the organization of a military force which will permit the recall of the French troops.[104]

By November the decision to abandon Maximilian was already pretty well formed. On the 15th of Novem-

[102] Vienna, National Archives, Metternich to Mensdorff, August 17, 1865, cited in Corti, II, 542.

[103] Paris, Min. des Aff. Etr., Corr. Pol., Mexique, vol. 64, September 21, 1865.

[104] *Ibid.*, October 24, 1865. Bigelow communicated Seward's instruction, it will be remembered, on October 5. See above, p. 497.

ber, Drouyn de l'Huys instructed Dano that France could not much longer be bound by the convention of Miramar, in view of its inexecution by the Mexican government, and that it would be forced to withdraw its troops if Mexico did not fulfil her financial engagements.[105] On November 22 Fould drew up an emphatic memorandum in the same sense. A week later came pessimistic despatches from Marshal Bazaine. Added to all these was the communication by Bigelow of Seward's famous No. 300, first on November 23, and, in more detail on November 28.[106] The instructions of the Emperor to the French commander in Mexico, written on November 29, ordering him to prepare for evacuation, and speaking sarcastically and bitterly of the unhappy Maximilian,[107] and the instructions of Drouyn to Dano of December 6,[108] which state in so many words that the limit of French sacrifices has been reached, while they may have been determined in part by other factors, yet bear an interesting relation in time to the news from Washington. It is worth noting, too, that the conciliatory interview of Bigelow and Drouyn of December 21 followed close on the reception of President Johnson's annual message in Paris; that the Christmas day conversation of Louis Napoleon and the American related itself to the appointment of Logan, and the sending of Schofield, and that the

[105] *Ibid.*, vol. 65, November 15, 1865.

[106] Bigelow, III, 240 *et seq.*, and 250 *et seq.*

[107] Gaulot, II, 201.

[108] Paris, Min. des Aff. Etr., Corr. Pol., Mexique, vol. 65, December 6, 1865.

French overtures of January 9 to the American government coincide with the despatch of Baron Saillard to Mexico. Taking all the evidence into consideration, it would appear easier to minimize than to exaggerate the rôle of the United States in bringing about the end of the Mexican experiment. An isolated or exclusive factor, it certainly was not; a factor constantly uppermost in the minds of Louis Napoleon and of his advisers in the second half of 1865 and the first months of 1866 it most assuredly was. The principles of the Monroe Doctrine had far more than an academic importance in the problem of Mexico.

The weight attached to the opinions of the United States in the spring of 1866 may be further illustrated by the correspondence with Austria. In the middle of March, while he was still awaiting an answer to his note of February 12, Seward received disquieting news from Motley, the American minister at Vienna. This news was to the effect that 4000 volunteers might be raised in Austria in the course of the year to sustain the rickety throne of Maximilian.[109] At the same time news of a similar color, less official and more highly colored, came from Bigelow. Seward replied by sending to Motley the note of February 12 to Montholon. " After reading that paper," he added, " you will be justified in saying that the American government and people would not be likely to be pleased with seeing Austria at this juncture assume the character of a protector to the foreign military power which, claiming the

[109] *Diplomatic Correspondence,* 1865, part 3, p. 830.

form of an empire, is attempted to be set up upon the supposed subverted foundations of the republic of Mexico." [110] But this was only the beginning. On April 6, having heard from Bigelow of the actual signing of a convention looking to the enrolment of the volunteers already mentioned, Seward advanced a step further. " It is thought proper that you should state," he now wrote, " that in the event of hostilities being carried on hereafter in Mexico by Austrian subjects, under the command or with the sanction of the government in Vienna, the United States will feel themselves at liberty to regard those hostilities as constituting a state of war by Austria against the republic of Mexico; and in regard to such war, waged at this time and under existing circumstances, the United States could not engage to remain as silent or neutral spectators." [111] Not yet satisfied, Seward drew up his famous No. 176. This document formally protested against the embarkation of any volunteers whatever from Austria to Mexico, and, in case such action was persisted in, it directed the American minister to demand his passports and leave Vienna. Before it was sent, it was discussed in a meeting of the cabinet. On the whole, it received the approval of Seward's colleagues. McCullough, the Secretary of the Treasury, opposed it, on the ground that he was opposed to war in general, and especially to a war for " a people as worthless as the Mexicans." [112] Speed, the Attorney-General, was also rather conserva-

[110] *Ibid.*, p. 831.
[111] *Ibid.*, p. 833.
[112] Welles, II, 485.

tive. But the rest of the President's advisers were decidedly in favor of its being sent; Dennison and Harlan, in particular, advocated a vigorous policy, and Welles took the same view, though he inquired a little naively, or maliciously, why so much stronger a tone was taken in relation to Austria than had been assumed towards France. The President's acquiescence can hardly be doubted. And so, after due deliberation, this third warning to the Austrian government went forth on its way to Vienna.

In the meantime John Lothrop Motley remained preternaturally calm. He could not take seriously the threat involved in the sending of a few thousand volunteers to Mexico. It did not enter his head (as it must enter the head of the sceptical historian) that Seward was taking a high tone for the simple reason that it seemed wholly possible to take it successfully, and to pile up treasures in the political Heaven at home. So impervious was he to the diplomatic, or the political, necessities of the occasion, on the receipt of the first of Seward's three instructions, that he wrote a long and argumentative despatch to Washington, indicating his reluctance to press the matter upon the attention of the Austrian government.[113] This despatch, with a candor which is unusual in diplomats, he showed to Count Mensdorff, the Austrian Foreign Minister. But Seward's No. 176 forced him to alter his tone. On May 6, in obedience to Seward's instructions, he sent to Mensdorff a formal protest against the sending of Austrian

[113] *Diplomatic Correspondence,* 1865, part 3, pp. 833-36.

troops to Mexico. The protest was carefully worded, and Motley strove to make it as palatable as possible. But there was none the less a clear assertion, not only of the point of view of his government, but of the principles of the Monroe Doctrine. " The feelings of the American people and its successive governments," wrote the American minister, " exhibited through the whole of their national career, and publicly manifested on many solemn occasions, in regard to forcible and armed interference by European powers with established institutions on the western continent, are, whether they be deemed reasonable or not, and whatever weight may be attached to them by European opinion, a matter of history and known to mankind. Such interference was long ago proclaimed, on the highest official authority, as of necessity to be considered a manifestation of an unfriendly disposition toward the United States. It is hardly expedient, therefore, on this occasion to consume more of your excellency's time by the exposition of a subject so familiar to you." [114]

To the statement of these views Count Mensdorff returned a wholly conciliatory reply. The moment was hardly propitious for any other. Austria was on the verge of a war with Prussia. It would have been silly to alienate the United States at such a moment. The advice proffered by the Duc de Gramont, the French minister at Vienna, to " act with the utmost prudence, and prevent the embarkation of the volunteers," was advice good enough to be taken. On the 20th of May,

[114] *Ibid.*, p. 843.

the Austrian minister indicated to Motley that, " without being able to agree with all the views developed in the many-times cited note," the necessary measures had been taken to meet the views of the United States.[115] Thus Seward in his relations with Austria, won a clear-cut and decisive victory. Austria, no more than France, was desirous of picking a quarrel with the government at Washington.

In the correspondence with Austria, and especially in the promptitude with which it was communicated to Congress, there was, one feels tolerably certain, a considerable infusion of domestic politics. It is not strange, indeed, that as the breach between President Johnson and the national legislature widened, Seward, who stood by the President, should seek to strengthen the hands of the Executive by a popular foreign policy; nor indeed, these considerations aside, was it unlike the wily man in the State Department to make frequent appeals to public opinion. If to some persons there may seem in this anxiety to please the public, and to be applauded by them, a little of the element of demagogy, it should be remembered that Seward had practised a long and masterly restraint in his dealings with France. And it should be remembered, too, that the very fact that Seward adopted the strong tone when he felt it safe to do so, and freely capitalized, or sought to capitalize, this appearance of bold policy, is striking evidence of the attachment to the Monroe Doctrine which the people of the United States manifested in 1865 and

[115] *Ibid.,* p. 845.

35

1866. There can be no doubt whatever that the Secretary of State struck a popular chord in his diplomatic correspondence.

Throughout the rest of 1866, a certain acrid character characterized diplomatic exchanges with France. On April 25, for example, replying to Montholon's assurances that the French forces would be withdrawn from Mexico, the Secretary of State, while expressing a desire for " a cordial renewal of the traditional friendship " none the less suggested " that the continuance of the intervention during the period limited will necessarily be regarded with concern and apprehension by the masses of our people, and perhaps by Congress," and added this still more disquieting paragraph:

" Under these circumstances our army of observation must also be continued in some proportion upon the southern bank of the Rio Grande. This situation will be not altogether conformable with our national sentiment and habits. Moreover, no one can certainly reckon upon the exercise of so much prudence on the part of commanders and forces confronting each other across a boundary as to remove all fears of unpremeditated disturbances and collisions. Therefore, the more promptly the intervention shall be brought to an end, the sooner and more complete will be the return of the cordial good feelings which both governments so earnestly desire." [116] On the 12th of May, on the basis of newspaper rumors indicating the departure of troops from France for Mexico, Seward instructed Bigelow to ask explana-

[116] *Ibid.,* 1866, vol. I, 78-79.

tions from Drouyn de l'Huys.[117] On August 16 he protested to Montholon at the nomination of Generals Osmont and Friand to be Minister of War and Minister of Finance in the government of Mexico.[118] On October 8 he informed Bigelow that " frequent incidents of various kinds, presented by the press in France and in Mexico as indicating a disposition on the part of the Emperor to depart from that engagement (*i. e.,* the engagement to withdraw from Mexico), have unavoidably produced a wide popular distrust of even the Emperor's sincerity in making the engagement, and of his good faith in fulfilling it." And in November came one of the most interesting and dramatic, if not one of the most important incidents, in the long history of the Mexican imbroglio.

There can be little doubt, after April, 1866, of the desire of the French government to get out of Mexico. In the debates in the Chamber in June, Jules Favre was allowed to attack the Mexican policy of the government in every phase without the voice of one of the ministers being raised in its defense; [119] Drouyn himself spoke to Bigelow of that " wretched, miserable Mexico; " [120] the American minister, in his correspondence with Seward, commented on the wide latitude allowed to the press in dealing with the problem; [121] and if further evidence of the inwards of French policy were needed,

[117] *Ibid.,* p. 306.
[118] *Ibid.,* pp. 381-2.
[119] Bigelow, III, 460.
[120] *Ibid.,* p. 461.
[121] *Ibid.,* p. 529.

it can be found in the promptitude with which the ap-
pointments of Generals Osmont and Friand to Mexican
government posts were declared to be inadmissible by
the government in Paris, and by the despatch of the
mission of General Castelnau to speed the evacuation.
Nor did the fall of Drouyn de l'Huys and the appointment of the Marquis de Moustier as minister of foreign affairs presage any change in French policy, as
Bigelow was assured in an interview with the new incumbent on October 11.[122] But military considerations
altered somewhat the French plans for evacuation, and
led to the decision to bring out all the troops in the
spring of 1867, instead of in three installments as stipulated in the preceding April. This possibility was first
brought within the possible purview of the American
government in an obscurely worded despatch of October
16 from Moustier to Montholon.[123] But it first came to
the attention of Seward through a communication of
Bigelow's of November 8,[124] which arrived in Washington only just before Congress was to begin its sessions. The Secretary of State must have known (indeed
Bigelow assured him) that there was nothing in this
change of plan which indicated a lack of good faith on
the part of Louis Napoleon. But none the less he took
a most extraordinary step. He despatched a long cablegram to Paris, at a cost of some $13,000, protesting
against the alteration in the French project of evacuation, and at the same time before it could have been

122 *Ibid.*, p. 575.
123 Published in *ibid.*, pp. 581-2.
124 *Ibid.*, *pp.* 598-600.

received in Paris, he gave it to the American press. " We cannot acquiesce : " he wrote boldly, " First, because the term next spring as appointed for the entire evacuation, is indefinite and vague. Second, because we have no authority for stating to Congress and to the American people that we have now a better guarantee for the withdrawal of the whole expeditionary force in the spring than we have hitherto had for the withdrawal of a part in November. Third, in full reliance upon at least a literal performance of the Emperor's existing agreement, we have taken measures, while facilitating the anticipated French evacuation, to cooperate with the republican government of Mexico for promoting the pacification of that country and for the early and complete restoration of the proper constitutional authority of that government. As a part of those measures, Mr. Campbell, our newly appointed minister, attended by Lieutenant-General Sherman, has been sent to Mexico in order to confer with President Juarez on subjects which are deeply interesting to the United States and of vital importance to Mexico." [125]

This was hardly more than a bald piece of domestic politics in the guise of a diplomatic note. Fortunately, perhaps, Bigelow recognized it as such. He never presented Seward's cablegram to the Quai d'Orsay; he transmitted only a mild interpretation of the same; and he accepted an equivocal reply.[126] So, too, did the Secretary of State himself. The episode has its principal

[125] *Ibid.*, pp. 609-11.
[126] The documents are in *ibid.*, pp. 612-18.

importance in the light which it throws on Seward's diplomatic methods, and on the public opinion which made such a political manoeuver possible or conceivable.

There are two other incidents in the course of the year 1866 which are of interest to the student of the Mexican question in its relation to the Monroe Doctrine. One of these is the debate which took place in the Senate in June on the motion to appropriate certain funds for the Paris exposition of 1867. To this motion Senator Grimes of Iowa offered an amendment making the appointment of any officer, or the payment of any funds, contingent on assurances by the French government that its troops would be " immediately withdrawn " from Mexico.[127] The diplomatic impropriety of any such suggestion is fairly obvious, and it seems probable that Grimes's whole object was political. But the debate which followed is none the less interesting on this account. For virtually every Senator who spoke either for or against the amendment alluded to the Monroe Doctrine, by name, and indicated his intense belief in its principles. The taking root of the declaration of 1823 in the public mind is thus once again interestingly illustrated.[128]

---

[127] *Cong. Globe,* 39th Cong., 1st Sess., p. 3138. The full text of the resolution is as follows: " Provided, however, That no officer shall be appointed and no money paid under the provisions of this resolution, until the Imperial Government of France shall first give ample and reliable assurances to the Government that the French troops and all French military officers shall be immediately withdrawn from the just territorial jurisdiction of the republic of Mexico."

[128] This debate is in *ibid.,* pp. 3155-3161.

The connection between domestic politics and the upholding of the Monroe Doctrine is also to be discovered in the extraordinary political manoeuver of Seward in the fall of the year, when President Johnson set out on his famous "swing around the circle." It occurred to the Secretary of State that it might be well to capitalize the stand which he had taken against France. He therefore invited Romero to accompany him. The Mexican guilelessly accepted. And so at the end of August, in company with the President, the Secretary, General Grant and numerous others, he set out from Washington. Everywhere he met with great popular enthusiasm for the cause of Mexico. In New York in a great banquet at which the mayor presided, he was importuned to speak. At Auburn he was presented to the crowd by Seward as the man " in whose behalf and with a view to the salvation of whose country, the President of the United States has indicated that foreign intervention must cease November 1 next." At Buffalo he was again presented, and the Secretary himself proposed three cheers for Mexico, which were given with a will. Similar scenes were enacted at Dunkirk, at Cleveland, at Toledo, at Detroit. But finally Romero began to suspect the truth. Perceiving that he was being exploited for purposes of domestic politics, he decided to be exploited no longer. Mildly objecting to the fact that his expenses had been paid for him wherever the Presidential party stopped, and declaring that his health would not stand the strain of the journey, he indicated to Seward his intention of returning to Washington.[129]

[129] For this whole episode, see Romero, VIII, 235-40.

But has there ever been, in the history of our diplomacy, a similar attempt to use the representative of a foreign power for purposes of domestic politics? William Henry Seward was a very able man, but his sense of the proprieties was, it must be confessed, rather extraordinary. On the other hand, it is safe to say that he would never have taken any such course had he not been sure that the diplomatic game with France was won, and that there was nothing further to fear.

Won, of course, it was by the fall of 1866. It is not necessary, indeed, to pursue further the melancholy history of the Mexican experiment. There is nothing in the period which runs from December, 1866, through the completion of the evacuation on March 12, 1867, and the collapse of Maximilian's government, and his own execution at Querétaro which would tend to throw further light on the relation of the whole matter to the Monroe Doctrine. The outstanding facts are by this time wholly clear; in France an increasing solicitude with regard to the attitude of the United States; in America an extraordinary and general interest in the principles of the Monroe Doctrine as applied to Mexico. There is more danger of minimizing than of exaggerating the historical significance of the great diplomatic shibboleth which we have been examining in its relation to the ill-fated experiment of Louis Napoleon in the New World.

Yet we must beware of a false general perspective with regard to the American view of the principles of 1823, in 1866; the French invasion of Mexico undoubtedly aroused the most vigorous opposition on the ground of those principles; but not all armed action in the New World was so jealously regarded. It will help us to attain a fairer and juster view of the exact status of the Doctrine at the end of the Civil War if before concluding this chapter, we turn for a little to consider the Spanish-Chilean war of 1866.

In this war neither public opinion nor governmental policy went beyond the limits which might have been indicated from the history of the ante-bellum period. Both, indeed, were, if anything rather more conservative than the history of that period might lead one to expect.

In the crisis in the relations of Spain and Peru in 1864 the sympathies of the people of Chile were, not unnaturally, upon the side of their fellow Americans. It seems fairly clear, moreover, that the attitude of the Chilean government reflected these sympathies, and led it to assume an attitude which deviated, in some measure, at least, from that of impartial neutrality.[130] The result was a very natural irritation at Madrid, and an irritation equally natural but still more overpowering on the part of Admiral Pareja, the Spanish commander in the waters of the Pacific. Had a better spirit been shown, this irritation could no doubt have been dissipated. Indeed, in May of 1865, the conciliatory Spanish

[130] For an excellent discussion of this matter, see Becker, II, 739 et seq. The Spanish grievances are here summed up, though not in the fullest detail. For the Chilean point of view, see Diplomatic Correspondence, 1866, vol. 2, pp. 349 et seq.

minister at Santiago and the Chilean foreign minister were on the verge of an agreement. But the stormy petrel, Pareja, refused to support these efforts at an accord; at home the Narváez ministry, disposed to seek a settlement, was supplanted by O'Donnell; and the new cabinet, perhaps anxious to recover the credit which its leader had lost in Santo Domingo, embarked upon the policy of prestige which has been so often, so foolishly, and oftentimes so ineffectually attempted by the chancelleries of both the Old World and the New. Accordingly, in September an ultimatum was despatched by the Admiral, acting under instructions, to the Chilean government, demanding, amongst other concessions, a salute of 21 guns; and when Chilean pride resisted this offensive demand, the Chilean coast was declared in a state of blockade, and a new and futile contest of arms initiated in the New World.

In relation to this contest, the attitude of Secretary Seward was from the first one very different from that assumed in the case of Mexico. In the struggle thus initiated, the good offices of the United States were more than once offered,[131] but the policy of the American government was most perspicuously stated in a des-

---

[131] *Diplomatic Correspondence*, 1865, part 2, p. 553, note to Perry, dated August 22, 1865, suggesting arbitration. *Ibid.*, 1866, vol. 2, p. 364, to Nelson, American minister to Chile, requesting him to offer his good offices when there is any chance of success, and *ibid.*, p. 426, sounding Asta Buruaga, the Chilean minister at Washington, as to a renewal of good offices. Also Washington, Dept. of State, Instructions, Chile, No. 9, June 2, 1866.

patch to Mr. Kilpatrick, the American minister at Santiago, and dated June 2, 1866. "The policy of the United States," wrote the Secretary, "in regard to the several Spanish-American states is, or ought to be, well known now, after the exposition it has received during the last five years. We avoid in all cases giving encouragement to expectations, which, in the varying course of events, we might find ourselves unable to fulfill; and we desire to be known as doing more than we promise rather than falling short of our engagements. On the other hand, we maintain and insist, with all the decision and energy which is compatible with our existing neutrality, that the republican system which is accepted by the people in any one of those states shall not be wantonly assailed, and that it shall not be subverted as an end of a lawful war by European powers. We thus give to those republics the moral support of a sincere, liberal, and, as we think, it will appear, a useful friendship. We could claim from foreign states no concession to our own political, moral, and material principles or interests, if we should not conform our own proceedings, in the needful intercourse with foreign states, to the just rules of the law of nations. We therefore concede to every nation the right to make peace or war, for such causes other than political or ambitious as it thinks right and wise. In such wars as are waged between nations which are in friendship with ourselves, if they are not pushed, like the French war in Mexico, to the political point before mentioned, we do not intervene, but remain neutral, conceding nothing to one belligerent that we do not concede to the other, and allowing to one belligerent what we allow to the other." [132]

This interesting despatch sums up much that ought to be summed up as to the Monroe Doctrine in 1866. It illustrates the fact, that despite his bluster, his fanfaronade, and his plays to the political galleries, the attitude of Seward with regard to the Doctrine was fundamentally conservative. Assaults upon its fundamental principles he would and did repel; but he did not believe, as have some American statesmen of later date, that any kind of armed action by a European state in the New World should be the occasion for the United States to assume a posture of defiance. In the dispute between Chile and Spain, he stuck to the orthodox and strict construction of the principles of 1823. The laws of neutrality were enforced strictly, indeed too strictly to satisfy the Chileans. [133] Even the Spanish bombardment of Valparaiso did not cause the United States to deviate from the course which it had marked out. [134]

The policy thus pursued, it may confidently be stated, was in accord with the views of the people of the United States. We are fortunate in having an excellent, if somewhat discouraged, analysis of American opinion in the reminiscences of Benjamin Vicuña Mackenna,

[132] *Diplomatic Correspondence,* 1866, vol. 2, p. 413.

[133] On this matter see Vicuña Mackenna, *Diez Meses de Misión á los Estados Unidos* (2 vols., Santiago, 1867), especially I, 437-92.

[134] Kilpatrick comments on the resentment of the Chileans at seeing the American squadron move out of the harbor, as the Spaniards prepared for action. *Diplomatic Correspondence,* 1866, vol. 2, p. 408.

Chilean publicist and man of letters, who was sent to the United States on a mission of propaganda toward the end of 1865.[135] On his arrival in New York Mackenna was at first successful in securing favorable notices on Chile in the press; but he marked with disgust that as soon as the British newspapers arrived, and it was seen that they took the same side, there was a marked tendency for the American dailies to "wipe their boots on our manifestos, and call us spoiled and disobedient children."[136] Turning to another kind of activity, the Chilean organized a great meeting in Cooper Union, on the subject of the Monroe Doctrine, and this meeting was held on January 6, 1866. The meeting was attended by many celebrities, and was a great success. It was opened by none other than Ephraim George Squier; William Cullen Bryant was called to the chair; letters were read from eminent public men, amongst them James A. Garfield and Schuyler Colfax, endorsing the Monroe Doctrine; but the press accounts of the occasion indicate quite clearly that it was Mexico, and not Chile, that was in the minds of the participants.[137] In Washington the war between Chile and Spain aroused the very slightest interest; it was never the subject of serious debate in Congress; and it does not seem strange that the disgusted agent of the Chilean government came to the disgusted conclusion that the

[135] Mackenna gives his instructions in I, *op. cit.,* 12-14. They are dated October 1, 1865.

[136] *Ibid.,* p. 248.

[137] *New York Herald,* January 8, 1866.

Monroe Doctrine was mostly humbug. What was not humbug, he wrote in his account of his mission, was simple plagiarism, a theft of ideas from George Canning and Thomas Jefferson.[138] While these severe judgments undoubtedly reflect in part the indignities to which Mackenna believed himself subjected in the United States (he was arrested for a violation of the neutrality laws),[139] they seem also to be borne out in fact. Of any sentiment looking toward intervention in the War of the Pacific on the part of the United States, I can find no trace. The American people were, in 1866, interested in matters much nearer home, and when their vision turned abroad, it turned, as we have seen, not towards Chile, towards Mexico.

In reverting to this latter question, there are certain concluding observations which may well be made. The French intervention in Mexico consolidated, or it may be gave expression to the consolidation of, American public opinion on the Monroe Doctrine. And the policy of Seward vindicated that policy abroad. In the case of France, as indeed in the case of Spain, we detect a growing respect for the American dogma in the events of 1861 to 1867. The great nation which had risen phoenix-like from the ashes of a Civil War, which had so successfully resisted domestic disunion and foreign intrigue, was, henceforth, when it willed, to speak with a new authority. If the day had not yet come when Europe was to give its final assent, its sanction even, to

[138] Mackenna, I, 412 et seq.
[139] For this episode, see ibid., pp. 437-68.

the conception of the Monroe Doctrine, it was at least true that the greatest perils to which that Doctrine has yet been subjected had passed.

On the other hand, it is to be doubted whether the defense of the Doctrine, in these days of Civil War, had notably strengthened the United States in its relations with Latin America. The policy of Seward had been by no means sufficiently vigorous to satisfy the exacting Romero; the policy of Seward in refusing the invitation to the Congress at Lima and in adopting a rigid neutrality in the war between Chile and Spain had given evidence of the limits set to the announced ideals of the United States; and a sceptical Latin might have been pardoned for believing that national egotism and national feeling would direct the diplomacy of the American government no less than that of any other nation. Noble as was the language in which Seward spoke to Louis Napoleon, resounding as were the periods of his diplomatic correspondence, they reflected no extraordinary altruism; and of all American diplomatic cant the most objectionable is that which pretends the contrary. Whatever else we may think or say with regard to the Monroe Doctrine, let us be honest enough to admit that it was, at the beginning, was in 1867, and has been ever since, an expression, not of international idealism, but of the interests, as statesmen and people have understood them, of the United States.

The evacuation of Mexico by the French marks an epoch in the history of the Monroe Doctrine. The sharp-

est challenge ever made to the principles of 1823 had
been completely defeated. The national sentiment of
the people of the United States, and their growing
attachment to the great dogma had been a potent, if not
a decisive influence in frustrating the designs of a first-
rate European power. No informed publicist, no responsible statesman, could henceforward ignore the
existence of a powerful prejudice amongst the American
people against the intervention of Old World states in
the affairs of the New. Never again (the statement has
been well weighed) was that prejudice directly and un-
yieldingly challenged. There were to be episodes in
which the Monroe Doctrine was to figure, and to figure
prominently, to be sure; there were even to be episodes
in which the American people believed its principles to
be in danger of flagrant violation; but there were to be
none where it was unqualifiedly challenged. The collapse of French policy in Mexico divides two separate
eras in the history of the great diplomatic principle
whose origins and developments we have been examining.

Illogical though it may seem therefore from one viewpoint, since it falls in the middle of an administration
and in the middle of the term of a great Secretary of
State, the discussion of the Mexican question may well
end this second volume. For the events which we have
just subjected to examination are the end of a great
development. As we look back across the forty years we
have traversed, we see a sight that may well arrest our
gaze. We are aware of the growth in the American

mind of a great principle of action, little noticed in the
thirties, revived in the forties, taking root in the fifties,
consolidated and vindicated in the sixties. We see that
principle gain in authority in Europe no less than in
America, forgotten in the thirties, distrusted and challenged in the forties, feared in the fifties, emerging
triumphant from an attempt to overthrow it in the
sixties. It is not our purpose to glorify that principle.
As yet, in the actual operation of American diplomacy,
fundamentally conservative, involving no absolute veto
on the political or military action of European states in
the New World, it none the less contained as developed
by a Polk, a Douglas, or a Buchanan the elements of
an aggressive and of an exclusive policy. It is already
easy to understand how it might be exaggerated to cover
ends which were far from the views of its framers and
to give a support to prejudices which neither are in accord with the interests of the United States nor with
its own well understood and properly restricted meaning.
But in the main it cannot be said, it could not be said
even by a severely hostile critic, that in the period from
1826 to 1867 the Monroe Doctrine had been seriously
abused. It had not led (though there were those who
would have liked to see it lead) to any questionable
policy of expansion. It had not prevented the vindication by European powers of their claims against American states. It had not impeded the innocent action of
European diplomacy in the New World.

There is a certain danger in the development of any
dogma. There is a threat to the soundest diplomatic

action in the growth of rigid formulae. Calhoun in his day and Seward in his were arguing a good case when they pleaded for a certain flexibility of mind in the application of the principles of 1823. But one may wonder whether in a democracy it is possible to get away entirely from catchwords. The Monroe Doctrine by 1867 had become such a catchword. Reflecting, as it seemed, at any rate, and still seems, to the majority of Americans, a not unsound conception of national interest, it has taken deep lodgment in the American mind. What we have witnessed is not merely a chapter in the history of American diplomacy. What we have witnessed is a chapter in the history of ideas, something vastly more important. In time no doubt those ideas may be modified. But the years that follow 1867 were most certainly to see no such modification. They were to see only the further development of the Monroe Doctrine, and a still deeper popular attachment to its principles. The history of the foreign policy of the United States down to our own time is impregnated with its spirit. The historian who seeks to analyze, in the field of politics, the ruling thoughts and prejudices of a great people, will, in the case of America, always be drawn in fascinated curiosity to the dogma which Monroe enunciated, which Polk endowed with new vitality, which Seward vindicated, and which, as Maximilian laid down his life at Querétaro, was still to have before it so interesting and important a future.

Bibliographical Note

Manuscript Materials:

The principal manuscripts used in this study are the collections of diplomatic correspondence in the archives of the various powers. I have made use of the files of the State Department, of the British Public Record Office, of the archives of the Ministère des Affaires Etrangères, and have had materials copied for me at the Archivo del Estado in Madrid and the Ministerio del Estado at Bogotá. Much important correspondence has been made available through the magnificent work of the Library of Congress in procuring transcripts from foreign archives; of major importance for this study are those of the Haus-archiv of the unfortunate Maximilian. The collections of the personal papers of American statesmen have also been drawn upon, but, for the purposes of this study, little material has been found with regard to the views of the Presidents or Secretaries of State which does not appear either in print or in the State Department.

Collections of Published Source Materials:

In the category of published source material of general value must be put the records of debates in the principal countries with which this study is concerned, the *Register of Debates* and *Congressional Globe* for the United States, Hansard's *Parliamentary Debates* for Great Britain, the *Archives Parlementaires* to July, 1839 and the *Moniteur Universel* 1839- for France, and *El Diario de las Cortes* for Spain. A mass of diplomatic correspondence, often not adequately exploited, is to be found in the Executive Documents, both House and Senate, and in the *British and Foreign State Papers*. Important citations with subject references are to be found in J. B. Moore (*A Digest of International Law*)

(8 volumes, Washington, 1906) especially Volume VI, pages 368 to 605. A considerable amount of newspaper and periodical material has been laid under contribution, as may be seen by references in the text or in the bibliography by sections.

Bibliography of Bibliographies

Besides the obvious bibliographical aids in diplomatic history, such, for example, as Adelaide R. Hasse, *Index to United States Documents relating to Foreign Affairs* (3 volumes, Washington, 1914) no student of the Monroe Doctrine should fail to acknowledge indebtedness to the admirable work of Herbert Kraus, *Die Monroe-Doktrin* (Berlin, 1913) with its extended bibliographical data, and to the bibliography prepared by Mr. H. H. B. Meyer of the Library of Congress, H. H. B. Meyer, *List of References on the Monroe Doctrine* (Washington, 1919).

Materials on Special Subjects

FALKLAND ISLANDS

A considerable mass of correspondence is to be found in *British and Foreign State Papers,* Volume XX, pages 311-441, and Volume XXII, pages 1366-94, and in Senate Executive Documents, 32nd Congress, 1st Session, Doc. 109. Of secondary works, of most importance are Julius L. Goebel, *The Struggle for the Falkland Islands. A Study in Legal and Diplomatic History* (New Haven, 1927), the best treatment, and Paul Groussac, *Les Iles Malouines. Nouvel Exposé d'un Vieux Litige* (Buenos Ayres, 1910). There is an excellent account of the whole controversy in Adolfo Saldías, *Historia de la Confederación Argentina—Rosas y su Epoca* (5 volumes, Paris, 1881-87).

FRANCO-BRAZILIAN BOUNDARY

An excellent collection of source materials is to be found in the proceedings of the arbitration commission which finally determined the question. See especially, *Les Frontières entre le Brésil et la Guyane Française. Mémoire présenté par les Etats-Unis du Brésil au Gouvernement de la Confédération Suisse, Arbitre chois selon les stipulations du traité conclu à Rio de Janeiro le 10 Avril, 1897, entre le Brésil et la France* (3 volumes, Paris, 1899), and also *Second Mémoire présenté par les Etats-Unis du Brésil au Gouvernement de la Confédération Suisse* (3 volumes, Paris, 1899). A good secondary account is in J. C. da Silva, *L'Oyapoc et l'Amazone. Question Brésilienne et Française* (2 volumes, Paris, 1899).

MONARCHY IN MEXICO BEFORE 1845

For political conditions prior to 1845 the following are especially useful: J. M. Gutierrez de Estrada, *Carta al S. E. Presidente de la República* (Mexico, 1840) and *Méjico y el Archiduque Fernando Maximiliano de Austria* (Mexico, 1862), able arguments for monarchy by one of its principal partisans, and D. J. Hidalgo, *Apuntes para Escribir la Historia de los Proyectos de Monarquía en México desde le Reinado de Carlos III hasta la Instalación del Emperador Maximiliano* (Paris, 1868). Other works containing interesting analyses of political conditions in Mexico are: E. K. H. Freiherr von Richthofen, *Die Aüssern und Inneren Politischen Zustände der Republik Mexico seit deren Unabhängkeit bis auf dis neueste Zeit* (Berlin, 1859), I. Löwenstern, *Le Mexique. Souvenirs d'un Voyage* (Paris, 1843), and L. M. del Rivero, *Méjico en 1842* (Madrid, 1844).

MONARCHY IN COLOMBIA

Documents connected with the movement for monarchy in Colombia are to be found in D. F. O'Leary, *Correspondencia de Estranjeros notables con el Libertador* (Madrid, Editorial America, 1920), and in *Hispania; politica, commercio, literatura, artes y ciencias* (5 volumes, London, 1912-16). Secondary material of value includes A. C. Rivas, *Ensayos de Historia Politica*

36

y *Diplomática. La Diplomacía de los Estados Unidos y La Monarquía en Colombia* (Madrid, 1916), and in D. G. Goebel, *William Henry Harrison* (Indianapolis, 1926). Some suggestive comment, drawn from the sources on the monarchical movement in Central America is to be found in Lorenzo Montufar, *Reseña Histórica de Centro-America* (7 volumes, Guatemala, 1881), IV, 70-80.

THE FRENCH INTERVENTION OF 1838 IN MEXICO

From the Mexican side, the most important published source material is that of Antonio de la Peña y Reyes, *La Primera Guerra entre México y Francia,* Volume XXVII, in *Archivo Histórico Diplomático Mexicano* (Mexico, 1927). On the French side, attention should be called to P. Blanchard and A. Dauzats, *San Juan de Ulúa. Relation de l'Expédition Française au Mexique, sous les ordres de M. le Contre-amiral Baudin, Suivi de notes et documents, et d'un aperçu général sur l'état actuel du Texas, par M. E. Massin* (Paris, 1839), the most important material, especially naval correspondence. The American Correspondence, as far as published, is to be found in House Executive Documents, 25th Congress, 3rd Session, Doc. No. 211. Secondary accounts of some value are those in G. L. Rives, *The United States and Mexico* (2 volumes, New York, 1913), and Paul Thureau-Dangin, *Histoire de la Monarchie de Juillet* (7 volumes, Paris, 1884-92).

INTERVENTION IN ARGENTINA

Instructions of the French minister with regard to the intervention in the Argentine are to be found in F. P. Guizot, *Histoire Parlementaire de la France* (5 volumes, Paris, 1863), III, which also sheds light on the debates. An Argentine view of the question is contained in Florencio Varela, *Sobre la Convención de 29 Octubre de 1840. Desarrollo y Desenlace de la Cuestión Francesa en el Rio de la Plata* (Montevideo, 1840). An excellent summary of events written by one who had a part in the later intervention is that of A. de Brossard, *Considérations Historiques et Politiques sur les Républiques de La Plata dans leur Rapports avec la France et l'Angleterre* (Paris, 1850). Of secondary works, special mention should be made of J. F. Cady, *Foreign Intervention in the Rio de la Plata 1838-50* (Philadelphia, 1929) with an excellent bibliography. Valuable also are Saldías, *op. cit.*, especially Volume III, pp. 298-320, M. A. Pelliza, *La Dictadura de Rosas* (Buenos Ayres, 1917), and C. A. Villanueva, *Historia de la República Argentina* (2 volumes, Paris, 1914). On the Argentine intervention, as indeed, on all interventions down to 1860, attention must be called to the useful article by Falcke, " Die Friedensblockade," in *Zeitschrift für internationales privat- und- öffentliches Recht,* XIX, 68-175.

POLK DOCTRINE AND ITS AFTERMATH

The Polk papers in the Library of Congress and the Buchanan papers in the library of the Pennsylvania Historical Society yield a little not to be found in the regular correspondence. Polk's diary, *Diary of James K. Polk*, edited by M. M. Quaife (4 volumes, Chicago, 1910) gives the reaction of the President, especially on the Oregon question, and the Buchanan writings, *Works of James Buchanan,* edited by J. B. Moore (12 volumes, Philadelphia, 1908-11), give all his most important instructions for the period 1845-49. E. D. Adams, *British Diplomatic Correspondence Concerning the Republic of Texas* (Texas State Historical Association, Austin, 1918) contains some interesting material. There are also a number of documents published in E. D. Adams, " English Interest in Annexation of Texas," *American Historical Review,* XIV, 744-64. The Guizot speeches are to be found in Guizot, *Histoire Parlementaire, op. cit.,* IV.

For the Anglo-French intervention in the Argentine see the *British and Foreign State Papers,* XXXIII, 930 *et seq.,* for the instructions to the British ministers. See also Eugène Guillemot. *Affaires de la Plata. Extrait de la Correspondence de M. Eugène Guillemot pendant sa mission dans l'Amérique du Sud* (Paris, 1849), and Brossard, *op. cit.*

For the Yucatan episode the works of Joaquin Baranda, *Recordaciones Históricas* (2 volumes, Mexico, 1913), and Eligio Ancona, *Historia de Yucatan desde la Época más Remota hasta Nuestros Dias* (4 volumes, Merida, Mexico, 1878-80) are valuable. See also an article by M. W. Williams, " Secessionist Diplomacy of Yucatan," *Hispanic American Historical Review*, X, 132-43.

The Flores project is described in C. Destruge, *La Expedición Flores- Proyecto de Monarquiá Americana,* 1846-7 (Guayaquil, 1906), and the Pan-American conference of 1847 receives special attention in J. M. Torres Caicedo, *Unión Latino-America* (Paris, 1865) with documents.

Brief comment on the monarchical plans of 1845-6 in Mexico is to be found in Antonio Pirala, *Historia Contemporánea de la España. Anales desde 1843 hasta la Conclusión de la Actual Guerra Civil* (6 volumes, Madrid, 1875-79). See also J. Becker, *Historia de las Relaciones Exteriores de España durante El Siglo XIX* (3 volumes, Madrid, 1924). The valuable correspondence of Nicholas Trist also throws some light on the problem, see Senate Executive Documents, 30th Congress, 1st Session, Doc. No. 52, and House Executive Documents, 30th Congress, 1st Session, Docs. Nos. 56, 60, 69.

CENTRAL AMERICA

On the question of Central America, there is much first-hand published material. Galindo's mission is to be found treated in Senate Executive Documents, 32nd Congress, 2nd Session, Doc. No. 27. Stephen's mission to Central America receives some attention in his book, J. L. Stephens, *Incidents of Travel in Central America, Chiapas, and Yucatan* (2 volumes, New York, 1848). The dispute over the Bay Islands is treated in E. G.

Squier, *Notes on Central America* (New York, 1855).
The occupation of San Juan in 1841 is dealt with in
House Executive Documents, 31st Congress, 1st Session, Doc. No. 75. There are important documents on
this subject also in *British Parliamentary Papers* for
1847-48. For the question of the inter-oceanic canal and
the Clayton-Bulwer treaty, information with regard to
the mission of Elijah Hise is to be found in " Letters of
Bancroft and Buchanan," *American Historical Review,*
V, 95-102, and in House Executive Documents, 31st
Congress, 1st Session, Doc. No. 75. Squier, *op. cit.,* is
also useful, and see also the *Democratic Review* for 1852.
British Parliamentary Papers for 1856 are very valuable, as are Senate Executive Documents, 34th Congress,
1st and 2nd Sessions, Doc. No. 25, and House Executive
Documents, 34th Congress, 1st Session, Doc. No. 1, and
35th Congress, 2nd Session, Doc. No. 2.

For the Bélly episode, see Felix Bélly, *L'Isthme
Américain. Notes d'un premier voyage* (Bruxelles,
1899), *Percement de l'Isthme de Panama par le Canal
de Nicaragua. Exposé de la Question* (Paris, 1858),
and *A travers l'Amérique Centrale. Le Nicaragua et le
Canal Inter-Océanique* (2 volumes, Paris, 1867).

The most important secondary works are M. W.
Williams, *Anglo-American Isthmian Diplomacy 1815-
1915* (Washington, 1916), an excellent study with bibliography, and I. D. Travis, *British Rule in Central
America: or a Sketch of Mosquito History* (No. 5 in
Publications of Michigan Political Science Association,
1895), and *The History of the Clayton-Bulwer Treaty*
(No. 8 in same series, 1900). Another suggestive work,
based on the archives of Colombia is Raimundo Rivas,
Colombia y los Estados-Unidos, 1810-1850 (Bogotá,
1915).

SANTO DOMINGO

The published source material on the question of
American relations with the Dominican Republic is
meager. The mission of Benjamin E. Green is covered
in Senate Executive Documents, 33rd Congress, 1st

Session, Doc. No. 12, and that of Robert M. Walsh in 32nd Congress, 1st Session, Doc. No. 113. For the period 1861-65, the series of *Papers Relating to Foreign Affairs, Accompanying the Annual Message of the President,* more commonly known as *Diplomatic Correspondence,* contain some of the principal exchanges between Seward and the American minister in Madrid. On the side of Spain, important material bearing on the intervention is to be found in *Documentos Relativos á la Cuestión de Santo Domingo. Sometidos al Congreso de los Diputados* (Madrid, 1865). These include the correspondence both of the minister of foreign affairs and of the minister of war. A first-hand account of the intervention is also to be found in El General Gándara, *Anexión y Guerra de Santo Domingo* (2 volumes, Madrid, 1884). Copious comments from Spanish newspaper opinion are to be found in Nuñez de Arce, *Santo Domingo* (Madrid, 1865), and Spanish views are to be found in Felix de Bona, *Cuba, Santo Domingo, y Puerto Rico* (Madrid, 1861) and S. Ferrer Couto, *Reincorporación de Santo Domingo á España. Breves consideraciones sobre esta acontecimento* (Madrid, 1861).

An interesting reflection of American public opinion with regard to the joint mediation is to be found in " Rumored Occupation of Santo Domingo," *Democratic Review,* 1853, and in B. C. Clark, *Remarks upon the United States Intervention in Haiti, with Comments upon the Correspondence connected with it* (Boston, 1853). French views on the Dominican question in the forties and fifties are to be found in Pelletier de St. Rémy, *Etude et Solution Nouvelle de la Question Haitienne* (Paris, 1846), and in articles by Gaston d'Alaux in *Revue des Deux Mondes,* XIX, 1851.

Of secondary works there is a decided dearth. Sumner Welles, *Naboth's Vineyard, The Dominican Republic 1844-1924* (New York, 1928) is the most thorough treatment of the history of the Dominican Republic and of its relations with the United States to be found in English and is written from the sources, containing excellent commentary and much material not to be found elsewhere. A useful general work by a Dominican historian is José Gabriel Garcío, *Compendio de la Historia de Santo Domingo* (3 volumes, Santo Domingo, 1896).

MEXICO AND THE UNITED STATES IN THE FIFTIES

For the preliminary period of the fifties source material of value is to be found in Antonio de la Peña y Reyes, *El Tratado Mon-Almonte,* Volume XIII, in *Archivo Histórico Diplomático Mexicano* (Mexico City, 1925), in *Documents Diplomatiques, 1862,* III, and in *Circulares y Otras Publicaciones hechas por la Legación Mexicana en Washington durante la Guerra de Intervención* (2 volumes, Mexico, 1868). See also an article by H. L. Wilson, " President Buchanan's Proposed Intervention in Mexico," *American Historical Review,* V (1900). Occasional references of value appear in G. M. Dallas, *Letters from London* (2 volumes, London, 1870). Secondary accounts of value are J. F. Rippy, *The United States and Mexico* (New York, 1926), and P. N. Garber, *The Gadsden Treaty* (Philadelphia, 1923).

The expedition of Raousset de Boulbon is treated by a contemporary and participant in E. Vigneaux, *Souvenirs d'un Prisonnier de Guerre au Mexique* (Paris, 1863), and by a secondary writer in W. O. Scroggs, *Filibusters and Financiers* (New York, 1916). Some of the correspondence having to do with this episode is in Senate Executive Documents, 33rd Congress, 2nd Session, Docs. Nos. 16 and 25, and in House Executive Documents, 35th Congress, 1st Session, Doc. No. 88.

FRENCH INTERVENTION IN MEXICO

The principal published materials from the American angle on the French intervention in Mexico are to be found in House Executive Documents, 37th Congress,

2nd Session, Doc. No. 100, 37th Congress, 3rd Session, Doc. No. 54, and 39th Congress, 1st Session, Doc. No. 73, Parts I and II. Many documents have been republished in *Diplomatic Correspondence*. Of large value also is the work of John Bigelow, *Retrospections of an Active Life* (5 volumes, New York, 1909). Bigelow was consul-general in Paris in 1861-65 and minister after April, 1865. Some light on the cabinet opinion with regard to the Mexican problem is to be found in Gideon Welles, *Diary of Gideon Welles* (3 volumes, New York, 1909).

On the French side, attention should be paid to the *Documents Diplomatiques* (Paris, 1861-67), and to the *Archives Parlementaires,* which also throw special light on the policy of Spain.

Of monumental significance is the great collection of the correspondence of Matías Romero, *Correspondencia de la Legación Mexicana en Washington durante la Intervención Extranjera* (10 volumes, Mexico, 1870-92). Of great value also is Genaro García and Carlos Pereyra, *Documentos inéditos ó muy raros para la historia de Mexico. Correspondencia secreta de los principales Intervencionistas Mexicanos* (36 volumes, Mexico, 1903).

Other books containing source materials of importance are: Egon Cesar Corti, *Maximilian and Charlotte of Mexico* (2 volumes, New York, 1928), which contains appendices with much interesting correspondence, especially the letters exchanged between Louis Napoleon and the Emperor Maximilian; P. Gaulot, *La Verité sur l'Expédition du Mexique* (3 volumes, Paris, 1889-90), which makes accessible important letters of the Emperor Napoleon to Bazaine, and G. Niox, *Expédition du Mexique* (Paris, 1874), which cites among other documents the instructions of June 5, 1863. The views of the French minister of foreign affairs are to be found, though not in very extensive form, in L. Thouvenel, *Le Secret de l'Empereur* (2 volumes, Paris, 1889), and those of the French minister of war, Marshal Randon, in J. L. Randon, *Mémoires du Marechal* (2 volumes,

Paris, 1875-7). An important collection of documents with comments is that of E. Lefèvre, *Documents Officiels Recueillis dans la Secrétairerie Privée de Maximilien* (2 volumes, Paris, 1870).

On the side of Spain particular attention should be called to Genaro Estrada, *Don Juan Prim y su Labor Diplomática en Mexico,* Volume XXV in *Archivo Histórico Diplomático Mexicano* (Mexico, 1928), and to E. Domenech, *Histoire du Mexique* (3 volumes, Paris, 1868).

Works reflecting public opinion in the United States, in France, or in Spain are: C. B. Boynton, *English and French Neutrality and the Anglo-French Alliance* (New York, 1864), John Jay, *Letter on the Relinquishment of the Monroe Doctrine* (New York, 1863), V. W. Kingsley, *French Intervention in America* (New York, 1863), Joshua Leavitt, *The Monroe Doctrine* (New York, 1863), and F. J. Parker, *The Mexican Empire and the American Union* (Boston, 1865) ; M. de La-Combe, *Le Mexique et les Etats-Unis* (Paris, 1863), M. Chevalier, *Mexique ancien et moderne* (Paris, 1864), P. L. Detroyat, *L'Intervention Française au Mexique* (Paris, 1868), anon., *La France, Le Mexique, et les Etats-Confédérés* (Paris, 1863), and Eugène Forçade, in *Revue des Deux Mondes,* XLVII (1863) *passim;* Fr. M. Tubino, *Un Trono en Méjico* (Madrid, 1862), and anon., *La Question in Méjico* (Madrid, 1862).

On army plans with regard to the intervention see, *Official Records of the Union and Confederate Armies.* J. Schofield, *Forty-Six Years in the Army* (New York, 1897), and Lew Wallace, *An Autobiography* (2 volumes, New York, 1906).

Of secondary works, Count Corti's, *op. cit.,* is a *chef d' oeuvre,* though written largely from one archive. The older work of Ernst Schmit Ritter von Tavera, *Geschichte der Regierung des Kaisers Maximilian und dis Französische Intervention in Mexico* (2 volumes, Vienna and Leipzig, 1903) is of great value. On Seward's policy, see J. M. Callahan, *Evolution of*

Seward's Mexican Policy, in West Virginia Studies in American History (Morgantown, 1908), and J. F. Rippy, *The United States and Mexico* (New York, 1926). The work of F. de P. Arrangoiz, *México desde 1808 hasta 1867* (4 volumes, Madrid, 1892) contains material not found elsewhere. In addition Lefèvre Domenech, and Niox, *op. cit.,* contain useful general commentary. See also the great works on the Second Empire, Pierre de la Gorce, *Histoire du Second Empire* (7 volumes, Paris, 1874) and Emile Ollivier, *L'Empire libéral* (18 volumes, Paris, 1895-1915).

Secondary material on Spanish policy is to be found in the excellent article H. Léonardon, " L'Espagne et la Question du Mexique," *Annales des Sciences Politiques,* XVI, 59-95, and J. Becker, *Historia de las Relaciones Exteriores de España durante El Siglo* XIX (3 volumes, Madrid, 1924).

Secondary works on public opinion in France are: F. E. Lally, *French Opposition to the Mexican Policy of the Second Empire,* in John Hopkins University Studies in Historical and Political Science, Series XLIX, No. 3 (Baltimore, 1931), and W. R. West, *Contemporary French Opinion on the American Civil War,* in the same studies, Series XLII, No. 1 (Baltimore, 1924).

Finally, a perspicacious analysis of the reasons for the French withdrawal from Mexico is C. A. Duniway, " Reasons for the Withdrawal of the French from Mexico," *Annual Report of the American Historical Association for 1902,* I, 313-328.

INDEX

Aberdeen, Lord, British Foreign Secretary, 33, 65; views on the Texan question, 66-71; views on California question, 82; 128, 230.

Abrantes, Viscount de, Special commissioner from Brazil to Europe, 128.

Acosta, Joaquín, New Granadan secretary of foreign affairs, 164.

Adams, British chargé, 57.

Adams, Charles Francis, American diplomat, 372, 423, 429; note from William H. Seward, 431-3.

Alamán, Lucas, Mexican Foreign Secretary, 23-4, 140, 319, 321-2.

Alberdi, J. B., Argentine jurist, 251.

Alexander, Tsar of Russia, 238.

Alfau, Felipe, special commissioner from Santo Domingo to Madrid, 280.

Allen, William, senator from Ohio, 103; Allen resolution, 104-7; 134, 217.

Almonte, General, Mexican reactionary, mission to Mexico, 382-3; 401.

Alto Vela, Island of, 283.

Alvarez, A., President of Mexico, 337.

Alvear, Carlos Maria de, Argentine minister to the United States, 56, 137.

Amapa, evacuation of by French, 21.

American Review, attitude toward message of 1845, 102.

Ancona, Eligio, Yucateco historian, 188.

Araguary River, 20.

Arce, Nuñez de, 304.

Argentine, the, rupture with American government over Falkland Islands, 6-7; monarchical projects, 1829, 36; French intervention in, 43 note, 49-55; Anglo-French intervention in, 83 f., 92, 127-40.

Arista, Mariano, President of Mexico, 319.

Arrangoiz, Francisco de Paula, Mexican reactionary, 141, 377, 393.

Astrada, General Berón de, 53.

Asunción, 139.

Atchison, D. R., senator from Missouri, 76.

Austria, and the Mexican intervention, 369-70, 394-6, 527 f.

Azua, 258.

Bacalar, seizure of, 189.

Badger, G. E., senator from North Carolina, 221, 223.

Baez, Buenaventura, Dominican politician, 256; friend of French protectorate over Santo Domingo, 257-60; 275; President of Santo Domingo, 278.

Bagby, Arthur P., senator from Alabama, 186.

Balance of Power, doctrine of, 64, 70-1, 73, 96, 98, 102-3, 113-14, 118-19, 135, 218.

Bancroft, George, American historian, on monarchy in Mexico, 436; 447-8.

Bankhead, Charles, British minister in Mexico City, 141-2, 145.

Barbachano, Miguel, Yucateco politician, 171, 188, 190.

Barclay, Anthony, British consul in New York, 195.

Maximilian, Emperor of Mexico, 357-8; name put forward by Louis Napoleon, 359; eager to found a throne in the New World, 367-8; 372; departure from Trieste, 379-80; 383, 391-4, 399; offered Mexican crown, 400; 402; signs convention of 1864, 403-4; 417, 430, 450, 457-9, 465, 476-8, 483, 485-6, 488, 494, 498-9; subsidizes American newspapers, 503; 506, 508-27.

Mazatlan, 342.

Mella, Ramón, sent to Spain to negotiate for Santo Domingo protectorate, 277.

Mendez, Santiago, leader of autonomist party in Yucatan, and question of a protectorate over Yucatan, 171-6, 188, 190.

Mensdorff, Count, Austrian foreign minister, interview with Motley, 529-30.

Mesilla Valley, 326.

Message of 1845, 62-125, especially, 86-9.

Metternich, Prince Richard, Austrian minister in Paris, 149, 238; conservative attitude toward Mexican expedition, 370, 394; 524.

Mexican War, 127, 137, 146, 169, 178.

Mexico, French blockade of, 40 f.; and the Texan question, 66-74; relations with United States, 135; clash of systems in, 318-56; intervention in, 357-548.

Mexico City, French entrance into, 392.

Miller, Jacob W., senator from New Jersey, denounces policy of President Polk, 183.

Miramar, 395-6; Convention of, 402-4.

Mofras, Duflot de, French traveler, opinion on monarchy in Mexico, 26.

Molé, L. M., Prime minister of France, 40; declares French do not intend to hold Martín García, 54.

Mon, Alexander, Spanish minister at Paris, assures Koerner that Spain will not retain Chincha Islands, 313; 353, 359; declares time is ripe for monarchy in Mexico, 376; replaced by General Concha, 386.

Mon-Almonte Convention, 352-4.

Monarchy, in Mexico, 23-29, 140-9, 318-548; in Ecuador, 150-4; in New Granada, 29-36.

Moniteur, 513.

Monroe Doctrine, first time so called, 223; first article under that title, 234.

Appealed to, by Central America (1834), 13, by the Argentine (1828), 38, by New Granada (1837), 39, by Ecuador (1840), 151, by Peru (1846), 154, by New Granada (1845), 160, 164-5, by Nicaragua (1847-8), 166, by Yucatan (1848), 173, by Nicaragua and Honduras (1849), 200, by Romero in behalf of Mexico (1862), 438, by Mackenna in behalf of Chile (1866), 543.

Criticized, by Whig newspapers, 102-3, in British press (1843-5), 110-13, 122-5, by Guizot, 114-17, in *Journal des Débats* (1846), 119, in Spanish note on Mexico, 144, by Calhoun, 178-83, and others in debate in 1848, 183-5, by Lord Palmerston (1849), 195, by Seward and others in debates of 1853, 218-20, by Lord Clarendon, 227-8, in debates of 1855, 233, in article in *North American Review,* 234-6, in *Revue Contemporaine,* 245-6, 336, 440-1, 451, 536, by Disraeli, 257-8, by Calderon Collantes, 300-1, in Spanish

ERRATA

Page 427, line 27—*for* Francis *read* Montgomery
Page 436, line 12—*for* Francis *read* Montgomery
Page 443, line 7—*for* son *read* grandson

ALBERT SHAW LECTURES ON
DIPLOMATIC HISTORY

1899. JOHN H. LATANÉ. The Diplomatic Relations of the United States and Spanish America. 1900. (Out of print.)

1900. JAMES MORTON CALLAHAN. The Diplomatic History of the Southern Confederacy. 1901. (Out of print.)

1906. JESSE SIDDALL REEVES. American Diplomacy under Tyler and Polk. 1907. $1.75.

1907. ELBERT JAY BENTON. International Law and Diplomacy of the Spanish-American War. 1908. $1.75.

1909. EPHRAIM DOUGLAS ADAMS. British Interests and Activities in Texas, 1838-1846. 1910. $1.75.

1911. CHARLES OSCAR PAULLIN. Diplomatic Negotiations of American Naval Officers, 1778-1883. 1912. $2.25.

1912. ISAAC J. COX. The West Florida Controversy, 1798-1813. 1918. $3.00.

1913. WILLIAM R. MANNING. Early Diplomatic Relations Between the United States and Mexico. 1916. $2.50.

1914. FRANK A. UPDYKE. The Diplomacy of the War of 1812. 1915. $2.75.

1916. PAYSON JACKSON TREAT. The Early Diplomatic Relations Between the United States and Japan, 1853-1865. 1917. $2.75.

1921. PERCY ALVIN MARTIN. Latin America and the War. 1925. $3.50.

1923. HENRY MERRITT WRISTON. Executive Agents in American Foreign Relations. 1929. $5.00.

1926. SAMUEL FLAGG BEMIS. Pinckney's Treaty: A Study of America's Advantage from Europe's Distress, 1783-1800. 1926. (Out of print.)

1927. BRUCE WILLIAMS. State Security and the League of Nations: A Survey of the Movement for State Security from the Treaty of Versailles to the Locarno Conference. 1927. $2.75.

1928. J. FRED RIPPY. Rivalry of the United States and Great Britain over Latin-America, 1808-1830. 1929. $2.75.

1931. CHARLES CALLAN TANSILL. The Purchase of the Danish West Indies. 1932. $3.50.

1932. DEXTER PERKINS. The Monroe Doctrine, 1826-67. 1933. $3.50.